When should I travel to get the best airfare?
Where do I go for answers to my travel questions?
What's the best and easiest way to plan and book my trip?

frommers.travelocity.com

Frommer's, the travel guide leader, has teamed up with **Travelocity.com**, the leader in online travel, to bring you an in-depth, easy-to-use resource designed to help you plan and book your trip online.

At **frommers.travelocity.com**, you'll find free online updates about your destination from the experts at Frommer's plus the outstanding travel planning and purchasing features of Travelocity.com. Travelocity.com provides reservations capabilities for 95 percent of all airline seats sold, more than 47,000 hotels, and over 50 car rental companies. In addition, Travelocity.com offers more than 2,000 exciting vacation and cruise packages. Travelocity.com puts you in complete control of your travel planning with these and other great features:

> **Expert travel guidance from Frommer's** - over 150 writers reporting from around the world!
>
> **Best Fare Finder** - an interactive calendar tells you when to travel to get the best airfare
>
> **Fare Watcher** - we'll track airfare changes to your favorite destinations
>
> **Dream Maps** - a mapping feature that suggests travel opportunities based on your budget
>
> **Shop Safe Guarantee** - 24 hours a day / 7 days a week live customer service, and more!

Whether traveling on a tight budget, looking for a quick weekend getaway, or planning the trip of a lifetime, Frommer's guides and Travelocity.com will make your travel dreams a reality. You've bought the book, now book the trip!

Travelocity.com
A Sabre Company

Frommer's

Also available from IDG Books Worldwide:

Beyond Disney: The Unofficial Guide to Universal, Sea World, and the Best of Central Florida, by Bob Sehlinger and Amber Morris

Inside Disney: The Incredible Story of Walt Disney World and the Man Behind the Mouse, by Eve Zibart

Mini Las Vegas: The Pocket-Sized Unofficial Guide to Las Vegas, by Bob Sehlinger

Mini-Mickey: The Pocket-Sized Unofficial Guide to Walt Disney World, by Bob Sehlinger

The Unofficial Guide to Bed & Breakfasts in California, by Mary Anne Moore & Maurice Read

The Unofficial Guide to Bed & Breakfasts in New England, by Lea Lane

The Unofficial Guide to Bed & Breakfasts in the Northwest, by Sally O'Neal Coates

The Unofficial Guide to Bed & Breakfasts in the Southeast, by Hal Gieseking

The Unofficial Guide to Branson, Missouri, by Eve Zibart and Bob Sehlinger

The Unofficial Guide to California with Kids, by Colleen Dunn Bates and Susan La Tempa

The Unofficial Guide to Chicago, by Joe Surkiewicz and Bob Sehlinger

The Unofficial Guide to Cruises, by Kay Showker with Bob Sehlinger

The Unofficial Guide to Disneyland, by Bob Sehlinger

The Unofficial Guide to Florida with Kids, by Pam Brandon

The Unofficial Guide to the Great Smoky and Blue Ridge Region, by Bob Sehlinger and Joe Surkiewicz

The Unofficial Guide to Golf Vacations in the Eastern U.S., by Joseph Mark Passov and C.H. Conroy

The Unofficial Guide to Hawaii, by Lance Tominaga

The Unofficial Guide to Las Vegas, by Bob Sehlinger

The Unofficial Guide to London, by Lesley Logan

The Unofficial Guide to Miami and the Keys, by Bob Sehlinger and Joe Surkiewicz

The Unofficial Guide to New Orleans, by Bob Sehlinger and Eve Zibart

The Unofficial Guide to New York City, by Eve Zibart and Bob Sehlinger with Jim Leff

The Unofficial Guide to Paris, by David Applefield

The Unofficial Guide to San Francisco, by Joe Surkiewicz and Bob Sehlinger with Richard Sterling

The Unofficial Guide to Skiing in the West, by Lito Tejada-Flores, Peter Shelton, Seth Masia, Ed Chauner, and Bob Sehlinger

The Unofficial Guide to Walt Disney World, by Bob Sehlinger

The Unofficial Guide to Walt Disney World for Grown-Ups, by Eve Zibart

The Unofficial Guide to Walt Disney World with Kids, by Bob Sehlinger

The Unofficial Guide to Washington, D.C., by Bob Sehlinger and Joe Surkiewicz with Eve Zibart

the Unofficial Guide® to the Southeast with Kids

1st Edition

Heidi Tyline King and Melanie M. Mize
with Nancy J. Worrell

Every effort has been made to ensure the accuracy of information throughout this book. Bear in mind, however, that prices, schedules, etc., are constantly changing. Readers should always verify information before making final plans.

IDG Books Worldwide, Inc.
An International Data Group Company
909 Third Avenue, 21st Floor
New York, New York 10022

Produced by Menasha Ridge Press

UNOFFICIAL GUIDE is a registered trademark of IDG Books Worldwide, Inc.

ISBN 0-7645-6218-5

ISSN 1531-1538

Manufactured in the United States of America

10 9 8 7 6 5 4 3 2 1

First edition

Contents

List of Maps

Introduction

The Dynamics of Family Travel

Dream vacations don't happen by chance—they take planning and forethought. With this in mind, here are three important points to remember:

Be flexible. From a flat tire to an unexpected visit to the emergency room, there are going to be some situations out of your control. They're inconvenient in everyday life; on the road, they can ruin the best-laid plans. Your children will feed off your attitude towards a situation, so just try to go with the flow. Your family will follow your lead. Later, it's often the mishaps that become the highlights of family road-trip memories.

Find a happy medium between the interests of adults and children. This seems self-explanatory, but the best vacations should be fulfilling for each family member. Take time to find out what each member wants to get from the vacation. It means taking stock of your children's passions and fears as well as your own. It also means attaching a budget to everyone's wishes. And it invariably means compromise.

Start by asking yourself some questions. Is this vacation a time for togetherness, for time alone for you while the children are entertained, or for a little of each? Are you a single dad who doesn't get to see the kids much? Are you an at-home mom who never gets a break? Are you looking for exhilarating adventures or a laid-back getaway? Do you want intellectual stimulation for you and the kids? How well do your kids handle spontaneity?

Once you determine each person's expectations, make a list that you can refer to during the trip. This will help you prioritize activities and give your children a firsthand experience with compromise and teamwork.

Because your family's dynamics change with every birthday, the answers may surprise you. One child may be more ready for adventure than you've realized, while another might be more ready for peace and quiet.

The journey is just as important as the destination. It's a cliché for a reason. Traveling allows children—and adults—to learn not only about new places, but also about themselves in a new environment and from a different perspective than the one they are accustomed to in everyday life. Your job as a parent is recognize and affirm your children in this new light and to help them discover other facets of their personalities as well. And don't forget, your vacation starts the minute you close your front door—not when you arrive at your destination. Too many parents don't realize that for children, the travel is a big part of the adventure.

THE PLEASURES OF PLANNING

It's best to decide what you want to do and come up with some options to start the ball rolling. Then call a family meeting and include your kids in the planning process. Let everyone ask questions. Show some brochures or books about the places you have in mind so they'll feel like they have enough information to be taken seriously. Pull out maps and a globe. Jump on the Internet. Teenagers in particular are quite vocal in expressing their choices and they appreciate it when they can influence the planning process. The getaway is much more enjoyable when everyone wants to be there.

Continue this shared planning time as the trip itself gets underway. Remember, your kids may not be able to easily visualize your destination or the flight or cab ride you'll take on the way. And if you're traveling from place to place during your vacation, each new day dawns on the unknown. Keep the brochures and guidebooks handy and break the itinerary down into manageable chunks. Offer an advance agenda every now and then, referring again to your original planning sessions ("Remember we thought that the Bubbling Brook Motel sounded like a good one?") and letting the kids develop anticipation rather than anxiety.

It's essential to be realistic when you plan a family vacation. Parents of young children may have to concede that the days of romantic sunsets are over for a while if there's a toddler tugging at their shorts. With infants and toddlers, the best vacations are the simple ones. They don't much need to see the sights; the idea is to be somewhere comfortable and intriguing for the adults, with a pleasant environment in which to relax and enjoy your children. Simple beach resorts are ideal for parents of this youngest group of kids. School-age kids revel in attractions created for their enjoyment—theme parks, amusement parks, arcades, and rides. The metropolitan regions can also be a blast with elementary-age kids. Teens may seem reluctant, but if a pilgrimage to a special point of interest for them (a certain skateboard shop, a movie-star hangout) is included, the whole trip becomes "worthwhile." And they thrive in safe, explore-it-on-your-own situations like Six Flags Over Georgia or the McWane Center in Birmingham.

Less is More Than Enough

Kids treasure moments, not places or days. As you plan, we urge you to leave plenty of downtime in the schedule. Some of our families' most memorable moments are simple breakfasts on the beach or early evening walks to nowhere when conversation naturally flows. Give your children plenty of room to run and play. A morning collecting seashells or an afternoon at the hotel pool can be more satisfying than standing in line at a crowded theme park attraction.

This good rule of thumb may sound stringent: No more than two activities in a day. If you spend the morning at the Aquarium of the Americas and plan dinner at a restaurant in New Orleans' French Quarter, go back to the hotel in the afternoon to rest and swim. If you're driving from Knoxville to Memphis, make your reservations for Graceland the next day. Then you can stop on the way for a leisurely picnic beside a cotton field or an afternoon stroll through the funny little town that time forgot. Remember that travel itself is an activity.

Also, plan some activities that allow you to take a break from each other. The quarters get a little close after a week together in a hotel room, particularly if children are of significantly different ages. Schedule an afternoon where mom and dad split duties, giving each other a break. Take advantage of child and teen programs offered in many resorts to make sure there's at least one evening alone with your spouse. Everyone benefits from a little elbow room.

Reconnections

Family vacations are a necessary indulgence in today's hurried-up world, a time for togetherness without the day-to-day distractions. Whether it's a car trip on a budget or a transcontinental flight, it's a time to reconnect with your family, especially teenagers. The best times are the serendipitous moments—a heart-to-heart conversation on an evening hike or silly "knock-knock" jokes while standing in line for a roller coaster. Roles are relaxed when schedules are flexible, and kids have the opportunity to see their parents as interesting companions instead of bossy grown-ups. We all can learn from one another when we take the time to listen and to see the world through a loved one's eyes.

A seasoned traveler friend once scoffed at the notion of traveling with young children, "since they don't remember anything." We couldn't disagree more. Given the open hearts and all the innocence of childhood, new impressions may sink in even more deeply with kids than with adults.

Children develop a greater understanding of the rest of the world as a result of visiting new places and experiencing new ideas. Siblings form a special bond when traveling together, a bond less likely to be formed at home, where they have separate classrooms, separate friends, separate rooms. As parents, it's essential to build in some fun in the trip for each member of the family. And as a family, we all need to remember to indulge our traveling companions from time to time. Remember, your responses to challenges on the road—delayed flights, long lines, unsatisfactory accommodations—will influence the way your children deal with frustrations. Be patient, be calm, and teach your children these important life skills.

Vacations are times for adventure, relaxation, shared experiences, time alone—whatever your family decides. Our goal with this book is to evaluate each destination, recognizing that your family has needs, based on ages, backgrounds, and interests, that are quite different from any other family's. We also hope to provide you with some structure to analyze those needs and create a vacation that works.

This book is not meant to be a compendium of every family-priced hotel or every advertised attraction, though we strive to cover a variety of interests for a variety of ages. Instead of compiling a family-travel Yellow Pages, we've edited out the less worthy places to better draw attention to the destinations that will make your trip a hit.

Dozens of families have contributed their opinions to this book. It is evaluative and opinionated, and it offers advice on the best ways for families to have fun together and strengthen relationships.

Survival Guide for Little Kids

Think Small.   Little ones love little pleasures: splashing in the hotel pool, playing hide-and-seek in the lobby, stacking rocks on the beach. Don't overload them.

Find Creative Transportation.   For young children, getting there is often more fun than being there. Planning ahead for your three-year-old to visit the pilot in the cockpit of your airplane will no doubt be more memorable to him than a day at the Grand Canyon. Seek out ferries, trolleys, shuttles, trains, surreys, and double-decker buses, and you'll be rewarded with a cheap thrill that's as fun for little ones as an amusement park ride.

Limit the Shopping.   Our rule at attractions is a firm one: no shopping, not even looking, until we are leaving the place. Young children can get consumed by and even panicky about choosing a souvenir, and they'll enjoy the museum or theme park more if they can focus on the activities, not the trinkets. Plus, you don't have to worry about losing your purchases or keeping up with shopping bags.

Give Them a Voice.   Even four-year-olds will benefit from feeling like they have some control over their vacation. When possible, let them make simple choices for the family, like "Should we walk to the beach or ride the trolley?"

Allow for Lots of Down Time. Bring books or quiet hobbies to amuse yourself during naps or play times. Remember, a child's ability to tackle the big world is much more limited than yours. And frankly, you'll find that you enjoy activities more when you are rested and stress-free.

Accept Some Slowness. It's stressful enough to get a kindergartener out the door to school each morning, so don't keep up the stress on vacation. If they're happy playing in their pajamas for an extra half hour, the museum can wait. Conversely, accept that the times you prefer to be more leisurely —like dinnertime—lead to impatience in children.

Survival Guide for School-Age Kids

Give Them Their Own Space. Whether it's a backpack, a carry-on train case, or one of those shoebag-like hanging pockets that fit over the car seat in front of them, each kid needs portable space of his or her own in which to stow gum, cards, books, disposable cameras, and souvenirs.

Make a New Routine. At least until middle school years, most kids do best with a certain amount of predictability, so it's a kindness to create little travel routines and rituals within your changed life. Knowing that your parents will always stop sight-seeing by 3 p.m. to swim (or will never check out without one last hour in the pool) is a comforting thought to many a fourth-grader. Knowing that they are allowed $5 spending money each day can do away with shopping anxiety. Taking turns as map reader can add some fun to a hundred-mile drive.

Avoid Eating Breakfast Out. Many savvy traveling parents never eat breakfast in a restaurant. School-age kids are at their brightest and best in the morning, and waiting for table service at a ho-hum restaurant can start the day on the wrong foot. Carry fruit, cereal, milk, and juice in coolers or to kitchenettes or spring for room service—it's the least expensive and most wonderfully indulgent time to do so.

Beware Befuddled Expectations. School-age kids are old enough to have some reference points and young enough to have great gaping holes in their mental pictures of the world. A seven-year-old might be thrilled with the idea of riding through an animal safari park but secretly worried about being attacked by a wild animal. Ask about their concerns, and address any misconceptions or fears.

Watch the Diet. It's fun to let vacation be a time of special treats, but over-indulgence in junk food, sweets, and caffeinated drinks may contribute to behavior changes in kids who aren't sleeping in their own beds and are full of adrenaline as it is.

Remember That Kids Hate Scenery.   Drive them through it if you must, but don't make them actually look at too much of it.

Give Them a Ship's Log.   A roll of tape and a blank book are all that's needed to turn ticket stubs, menus, brochures, and postcards from a clutter of trash into a wonderful scrapbook that's always ready to be shared and enjoyed.

Hotels and Motels Are Not Just for Sleeping.   Allow time for getting ice, playing in the pool, reviewing all items and prices in the minibar, packing and unpacking, using the hairdryer, putting laundry into the laundry bags, trying out the vending machines, etc.

Hit the Playgrounds.   Check your maps and ask ahead about public playgrounds with climbing and sliding equipment. On days when you'll be sight-seeing, driving, or absorbing culture, allow for an hour's lunch or rest stop at the playground. Even on city vacations, try to set aside at least one day for pure physical fun at a beach, water park, or ski slope.

Just Say Yes to Ranger Tours.   These tours are often designed with school kids in mind, and they are a good source of up-to-date park information. On your own, you would probably never learn about nesting bald eagles or baby sea turtle migration.

Survival Guide for Teenagers

Don't Try to Fool Them.   Don't try to tell teenagers they'll have more fun with you than with their friends. They won't. But if you offer them the possibility of doing things they might want to tell their friends about later, they'll be more interested.

Respect Their Culture.   Let your teenagers play an active role in planning the vacation. Ask their opinion of your arrangements. Often a teen will have a great suggestion or an alternative that you may not have considered. And look for pop culture landmarks—movie locations, palaces of fashion or music or sport. Add a ball game to the itinerary.

Night Moves.   A vacation is a great time to go with your teenager to a music club or a midnight movie, or on a moonlight hike. Go to the theater or the ballet or check out a jazz club. If you have other kids needing earlier bedtimes, let the parents switch-hit on going out at night with the older kids.

Give Them Options.   You don't need to go everywhere with everyone. If your younger child wants to see the dinosaurs at the museum, this is the time for a split plan: Father and son see the dinosaurs, mother and daughter shop or take in a movie or a play. If you have teenagers who appreciate their sleep time, let them snooze late at least one morning. Slip out with younger siblings to take a walk or read a book. Also, set wake-up time before everyone says good night so that there are no grouchy morning risers (at least not because they've been awakened too early).

Give Them Freedom.   Before age 12, kids are bound to parents, preferring to stay in your orbit; when adolescence hits, they're programmed to push away from you. Choose a vacation spot that is safe and controlled enough to allow them to wander or spend time with other teenagers. If you can't do that, look for an afternoon or evening at a controlled hangout place like Columbus, Georgia's Hollywood Connection. Sign them up for a bayou tour in Baton Rouge; let them spend an afternoon alone at the hotel swimming pool.

Compromise on the Headphone Thing.   Headphones can allow teens to create their own space even when they're with others. While that can be a safety valve, try to agree before the trip on some non-headphone parameters so you don't begin to feel as if they're being used to keep other family members and the trip itself at a distance. If you're traveling by car, take turns choosing the radio station or CD for part of the trip.

Don't Make Your Teenager the Built-in Babysitter.   It's a *family* vacation—a time for reconnecting, not for avoiding the kids. A special night out for parents also should be special for the children; let them order videos and room service, for example, or participate in age-appropriate hotel programs.

Make Peace with Shopping.   Look for street markets and vintage stores; spend some time in surf shops and record stores. If you go with your teenager, you may find that the conversation in such an environment flows easily. Or hit the outlets—many a summer vacation has included a day of back-to-school shopping.

Just Say Yes to at Least One Big-Ticket Excursion.   Teenagers will get a lot out of a half-day adventure. What initially look like expensive tours (often available through the hotel sports desk or concierge) can turn out to be memorable and important experiences for kids—experiences that parents are often not able to offer by themselves. A raft ride, a desert jeep tour, a kayak and snorkel trip, a horseback trail ride—these are the stuff that memories are made of.

A Word on Homework

If you're traveling during the school year, homework is unavoidable. Consider strategies such as bringing along a laptop computer, scheduling vacation fun in half-day chunks so that your child gets some work and some play, and/or a marathon session in a library at the vacation spot. You can also shamelessly beg the teacher for a reprieve, but make that a last resort.

The Secret to Visiting Art Museums

Room after room of paintings and sculptures are numbing to children (and to some adults). They need a focal point and a sense of adventure. Before your visit, find out what some of the major works on display are, and locate pictures of them (perhaps the museum will mail you a brochure with pictures, or you can look online or get an art book from the library). Let each child pick one or two works to sleuth out. They can learn a little about the artist and the work in question, and then when you visit the museum, they can go on a hunt for "their" artwork.

Another option is to schedule time with a docent, emphasizing that the tour be directed toward your child's age. Docents can give you the inside scoop on artists (many of whom have crazy lives that will interest children) as well as the context of a particular piece of artwork.

A Few Words for Single Parents

Because single parents generally are working parents, planning a special getaway with your children can be the best way to spend some quality time together. But remember, the vacation is not just for your child—it's for you, too. You might invite along a grandparent or a favorite aunt or uncle; the other adult provides nice company for you, and your child will benefit from the time with family members.

Don't try to spend every moment of the trip with your children. Instead, plan some activities for your children to be with other children. Look for hotels with supervised activities, or research the community you'll be visiting for school-vacation offerings at libraries, recreation centers, temples, or churches. Then take advantage of your free time to do what you want to do: Read a book, have a massage, take a long walk or a catnap.

Tips for Grandparents

A vacation that involves multiple generations can be the most enriching experience for everyone, but it is important to consider the needs of each family member, from the youngest to the oldest. Here are some particulars:

- If you're planning to travel alone with your grandchildren, spend a little time getting to know them before the vacation. Be sure they're comfortable with the idea of traveling with you if their parents are not coming along.

- It's best to take one grandchild at a time, two at the most. Cousins can be better than siblings because they don't fight as much.

- Let your grandchildren help plan the vacation, and keep the first one short. Be flexible and don't overplan.

- Discuss mealtimes and bedtime. Fortunately, many grandparents are on an early-dinner schedule, which works nicely with younger children. Also, if you want to plan a special evening out, be sure to make the reservation ahead of time. Stash some crayons and paper in your bag to keep kids occupied.

- Gear plans to your grandchildren's age levels, because if they're not happy, you're not happy.

- Choose a vacation that offers some supervised activities for children in case you need a rest.

- If you're traveling by car, this is the one time we highly recommend headphones. Teenagers' musical tastes are vastly different from most grandparents', and it's simply more enjoyable when everyone can listen to their own style of music.

- Take along a nightlight.

- Carry a notarized statement from parents for permission for medical care in case of an emergency. Also, be sure you have insurance information.

- Tell your older grandchildren about any medical problems you may have so that they can be prepared if there's an emergency.

- Many attractions and hotels offer discounts for seniors, so be sure you check ahead for bargains.

- A cruise may be the perfect compromise—plenty of daily activities for everyone, but shared mealtimes.

If planning a child-friendly trip seems overwhelming, try Grandtravel (800) 247-7651, a tour operator/travel agent aimed at kids and their grandparents.

For Travelers with Disabilities

Facilities for the physically challenged are plentiful throughout the Southeast. All public buildings have some form of access for those who use wheelchairs. In addition, many public buses are equipped with wheelchair lifts. Most of the state's attractions offer facilities and services for those with physical challenges, and many hotels have specially equipped rooms.

Almost every major city in each state has guides for the physically challenged. Visit state and city web sites or call ahead for specific information.

How the *Unofficial Guide* Works

ORGANIZATION

Our informal polls show that most families tend to choose a vacation spot based on geography—a place that's new and different, or familiar and comfortable. So we've divided the Southeast by states into eight regions, with

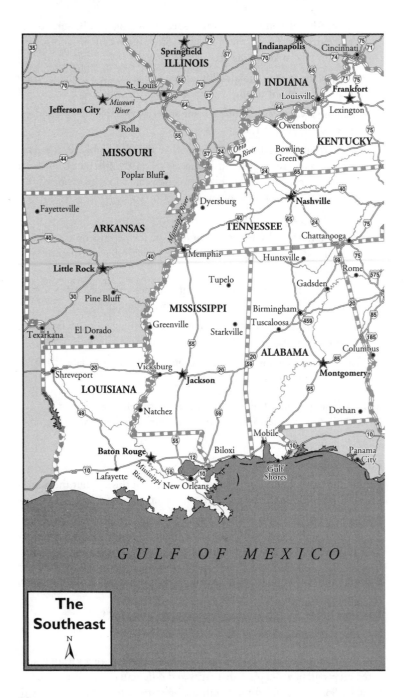

The Southeast

N

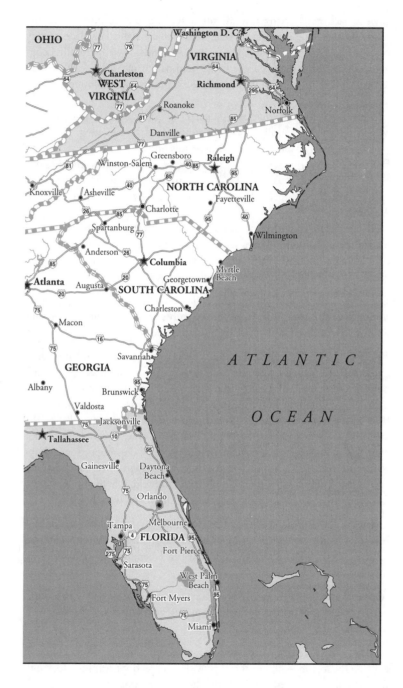

cities in each state serving as a hub for activities and attractions in the surrounding area. The chapters are organized alphabetically. For places to stay within those regions—resorts, hotels, campgrounds—see the Family Lodging sections within each chapter. Child- and parent-pleasing restaurants are recommended in the Family-Friendly Restaurants sectionsfound in each chapter.

The states covered include: Alabama, Georgia, Kentucky, Louisiana, Mississippi, North Carolina, South Carolina, and Tennessee.

Each regional chapter reviews outdoor adventures and attractions ranging from theme parks to science museums. We've also included serendipitous sidebars on offbeat places that you'll want to know about, from Elvis Presley's birthplace in Tupelo, Mississippi, to a glow-worm canyon in north Alabama.

If you're looking for some healthy family bonding, stretch beyond the man-made attractions. Have a sense of adventure, and plan some activities that are new and exciting—not necessarily strenuous, but memorable. Each region has specific spots for the following activities:

Camping. We've selected a few choice family-friendly campgrounds throughout the Southeast. If it's your family's first experience, you might opt for a cabin; we list them in many state parks.

Biking. Cycling is one of the best ways to experience an area firsthand, and it can be enjoyed year-round in much of the Southeast. Keep in mind, however, that much of the region has high humidity in the summer, making spring and fall the best times for cycling adventures. For beginners, we have recommended miles of paved bicycle trails; older kids will like the mountain-biking spots we've found. You don't even have to bring your own bike; you can rent one at many resorts and bike shops. Some shops rent trailers for small children (age 5 and younger) to travel safely behind you—they're much safer than bicycle seats. Know that helmets are the law for children, and it is strongly advised that all cyclists wear helmets.

Hiking. The Southeast offers an array of diverse geographical settings for hikes, including pine forests, canyons, and mountains. We've concentrated on the easiest spots suitable for kids that can be enjoyed by families of all interests and fitness levels.

Kayaking and White-Water Rafting. The Southeast is blessed with a number of rivers and streams ideal for bonding adventures for families with kids older than five or six years of age.

Fishing. Take your pick of waterways: Rivers, lakes, streams, and, of course, the ocean—all of these provide ample opportunities for both novice and experienced anglers throughout the Southeast.

The *Unofficial Guide* Rating System for Attractions

Our system includes an Appeal by Age Group category, indicating a range of appeal from one star ★: Don't bother, up to five stars ★★★★★: Not to be missed.

WHAT'S "UNOFFICIAL" ABOUT THIS BOOK?

The material in this guide originated with the authors and researchers and has not been reviewed, edited, or in any way approved by the attractions, restaurants, and hotels we describe. Our goal is to help families plan a vacation that's right for them by providing important details and honest opinions. If we've found a family-oriented destination to be dreary or a rip-off, we simply don't include it.

Readers care about the author's opinion. The author, after all, is supposed to know what he or she is talking about. This, coupled with the fact that the traveler wants quick answers (as opposed to endless alternatives), dictates that authors should be explicit, prescriptive, and, above all, direct. The *Unofficial Guide* tries to do just that—it spells out alternatives and recommends specific courses of action. It simplifies complicated destinations and attractions and allows the traveler to feel in control in the most unfamiliar environments. The objective of the *Unofficial Guide* is not to have the most information or all of the information, but to have the most accessible, useful information, unbiased by affiliation with any organization or industry.

This guide is directed at value-conscious, consumer-oriented families who seek a cost-effective, though not spartan, travel style.

Letters and Comments from Readers

We expect to learn from our mistakes, as well as from the input of our readers, and to improve with each book and edition. Many of those who use the *Unofficial Guides* write to us asking questions, making comments, or sharing their own discoveries and lessons learned. We appreciate all of the input, both positive and critical, and encourage our readers to continue writing. Readers' comments and observations are frequently incorporated into revised editions of the *Unofficial Guide* and will contribute immeasurably to its improvement.

How to Write the Author

Heidi King
The Unofficial Guide to the Southeast with Kids
P.O. Box 43673
Birmingham, AL 35243

When you write, be sure to put your return address on your letter as well as on the envelope—sometimes envelopes and letters get separated. And remember, our work takes us out of the office for long periods of time, so forgive us if our response is delayed.

Getting Ready to Go

WEATHER AND WHEN TO GO

Climate in the Southeast fluctuates tremendously from state to state, and even within states, you'll find distinct variations. In general, it is a temperate part of the country suitable for year-round visiting.

Regardless of your destination, there's no getting around the humidity that characterizes southern summers. It generally begins in mid-May and doesn't let up until September; the duration can be longer for states in the Deep South and those along the coast. Unfortunately, many theme parks are open only during the summer months, making the humidity impossible to avoid. Remember to drink plenty of water and take along towels and cloths you can wet in an ice chest to press on your face and neck.

If you plan to camp, spring and fall are ideal, not only because of the break in humidity, but also because of the lack of mosquitoes. For beach trips, summer is the most popular time for travel, as all shops and restaurants are open for business. The choices are fewer in spring and fall, but these shoulder seasons offer lower rates and mild weather. If you plan to hike, be aware that parts of the Appalachian Trail and paths through the Great Smoky Mountains are closed during the winter months.

Snow is rare in most parts of the Southeast, so much so that if the sky looks threatening, schools and businesses will close. Much of the reason is because the threat is so small that equipment is not as essential as it is in northern cities. Another reason is that snow in the South is often accompanied by sheets of ice underneath, making driving conditions extremely hazardous. As in other parts of the country, the farther north you go, the more likely you will encounter snow and colder temperatures. Virginia, North Carolina, and Tennessee are the most likely snow spots.

In general, popular tourist sights are busier on weekends than weekdays, and Saturdays are busier than Sundays. Locals say the least crowded time to visit theme parks is on a rainy weekday in the winter (if the park is open during the winter). And don't be surprised to find restaurants and attractions that close on Sundays; the Southeast has deep religious roots that continue to influence everyday life. The same goes for buying alcohol; some cities just don't sell the stuff on Sundays, and those that do often have a designated window of time in which you can buy.

Of course, family travel schedules often center around school holidays, which tend to be the busiest times to travel. But consider taking your children out of school for special family trips—a well-planned week of family travel is just as enriching as five days in a classroom. Make it clear that traveling is a privilege, and agree that all missed work must be made up upon return. Talk with teachers ahead of time.

PACK LIGHT

We limit ourselves to one carry-on bag each and a backpack, no matter what the duration of the trip or how we are traveling. (The exception is a ski or snow trip, which demands bulky clothes.) If you have small children, stashing an extra T-shirt and pair of shorts in your backpack comes in handy in emergencies. A trip in the Southeastern United States is generally casual, though you may want to pack one nice outfit for dressing up for a special evening out.

T-shirts, shorts, and bathing suits are ideal for summer months; they can also be worn in the spring and fall in many parts of the Southeast. Just be sure to pack a light jacket or sturdy sweatshirt in case the nights are cool. In the winter, jeans and layered tops are good choices; you may want to pack winter coats just in case. And don't forget a raincoat; the cold and damp of a Southeastern winter rain is miserable.

Take along a small bottle of detergent for hand-washing. The vacation is much more enjoyable if you don't have a bunch of bags to haul around busy airports or hotel lobbies.

Let your children pack their own backpack, then ask them to wear it around the house to test how comfortable it will be on a long trip. Of course, you should check their bags before departure, just to be sure the essentials are all there.

Finally, you may want to take along a "surprise bag" for young travelers. Sticker books, a card game, or a new book are perfect, lightweight diversions to bring out when everyone's patience is wearing thin.

WHAT TO TAKE WITH YOU: A CHECKLIST

No matter what your means of transportation, be sure you take along (and have handy at all times):

- Sunglasses and hats to protect you from the sun.
- Sunscreen, at least SPF 15.
- Emergency information—who to contact at home in case of an accident or emergency, medical insurance cards, and your pediatrician's telephone number (they can often diagnose and call in a

prescription by phone). Make copies and tuck them into two different places in case you lose one set.

- A travel-size bottle of antibacterial gel (the kind that doesn't require water).

- Basic first-aid kit—children's aspirin and aspirin substitute, allergy medication, Dramamine for motion sickness, bandages, gauze pads, a thermometer, cough syrup, decongestant, medication for diarrhea, antibiotic cream, tweezers, and fingernail scissors.

- Insect repellent.

- Plastic bags for quick storage and wet clothes.

- Prescription medications.

- Unscented baby wipes that can be used for any cleanup.

- A small sewing kit with scissors.

- A small nightlight to ease fear of darkness.

- A couple of extra paperback books, especially for teenagers.

- A folding cooler, or better yet, one with wheels. Perfect for carrying fruit, drinks, even sandwiches to theme parks, on walks, or in the car.

- Lightweight windbreakers for cool evenings at the beach.

- Inexpensive rain ponchos for surprise rainstorms.

- Comfortable walking shoes for nature trails, botanical gardens, and beachside strolls (as well as theme parks).

- Children should bring along some cash of their own, even just a few dollars. Tell them it is theirs to spend on souvenirs or whatever they choose. When it's their money, they're much more judicious shoppers.

- A sense of humor. Traveling with children can be trying at times.

REMEMBERING YOUR TRIP

When you choose a destination, write or call for information (listed at the beginning of each chapter). The travel brochures can later be used as part of a scrapbook commemorating your trip.

Purchase a notebook for each child and spend time each evening recording the events of the day. If your children have trouble getting motivated or don't know what to write about, start a discussion; otherwise, let them write, draw, make lists—whatever they want to remember the day's events.

Collect mementos along the way and create a treasure box in a small tin or cigar box. Months or years later, it's fun to look at postcards, seashells,

Traveling with Pets

If your pet is a vital part of the family, plan a trip where Fido can participate. Here are some helpful tips about traveling with pets from the ASPCA and Tom Scott of AAA-Alabama.

- Pets who are very young, very old, pregnant, sick, injured, prone to biting or excessive vocalizing, or who cannot follow basic commands should not travel.
- Make sure your pet has proper identification on its collar.
- While in the car, pets are safest when secured in pet carriers.
- If your pet can't actively participate in the trip, such as visiting a theme park, it should stay home.
- Before leaving, get a clean bill of health from your veterinarian, making certain the pet is up-to-date with vaccinations or inoculations. You should also take along documentation of rabies vaccinations and other medical records.
- Pack for your pet. Make sure you have an ample supply of any medications your pet is taking. Bring along your pet's prescriptions, the name and phone number of your pet's veterinarian, and get a reference for a vet in the area you will be visiting. Don't forget to pack food, water, the pet's bowls, and favorite toys. Pack a leash and a collar with an ID tag, and always leash your pet before opening the vehicle door.
- Train your pet for trips by car. Take short drives prior to your vacation so your pet can adjust to car travel. This will also give you a clue about how the pet might be affected by motion sickness.
- Become familiar with your travel destination's quarantines, restrictions, required documentation, and potential safety risks both at your destination and along the travel route.
- Ask questions when making hotel/motel reservations. You will find some lodging facilities do not allow pets or have size limitations, require you to hire a pet sitter, or require you to crate your pet.
- Never leave an animal in a parked car. Plan to visit a rest stop every two hours or so to give you and your pet a drink, rest break, and chance to stretch.
- Don't let your animal lean out the window. Road debris, flying objects, or tree limbs can cause severe injury to your pet.
- To prevent car sickness, feed your pet a light meal four to six hours before departing. Do not give a pet food or water in a moving vehicle.

Traveling with Pets (continued)
Information on accommodations and helpful tips for traveling with pets are available from the following: ■ AAA's *Traveling With Your Pet: The AAA Petbook* is a good resource for families who plan to travel with a pet. AAA members also have free access to AAA TourBooks which list lodging facilities allowing pets. ■ www.geocities.com/heartland/ranch/1146, with information about lodging, from bed and breakfasts to five-star resorts. ■ www.takeyourpet.com, a comprehensive listing of lodging as well as general pet-friendly travel information. ■ www.travelingdogs.com/vacindex.html, for tips on planning a pet vacation and finding places to stay.

or ticket stubs to jump-start a memory. We used seashells from a trip to Jekyll Island off Georgia's coast to create a wind chime for our back porch.

Add inexpensive postcards to your photographs to create an album, then write a few words on each page to accompany the images. Better yet, purchase postcards, let your children write about their travels on them, and then mail the postcards home. It's a great surprise when you return from your trip and makes for a neat memory of your travels.

Give each child a disposable camera to record his or her version of the trip. A five-year-old might capture images taken entirely below the waist, but it is his version of the world—and a priceless commentary at that.

Today, many families travel with a camcorder. Just make sure you don't end up viewing the trip through the lens rather than enjoying the sights. Record a few moments of major sights (too much is boring anyway). Let the kids tape and narrate.

Even better, take along a digital camera or video cam so that you can download photos from your trip and email them to everyone back home. You can either wait to do this when you return from your vacation or find places along the way to dispatch your prints. Many hotels have business centers or can refer you to a nearby copy shop with Internet access. Just be sure to take along any plugs or adapters required to hook your camera into the computer.

You can also carry a palm-sized tape recorder and let everyone describe their experiences. Hearing a small child's voice years later is endearing, and those recorded descriptions will trigger an album's worth of memories.

GETTING THERE

By Car

Driving is certainly the most economical way to travel, and in the South, it's the most practical. Still, if you're covering a lot of miles, it's time-consuming and can try the patience of every passenger. For starters, don't pull any punches with your kids about how long you'll be in the car.

If it's a long trip, leave before daylight. Take along small pillows and blankets (we use our children's baby blankets), and let the kids snooze. When they're fully awake a few hours down the road, stop for breakfast and teeth brushing.

Or opt for leaving after dark. Have a nice dinner and get the children bathed and dressed in pajamas. Provide plenty of quiet activities like books or coloring to allow them time to mellow out before going to sleep.

Be sure to pack books, crayons and paper, and a couple of laptop games (though not the electronic kind with annoying beeps). Parents can stash a few surprises to dole out along the way: Sticker books, action figures, magazines. A beach ball that can be deflated, a Frisbee, or a Koosh ball are perfect for impromptu play times at rest stops.

Be sure you have maps, and chart your trip before you leave home. Share the maps with the children so that they'll understand the distance to be covered.

The Southeast is connected by a series of interstates, many of which provide the same disinfected view of the countryside. When possible, take state highways and back roads that zigzag through the South's charming towns and gorgeous scenery; it's more entertaining and easier to stop on a whim. Some general pointers:

- Yellow signs indicate warning or directions; green signs are for free-way directions and street names; orange signs signal roadwork or detours; brown signs indicate parks, campsites, and historic sites; blue signs provide non-driving information; and red-and-white signs mean do not enter or wrong way.

- Speed limits and distances are provided in miles, not kilometers.

- Roads stretching from east to west have even numbers, while those stretching north to south have odd numbers.

- Rest areas can be found all along major highways and interstates, and many—though not all—are open around the clock. Most state rest areas have restrooms, public telephones, and security for at least a portion of the day.

Seat belts for drivers and front-seat passengers are the law. Child safety seats are mandatory for children under four years of age or 40 pounds.

Snacks are great, but leave the drinks (preferably water, since it doesn't stain or get sticky when spilled) until the last moment, or frequent rest room stops will prolong the journey. Pack a picnic for mealtimes, and everyone can take a walk or stretch.

Small pillows and your own CDs or tapes make the journey peaceful. Take turns and let everyone choose a favorite. If kids fight over music, make them take turns choosing. To solve seat fights, rotate turns, either weekly or daily, for who gets to choose a seat first.

Don't forget to always lock your car, and never leave wallets or luggage in sight. Keep valuables locked in the trunk.

By Train

Amtrak serves several major cities in the Southeast, with stops in smaller towns along the way. The best resource is to access the website at www.amtrak.com. You can also call (800) USA-RAIL for reservations and route information.

For youngsters, train trips are interesting for about the first hour. Afterwards, occupy their time with books, games, and activities. Otherwise, it's a leisurely and relatively inexpensive way to travel, with time to unwind and spend quality moments with your family. You can stand up and stretch or go for a walk, and there's more leg room than in an airplane or car (and no traffic jams). Many trains offer sleeping and dining cars, but some trips can be extremely long, and the fare is not much less than cut-rate airfares. If you opt for a longer trip, book first-class and a sleeping car.

Train stations are generally not close to major attractions, so car rentals need to be arranged in advance.

Amtrak offers a children's discount—kids ages 2–15 ride for half-price when accompanied by a full-fare-paying adult. Each adult can bring two children for the discount; children under two years of age ride for free.

By Plane

According to a survey by the Travel Industry Association of America, nearly one-fourth of all trips taken in 1998 included children. These aren't just family vacations—children accompanied parents on 16 percent of all business trips taken the same year.

Every major city in the Southeast is served by major airlines, so choosing a flight is a matter of time and economics. But with more children on the go, it is important that parents to be informed of how to make air travel easier and hassle-free. Christine Turneabe Connelly with Southwest Airlines has the following recommendations:

- Book as far in advance as possible to save hundreds of dollars (for a family of four) and to ensure that your family is seated together for the flight.

- Request bulkhead seats for small kids who won't be entertained by a movie but might be able to move around a bit. Although far-front seats are preferred for the most part, inquire as to how the movie is shown; if you're more than a few rows back from a small screen, it can be hard to enjoy the film.

- Timing is everything, so arriving early at the airport is a must. Families should arrive at least one hour ahead of the scheduled departure so that they have plenty of time to check luggage, go through security, and make any necessary pit stops in the airport. Parents also can use this time to give their children a chance to get a feel for the airport. Whether traveling alone or with the entire family, it's a good idea to have all children carry identification and a small amount of cash for emergencies.

- Dress for comfort. Pack extra disposable diapers for babies and dress children in layers, as the temperature may fluctuate during the flight.

- Ease fears by having children listen carefully to the flight attendants' safety announcements, and make sure they understand the information and know where to go in case of an emergency.

- Earphone-style cassette and CD players may be used at certain times; however, radios may not be operated during flight.

- Take-off and landing bother some children's ears, particularly if they have a cold. Look for plastic earplugs designed to ease ear-pressure pain. They come in children's sizes and are available at travel stores, drug stores, and airport sundry stores. One pair lasts for two plane flights at least; they cost two or three dollars per pair. You can also take along gum for older children or a bottle or sipper cup for babies and toddlers. A washcloth heated with hot water from a thermos and held to ears will also help the younger ones who can't tolerate earplugs. A flight attendant friend swears that squirting children's nose drops into each ear will open the ear canal during flight. If possible, book your flights around nap times, which ensures a peaceful flight for you and a happy child as you land.

- Pack a few nutritious snacks, like pretzels, dried fruit, or crackers, and a small bottle of water. Food and beverage service takes a while on a packed flight (and food isn't always served). If you or your child wants or needs a special meal, be sure to call the airlines at least 48 hours in advance to request it.

- Bring your own child safety seat; though airlines allow children under two years of age to fly free on a parent's lap, it's much safer if they're strapped in a safety seat (and they're much more likely to nap, giving you a break). A car seat must have a visible label stating it is approved for air travel.

IF YOU RENT A CAR

Almost all major car rental companies can be found at airports in major cities, but while the car is king throughout the Southeast, you should shop around for competitive prices before leaving home. Recreational vehicles, four-wheel-drives, and convertibles can be rented, though they are considerably more expensive. To rent a car, you will need a valid driver's license, proof of automobile insurance, and a major credit card. Most companies have minimum age requirements. Confirm all reservations in advance.

Ask about extras. Many companies offer cellular phones, ski racks, electronic area maps, and child safety seats.

If there are more than four in your family, you might want to consider renting a minivan. They cost a little more, but the comfort is worth it.

Car Rental Companies	
Advantage (800) 777-5500	**Enterprise** (800) 325-8007
Alamo (800) 327-9633	**Hertz** (800) 654-3131
Avis (800) 831-2847	**National** (800) 227-7368
Budget (800) 527-0770	**Thrifty** (800) 367-2277
Dollar (800) 800-4000	

RV Rental Companies
Cruise America (800) 327-7799
Go Vacations, Inc. (800) 487-4652
Recreation Vehicle Rental Association (800) 336-0355
Rental Management Systems (818) 960-1884

Family Lodging
HOTELS, MOTELS, AND RESORTS

In each regional chapter you'll find our favorite family-friendly hotels, motels, and resorts. Note that we said favorite family-friendly hotels, not favorite hotels—many wonderful retreats were excluded because they're aimed at romantics or businesspeople and they'd make parents of an energetic four-year-old feel out of place. We've reviewed only places that particularly catch our fancy or seem suitable for families, and we've strived to find places with character. If you don't see an accommodation in the region you wish to visit, call the 800 number of your favorite chain to find out what they can offer.

Tips on Hotels, Motels, and Resorts with Kids

First, there has to be a pool. After that, you get some choices.

One room or two? Large or small? Upscale hotel or basic motel? Old or new? There are pros and cons with each of these overnight options, and we've found that on different days on the same vacation, we might make different choices.

Overall, one of the hardest things for some of us parents to adjust to is being awake when the kids are asleep but not wanting to leave them alone in the room. Although adjoining rooms are a good option in some hotels, they're not offered everywhere, and the choice between one or more rooms for a family always seems to come up.

So we try, on an extended family vacation during which we're moving from place to place, to book ourselves into several different kinds of facilities and find different solutions. In a hub city where we're not expecting to be in a picturesque setting, we look for a business-suite chain, especially on the weekends, when discounts are often offered (but check to see that all amenities, like breakfasts, continue). The price for a spacious suite may be the same as for a cramped room at the motel down the street, and it's great to be able to watch the late show while the little ones snooze.

Big landmark hotels or luxury hotels with character are worth the splurge for us if the location is workable, and they might come at the end of a road trip, when the only choices in small-town stops on the way have been inexpensive roadside motels. Kids like the excitement of big hotels (it's almost like a theme park) and even enjoy "the neat old stuff" in some establishments. And room service is God's gift to traveling parents. But always ask about the executive, concierge, or butler floor in this kind of establishment, because the lounge areas often offer breakfast, coffee, snacks, and wine at various hours. For one thing, it's convenient for grabbing a muffin for a kid in the room; for another, it's a place for parents to escape to, like a living room, without being far away.

The all-American motel is, of course, a favorite with families. No need to find a bellman—you park in front of your room and unload only what you need. Kids love roaming the corridors for ice, soda machines, and the spotting of other children. Lack of towel-service poolside may be compensated for by the existence of a coin laundry. At this kind of hostelry, we might opt for one room, but we'd request a room near the pool with a patio or veranda. Proximity to the pool allows older kids to come and go; the patio extends the living space nicely.

CAMPING

We've included a small but choice collection of southeastern campgrounds that are easily accessible, fun for children, and not too demanding of parents (we consider bathrooms and running water, for instance, to be essential). Camping can be a wonderful family experience, slowing down the pace so you can all take pleasure in the small things, from fishing in a stream to chasing butterflies. And, of course, camping takes you to some of the South's most beautiful places for very little money.

Nearly all the campgrounds we list are state properties, and all are popular. For those that take reservations, make them early.

Tips on Camping with Children

If you are regular campers and your children are used to it from birth, you'll be happy at any of the campgrounds we recommend. If you're not regular campers, we'd recommend the motel option while your children are between infancy and at least three, maybe four years of age.

Camping is a superb opportunity to teach children independence and self-reliance. If they're all expected to pitch in, and the adventure aspect is played up, they'll help prepare food, pitch tents, and do all the camp chores. To maximize your family's safety and comfort, we recommend the following camping tips:

- No one is allowed to leave the campsite (even to go to the bathroom) without a whistle. Children wear the whistle around their necks; adults can carry it as they like. The whistle is blown only in an emergency, which can range from a twisted ankle to getting lost.
- Hats and sunscreen must be worn on all outings.
- Water must be carried on all outings.
- No playing, exploring, or hiking until the morning campsite is tidied and breakfast dishes are done.

Finally, recognize that camping is tiring, and after a few days of sleeping on the ground, tempers of both children and adults can get frayed. After two or three nights of roughing it, nothing cheers a family up like clean hotel sheets, a swimming pool, and a restaurant hamburger.

WHAT TO LOOK FOR IN A HOTEL

Some families want every moment planned; others just want advice on interesting hotels that other families recommend. Many of our recommendations are suites or apartments, since the best vacations give everyone a space of their own. Four in a hotel room is economical, but adjoining rooms or an apartment or condominium may save your sanity and be worth the extra dollars.

Here are some important questions you might want to ask before booking a reservation:

- Do kids stay free?
- Is there a discount for adjoining rooms? How much?
- Can you rent cribs and rollaway beds?
- Does the room have a refrigerator? A microwave?
- Is the room on the ground floor? (Particularly important if you have small children.)
- How many beds in the room?
- Is there a swimming pool? Is there a lifeguard? Is the pool fenced?
- How close is your room to the pool?
- Are there laundry facilities on the premises?
- Is there a kid-friendly restaurant? A breakfast buffet? Other kid-friendly restaurants nearby?
- Is there a supervised children's program? What are the qualifications of the staff? How much does it cost? How do you make a reservation?
- Is there in-room baby-sitting? What are the qualifications of the caregivers? How much does it cost per hour? How do you make a reservation?
- Are the rooms childproofed? Can patio or balcony doors be securely locked and bolted?
- Is there an on-site doctor or a clinic nearby that the hotel recommends?

WHAT'S IN A ROOM?

Here are a few of the things we check:

Room Size.   A large and uncluttered room is generally preferable for families, especially if you are taking advantage of the "kids stay free with parents" deal offered at many hotels. Ask if the hotel has suites, or if they will offer you a discount on an adjoining room for children.

Temperature Control and Ventilation.   The guest should be able to control the temperature of the room. The best system, because it's so quiet, is central heating and air-conditioning, controlled by the room's own thermostat.

The vast majority of hotel rooms have windows or balcony doors that have been permanently secured shut. Though there are some legitimate safety and liability issues involved, we prefer windows and balcony doors that can be opened to admit fresh air.

Childproof Your Room
When you arrive at the hotel, some childproofing may be in order. Be sure that both the front door and any patio or balcony doors and windows can be securely locked and bolted. Some hotels offer electrical outlet coverings if you have toddlers, and protective covers for sharp furniture corners. They will also remove glass objects or other knick-knacks that might be easy for a toddler to break. And if the minibar is stocked with junk food and alcoholic beverages, it should be locked.

Safety. Every room should have a fire or smoke alarm, clear fire instructions, and preferably a sprinkler system. Bathtubs should have a nonskid surface, and shower stalls should have doors that either open outward or slide side-to-side. Bathroom electrical outlets should be high on the wall and not too close to the sink. Balconies should have sturdy, high rails.

Noise. Most travelers have been kept awake by the television, partying, or amorous activities of people in the next room, or by traffic on the street outside. Better hotels are designed with noise control in mind. Wall and ceiling construction are substantial, effectively screening routine noise. Carpets and drapes, in addition to being decorative, can also absorb and muffle sounds. Mattresses mounted on stable platforms or sturdy bed frames do not squeak, even when challenged. Televisions enclosed in cabinets, and with volume governors, rarely disturb guests in adjacent rooms.

Lighting. Poor lighting is an extremely common problem in American hotel rooms. The lighting is usually adequate for dressing, relaxing, or watching television, but not for reading or working. Lighting should be bright over tables and desks and alongside couches or easy chairs. If you're sharing a room with children, ask for one with separate lights over the beds, so you can stay up reading after the kids have lights-out.

Furnishings. At bare minimum, the beds must be firm. Pillows should be made with hypoallergenic fillers, and, in addition to the sheets and spread, a blanket should be provided.

With a family of four or more sharing a hotel room, you may not have enough dresser space to give everyone more than one drawer. You can request extra luggage racks if there is wall space to accommodate.

Many well-designed hotel rooms have a sleeper sofa, which is invaluable for families. Other family-friendly amenities to look for include a small refrigerator, a microwave, a digital alarm clock, and a coffeemaker.

Bathrooms. Two sinks are better than one, and you cannot have too much counter space. A sink outside the bath is a great convenience when families are bathing and dressing at the same time.

Overall Appearance.   We recommend that you ask to be sent a photo of a hotel's standard guest room before you book, or at least get a copy of the hotel's promotional brochure or look up the property on the Internet. Be forewarned, however, that some hotel chains use the same guest room photo in their promotional literature for all hotels in the chain and that the guest room in a specific property may not resemble the photo in the brochure. When you or your travel agent calls, ask how old the property is and when the guest room you are being assigned was last renovated. If you arrive and are assigned a room inferior to that which you had been led to expect, demand to be moved to another room.

CHILDREN'S PROGRAMS

Many large hotels offer supervised programs for children, some complimentary, some with fees. We've included several throughout the Southeast that offer exemplary activities.

If you decide to take advantage of the kids' programs, call ahead for specific children's events that are scheduled during your vacation. Ask about cost and the ages that can participate; the best programs divide children into age groups. Make reservations for activities your child might enjoy (you can always cancel after arrival).

After check-in, stop by and visit with the kids' program staff. Ask about counselor-child ratio and whether the counselors are trained in first aid and CPR. Briefly introduce your children to the staff and setting, which typically will leave them wanting more, thereby easing the separation anxiety when they return to stay.

Some hotels offer in-room baby-sitting, but if your hotel does not, there is a national, nonprofit referral program called Child Care Aware that will help you locate a good, dependable sitter. You can call (800) 424-2246, Monday-Friday, 8:30 a.m.–4:30 p.m.

Be sure to ask if the sitter is licensed, bonded, and insured. To ease your children's anxiety, tell them how long you plan to be away, and be sure they feel good about the person who will be caring for them. Finally, trust your own instincts.

CHAIN HOTEL TOLL-FREE NUMBERS

This guidebook gives details on some of the hotels in the Southeast with outstanding children's programs. However, for your convenience we've listed toll-free numbers for the following hotel and motel chains' reservation lines:

Best Western	(800) 528-1234 United States and Canada
	(800) 528-2222 TDD
Comfort Inn	(800) 228-5150 United States

Courtyard by Marriott	(800) 321-2211	United States
Days Inn	(800) 325-2525	United States
Doubletree	(800) 528-0444	United States
Doubletree Guest Suites	(800) 424-2900	United States
Econo Lodge	(800) 424-4777	United States
Embassy Suites	(800) 362-2779	United States and Canada
Fairfield Inn by Marriott	(800) 228-2800	United States
Four Seasons	(800) 332-3442	
Hampton Inn	(800) 426-7866	United States and Canada
Hilton	(800) 445-8667	United States
	(800) 368-1133	TDD
Holiday Inn	(800) 465-4329	United States and Canada
Howard Johnson	(800) 654-2000	United States and Canada
	(800) 654-8442	TDD
Hyatt	(800) 233-1234	United States and Canada
Loew's	(800) 223-0888	United States and Canada
Marriott	(800) 228-9290	United States and Canada
	(800) 228-7014	TDD
Quality Inn	(800) 228-5151	United States and Canada
Radisson	(800) 333-3333	United States and Canada
Ramada Inn	(800) 228-3838	United States
	(800) 228-3232	TDD
Residence Inn by Marriott	(800) 331-3131	United States
Ritz-Carlton	(800) 241-3333	United States
Sheraton	(800) 325-3535	United States and Canada
Stouffer	(800) 468-3571	United States and Canada
Wyndham	(800) 822-4200	United States

Family-Friendly Restaurants

Face it: Adults and kids have different opinions on what constitutes a good restaurant. We like comfort, good service, creative cooking, and a nice glass of wine. They like noise, cups with lids, and as much fried food as possible. Hence the challenge: To put together a roster of restaurants throughout the Southeast that make both parents and children happy. We had more success in some areas than others; areas in some states don't have much more than coffee shops and chains, so you'll have to make do. Other areas, however, (especially New Orleans, Atlanta, Memphis, and Raleigh) are rich in kid- and parent-friendly dining.

You'll note that most major chain restaurants and all the chain fast-food restaurants are not found in the listings that follow. We encourage you to skip McDonald's whenever possible and make the effort to patronize local places—not only is it better for your health, but also you're more likely to get a feel for an area when you sit with the locals and eat a burrito, dim sum, or pancakes. As for the big chain restaurants, we find most of them to be soulless and dull, though hard to beat for consistency and predictability.

The major tourist areas all seem to have Hard Rock Cafes and Planet Hollywoods, but we cover those rarely—after all, if you've been to one Hard Rock, you've been to them all. Your hotel can steer you to one of them.

Tips on Dining Out with Children

Be Realistic about Age Limits.   We ate at elegant restaurants when our children were sleeping infants in car seats. By the time toddlerhood hit, we restricted ourselves to quality fast food (like taquerias), child-friendly ethnic restaurants (Chinese, Cuban, Mexican, etc.), and takeout food enjoyed in park picnic areas. We began restaurant-training in earnest at about age four, the dawn of a years-long process of gentle reminding about napkins on laps, feet off chairs, and proper butter knife etiquette. We expect to have achieved success around the junior year of college.

Don't Battle a Picky Eater.   You'll never win this one. If everything looks yucky to them, get them some plain rice and plain bread. Enjoy your food with gusto, and if the kids get hungry enough, they'll break down and ask to try some.

Look Beyond the Children's Menu.   The vast majority of children's menus are monotonous and unhealthy, consisting mostly of burgers, deep-fried chicken, and french fries. Encourage experimentation in the grown-up menu, and ask if it's possible to order smaller portions of the "adult" food.

Remember the Tailgate.   We had more fun eating on a tailgating vacation than perhaps any other. Grocery stores, delis, upscale gourmet shops, and mini-marts are all stocked with foods that seem almost too decadent to buy at home—but if you're tailgating, you have to go for the convenience foods. So we'd get takeout salads and chicken, made-to-order sandwiches, sushi, poached salmon, fresh baguettes, imported cheeses, and exotic fruits. The price was still less than a bad meal at a roadside coffee shop.

Watch the In-Betweeners.   When they feel too old for (or don't like) the children's menu but can't really eat a big meal, some parental diplomacy is in order, or the in-betweener will be taking one bite from a huge order of whatever and then stopping, overwhelmed. Some kids will agree to splitting or sharing a meal, but let them choose most of it. Sometimes it's just a matter of ordering three meals for four people, so you avoid huge quantities of leftovers (which you can't take home when traveling) and yet allow for some tasting of different things.

Soup, Soup, Soup.   Not only is it comforting and homey, but soup is often a tasty, nutritious, affordable basis for a kid's meal that needs only an appetizer to complete it.

Let Them Be Weird.   One man we know is still grateful to his parents for letting him order hamburgers at breakfast—and conversely, how many people are cheered up by a nice breakfast at 7 p.m.? As much as possible, let your kids enjoy the get-what-you-want pleasure of restaurant eating as part of their vacation. Remember, they're also missing home, routine, and the certainty of their daily meal rituals.

Special Challenges to a Southeast Vacation

The summer is naturally the most popular time for travel in the Southeast, and even during the shoulder seasons, it can be unbearably hot. Before starting off on a day of touring or a visit to the beach, parents should keep some things in mind.

Overheating, Sunburn, and Dehydration.   Due to the Southeast's temperate climate, parents with young children on a day's outing need to pay close attention to their kids. The most common problems of smaller children are overheating, sunburn, and dehydration. A small bottle of sunscreen carried in a pocket or fanny pack will help you take precautions against overexposure to the powerful sun. Be sure to put some on children in strollers, even if the stroller has a canopy. Some of the worst cases of sunburn we have seen were on the exposed foreheads and feet of toddlers and infants in strollers. To avoid overheating, rest at regular intervals in the shade or in an air-conditioned museum, hotel lobby, restaurant, or public building.

Don't count on keeping small children properly hydrated with soft drinks and water-fountain stops. Long lines at popular attractions often make buying refreshments problematic, and water fountains are not always handy. What's more, excited children may not inform you or even realize that they're thirsty or overheated. We recommend renting a stroller for children six years old and younger, and carrying plastic water bottles.

Blisters.   Blisters and sore feet are common for visitors of all ages, so wear comfortable, well-broken-in shoes or sandals. If you or your children are usually susceptible to blisters, carry bandages for your feet. When you feel a hot spot, stop, air out your foot, and place a bandage over the area before

Time Zones
Louisiana, Mississippi, and Alabama are in the Central Standard Time zone (CST). Georgia, Tennessee, North Carolina, South Carolina, and Virginia are in the Eastern Standard Time zone (EST).   Daylight Savings Time is observed from the first Sunday in April until the last Sunday in October, when clocks are forwarded one hour to take advantage of daylight.

a blister forms. Moleskin is available by name at all drugstores. Sometimes small children won't tell their parents about a developing blister until it's too late. We recommend inspecting the feet of preschoolers two or more times a day.

Sunglasses.   If you want your smaller children to wear sunglasses, it's a good idea to affix a strap or string to the frames so the glasses won't get lost and can hang from the child's neck while she's indoors.

Bug Spray.   Accept it—bugs of all sorts are quite prevalent in the South-east, and several itchy bites can make even the toughest adult miserable. Buy kid-safe repellent, preferably without Deet, or opt for other options like Avon's Skin So Soft lotion. If you'll be hiking in the woods, experts recommend long sleeves and pants, all coated with spray. It's a toss-up— either swelter in the clothing or take the risk of carrying home a tick. We recommend thorough, nude-body checks after a day in the woods.

Beach Safety.   To avoid a severe sunburn that can ruin a child's—and your—vacation, follow this advice offered by Larry Pizzi, operations supervisor of the Miami Beach lifeguards: "Put your kids in light or pastel-colored T-shirts—they'll tan right through the shirts—gob the sunscreen on exposed skin, and give 'em little hats. Be particularly careful on windy days, because kids don't feel the sun burning."
   More advice: "Don't let little kids swim alone—it's still the ocean out there," Pizzi says. "And don't leave your children alone on the beach—it's easy for them to get disoriented."

Seasickness.   Seasickness can occur any time the body experiences motion other than on-foot. As a result, almost 90 percent of people suffer from some level of seasickness. Scientists think the condition is caused by sensory mis-match in the brain, when the vestibular system of the inner ear sends mes-sages about body position and movement that contradict information relayed by the eyes. This confuses the brain and causes dizziness, blurry vision, nausea, and other side effects. To counter these unwanted symptoms:

- Try nonprescription drugs designed to keep the symptoms under control. To be effective, most drugs should be taken at least an hour before the boat leaves the dock.

- Keep a broad view of the horizon in sight and walk around to try and adjust to the motion of the boat. Avoid reading and lying down.

- Ask to join the captain so you can focus on the boat's course. This is the same reasoning behind the fact that most automobile drivers never get carsick because they are focused on the road in front of them.

- Avoid alcoholic beverages.

- Consider purchasing a Sea Band that controls pressure on the acupuncture points (the neikuan point) in your wrists.

Safety

- Discuss safety with your family before you leave home.

- Discuss what to do if someone gets lost. If you are going to a crowded theme park or anywhere that there's a possibility you and your children could get separated, write your children's name on adhesive tape and tape it inside their shirts. Be sure that young children know their full name, address, and phone number (with area code).

- Carry photos of your kids for quick ID.

- Travelers' checks are the easiest way to protect your money.

- In emergencies, call 911 for assistance in reaching paramedics, law enforcement, or the fire department.

- Teach your children to find the proper authorities if they are lost. Tell them to approach a security guard, a store clerk, or "a grown-up who is working where you're lost."

- Before heading out for a stroll, if you are unsure about the safety of an area, ask the front desk manager or concierge in your hotel.

- Always lock your car when it is parked.

- Always try to keep your gas tank full.

- At night, try to park your car under a streetlight or in a hotel parking garage. Never leave wallets, checkbooks, purses, or luggage in the car. It's best to lock your luggage out of sight in the trunk.

- Keep your wallet, purse, and camera safe from pickpockets. A fanny pack, worn around the waist, is the most convenient way to stash small items safely.

- Leave your valuables at home, and if you must bring them along, check with your hotel to see if there is a safe.

- Be sure you lock sliding doors that lead to your hotel balcony or porch while you are in your room and always when you leave. Never open the hotel room door if you are unsure about who is at the door.

- Keep medicine out of reach of small children; it's easy to forget and leave it out in hotel rooms.

- Check with the front desk, hotel security, or guest services at attractions for lost property. Report lost or stolen travelers' checks and credit cards to the issuing companies and to the police.

- Crime can happen anywhere, so use common sense and take necessary precautions.

Part One

Alabama

As a destination, Alabama rarely makes it to the top of travel wish lists. It doesn't offer the glitz and glamour of neighboring Tennessee's cities, and it has yet to reach the high-profile status of Georgia and its Olympian Atlanta. Yet anyone who considers a trip to the South would be remiss to bypass "the Heart of Dixie."

Alabama is laid-back and low-key. Its four largest cities, Birmingham, Huntsville, Montgomery, and Mobile, are as cosmopolitan as any others in the South, but sprinkled between these metropolises are cozy, small towns where high school football and dinner on the ground after Sunday church services are vital parts of everyday life.

Another Alabama advantage is the diversity in geography. There are mountains in the northeast (the foothills of the **Appalachians**), sugar-white beaches in the south, and plenty of lakes and rivers in-between.

For families, an Alabama vacation can be completely different from one day to the next. We recommend giving yourself plenty of time to stop along the way. Part of Alabama's charm is that the journey rather than the destination can become the most memorable part of your trip. Experiencing how other people live through simple activities like picnicking in a cow pasture and slurping milkshakes at a quaint downtown soda fountain are just as enriching as museums and theme parks.

Because the South is essentially a driving destination, you are going to need a car to get anywhere in most cities and to travel from one city to the next. With this mind, plan your trip with the four major cities as interval stops on your itinerary.

In **Birmingham**, take in all the big-city attractions, such as VisionLand, Alabama's first amusement park, and the Civil Rights Institute. **Montgomery** is also a hot spot for Civil Rights history, with the Civil Rights Memorial and the first White House of the Confederacy. **Huntsville** is best

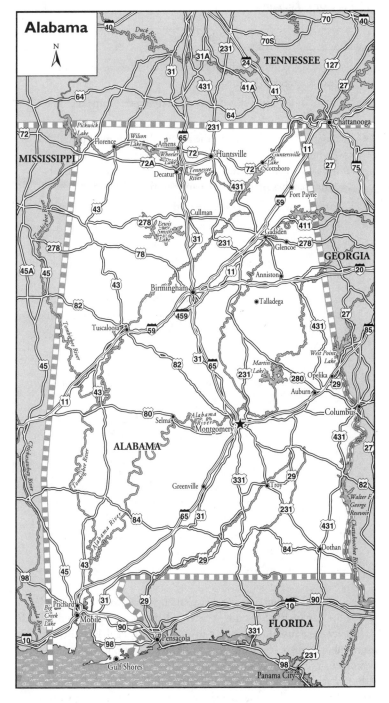

Alabama

N

Kids' Beat

- Alabama was named from an Alibamu Indian word and means "I clear the thicket."

- The state bird is the yellowhammer; state flower: camellia; state tree: southern pine.

- Alabama has two nicknames: the Heart of Dixie and the Yellowhammer State, so-named because soldiers during the Civil War embellished their uniforms with yellow trimmings that resembles the wing patches of the yellowhammer, the state bird.

- Alabama is the 30th-largest state in the Union.

- The Boll Weevil Monument, erected in 1919 as the first statue ever erected to an insect pest, is located in Enterprise.

- Parts of the Steven Segal movie *Under Siege* were filmed at the battleship *USS Alabama*.

- Alabamian George Washington Carver invented many products from peanuts, including linoleum, peanut-oil shampoo, gasoline, cherry punch, face bleach and tan remover, buttermilk, and dry coffee.

- Forty percent of the total peanuts produced in the United States are grown in southern Alabama within a 100-mile radius of Dothan.

- In 1910, Wilbur and Orville Wright established the world's first flying school at the site now known as Maxwell Air Force Base in Montgomery.

- Kudzu is a fast-growing vine that covers more than seven million acres of the Deep South. It was first introduced at the 1876 Centennial Exposition as an ornamental garden plant and later promoted as an animal food and for erosion control. Because it will grow over virtually any surface (cars, houses, street signs. . .), people are now trying to get rid of it.

known for the U.S. Space & Rocket Center, while **Mobile** is a good place to visit the Exploreum Museum of Science before heading off to the beach.

In-between, **Tuscaloosa** sports an outstanding Paul Bear Bryant Museum full of Alabama football facts. **Ave Maria Grotto** in Cullman features a garden of miniatures built by a monk using marbles, tail pipes, and other garbage scraps. And at the **Dismals Canyon** in Phil Campbell, your youngsters will ooh and ah at the incredible "Dismalites," twinkling worms that glow in the dark along the canyon walls.

Alabama's Not-to-Be-Missed Attractions	
Huntsville	Earlyworks
	U.S. Space & Rocket Center
	Ave Maria Grotto
Birmingham	Birmingham Civil Rights Institute
	McWane Center
	Birmingham Museum of Art
	Rickwood Caverns State Park
	Robert Trent Jones Golf Trail
	VisionLand
Mobile	Bellingrath Gardens & Home
	The Estuarium at the Dauphin
	Island Sea Lab
	USS Alabama Battleship
	Memorial Park
Montgomery	Alabama Cattleman's Mooseum
	Alabama Shakespeare Festival
	Civil Rights Memorial
Gulf Shores/	Fort Morgan State Historic Site
Orange Beach	

The climate is usually cooperative to vacation plans. Temperature differences between the northern and southern areas of the state vary only slightly. Highs can reach the 90s during the summer and will more than likely be accompanied by the South's infamous humidity, but winters are mild. When it does threaten to snow, school can be dismissed and roads can sometimes be closed.

GETTING THERE

By Plane.   The largest airport in the state is the Birmingham International Airport, located about five miles from downtown and accessible from all interstate roads, (205) 595-0533. This is where you'll probably have the best luck with reasonable airfares and the largest variety of carriers. Some travelers take advantage of the lower airfares at Hartsfield International Airport in Atlanta, then rent a car and drive to Alabama. (The state line is an hour from the airport.) Other airports can be found in Dothan off Napier Field Road, (334) 983-3594; Huntsville on Glenn Hearn Boulevard, (256) 772-

9395; Mobile on Airport Boulevard, (334) 633-4510; Montgomery on Highway 80, (334) 281-5040; and Muscle Shoals at 1687-T Ed Campbell Drive, (256) 381-2869. Tuscaloosa's airport is currently closed to commercial traffic; visitors must fly into Birmingham and then drive about 45 minutes to Tuscaloosa.

By Train.   Passenger trains serve Anniston, Atmore, Birmingham, Mobile, and Tuscaloosa on a limited basis. Information on train schedules is available at (800) 872-7245 or (205) 324-3033.

By Car.   Interstate 65 divides the state in half from north or south, I-59 also travels north to south in the northeastern corner of the state, I-20 bisects central Alabama from west to east, and I-85 provides a west-to-east route from Montgomery to Atlanta. These are the major jumping-off points for many of the state roads and highways that lead through rural Alabama. For reference, driving the major highways from Huntsville to Birmingham takes about an hour and a half; Birmingham to Montgomery, about two hours; and Montgomery to Mobile, about three and a half hours. For exact directions, the state Website, www.touralabama.org, can give you exact directions to your destination; all you have to do is enter the address of your starting point and your destination. Another helpful page on the site is a list of road construction sites throughout the state. Alabama law requires all front-seat occupants to buckle up, and children younger than six years of age must be restrained in federally approved safety restraints. Four- and five-year-olds may use safety belts instead of child safety seats, which are mandated for children ages three and younger.

How to Get Information before You Go

State

Alabama Bureau of Tourism and Travel, P.O. Box 4927, Montgomery 36103-4927; (800) ALABAMA; (334) 242-4169; www.touralabama.org

AAA Alabama Motorists Association, 2400 Acton Road, Birmingham 35243; (205) 978-7000

Bed & Breakfast Association of Alabama, P.O. Box 707, Montgomery 36101; (800) 965-7321; www.bbonline.com/al/bbaa

Regional

Alabama Mountain Lakes Association, P.O. Box 1075, Mooresville 35649; (800) 648-5381; www.almtlakes.org

Alabama Gulf Coast Area Convention & Visitors Bureau, 23685 Perdido Beach Boulevard, Orange Beach 36561; (800) 982-8562; www.gulfshores.com

Tallacoosa Highland Lakes Association, 1240 Mahaffey Road, Eastaboga 36260; (256) 831-8409

Local

Auburn-Opelika Convention & Visitors Bureau, 714 East Glenn Avenue, Auburn 36830; (800) 321-8880; www.auburn-opelika.com

Greater Birmingham Convention & Visitors Bureau, 2200 9th Avenue North, Birmingham 35203; (800) 458-8085; www.birminghamal.org

Decatur Convention & Visitors Bureau, 719 6th Avenue SE, Decatur 35601; (800) 524-6181; www.decaturcvb.org

Dothan Area Convention & Visitors Bureau, 3311 Ross Clark Circle NW, Dothan 36303; (334) 794-6622; www.dothanalcvb.com

Florence/Lauderdale Tourism, One Hightower Place, Florence 35630; (256) 740-4141; www.flo-tour.org

Gulf Coast Chamber of Commerce, P.O. Box 3869, Gulf Shores 36547; (334) 968-6904; www.alagulfcoastchamber.com

Huntsville/Madison County Convention and Visitors Bureau, Von Braun Civic Center, 700 Monroe Street, Huntsville 35801; (800) SPACE-4-U or (256) 551-2230; www.huntsville.org

Mobile Area Convention & Visitors Corporation, P.O. Box 204, Mobile 36601-0204; (800) 5-MOBILE; www.mobile.org

Montgomery Area Chamber of Commerce, 401 Madison Avenue, Montgomery 36104; (334) 261-1100; www.montgomery.al.us

Tuscaloosa Convention and Visitors Bureau, 1305 Greensboro Avenue, Tuscaloosa 35401; (800) 538-8696; www.tcvb.org

More Alabama Websites
Alabama History   www.alabamastuff.com
Alabama Symbols   www.geobop.com/world/na/us/al
Alabama's Part in the Civil War   www.tarleton.edu/~kjones/ alabama.html
Alabama History On-Line   www.archives.state.al.us/aho.html
Alabama Experience   www.cptr.ua.edu/alex

Family Outdoor Adventures

▲ - Camping

♥ - Author's favorite

▲ - *Cheaha Mountain, Lineville*   Few people realize that Alabama has both beaches and mountains. Located in the northeastern part of the state, Cheaha Mountain is the tallest mountain in Alabama with a peak reaching 2,407 feet. Surrounded by the Talladega National Forest, Cheaha State Park Resort is located here and offers a variety of outdoor activities such as hiking, a wildflower garden, fishing, swimming, the Cheaha Mountain Express bike trail, and boating on Cheaha Lake. Kids especially enjoy the Nature Center's wildlife and backpacking workshops. Park admission is $1 per person; hours are daily until sunset. There are 73 campsites; cost is $14.56, or $7 for primitive sites. The park also features 15 family cottages that cost from $51 for two people to $74 for eight people per night, and a hotel with 31 rooms that cost from $61 to $76 per night. Located in Lineville off I-20; (800) 846-2654 or (256) 488-5111.

▲ ♥ - *Gulf Beaches*   Alabama's beaches rival those of northwest Florida. The water is clear and the sand is white quartz that has been polished like glass by the undulating waves in the Gulf. Various minerals cause color fluctuations, but since these beaches are created with only hard, crystal-clear quartz, they have the look and texture of sugar—so much so that rumors abound about shysters during World War II trying to pass the sand off as sugar.

Some say the sand is so fine because it is hundreds of miles away from its source—the Appalachian Mountains. Over hundreds of thousands of years, quartz from granite formations from the mountains weathered away then washed down to riverbeds and into the ocean. This journey pummeled the pieces into small bits and buffed raw edges smooth.

There's plenty to do along these 62 miles of sea and sand, including camping, swimming, sunbathing, fishing, hiking, and water sports. Gulf Shores, Orange Beach, and Dauphin Island have beach points of entry that are free; admission is charged for state park access; (334) 948-7275.

▲ - *Moundville Archaeological Park, Moundville*   A visit to Moundville Archaeological Park is a good way to get acquainted with Alabama's rich Native American history. This site was once home to a large Mississippian settlement on the Black Warrior River. The park's main attraction, the 26 prehistoric Indian mounds, will look like nothing more than grassy hills to kids, but other points of interest include the Jones Archaeological Museum with artifacts unearthed during the 1930s excavations. One of the more interesting findings is that 85 percent of the Moundville Indians had deformed skulls; as children, boards were fastened to their heads to cause sloped foreheads.

You can watch videos on Native American life in the museum theater, visit a reconstructed Indian village, and view life-size dioramas of ancient Indian rituals in the Temple Mound. There is also a picnic area and a boardwalk nature trail winding through the forest and along the river. A solid game plan would be to spend the morning exploring the park and then wind up your visit with a picnic. Each of the 31 spaces in the wooded campground costs $10 a night and is equipped with water, electrical hookup, RV pads, and grills. Park admission is $4 for adults, $2 for children; hours are daily from 8 a.m. to 8 p.m.; museum hours are daily from 9 a.m. to 5 p.m. Located 13 miles south of Tuscaloosa on Moundville Parkway; (205) 371-2572.

▲ - *Oak Mountain State Park, Pelham*   Alabama's largest state park is conveniently located on the outskirts of Birmingham. Besides a fabulous amphitheater that frequently hosts nationally known performers, the park offers 10,000 acres for outdoor exploration. Small children will enjoy the petting farm; older kids will get a kick out of renting paddle boats and canoes at the manmade beach or renting a horse and traversing the park's equestrian trails. Golf, a marina, tennis, fishing, interpretive nature trails and hiking trails, and a bicycle motocross track are also in the park. Park admission is $1 per person, children ages 5 and younger get in free. Hours are daily from 7 a.m. to 9 p.m. There are 91 campsites that cost $10.55 or $14.43 per night with gas/electric hook-ups and ten cottages that cost $114 per night. Located 15 miles south of Birmingham; (205) 620-2524 or (205) 620-2520.

▲ - *Rickwood Caverns State Park, Warrior*   Here's your chance to go underground! Your kids will love walking along the "miracle mile" of underground caverns at this state park. The limestone formations are the highlight — they're over 260 million years old, and you can see where new formations are being created as mineral-rich water droplets build colorful structures and flowstones next to the established formations. The pathways you walk along through the caves are also natural, carved out by water millions of years ago. Some of the passages are dimly lit but open into lighted "rooms." The walk takes about 45 minutes.

Afterwards, hike one of the two nature trails, visit the gift shop, or swim in the park's swimming pool (open only during the summer). Stay overnight in one of the 13 campsites; cost is $12.60 per night. There is also a picnic area and snack bar. Park admission is $1 for ages 6 and older; hours are 7:30 a.m.untilsunset. Located near Birmingham off I-65 and Exit 284; (205) 647-9692; www.bham.net/rickwood.

Robert Trent Jones Golf Trail   The golfers in the family won't want to miss one of Alabama's unique attractions, the Robert Trent Jones Golf Trail. With 18 courses spread out over seven locations, the Trail stretches from the Appalachian Mountains of northern Alabama to the flatlands surrounding Mobile Bay in the south. Each course is slightly different, showcasing the natural beauty and geography found in each part of the state. Several courses offer a golf academy for both children and adults. Prices and hours vary for each course; children get half-off the rack rates. For tee times and information, call (800) 949-4444; www.rtjgolf.com.

Calendar of Festivals and Events

January

Fury on the Gulf, Dauphin Island   This event is held annually on a weekend close to January 11, the date in 1861 when Alabama seceded from the Union. Visitors can watch as Confederates gallantly defend the port of Mobile in a re-enactment of the Battle of Mobile. Hosted by the 21st Alabama Infantry Company D, the event takes place at Fort Gaines Historic Site and also includes a candlelight tour; (334) 861-6992.

Dr. King Birthday Celebration, Birmingham   A variety of special activities and programs take place at the Birmingham Civil Rights Institute in honor of Dr. Martin Luther King Jr.'s birthday; (205) 328-9696.

February

Mardi Gras, Mobile   A two-week extravaganza of parades and formal balls that culminates on Fat Tuesday. Parade times and routes vary daily; (334) 415-2017.

Black Heritage Festival, Anniston   The Anniston Museum of Natural History hosts the annual celebration of Alabama's rich African-American heritage. The festival features song, dance, storytelling, craft demonstrations, and orations. This event is the area's largest and longest-running celebration of Black History Month; (256) 237-6766.

March

Battle of Horseshoe Bend Anniversary, Tallapoosa County near Daviston   This annual event at the Horseshoe Bend National Military Park commemorates the March 27, 1814 battle between Andrew Jackson's Tennessee army and the Red Stick Creeks of Menawa. There are living history demonstrations on a soldier's life and flintlock musketry, encampments where volunteer "soldiers" and "laundresses" of the platoon pitch canvas tents and kindle log fires for cooking, and solder drills complete with live volleys of black powder musketry; (256) 234-7111.

April

Indian Dance Festival, Childersburg One of the South's top festivals, this event at DeSoto Caverns Park attracts hundreds of Native Americans from across the U.S. to celebrate their culture and traditional values. Storytelling, making blowguns and arrowheads, basket weaving, singing, demonstrations of how Native Americans used to live, samplings of Native American foods, pony rides, a petting zoo, and booths of authentic handmade crafts are among the activities. The Atlanta-based Southeast Tourism Society (STS) picked the dance festival as one of the top 20 events in the South; (800) 933-CAVE.

Birmingham International Festival, Birmingham Formerly the Birmingham Festival of Arts, this annual festival salutes a different country each year. Fun for the whole family, the festival lets attendees experience the culture of the chosen country through performances, art, food, crafts, and musicians. Special children's activities are held, along with Ciclismo, America's Richest Masters Bike Race; (205) 252-7652.

Battle of Selma Re-enactment, Selma Thousands of authentically costumed and equipped soldiers and cavalry of the Blue and Gray clash once again in this re-enactment that portrays the sealing of the Confederacy's doom. Weekend activities for this annual event are held at Battlefield Park and include campfire visits, a grand ball at Sturdivant Hall, and, of course, the battle itself; (800) 45-SELMA or (334) 875-7241.

May

Jubilee Cityfest, Montgomery Designated by the American Bus Association as one of the top 100 Events in North America, the Jubilee Cityfest features more than 70 acts performing on six musical stages. Musical styles range from gospel, pop, jazz, blues, and country to classical. In addition, there are a variety of foods plus arts and crafts; (334) 834-7220.

Annual Blessing of the Fleet, Bayou La Batre Seafood dinners, arts and crafts, a land parade, a decorated boat parade and blessing, exhibits, and contests round out this annual event; (334) 824-2415.

June

Cahaba Riverfest, Centreville This all-day festival on the banks of the Cahaba River features canoe rides, prizes, food, music, and water education activities; (334) 322-5326.

Frontier Day Celebration, Florence   Celebrate the life and craftsmanship of early settlers with arts and crafts of the period, educational demonstrations, and dulcimer music—all by artisans and musicians in costumes typical of the frontier period. The event is held at Pope's Tavern; (256) 760-6439.

City Stages, Birmingham   This annual outdoor music festival in and around Linn Park has 16 stages and performance areas along 18 blocks and includes a children's festival, dance-o-rama stage, gospel fest, and classical music oasis; (205) 251-1272.

Old Alabama Town's Storytelling Fest, Montgomery   Join noted local and regional authors and storytellers for an afternoon of stories, fun, food, and family; (888) 240-1850.

Helen Keller Festival, Tuscumbia   This summer festival, held in downtown Tuscumbia, includes athletic events, a huge arts and crafts show, art competition, storytelling, musical concerts, a parade, sidewalk sales, educational events, and presentations of *The Miracle Worker*, a play about Helen Keller's life; (256) 383-4066.

July

Spirit of America Festival, Decatur   This Fourth of July celebration at Point Mallard Park has games for the children, a presentation of the Audie Murphy Patriotism Award, a huge fireworks display, and the Miss Point Mallard Scholarship Pageant; (800) 524-6181.

August

W.C. Handy Music Festival, Florence   This is a weeklong celebration of the musical heritage of northwest Alabama honoring Florence native W.C. Handy, "The Father of the Blues." There are approximately 150 events held in conjunction with the festival throughout the Shoals area (Florence, Sheffield, Tuscumbia, Muscle Shoals, Russellville, and others); (256) 766-7642.

September

World's Largest Peanut Boil, Luverne   Crenshaw Shriners boil more than 14 tons of peanuts fresh from the field in stainless cookers; (334) 335-4809.

Mule Day, Winfield   This mule-and-horse parade is a town tradition, with arts and crafts booths, a flea market, an antique car display, music, dancing, and lots of food and fun; (205) 487-8841.

October

Sidewalk Moving Picture Festival, Birmingham   Weekend festival of independent film. Free outdoor street carnival with live music, performers, games, and entertainment, with elaborate children's area and amusements. One-time wristband purchase required to see any (or all) of a hundred films showing continuously in a half-dozen venues. 1911 27th Avenue South, Birmingham, AL 35209; (205) 871-2927; www.sidewalkfest.com.

Kentuck Festival of the Arts, Northport   More than 30,000 visitors turn out for this two-day, outdoor, juried art festival. In addition to the more than 300 booths of arts and crafts, there are musicians, children's art activities, folk artists who demonstrate expert traditional craftsmanship, a petting zoo, storytelling, and Southern and ethnic food specialties; (205) 758-1257.

Bayfest Music Festival, Mobile   Continuous music all weekend long is the hallmark of this festival. More than 100 musicians from around the United States perform annually; (800) 566-2453.

National Shrimp Festival, Gulf Shores   This annual event is one of Gulf Shores' signature festivals. In all, the event lasts four days and is jam-packed with music, arts and crafts, fine arts, seafood, children's art activities, and a sandcastle contest on the beach; (334) 968-6904.

Halloween Ghost and Goblin Train, Calera   Passengers board the train at the Heart of Dixie Railroad Museum and take a 30-minute ride through spooky encounters in a Halloween forest; (800) 943-4490.

November

National Peanut Festival, Dothan   A ten-day fair featuring top-name entertainment, agricultural and livestock displays, and a dazzling parade; (334) 793-4323.

December

Tannehill Village Christmas, McCalla   The historic cabins at Tannehill are decorated 1800s-style with different activities in each one. There are storytelling events, music, Santa, and old-fashioned crafts; (205) 477-5711.

Christmas on the Alabama River, Selma   Watch a parade of lighted boats as they float down the Alabama River. There are also fireworks; (800) 45-SELMA

First Night, Mobile   A multimedia, multicultural event that combines the magic of the arts with the thrills of a nonalcoholic, family-oriented New Year's Eve celebration. From the opening procession to the midnight fireworks over the river, more than 80 acts on the streets and in venues fill downtown; (334) 470-7730.

Huntsville

Huntsville was founded in 1805 by pioneer John Hunt, and in 1819, the first leaders of the Alabama Territory met here to elect the first governor and legislature. Later, the city became an important center for cotton trading, and many planters and merchants relocated here from the original 13 Colonies. Because of their loyalty to the Union, the town was spared from destruction during the Civil War. Therefore, Huntsville has the state's largest collection of antebellum homes.

Today, Huntsville has a high tech image, one that was born in the 1950s when the city played a strategic part in the development of the U.S. space and rocket industry. Here, a team of scientists, led by German scientist Wernher von Braun, created the rocket that orbited America's first satellite and helped develop the technology which put the first American in space and transported the first astronauts to the moon. It's no surprise that the **U.S. Space & Rocket Center** is the top attraction in Alabama—over 400,000 people visit annually.

Only 20 miles from the Tennessee state line in north Alabama, Huntsville's climate is temperate, though the city does catch colder weather in the winter than other Alabama cities simply because of its location at the foothills of the **Appalachian Mountains.** These mountains create Huntsville's rolling topography—hills perfect for biking and hiking. As for day trips, Huntsville is 217 miles from Atlanta, 110 miles from Nashville, and only 96 miles from Birmingham. If you are driving into Alabama, Huntsville is a good place to begin your trek through the state.

If you only have a weekend to explore the city, we recommend planning a day at the U.S. Space & Rocket Center and a day at all of the **Earlyworks** attractions. Depending on the season, you might also consider catching a Huntsville Stars baseball game or a Channel Cats ice hockey game. Tourist information centers are located at the von Braun Center on Monroe Street and the Huntsville International Airport. Both are open daily.

Note: The area code for Huntsville and the surrounding areas in northern Alabama recently changed from 205 to 256.

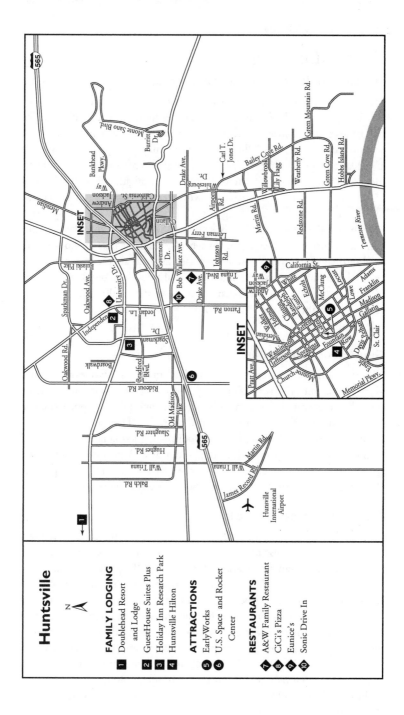

Huntsville

N

FAMILY LODGING

1 Doublehead Resort
   and Lodge
2 GuestHouse Suites Plus
3 Holiday Inn Research Park
4 Huntsville Hilton

ATTRACTIONS

5 EarlyWorks
6 U.S. Space and Rocket
   Center

RESTAURANTS

7 A&W Family Restaurant
8 CiCi's Pizza
9 Eunice's
10 Sonic Drive In

Family Lodging

Doublehead Resort and Lodge, Town Creek

Saddle up and head 45 minutes west of Huntsville to Doublehead Resort and Lodge, one of the few dude-style ranches found in the Southeast. The main lodge was handcrafted from cedar and features a 5,000-square-foot deck that overlooks Lake Wilson. For private, fully equipped quarters, there are cedar cottages around the lake, with front porches complete with hammocks. While you could limit your stay to overnight, this is the kind of place that is a destination unto itself, with plenty of opportunities to catch up on quality family time. Hang out for a couple of days and play beach volleyball at the white-sand beach, swim and water-ski in the lake, try your hand at shooting sport clays, go horseback riding, or play air hockey and pool in the game room. Western weekends are held at certain times of the year, with roping lessons, calf branding, trail rides, hoedowns, and chuckwagons. Rates start at $150 for cabins in the winter; $200 for cabins in the summer. County Road 314; (800) 685-9267 or (256) 685-0224; www.doublehead.com.

GuestHouse Suites Plus

Clean, affordable, and centrally located to many Huntsville attractions, GuestHouse Suites Plus offers privacy and convenience for parents. Each room has a separate living area with a fireplace and fully equipped kitchen, and the exterior doors open to an inside corridor. There is also a complimentary continental breakfast, an outdoor pool, guest laundry on-site, and a complimentary airport shuttle. Rates start at $63 in both summer and winter. 4020 Independence Drive, three miles from the U.S. Space & Rocket Center; (800) 21-GUEST or (256) 837-8907; www.guesthouse.net.

Holiday Inn Research Park

No surprises here—just a modest room at an affordable price. The main reason to stay is because of the location; it's only two miles from the U.S. Space & Rocket Center and adjacent to the mall. If you reserve your room well in advance, you can request adjoining rooms. The property also has refrigerators for rent at $5 per night, and you can choose between a room with an exterior door (convenient for packing and unpacking) or one that opens onto an interior corridor or onto the courtyard where the pool is located. There is also an outdoor pool and complimentary airport shuttle. As with other Holiday Inns, kids ages 12 and younger eat free from the Kids Menu in the restaurant, and room service is offered. Rates start at $69 per night year-round. 5903 University Drive; (800) HOLIDAY or (256) 830-0600; www.basshotels.com/holiday-inn.

Huntsville Hilton

Huntville's only downtown hotel is within walking distance of all downtown attractions, including the Big Spring International Park, the von Braun Civic Center, and the historic district. An outdoor pool, on-site restaurant with room service, and jogging and biking trails are among the amenities offered. The hotel also features suites, though you should book in advance to ensure availability. Rates begin at $99 for a standard room year-round, but you can often find lower rates (as low as $63) on their website. One other note: The hotel has just completed an extensive renovation, so it's now one of the nicer chain hotels in northwest Alabama. 401 Williams Avenue; (800) 774-1500 or (256) 533-1400; www.hilton.com.

Attractions

EarlyWorks

(Includes Alabama Constitution Village and the Historic Huntsville
   Depot); 404 Madison Street, Huntsville; (800) 678-1819
   www.earlyworks.com

Hours: Monday–Saturday from 9 a.m.–5 p.m.

Admission: Combo tickets for Constitution Village, Historic Huntsville
   Depot, and EarlyWorks: $13 adults, $10.50 children ages 4–17, $12
   seniors; tickets for individual attractions begin at $6 adults and $3.50
   children ages 4–17; Trolley Tour is $2 adults, $1 seniors and children
   ages 4–17

Appeal by Age Group:

Pre- school	Grade School	Teens	Young Adults	Over 30	Seniors
★★★	★★★★	★★★	★★★	★★★	★★★

Average Touring Time: 5 hours; 1½ hours for EarlyWorks, 1 hour for
   Alabama Constitution Village, and 1½ hours for Historic Huntsville
   Depot

Minimum Touring Time: 30 minutes for EarlyWorks, 30 minutes for
   Alabama Constitution Village, 1 hour for Historic Huntsville Depot

Rainy Day Touring: Recommended for EarlyWorks and Historic
   Huntsville Depot; not recommended for Alabama Constitution Village

Author's Rating: ★★★★   A good balance of non-participatory exhibits
   and interactive activities

Services and Facilities:

Restaurants No	Wheelchair rental No
Alcoholic beverages No	Baby stroller rental No
Disabled access Yes	

Lockers No   Rain check N/A
Pet kennels No   Private tours Yes

Descriptions and Comments   EarlyWorks is the interactive history equiva-
lent of the science museums popping up all over the country. The complex
is actually home to four separate attractions. EarlyWorks is the South's
largest hands-on history museum, with interactive architectural exhibits,
giant-sized instruments, a talking story tree, and the kids' favorite—a gang-
plank that you walk from a 46-foot keelboat.

Alabama Constitution Village, where the founding fathers first met to
elect a governor and legislature, is a nineteenth century, living-history village. The houses display period furnishings and household equipment, and
with the help of villagers dressed in period clothing, children can participate in activities like working in a cabinetmaker's shop. This is also the site
of eight reconstructed Federal-style buildings and the actual site where the
early delegates met to establish Alabama's statehood.

The Historic Huntsville Depot, one of the nation's oldest remaining railroad structures, is the boarding point for the trolley ride that carries guests
through historic downtown Huntsville. Kids can climb aboard locomotives
and view the state's largest public model railroad at the Depot.

If you're going to try and see it all, spend the morning at Alabama Constitution Village, take the trolley at midday and catch lunch, and finish your
day at EarlyWorks.

U.S. Space & Rocket Center

One Tranquility Base, Huntsville; (800) 63-SPACE or (205) 837-3400
   www.ussrc.com

Hours: Open daily from 9 a.m.–5 p.m.; until 6 p.m. during summer

Admission: $14.95 adults, $10.95 children ages 3–12, free ages 2 and
   younger; IMAX is $6.50 adults, $5.50 children ages 3–12

Appeal by Age Group:

Pre-school	Grade School	Teens	Young Adults	Over 30	Seniors
★★★	★★★★★	★★★★★	★★★★★	★★★★★	★★★★★

Average Touring Time: 3½ hours

Minimum Touring Time: 1½ hours

Rainy Day Touring: Recommended

Author's Rating: ★★★★★   Fantastic tour of science and space

Services and Facilities:

Restaurants Yes   Disabled access Yes
Alcoholic beverages No   Wheelchair rental Yes

Baby stroller rental Yes

Lockers No

Pet kennels Yes

Rain check N/A

Private tours Yes

Description and Comments The U.S. Space & Rocket Center is a parent's dream: Kids are so overwhelmed by the hands-on, interactive exhibits that they remain attentive for the entire tour. And a bonus is the fact that they are getting a science lesson about physics and space without ever realizing it.

This is the world's largest space-travel attraction, and as such, there are space-travel simulators and displays unlike any others. In the interactive Outpost in Space, learn all about life on a space station. The Journey to Jupiter is a motion-based simulated flight with asteroids hurling toward you, while Mars Mission is a simulator that takes you on a journey across the Red Planet. Rocket Park, the NASA Bus Tour, and an IMAX theater are also not to be missed. No age group is left out, though activities for preschoolers are limited. Kids Cosmos blasts the little ones into an "energy depletion zone" for a gentle landing on the moon, and the Space Station Crawl Structure lets them explore on their own. If your kids get hooked, there are summer and weekend space camps available for in-depth instruction and experiences. The center is located at Exit 15 off I-565.

Side Trips

Butterflies and Biospheres The Huntsville-Madison County Botanical Garden is not high on the list of kids' activities in the city, but if you find yourself with extra time, stop by and tour the 80-foot-long, screened-in butterfly house. The exhibit is filled with dazzling butterflies of a variety of species, and informative markers explain the life cycle of these beautiful creatures. The butterfly house is open from Memorial Day to Labor Day. There is also a NASA–influenced Center for Biospheric Education and Research with an astronaut garden complete with demonstrations in hydroponics and other ways that astronauts grow food in outer space. Located at 4747 Bob Wallace Avenue between the U.S. Space & Rocket Center and Jordan Lane; (256) 830-4447; www.hsvbg.com.

Point Mallard Park, Decatur Kids love the water, and at Point Mallard's J. Gilmer Blackburn Aquatic Center in Decatur, the first water park in the state, there are plenty of creative ways to get wet. Among the favorites: The wave pool (the nation's first), the three-flume Sky Pond water slide, the sandy beach at Flint Creek, the Olympic-size pool, and the Duck Pond Kiddie Pool. There are concession areas throughout the park, but it's easier to pack a picnic lunch and set up camp on one of the grassy areas. Other features in the 750-acre park include an 18-hole championship golf course, 200 acres along the banks of the Tennessee River for hiking and camping, and indoor ice skating in the winter. Located in Decatur, a 25-minute drive from Huntsville, at 1800 Point Mallard Drive; (800) 669-WAVE or (256) 350-3000.

Dismals Canyon, Phil Campbell   Named a National Historic Site by the National Geological Society, the Dismals offer a natural bridge, waterfalls, a flourishing arboretum, and cool, clear streams in one of the oldest untouched forests east of the Mississippi River. Visitors can hike, canoe, or swim in the canyon, but the highlight of the visit is spotting the "Dismalites," twinkling worms that glow in the dark, giving the canyon its mysterious reputation. Located about two hours from Huntsville in Phil Campbell off Highway 43; (800) ALABAMA.

Ivy Green, Tuscumbia   By itself, kids will write this off as another old house-turned-museum. But take them to the back of the cottage to see and touch the very well where Helen Keller first began to understand sign language, and they'll understand what the fuss is all about. The museum contains original furniture of the Keller family and many of Helen's personal mementos and books, including her complete library of Braille books and her Braille typewriter. There is also a gift shop on the property. In the summer, an hour-and-a-half play called *The Miracle Worker* is presented outdoors behind the Kellers' home. Located about one hour from Huntsville at 300 West North Commons in Tuscumbia; (205) 383-4066.

Ave Maria Grotto, Cullman   Alabama's only Benedictine abbey is the home of Ave Maria Grotto, a garden of miniatures crafted from broken fluorescent bulbs, pieces of shiny mufflers, and toilet bowl floats. Brother Joseph Zoettl, who lived at St. Bernard's abbey for over 60 years, built the more than 125 detailed miniatures. The Leaning Tower of Pisa, Noah's Ark, and St. Peter's Basilica are but a few of the replicas scattered along the rocky landscape that once served as the Abbey's rock quarry. Located in Cullman, a 30-minute drive from Huntsville, at 1600 Saint Bernard Abbey Drive; (256) 734-4110.

Looney's Tavern, Double Springs   Not all Southerners were interested in seceding from the Union. This outdoor drama highlights those in the hill country of North Alabama's Winston County, who actually tried to secede from the state. The production takes place nightly during the summer; for daytime diversions, take a riverboat ride on Smith Lake, play the miniature golf course, and mill through the countrified gift shops. There is also an indoor musical presentation about the Civil War. Located on Highway 278 in Double Springs, about one-and-a-half hours from Huntsville; (205) 489-5000.

Family-Friendly Restaurants

A&W FAMILY RESTAURANT

2110 Drake Avenue, Huntsville; (256) 883-9250

Meals served: Lunch and dinner
Cuisine: American
Entrée range: $3.59 and up
Kids menu: Yes
Reservations: Not accepted
Payment: Cash only

In business for 30 years, this landmark old-fashioned malt shop is known for its Coney dogs made with homemade chili and onions and, of course, A&W Root Beer Floats. It also has fish and chicken sandwiches and dinners.

CICI'S PIZZA

4925 University Drive, Huntsville; (256) 864-2224
10004 South Memorial Parkway, Huntsville; (256) 885-1595
www.cicispizza.com

Meals served: Lunch and dinner
Cuisine: Italian/pizza buffet
Entrée range: $2.99 and up
Kids menu: No
Reservations: Not accepted
Payment: All major credit cards accepted

This all-you-can-eat buffet chain can't be beat for families with a penchant for pizza. When you're beat from touring the town, CiCi's is an easy place for dinner.

EUNICE'S

1004 Andrew Jackson Way, Huntsville; (256) 534-9550

Meals served: Breakfast
Cuisine: American
Entrée range: $1–7
Kids menu: No, but will prepare small portions
Reservations: No
Payment: Cash or check

You'll be hard-pressed to find better Southern food around Huntsville. Since the 1960s, Eunice has served good old-fashioned Southern breakfasts for her local followers as well as astronauts and presidents. Her specialties are homemade biscuits and gravy made from her mother's recipe, and country ham-and-cheese grits are also popular. Though she doesn't have a kids' menu, she will prepare small portions for children.

SONIC DRIVE-IN

3222 Bob Wallace Avenue, Huntsville; (256) 539-4004

Meals served: Lunch and dinner
Cuisine: American
Entrée range: $3.50 and up
Kids menu: Yes
Reservations: Not accepted
Payment: All major credit cards accepted

It's a chain, but forget the hassle of going in to eat—just sit back and let dinner come to you. This drive-in serves up the usual hamburgers, fries, and shakes, but you can also get tater tots with cheese, chili pies, hot dogs, and chicken sandwiches.

Birmingham

When Birmingham was founded in the late 1800s, people began calling it the Magic City because it sprang like magic from a railroad junction. Today, few people realize that Birmingham is a cosmopolitan city sprawled along the foothills and literally carved into the sides of **Red Mountain.** With most of the amenities of its Southern cousin, Atlanta, but without the hassle of that city's urban sprawl, Birmingham packs enough clout to attract major events such as Olympic soccer and a world-renowned Asian art exhibit, plus national companies such as Books-A-Million and Southern Progress Corporation, publisher of *Southern Living* magazine.

Your first inclination about the city might be to remember the images of George C. Wallace, hooded Klansmen, and protesters being sprayed with fire hoses and attacked by police dogs. This is the Birmingham indelibly stamped on the minds of millions who witnessed, via television, the civil rights demonstrations of the 1960s. But for the past 30 years, while other Southern cities have basked in the media spotlight, Birmingham has sat in the shadows, working quietly to mend its reputation for ignorance and intolerance.

Memorials have been erected to remember the tumultuous events of the Civil Rights era. The **Birmingham Museum of Art** has undergone a multi-million-dollar renovation. A dilapidated iron foundry, **Sloss Furnace,** has been restored as the only national landmark of its kind, and urban parks and architecturally rich inner-city communities have been revitalized.

These are but a few of the visible changes throughout the city. Attitudes have also changed. Birmingham's first black mayor was in office for four straight terms. Community culture has a strong influence in city planning. And as home to influential medical facilities such as the University of Alabama in Birmingham Hospital and HealthSouth, Inc., the city has positioned itself as an international leader in medical research and technology.

Oh, you'll still see pickup trucks sporting Confederate flags and gun racks cruising along the highways—only now they're sandwiched between

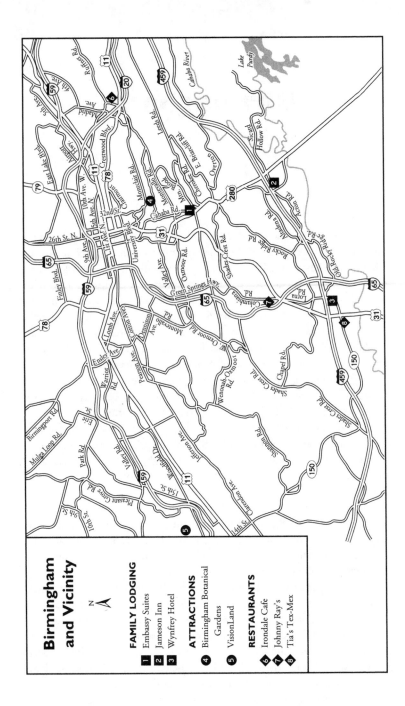

Birmingham and Vicinity

N

FAMILY LODGING

1 Embassy Suites
2 Jameson Inn
3 Wynfrey Hotel

ATTRACTIONS

4 Birmingham Botanical Gardens
5 VisionLand

RESTAURANTS

6 Irondale Cafe
7 Johnny Ray's
8 Tia's Tex-Mex

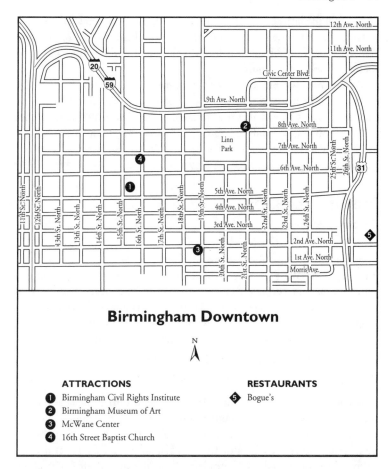

Birmingham Downtown

N

ATTRACTIONS

① Birmingham Civil Rights Institute
② Birmingham Museum of Art
③ McWane Center
④ 16th Street Baptist Church

RESTAURANTS

⑤ Bogue's

Mercedes and BMWs. Coffee houses with cappuccino and iced latte are becoming as popular as mom-and-pop diners serving grits and barbecue. Birmingham is a young city in terms of both economic growth and the age of its population, and this gives it the unmistakable feel of a city on the move.

During the day, your family will discover a bustling city brimming with art galleries, museums, and plenty of shopping—and that includes specialty toy stores for the kids. Skyscrapers are clustered along downtown streets, while family-favorite chain restaurants and local cafes are scattered throughout the suburbs.

At night, a breathtaking view of the city is visible from any of the numerous neighborhoods and streets perched along the ridge and tucked into the crevices of the mountain.

Deep in the heart of Dixie, Birmingham enjoys a temperate climate, yet still experiences seasonal changes, from the brilliant display of red and golden leaves in the fall to the colorful explosion of budding trees and flowers in the spring and summer.

Birmingham is centrally located within the state and enjoys proximity to other hot spots in the South. Only a three-hour drive from Nashville or Atlanta, it makes an easy day trip from either city. The Gulf Coast beaches are four hours away, and you can head for the Appalachian foothills of northern Alabama by driving a couple of hours northeast to Lookout Mountain.

Family Lodging

Embassy Suites

Yes, it's a chain, but the roomy accommodations work well for families. Rooms come complete with a private bedroom, separate living area for watching television, and refrigerator and wet bar for quick snacks. You also get a complimentary, cooked-to-order breakfast. The kicker: Kids ages 18 and younger stay free. Rates start at $109 in both summer and winter. 2300 Woodcrest Place, Birmingham, between Mountain Brook and Homewood, three miles from Brookwood Mall and four miles from downtown; (800) EMBASSY or (205) 879-7400; www.embassy-suites.com.

Jameson Inn

This colonial-style inn is nothing fancy, but you can't beat its affordable price and location next to VisionLand in Bessemer. The setup is that of a traditional motel, with doors opening to the outside. There is also a swimming pool, fitness center, and free continental breakfast. Rates average around $60 year-round. 5021 Academy Lane at Exit 108 off I-459; (800) JAMESON or (205) 428-3194; www.jamesoninns.com.

La Quinta Inn & Suites

Standard hotel rooms and suites can be found at this Homewood area inn, and the best part is the recent remodeling. All rooms have new furniture and linens, and the bathrooms have been refinished as well. Extended-stay rooms have king-size beds, microwaves, refrigerators, and recliners. Rates begin at $89. 60 State Farm Parkway; (800) 531-5900, (205) 290-0150; www.laquinta.com.

Radisson Hotel

The Radisson is conveniently located downtown near the university's medical center and Five Points South's restaurants. The hotel has a pool, exercise room, restaurant, sauna, and three suites. Rates start at $88. 808 South 20th Street; (800) 333-3333, (205) 933-9000; www.radisson.com.

Wynfrey Hotel

With its AAA Four Diamond, Mobil Four Star, and Preferred Hotel status, the Wynfrey Hotel is somewhat swanky for small kids, but you'll see plenty here because of the hotel's location—it's attached to the Riverchase Galleria, a large mall with 250 stores, 20 restaurants and ten theaters. The hotel is also close to Oak Mountain State Park, Metropolitan Stadium, and the Robert Trent Jones Golf Trail. Rates range between $164–250 year-round, with fall weekend prices increasing due to football bookings. 1000 Riverchase Galleria, 15 minutes south of downtown Birmingham and 26 miles from the Birmingham International Airport; (800) 476-7006 or (205) 987-1600; www.wynfrey.com.

Attractions

Birmingham Botanical Gardens

2612 Lane Park Road, Birmingham; (205) 879-1227

Hours: Open daily from sunup to sundown

Admission: Free

Appeal by Age Group:

Pre-school	Grade School	Teens	Young Adults	Over 30	Seniors
★	★★	★★★	★★★	★★★	★★★★

Average Touring Time: 2 hours

Minimum Touring Time: 1 hour

Rainy Day Touring: Not recommended as most exhibits are outdoors

Author's Rating: ★★★   A pretty place for a picnic

Services and Facilities:

Restaurants Yes	Lockers No
Alcoholic beverages Yes	Pet kennels No
Disabled access Yes	Rain check N/A
Wheelchair rental No	Private tours No
Baby stroller rental No	

Description and Comments   No doubt some children find horticulture boring, but we wanted to be sure and mention the Gardens because it's a popular attraction in Birmingham and a great place for a low-key family picnic. Located in the heart of the city, this 67-acre park is a celebration of nature, with both exotic and native gardens to visit. The most recent addition is the

Japanese Cultural Center, which includes a replica of a fourteenth century teahouse and a performance pavilion for ongoing Japanese cultural events.

Birmingham Civil Rights Institute

520 16th Street North, Birmingham; (205) 328-9696

Hours: Tuesday–Saturday, 10 a.m.–6 p.m.; Sunday, 1–5 p.m.

Admission: $5 adults, $2 seniors, $1 college students (with I.D.), free for children ages 17 and younger

Appeal by Age Group:

Pre-school	Grade School	Teens	Young Adults	Over 30	Seniors
★	★★★	★★★★★★	★★★★★	★★★★★	★★★★★

Average Touring Time: 2½ hours

Minimum Touring Time: 1½ hours

Rainy Day Touring: Recommended

Author's Rating: ★★★★★ Informative, with engaging exhibits and recorded narrative

Services and Facilities:

Restaurants No	Lockers No
Alcoholic beverages No	Pet kennels No
Disabled access Yes	Rain check N/A
Wheelchair rental No	Private tours By appointment
Baby stroller rental No	only

Description and Comments Instead of sweeping past indiscretions under the rug, the Birmingham Civil Rights Institute exposes life in Birmingham during the "separate but equal" days of Jim Crow. Lifelike figures and detailed exhibits depict slices of everyday life during segregation, and the tense moments of the Civil Rights Movement are recaptured on film. The self-paced journey ends with visitors joining a procession of animated figures celebrating the victories of the civil rights struggle and with an exhibit displaying contemporary human rights issues around the world. The Institute is located in the historic Civil Rights District.

Note: A few of the exhibits might be disturbing for younger children.

Birmingham Museum of Art

2000 8th Avenue North, Birmingham; (800) 277-1700, (205) 254-2565 artsbma.org

Hours: Tuesday–Saturday, 10 a.m.–5 p.m.; Sunday, noon–5 p.m.

Admission: Free

Appeal by Age Group:

Pre-school	Grade School	Teens	Young Adults	Over 30	Seniors
★	★★	★★★	★★★	★★★	★★★

Average Touring Time: 3½ hours

Minimum Touring Time: 1½ hours

Rainy Day Touring: Recommended

Author's Rating: ★★★ A manageable art museum that doesn't overwhelm; call ahead and schedule a tour with a docent for the most fulfilling experience

Services and Facilities:

Restaurants Yes	Lockers No
Alcoholic beverages No	Pet kennels No
Disabled access Yes	Rain check N/A
Wheelchair rental No	Private tours By appointment
Baby stroller rental No	only

Description and Comments The largest municipally owned art museum in the Southeast underwent a multimillion-dollar expansion earlier this decade. It features an outstanding permanent art collection of over 17,000 works from many diverse cultures, especially European, American, Asian, and African. Unless your children are art enthusiasts, it won't be one of their favorite stops, but it is a good place to introduce them to art. Don't miss the multilevel sculpture garden and the Beeson Collection of Wedgwood china.

McWane Center

200 19th Street North, Birmingham; (205) 714-8300; www.mcwane.org

Hours: June–August: Monday–Friday, 9 a.m.–6 p.m.; Saturday, 9 a.m.–6 p.m.; Sunday, noon–6 p.m. September–May: Monday–Friday, 9 a.m.–5 p.m.; Saturday, 9 a.m –6 p.m.; Sunday, noon–5 p.m.

Admission: Adventures Halls: $7 ages 13–59, $6.50 ages 6–12 and seniors, $5.50 children ages 3–5, free ages 2 and younger. Call for IMAX and combo prices.

Appeal by Age Group:

Pre-school	Grade School	Teens	Young Adults	Over 30	Seniors
★★★	★★★★★	★★★★★	★★★★	★★★★	★★★★

Average Touring Time: 3 hours for tour; 45 minutes for IMAX film

Minimum Touring Time: 1½ hours

Rainy Day Touring: Recommended

Author's Rating: ★★★★★
Services and Facilities:

Restaurants Yes	Lockers No
Alcoholic beverages No	Pet kennels No
Disabled access Yes	Rain check N/A
Wheelchair rental No	Private tours No
Baby stroller rental No	

Description and Comments   Science becomes an adventure at the McWane Center, where kids can take in the World of Water, a 6,500-square-foot exhibition with interactive aquarium exhibits; the Challenger Learning Center Alabama, with space-mission simulations; and ScienceQuest, an assembly of interactive science exhibits including a ten-foot-tall tornado. There is also an IMAX theater.

VisionLand

5051 Prince Street, Birmingham; (205) 481-4750
  www.visionlandpark.com

Hours: Open daily during summer from 10 a.m.–10 p.m.; open weekends only in April, May, September, and October from 10 a.m.–9 p.m.

Admission: $22 adults, $18 children and seniors

Appeal by Age Group:

Pre-school	Grade School	Teens	Young Adults	Over 30	Seniors
★★★	★★★★	★★★★	★★★★	★★★	★★★

Average Touring Time: 1 day
Minimum Touring Time: 3 hours
Rainy Day Touring: Not recommended
Author's Rating: ★★★★
Services and Facilities:

Restaurants Yes	Lockers Yes
Alcoholic beverages No	Pet kennels No
Disabled access Yes	Rain check No
Wheelchair rental Yes	Private tours No
Baby stroller rental Yes	

Description and Comments   Alabama's first amusement park was inspired by Birmingham's early steel industry, and many of the rides in the water park have an industrial theme. Yet this reference is lost on kids who are more concerned with the park's various rides. There are four themed areas that include a seven-acre water park for all ages and the Rampage, a wooden roller coaster. Other favorites include the Dino Domain by Dinamation, with 36 species of life-sized, animated dinosaurs, and The Mine Shaft, a series of four enclosed dark tubes with twists and turns that end with a big splash. Because the park is new, there are not as many rides as in other amusement parks, but it is less crowded and the lines are shorter.

Side Trips

16th Street Baptist Church   This is the historic site of the tragic 1963 bombing that killed four girls and prompted the worldwide outcry against racial violence. While its tragic history may be disturbing for young children, visiting the site brings the past alive for teens and young adults. The church, newly renovated, still open for worship on Sundays, and you can often catch the minister there during the week. If you call for an appointment, he will be glad to give you a quick tour of the facility. Located downtown at 1530 6th Avenue North; (205) 251-9402.

Desoto Caverns, Childersburg   What makes this fascinating park different from other geological gems is the plethora of kids' activities designed to help them appreciate the rock formations and caverns found throughout the park. You'll find an inflatable cave for jumping and hopping; a simulated-cave crawl tunnel; a simulated, horizontal cave wall climb; a life-size lost-trail maze; water balloon stations; and panning for gemstones.

Before you allow the kids to expend some energy, take them on a cave tour. As the first officially recorded caves in the United States, DeSoto Caverns have a rich Native American history. The caverns were once a center of activity for the Creek Indian nation, and there is a prehistoric Native American habitat and burial ground over 2,000 years old found on-site. During the Civil War, the Confederacy used the caverns as a gunpowder mining center, and during Prohibition the caverns hid moonshine stills. Today, the park presents a spectacular laser-light and sound show inside the onyx cathedral, an actual cavern larger than a football field and taller than a 12-story building. There is also a nice gift shop in the park with affordable items for children. The Caverns are a 45-minute drive from Birmingham, making this a nice day trip. Located at 5181 DeSoto Caverns Parkway in Childersburg; (800) 933-2283 or (256) 378-7252.

Family-Friendly Restaurants

BOGUE'S

3028 Clairmont Avenue, Birmingham; (205) 254-9780

Meals served: Breakfast and lunch
Cuisine: Hearty southern fare
Entrée range: $2.50–9 for breakfast; $5.40–6.40 for lunch

Kids menu: No
Reservations: Not accepted
Payment: Cash only

The owners describe this place as a businessman's restaurant, with hefty helpings of hearty southern fare. Bogue's has been around for more than 50 years and has had only two owners. For breakfast, don't miss the homemade biscuits and good country ham. Omelets with vegetables or shrimp Creole are also favorites. At lunch, it's a meat-and-potatoes kind of place, with a daily special ranging from short ribs to country-fried steak. Kids are welcome, along with "anybody else who has money in their pocket."

IRONDALE CAFE

1906 First Avenue North, Birmingham; (205) 956-5258
www.whistlestopcafe.com

Meals served: Lunch
Cuisine: Southern
Entrée range: $2.20–2.75
Kids menu: No, but serves half orders
Reservations: Not accepted
Payment: V, MC, D

This local favorite was Fannie Flagg's inspiration for the book *Fried Green Tomatoes*, though in the book it was called the WhistleStop Cafe. The restaurant is known for its good home cooking, which includes the dish that made it famous, plus fried chicken reputed to be the best in the South. Owners Bill and Mary Jo McMicheal also have a variety of "WhistleStop" products you can buy, including a cookbook with The Irondale Cafe's Original WhistleStop Recipes.

JOHNNY RAY'S

1460 Montgomery Highway, Birmingham; (205) 823-7437

2252 Pelham Parkway; (205) 985-7675

3431 Colonnade Parkway; (205) 967-0099;
www.johnnyrays.com

Meals served: Lunch and dinner
Cuisine: Barbecue
Entrée range: $2.45–10.99
Kids menu: Yes
Reservations: Not accepted

Payment: All major credit cards accepted

While Dreamland, a spin-off of the renowned Tuscaloosa barbecue joint, is more popular among adults, kids will enjoy Johnny Ray's because the barbecue is spicy-sweet with minimal bite. The restaurant has delicious homemade chocolate, coconut cream, and lemon pies—the best you'll find in Alabama.

LOVOY'S

420 Greensprings Highway, Birmingham; (205) 942-9866

Meals served: Dinner
Cuisine: Italian
Entrée range: $7.95 and up
Kids menu: No, but will serve child's portions
Reservations: Accepted
Payment: All major credit cards accepted

A Birmingham mainstay, Lovoy's has been serving authentic Italian cuisine for 36 years. Ziti, chicken parmesan, lasagna, and fettuccine Alfredo are some of the most requested dishes. It's casual and noisy, so kids will feel right at home.

THE ORIGINAL PANCAKE HOUSE

1931 11th Avenue South, Birmingham; (205) 933-8837

Meals served: Breakfast and lunch
Cuisine: American
Entrée range: $4 and up
Kids menu: Yes
Reservations: Not accepted
Payment: All major credit cards accepted

The name says it all. This is where you can get a piping hot stack of hotcakes or French toast, or one of those puffy German pancakes called a "Dutch Baby" that comes topped with powdered sugar and lemon drizzles. In all, there are 15 varieties of pancakes, made from scratch at any time of the day.

THE PURPLE ONION

1717 10th Avenue South, Birmingham; (205) 933-2424
1931 Second Avenue North, Birmingham; (205) 252-4899
1550 Montgomery Highway, Hoover; (205) 823-1069

5614 Chalkville Road, Trussville; (205) 856-2424

Meals served: Lunch and dinner
Cuisine: Middle Eastern
Entrée range: $5.95 and up
Kids menu: Yes
Reservations: No
Payment: All major credit cards accepted

A Middle Eastern menu gives this place a decidedly different flair, and you might be surprised how much kids seem to like the kebabs, chicken pita roll-ups, and hummus and chips. The kids' menu also has the old stand-bys—cheeseburgers and chicken fingers. Hours vary for each restaurant, with some open all night.

SILVERTRON CAFE

3813 Clairmont Avenue, Birmingham; (205) 591-3707

Meals served: Lunch and dinner
Cuisine: American
Entrée range: $5.95 and up
Kids menu: Yes
Reservations: Accepted
Payment: All major credit cards accepted

Expect generous portions of perennial favorites at this popular neighborhood hangout. Pastas with homemade sauces, a variety of salads, burgers topped with everything from chili to bleu cheese, and fajitas round out the menu.

TIA'S TEX-MEX

3630 Galleria Circle, Birmingham; (205) 403-0772
www.tiastexmex.com

Meals served: Lunch and dinner
Cuisine: Mexican
Entrée range: $5.79–25.99
Kids menu: Yes
Reservations: Accepted
Payment: All major credit cards accepted

Tia's offers informal Mexican dining in a boisterous atmosphere. Another plus is its location next to the Riverchase Galleria. Look for signature dishes such as fajitas, quesadillas, and jalapeno hot rings. For the kids, the menu features traditional Mexican dishes like mini tacos and American cuisine such as corndogs and grilled cheese sandwiches.

Mobile

If you are planning a trip to Mobile in southern Alabama, get ready to see lots of water. This is one of America's oldest ports, and **Mobile Bay** on the Gulf Coast has shaped the culture and feel of the city for three centuries. Its deep bay, harbor, and the barrier islands of Gulf Shores and **Dauphin Island** made the city an attractive military site and active port from its beginning, and an asset to early settlers who were privy to the finer imports from Europe, England, the Mediterranean, and the Orient. Mobile also has a reputation for receiving more annual rainfall than any other American city—with an average of 64 inches annually since 1961.

Yet don't let its rainy reputation put a damper on your travel plans. Mobile is steeped in history, with a rich Southern tradition influenced heavily by French, African, Spanish, Creole, and Celtic cultures. In the late 1700s, travelers from across Colonial America came to see the azaleas that Fifse Langlois brought from his father's garden in Toulouse, France. Later, farmers and their families traveled to the city by steamboat to ship cotton throughout the world. And it was here, not in New Orleans, that the first North American Mardi Gras celebration was held.

If you can stand the heat and humidity of the summer, Mobile is an excellent year-round destination for families. Otherwise, plan your visit for fall and spring, when the temperatures are mild and the wind is less chilly than in winter. There are museums, Civil War sites, and of course, plenty of activities on the water to fill your days. Boating and fishing are perennial favorites, and beach bums can head to the white, sandy shores of Dauphin Island and Gulf Shores for a day of fun in the sun.

Mobile is also a great jumping-off point for Gulf Coast excursions. New Orleans is 144 miles to the west, Pensacola, Florida, lies 60 miles to the east, and Birmingham is 260 miles north.

For weekend trips, spend the first morning at the *USS Alabama* **battle-ship;** head to the beach at Gulf Shores in the afternoon. The **Gulf Coast Exploreum** and the **Estuarium** are good choices for day two.

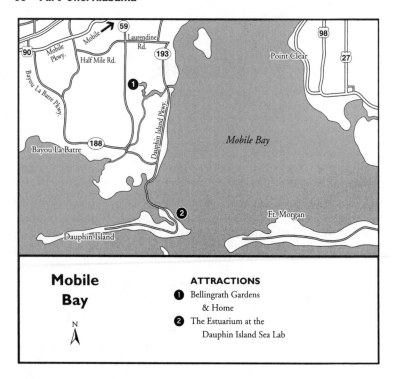

Mobile Bay

N
Λ

ATTRACTIONS
1. Bellingrath Gardens & Home
2. The Estuarium at the Dauphin Island Sea Lab

Family Lodging

Adam's Mark Mobile

Primarily a hotel for business meetings, the Adam's Mark Mobile is not the sort of hotel where you feel comfortable letting your children run around the lobby, but it is in a good location and many of the amenities are conducive to family travel. This particular property has 375 standard rooms and 12 suites complete with in-room wet bars and refrigerators. The hotel features a health club with whirlpool and sauna, an outdoor pool with a deck, nearby golf courses, and express checkout. The hotel recently underwent a $1.6 million renovation. Rates begin at $85. 64 South Water Street; (800) 444-ADAM or (334) 438-4000; www.adamsmark.com.

Radisson Admiral Semmes Hotel

More upscale than most of the selections in this guide, we included this hotel because of its downtown location, just ten minutes from the battleship and in the heart of the downtown historic district. It also helps that the accommodations are roomy and comfortable. Named for Admiral Raphael Semmes, the commander of the Confederate ship *Alabama*, the hotel first opened in 1940. Hurricane Frederic caused massive damage in 1979, but in

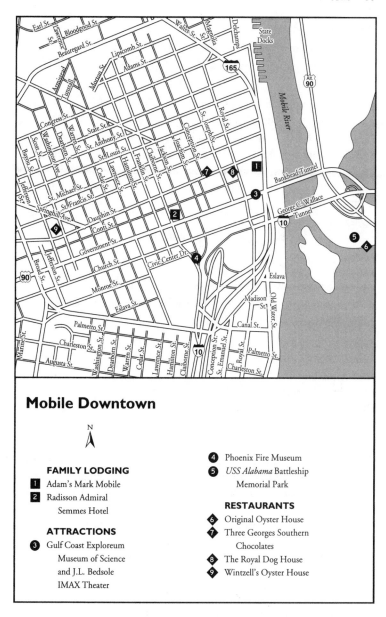

Mobile Downtown

N
↑

FAMILY LODGING

1. Adam's Mark Mobile
2. Radisson Admiral
   Semmes Hotel

ATTRACTIONS

3. Gulf Coast Exploreum
   Museum of Science
   and J.L. Bedsole
   IMAX Theater

4. Phoenix Fire Museum
5. *USS Alabama* Battleship
   Memorial Park

RESTAURANTS

6. Original Oyster House
7. Three Georges Southern
   Chocolates
8. The Royal Dog House
9. Wintzell's Oyster House

1985 the hotel reopened in its original splendor. Though it is a historic landmark, it's kid-friendly, with room service, a pool and whirlpool, and a limited number of suites. Rates begin at $109. 251 Government Street; (800) 333-3333 or (334) 432-8000; www.radisson.com.

Attractions

Bellingrath Gardens & Home

12401 Bellingrath Road, Theodore; (800) 247-8420 or (334) 973-2217
   www.bellingrath.org

Hours: Open daily from 8 a.m. to dusk; cruise schedule varies—call
   ahead for up-to-date schedule

Admission: Gardens, museum, and river cruise combination package:
   $18.95 adults, $13.95 children ages 5–11, and free for children ages 4
   and younger. Gardens and museum package or gardens and river cruise
   package: $13.95 adults, $9.95 children ages 5–11, and free children 4
   and younger

Appeal by Age Group:

Pre-school	Grade School	Teens	Young Adults	Over 30	Seniors
★	★★	★★★	★★★	★★★★	★★★★

Average Touring Time: 3½ hours for all attractions

Minimum Touring Time: 1 hour for gardens, cruise, or museum only

Rainy Day Touring: Not recommended

Author's Rating: ★★★

Services and Facilities:

Restaurants Yes	Baby stroller rental Yes
Alcoholic beverages No	Lockers No
Disabled access On main deck	Pet kennels Yes
only	Rain check No
Wheelchair rental Yes	Private tours No

Description and Comments   Kids might not jump up and down about the
prospect of visiting the 65 acres of Alabama's oldest public gardens, but
offer them the opportunity to take a river cruise along the Fowl River and
they might go along with your plans. Bellingrath is noted for its gardens,
which feature a nature walk, conservatory, and rose garden. The museum
is in a historic house built by the Bellingrath family and is still furnished
with much of their period furniture. The river cruise aboard the *Southern
Belle* is a favorite for children, as is the Ecological Bayou Boardwalk with a
view of a southern bayou.

The Estuarium at Dauphin Island Sea Lab

101 Bienville Boulevard, Dauphin Island; (334) 861-2141
   www.disl.org

Hours: October–May, Monday–Saturday from 9 a.m.–5 p.m., Sunday
   from 1–5 p.m.; June–September, Monday–Saturday from 9 a.m.–

6 p.m., Sunday 1–6 p.m.

Admission: $6 adults, $3 children ages 5–18, free for children ages 4 and younger, $5 seniors

Appeal by Age Group:

Pre-school	Grade School	Teens	Young Adults	Over 30	Seniors
★★★★	★★★★	★★★	★★★	★★★	★★★

Average Touring Time: 1½ hours

Minimum Touring Time: 45 minutes

Rainy Day Touring: Recommended

Author's Rating: ★★★

Services and Facilities:

Restaurants No	Baby stroller rental No
Alcoholic beverages No	Lockers No
Disabled access Yes	Pet kennels No
Wheelchair rental Yes, complimentary	Rain check N/A
	Private tours No

Description and Comments From the outside, The Dauphin Island Sea Lab, Alabama's marine research and education institution, doesn't look so hot. But on the inside, the new estuarium with its visual displays and engaging interactive exhibits brings the four main ecosystems and the inhabitants of the Mobile estuary system to life. Things to see include Native American artifacts; the *Miss May,* a boat on land that kids can climb through and explore; the Living Marsh Boardwalk; and a "touch lab" with marine life that children can pick up for a closer look.

Gulf Coast Exploreum Museum of Science and J.L. Bedsole IMAX Theater

65 Government Street, Mobile; (877) 625-4FUN or (334) 208-6873
www.exploreum.com

Hours: Monday –Thursday, 9 a.m. –5 p.m.; Friday–Saturday, 9 a.m.– 9 p.m.; Sunday, noon–5 p.m.

Admission: Exploreum exhibits or IMAX: $6.75 adults, $5.75 youths and seniors, and $5.25 children; tickets for both are $10 adults, $9 youths and seniors, and $8 children

Appeal by Age Group:

Pre-school	Grade School	Teens	Young Adults	Over 30	Seniors
★★★★	★★★★	★★★★	★★★★	★★★★	★★★★

Average Touring Time: 2½ hours

Minimum Touring Time: 1½ hours

Rainy Day Touring: Recommended

Author's Rating: ★★★★ Great for educational play

Services and Facilities:

Restaurants Yes	Baby stroller rental No
Alcoholic beverages No	Lockers No
Disabled access Yes	Pet kennels No
Wheelchair rental Yes, compli- mentary	Rain check N/A
	Private tours Yes

Description and Comments Located off I-10 in the heart of historic downtown Mobile, this hands-on museum gives children the chance to explore basic theories in science through magnets, microscopes, and interactive exhibits—more than 50 in all. Younger kids are drawn to Hands On Hall, where they can construct bridges, play with lasers, and experiment with animation techniques. Teenagers like the IMAX theater and its in-your-face, adventure-oriented films.

Phoenix Fire Museum

203 South Claiborne Street, Mobile; (334) 208-7554

Hours: Tuesday–Saturday, 10 a.m.–5 p.m.; Sunday, 1–5 p.m.

Admission: Free

Appeal by Age Group:

Pre- school	Grade School	Teens	Young Adults	Over 30	Seniors
★★★	★★★	★★★	★★★	★★★	★★★

Average Touring Time: 45 minutes

Minimum Touring Time: 30 minutes

Rainy Day Touring: Recommended

Author's Rating: ★★★

Services and Facilities:

Restaurants No	Baby stroller rental No
Alcoholic beverages No	Lockers No
Disabled access Yes, first floor only	Pet kennels No
	Rain check N/A
Wheelchair rental No	Private tours Yes

Description and Comments The original home of the Phoenix Volunteer Fire Company No. 6, this museum (part of the Museum of Mobile) houses a unique collection of colorful, authentic steam engines and fire trucks from the 1800s and 1900s. There are exhibits on how early firemen lived and a display of fire-fighting equipment, including early fire horns that predated the sirens of today. The original fire pole is still in place. Kids will enjoy this unique look at history but will be disappointed because they can't sit on any of the fire trucks or slide down the pole. The only consolation is getting their picture made with a large Dalmatian, but even that isn't real.

USS Alabama Battleship Memorial Park

2703 Battleship Parkway, Mobile; (800) 426-4929 or (334) 433-2703
www.ussalabama.com

Hours: Open daily from 8 a.m.–5 p.m.; until 8 p.m. from May–August; closed Christmas

Admission: $8 ages 12 and older, $4 ages 6–11; free for children ages 5 and younger; parking is $2 per car

Appeal by Age Group:

Pre-school	Grade School	Teens	Young Adults	Over 30	Seniors
★★★★	★★★★★	★★★★★	★★★★★	★★★★★	★★★★★

Average Touring Time: 2 hours

Minimum Touring Time: 1 hour

Rainy Day Touring: Not recommended

Author's Rating: ★★★★ You could easily spend a day at the park; the film is especially interesting

Services and Facilities:

Restaurants Yes	Baby stroller rental No
Alcoholic beverages No	Lockers No
Disabled access On main deck only	Pet kennels Yes
	Rain check No
Wheelchair rental Yes	Private tours No

Description and Comments The war buffs in your family will think they've died and gone to heaven at this memorial park. The *USS Alabama* was commissioned in 1942 and saw action in World War II against the Germans off the coast of England and against the Japanese in the South Pacific before retiring to Alabama in 1965. The battleship is open for tours, as is the *USS Drum*, a WWII submarine. You can also tour 21 combat aircraft, including an A-12 "Blackbird" spyplane and the P51-D Mustang Redtail, the plane flown by the Tuskegee Airmen. Don't miss the flight simulator in the Aircraft Pavilion and the film that shows onboard the battleship continuously throughout the day. It features interviews with soldiers who served on the *Alabama*. The gift shop is really nice, with items in all price ranges for kids to purchase.

MUSEUM OF MOBILE

Mobile was founded in 1702 and has a long, storied history under six flags. At this writing, much of the city's history is chronicled in the Museum of

Mobile, but in the fall of 2000, the Museum will split into two buildings and reopen as the Museum of Mobile at 111 South Royal Street (the Southern Market/Old City Hall building) and the Mardi Gras Museum at the present site of 355 Government Street.

The Museum of Mobile will become five times larger with the move and will feature 300 years of Mobile history, including Native American interpretations, Civil War exhibits, and displays about slavery in Mobile. The museum also has a fine collection of carriages from the 1800s and 1900s. Among the more fascinating items: A Native American canoe dating to 1320 and the sword of admiral Raphael Semmes, the only officer in U.S. history to serve as an admiral in the Navy and a general in the Army.

The Mardi Gras Museum will highlight the origins of Mobile's Mardi Gras—the oldest in the United States—and the history of subsequent Mardi Gras. There will be displays of gowns and trains, old photos, throws, crowns, and scepters. There is also talk about turning the present carriage house into an exhibit of Mardi Gras floats, with actual floats on display along with information about how the floats are made.

The Conde Fort, a bicentennial reproduction of a fort that stood in the same place in the 1700s, the Phoenix Fire Museum, and the Carlen House—an 1840s Creole cottage, also fall under the umbrella of the Museum of Mobile and will remain open during the reconfiguring of the main museum and the Mardi Gras Museum; (334) 208-7569.

Side Trip

Dauphin Island   Dauphin Island, a nearby barrier island, is an easy, fun day trip for families. Begin with a ferry ride on the Mobile Bay Ferry ($23 roundtrip for all autos), then catch an island cruise that highlights major attractions, such as Fort Gaines and the Audubon Bird Sanctuary, from the water. If you're lucky, dolphins might actually swim along with the boat during your cruise. Should you wish to stay the night, you can camp at the Dauphin Island Campground (phone (334) 861-2742) and have access to a secluded Gulf beach via a boardwalk and to the 160 acres of walking trails throughout the Audubon Bird Sanctuary. Located 33 miles from Mobile; (334) 861-5524.

Family-Friendly Restaurants

ORIGINAL OYSTER HOUSE

1175 Battleship Parkway, Mobile; (334) 626-2188

Bayou Village Shopping and Dining Center, Gulf Shores; (334) 948-2445 www.theoysterhouse.com

Meals served: Lunch and dinner
Cuisine: Seafood
Entrée range: $6.95–15.95
Kids menu: Yes
Reservations: Yes, for six or more
Payment: All major credit cards

The good thing about eating here is that you don't have to dress up. The atmosphere is casual, and at the Bayou Village location (only a couple of blocks north of the beach), kids can feed the fish in the canal while you wait. And waiting is not uncommon. Sometimes it can take up to 45 minutes to be seated, but if you like seafood, you won't be disappointed. The house specialties are seafood gumbo and create-your-own-platters, where you can choose from a variety of baked, fried, steamed, or broiled selections. For kids, there's shrimp, crab claws, fish, and pizza. The Battleship Parkway location, where you can see the ship from the restaurant, also features the Half Shell Steamer, an extremely laid-back dining room serving steamed seafood specialties.

THREE GEORGES SOUTHERN CHOCOLATES

226 Dauphin Street, Mobile; (800) 669-5175 or (334) 433-6725
www.3georges.com

Meals served: N/A
Cuisine: Candy and chocolate
Entrée range: N/A
Kids menu: N/A
Reservations: N/A
Payment: All major credit cards

What the heck, you're on vacation, so you might as well indulge your sweet tooth at the city's oldest candy company. Pralines, divinity, fudge, heavenly hash, and pecan and cashew candies are among the company's specialties, and all are handmade on the premises. Three Georges is a Mobile landmark and dates to 1917 when Georgio Pappalamprous and his two friends, also named George, opened a candy store.

THE ROYAL DOG HOUSE

5 North Royal Street, Mobile; (334) 432-5217

Meals served: Breakfast and lunch

Cuisine: Hot dogs
Entrée Range: $1.80 and up
Kids Menu: Yes
Reservations: Yes
Payment: Cash and checks

In business for over 30 years, this is the place to get a hot dog dressed just the way you like it. The Royal Dog is the favorite, topped with chili, cole slaw, cheese, sauerkraut, pickles, onions, and salsa. The daily special is a hot dog with chips and a drink for $3.05. Breakfast includes grits, eggs, ham, and toast.

WINTZELL'S OYSTER HOUSE

605 Dauphin Street, Mobile; (334) 432-4605

Meals served: Lunch and dinner
Cuisine: Seafood
Entrée range: $6.95–18
Kids menu: Yes
Reservations: Yes
Payment: All major credit cards except Discover

Founded in 1938, Wintzell's has been known for its seafood for over 60 years. Oysters are a customer favorite—you can have them fried, stewed, or nude—but virtually every other kind of seafood is also featured on the menu. For kids, the restaurant offers fish and fries, popcorn shrimp, chicken, and other pint-sized entrees.

Gulf Shores/ Orange Beach

Alabama's beaches rival those of northwest Florida. The water is clear and the sand is white—due to its mineral content. Other beaches are made up of a variety of minerals, hence the variations in color, but the Gulf sand is nothing but pure quartz.

Another unique characteristic of Gulf sand is its texture. Over hundreds of thousands of years, quartz from granite formations from the Appalachian Mountains weathered away then washed down to riverbeds and into the ocean. This journey pummeled the pieces into small bits and buffed the raw edges smooth, creating extremely fine sand.

What this means for visitors is a chance to plan on some of the finest beaches in the country—32 miles of sea and sand for sunbathing and romping in the waves.

The Gulf Shores/Orange Beach area is a small strip of land sandwiched between Mobile Bay and the Intracoastal Waterway on the west and Perdido Bay on the east. Besides the beaches, outdoor enthusiasts will have a heyday playing golf and tennis and fishing in freshwater lakes and in the salty Gulf. Shopping and eating are other favorite pastimes.

Lodging

Holiday Inn Express, Gulf Shores–On the Beach

Probably the biggest advantage to staying at this beachfront hotel is that you can sit in the shade and watch your kids frolic from the pool to the beach. All rooms have a balcony overlooking the Gulf—a nice feature but one that poses safety concerns for parents of small children. There are also 29 suites with kitchenettes and separate sitting areas; book early. Rates start at $65 during the off-season. 365 East Beach Boulevard; (800) HOLIDAY; (334) 948-8240; www.basshotels.com.

Condos and Beach House Rentals

Like Panama City Beach in Florida, Alabama's Gulf Coast is a mix of swanky hotels, mom-and-pop hotels, and condos of all shapes and sizes. If you're interested in having more than just a bed and television, consider renting a house or condo. Many realty companies have services available for guests interested in renting, and the Gulf Coast Convention and Visitors Bureau can provide you with a list. Here are a few to try: Kaiser Realty, Inc., (800) 225-4853, www.kaiserrealty.com; Bender Realty, Inc., (800) 528-2651, www.gulftel.net/bender; Gulf Coast Reservations, (800) 423-GULF, www.gulfcoastres.com.

Attractions

Bon Secour Wildlife Refuge

State Highway 180 at 13 mile marker; (334) 540-7720

Hours: Daily, dawn to dusk

Admission: Free

Appeal by Age Group:

Pre-school	Grade School	Teens	Young Adults	Over 30	Seniors
★★★★★	★★★★★	★★★★★	★★★★★	★★★★★	★★★★★

Average Touring Time: 2 hours

Minimum Touring Time: 1 hour

Rainy Day Touring: Not recommended

Author's Rating: ★★★★★ Pristine and pretty

Services and Facilities:

Restaurants No	Lockers No
Alcoholic beverages No	Pet kennels No
Disabled access Yes	Rain check No
Wheelchair rental No	Private tours No
Baby stroller rental No	

Description and Comments Bon Secour is what the Gulf Coast used to look like before development took over. The 6,200-acre refuge is home to a variety of native plants and animals, all protected in this pristine habitat. Your family, however, can take advantage of this unspoiled retreat by trekking on the Pine Beach Trail to a secluded sliver of shoreline. There are few people who know of or visit this place, so you could conceivably have the beach to yourself. One reason might be the hike; it's two miles one way. Another option is to hike the one-mile-loop Jeff Friend Trail or fish in the

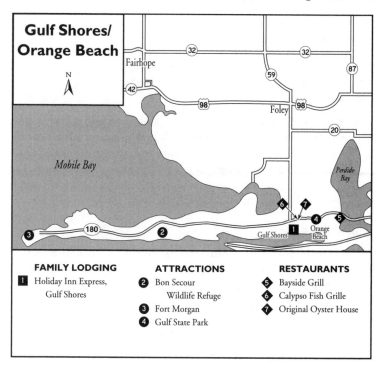

Gulf Shores/ Orange Beach

N

Fairhope

Mobile Bay

Foley

Perdido Bay

Gulf Shores

Orange Beach

FAMILY LODGING

1 Holiday Inn Express, Gulf Shores

ATTRACTIONS

2 Bon Secour Wildlife Refuge

3 Fort Morgan

4 Gulf State Park

RESTAURANTS

5 Bayside Grill

6 Calypso Fish Grille

7 Original Oyster House

40-acre Gator Lake. There is a visitors center in the refuge, but it's open only during the week. Otherwise, amenities are limited. If you plan to stay a while, take plenty of liquids and snacks.

Fort Morgan State Historic Site

51 Highway 180 West; (334) 540-7125 or (334) 540-7127

Hours: Site: Daily 8 a.m.–6 p.m.; Museum: Daily 9 a.m.–5 p.m.

Admission: $3 adults, $1 children, free for children ages 6 and younger

Appeal by Age Group:

Pre-school	Grade School	Teens	Young Adults	Over 30	Seniors
★★★	★★★	★★★	★★★	★★★	★★★

Average Touring Time: 2 hours

Minimum Touring Time: 1 hour

Rainy Day Touring: Not recommended

Author's Rating: ★★★

Services and Facilities:

Restaurants No	Lockers No
Alcoholic beverages No	Pet kennels No
Disabled access Yes	Rain check No
Wheelchair rental Yes	Private tours Yes
Baby stroller rental No	

Description and Comments   This fort has a long history of military service stretching from the early 1800s to World War II. Today, its colorful past is retold by living history interpreters, who take you through the fort on a narrated tour. In addition to the fort, there are picnic facilities and a beach. The beach is nice and secluded, but there is no lifeguard on duty. On Tuesday nights during the summer, candlelight tours of the fort are conducted.

Gulf State Park

20115 State Highway 135; information (334) 948-7275, campground
reservations (334) 948-6353, hotel reservations (800) 544-4853

Hours: Daily 7 a.m.–sundown

Admission: $2 per car, charges vary for other activities and areas

Appeal by Age Group:

Pre-school	Grade School	Teens	Young Adults	Over 30	Seniors
★★★★★	★★★★★	★★★★★	★★★★★	★★★★★	★★★★★

Average Touring Time: 1 day

Minimum Touring Time: ½ day

Rainy Day Touring: Not recommended

Author's Rating: ★★★★

Services and Facilities:

Restaurants No	Lockers No
Alcoholic beverages No	Pet kennels No
Disabled access Yes	Rain check No
Wheelchair rental No	Private tours No
Baby stroller rental No	

Description and Comments   Gulf State Park has all the outdoor activities and facilities you would expect from a state park, plus resort-style amenities like a hotel, swimming pool, and golf. There are 6,100 acres in all, and the beach is by far the most popular activity. Parents will be happy to know that lifeguards are on duty during the day.

The park has three freshwater lakes, all relatively close to the beach, so anglers will have plenty of saltwater and freshwater fishing options. Lake Shelby, the largest lake at 900 acres, is noted for bass, bream, crappie, and two kinds of catfish. The lake also has boat launches and swimming areas.

A 25-foot pier is perfect for anglers who prefer saltwater fishing in the Gulf.

The park also has an 18-hole golf course, a picnic area, a camp store, and tennis courts.

Our suggestion for a perfect day is to arrive early, stake out a spot on the beach, and spend the morning playing in the waves. At midday, head over to the beach pavilion for an informal picnic lunch, then spread out blankets in the shade for a catnap. When the afternoon sun is at its hottest, ride along the eight miles of bike trails (watch out for alligators), check out one of the special kids programs at the nature center, or take a canoe trip into the wetlands to see native plants and wildlife.

Park accommodations include a resort, cabins, and a campground. One note: The resort rooms are in need of renovation, but the cabins have all been remodeled. These tend to stay booked during the summer so make reservations well in advance. If you prefer more rustic accommodations, there are campsites throughout the park.

Side Trips

Fishing on the Gulf Coast   With so many places to cast a line, avid anglers will think they have died and gone to heaven along the Gulf Coast. There are more than 100 deep-sea fishing charter boats in the area and a variety of excursions to choose from. Half-, full-, or multi-day trips are available. Marlin, tuna, barracuda, wahoo, sailfish, mackerel, and shark are among the sport fish found in the Gulf from May to December. If you're not a serious angler but would still like to try your luck, consider a party boat that takes out up to 35 people out.

Another option is freshwater fishing in the abundant lakes, rivers, and streams. The Bon Secour River and the 700-acre, freshwater Lake Shelby are two favorites. Speckled trout, black and striped bass, bream, and red drum are some of the catches.

A license is required to fish in Alabama; contact the Alabama Gulf Coast Convention and Visitors Bureau for more information; (800) 745-SAND; www.orangebeach.com.

Bird-watching   The Gulf Coast is part of the Mississippi Flyway, and as such, is one of the major routes for migratory birds. Royal terns, tricolored herons, great egrets, tree swallows, herring gulls, mallard ducks, and long-billed curlews are but a few of the birds you might see.

The Alabama Coastal Birding Trail was created to make it easier to observe birds in migration. The trail is a series of loops that can easily take a half-day or longer to complete. Our suggestion is to drive a bit, get out at one of the suggested observation sites, and stay until you see activity.

Spring and fall are the best times to observe birds. Monarch butterflies migrate along the same route in the fall. There are several public areas designated as observation points. Fort Morgan, Bon Secour National Wildlife Refuge, and Perdido Pass are all good observation sites. If you're serious about spotting our feathered friends, contact the Hummer/Bird Study Group (phone (205) 681-2888, www.hbsg.org), a local group that meets to place identification bands on birds as they come through. Once a bird has been banded, it is set free to continue its journey.

A complete guide to birds and the Alabama Coast Birding Trail is available from the Gulf Coast Convention and Visitors Bureau; (800) 745-SAND; www.orangebeach.com.

The Golf Coast   Whether you're just getting the swing of golf or you're the next Tiger Woods, the Gulf Coast is a good place to unpack your clubs. There are 13 championship courses in the area, and one is bound to suit your style. Craft Farms (phone (800) 327-2657, www.craftfarms.com) has three courses to play. Cotton Creek, designed by Arnold Palmer, has water and bunker features along with Bermuda grass fairways and greens for speed. Hole 5 is rated one of the top ten in the state. Cypress Bend at Craft Farms is the newest addition, with staggered tee boxes and sprawling bunkers. Larry Nelson designed the Woodlands at Craft Farms. Rolling fairways between marshlands and woods offer a challenge to players of all levels.

Lost Key Golf Club (phone (888) 492-1300, www.lostkey.com), also an Arnold Palmer Course, is on Perdido Key and is considered an Audubon Sanctuary Course because of its environmental focus areas for wildlife conservation, habitat enhancement, water quality, and conservation. Kiva Dunes (phone (888) 540-7000, www.kivadunes-golf.com), designed by Jerry Pate, is a links-style course that was named the second-best public course in America by Golf Digest. For more information, contact the Gulf Shores Golf Association at (800) 745-SAND; www.golfgulfshores.com.

Family-Friendly Restaurants

BAYSIDE GRILL

Canal Road at Sportsman Marina, Orange Beach; (334) 981-4899

Meals served: Lunch, dinner, Sunday brunch
Cuisine: Seafood
Entrée range: $6.95–19.95
Kids menu: Yes
Reservations: Yes, for six or more
Payment: All major credit cards

Wood-grilled fish, shrimp, steaks, chicken, and ribs—all cooked with Creole or Caribbean flair—round out the grown-up fare at this casual seafood grill. The kids' menu covers all the usual bases, with chicken, fish, hamburgers, and spaghetti as popular choices.

CALYPSO FISH GRILLE & MARKET

27075 Marina Road, Gulf Shores; (334) 981-1415

Meals served: Lunch and dinner
Cuisine: Seafood
Entrée range: $7.95 and up
Kids menu: Yes
Reservations: Yes
Payment: All major credit cards

This is the laid-back, Jimmy Buffett–style kind of place where you could while away the afternoon. Located waterfront near the Orange Beach Marina, the Calypso serves fresh seafood, salads, and the famous Calypso Burger. For kids, you'll find junior burgers, chicken tenders, and grouper fingers.

ORIGINAL OYSTER HOUSE

1175 Battleship Parkway, Mobile; (334) 626-2188
Bayou Village Shopping and Dining Center, Gulf Shores; (334) 948-2445
www.theoysterhouse.com

Meals served: Lunch and dinner
Cuisine: Seafood
Entrée range: $6.95–15.95
Kids menu: Yes
Reservations: Yes, for six or more
Payment: All major credit cards

The good thing about eating here is that you don't have to dress up. The atmosphere is casual, and at the Bayou Village location (only a couple of blocks north of the beach), kids can feed the fish in the canal while you wait. And waiting is not uncommon. Sometimes it can take up to 45 minutes to be seated, but if you like seafood, you won't be disappointed. The house specialties are seafood gumbo and create-your-own-platters, where you can choose from a variety of baked, fried, steamed, or broiled selections. For kids, the menu features shrimp, crab claws, fish, and pizza. The Battleship Parkway location, where you can see the ship from the restaurant, also features the Half Shell Steamer, an extremely laid-back dining room serving steamed seafood specialties.

Montgomery

Montgomery is a hotbed of history in the state of Alabama. In 1540, Hernando de Soto staked a Spanish flag on the banks of the Alabama River. French settlers claimed the territory when they established Fort Toulouse in 1717. In 1819, East Alabama and New Philadelphia merged to form the city, and it was chosen as the state capital in 1846. That's when all the juicy historical events began to happen. Jefferson Davis was sworn in on the state capitol steps in 1861, and the Civil War broke out shortly thereafter.

Almost 100 years later, in 1965, Dr. Martin Luther King Jr., culminated his Civil Rights March from Selma in the exact same spot—a struggle that began when Rosa Parks refused to give up her seat on a Montgomery city bus.

The significant role of these two related but contrasting events, the Civil War and the Civil Rights Movement, continue to influence the atmosphere of Montgomery. Today, the birthplace of the American Civil War and the Civil Rights Movement offers several attractions for guests interested in either historical realm, and it serves as a hub for itineraries that include jaunts to some of the other attractions nearby. Like other parts of Alabama, the south-central area has a slew of backroads to meander along, but if you are limited by time, hit the high points in Montgomery and take in what you can while traveling from one city to the next. It's about one-and-a-half hours from both Dothan and Birmingham and two hours from Atlanta.

For a day in town, begin at the **Visitors Center** at 401 Madison Avenue (at the corner of North Hull Street) and plan to spend the morning walking the three-block area surrounding the capitol, where many of the historical attractions are located. Montgomery is one of the few cities that offers free designated parking for visitors, and it's right at the front door of the state capitol building. Just ask for a pass at the Visitors Center. Eat lunch at the **Montgomery Zoo,** then wind up at the **Alabama Shakespeare Festival** for an evening play. For most of the year, the weather is pleasant, averaging 65.6 degrees.

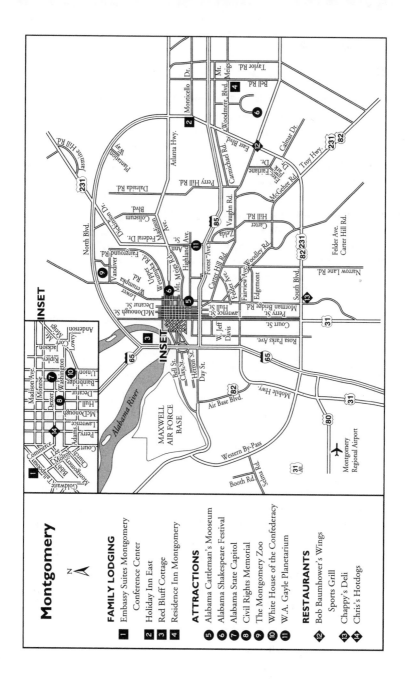

Montgomery

N

FAMILY LODGING

1. Embassy Suites Montgomery
   Conference Center
2. Holiday Inn East
3. Red Bluff Cottage
4. Residence Inn Montgomery

ATTRACTIONS

5. Alabama Cartleman's Mooseum
6. Alabama Shakespeare Festival
7. Alabama State Capitol
8. Civil Rights Memorial
9. The Montgomery Zoo
10. White House of the Confederacy
11. W.A. Gayle Planetarium

RESTAURANTS

12. Bob Baumhower's Wings
    Sports Grill
13. Chappy's Deli
14. Chris's Hotdogs

85

Family Lodging

Embassy Suites Montgomery Conference Center

Besides its family-friendly accommodations, this hotel is located in the heart of Historic Downtown Montgomery in front of Union Station, riverfront parks, and the *Betsy Ann* Riverboat. It is also just blocks from the State Capitol Complex, a historic museum, and theatres, and it is next to the Montgomery Civic Center.

Expect roomy accommodations, complete with a private bedroom, separate living area for watching television, and refrigerator and wet bar for quick snacks. This setup works well for families. You also get a complimentary, cooked-to-order breakfast, and kids age 18 and younger stay free. Rates start at $125 in both summer and winter. 300 Tallapoosa Street; (800) EMBASSY or (334) 269-5055; www.embassy-suites.com.

Holiday Inn East

Located on the east side of town, this hotel is convenient to downtown attractions, the Shakespeare Festival, and an ice rink. It is one of the "Holidome" hotels, featuring a heated indoor pool, whirlpool, sauna, sundeck, fitness center, and free game room with pool tables, hockey, Foosball, and pingpong. There are both standard and suite rooms; book suites directly through the hotel. As with other Holiday Inns, kids ages 11 and younger eat free from the Kids Menu in the restaurant, and room service is available. Rates start at $99 per night year-round. 1185 Eastern Bypass; (800) HOLIDAY or (334) 272-0370; www.basshotels.com/holiday-inn.

Red Bluff Cottage

Only eight blocks from downtown, this bed and breakfast inn is one of the few in the country that actually caters to families. There are four guest rooms; the Plaid Room and the Children's Room combine to create a suite with a large private bath. There are also several common areas where families can relax and take in views of the Alabama River. A crib is available, the yard is large enough for kids to work off some energy, and a full breakfast is provided. Rates start at $65 per night. 551 Clay Street; (800) 551-CLAY or (334) 264-3054; www.bbonline.com/al/redbluff.

Residence Inn Montgomery

This is another hotel that primarily caters to business travelers. The appeal to families comes from the fact that each room is a suite with a full kitchen and an optional fireplace. Pets are permitted, though additional charges may apply. There is an outdoor pool. The choice location is only a half-mile from the Shakespeare Festival and the Museum of Fine Arts, and five miles from the state capitol and Civil Rights Memorial. Rates begin at $85 year-round; (800) 331-3131 or (334) 270-3300; www.residenceinn.com.

Attractions

Alabama Cattleman's Mooseum

201 South Bainbridge Street, Montgomery; (334) 265-1867

Hours: Monday–Friday from 8 a.m.– 4 p.m.

Admission: Free

Appeal by Age Group:

Pre-school	Grade School	Teens	Young Adults	Over 30	Seniors
★★★★	★★★★	★★★★	★★★★	★★★★	★★★★

Average Touring Time: 40 minutes

Minimum Touring Time: 30 minutes

Rainy Day Touring: Recommended

Author's Rating: ★★★★

Services and Facilities:

Restaurants No	Lockers No
Alcoholic beverages No	Pet kennels No
Disabled access Yes	Rain check No
Wheelchair rental No	Private tours No
Baby stroller rental No	

Description and Comments   Full of kitsch and charisma, this "mooseum" is the sort of place kids love. Sponsored by the Alabama Cattleman's Association, the museum exists to tell the story of cows, particularly their relevance to the state of Alabama. They have put a lot of work into this place, and it takes a high tech approach to storytelling. The Rodeo Room highlights the history of the rodeo. Adam Bainbridge, a state-of-the-art talking mannequin, sits at the entrance of the museum to introduce children to exhibits and bovine history. There is a presentation of all products made from cows (including automobile tires and Jell-O). Headsets along the way feature cow-related audios, such as classes in cattle management or an auctioneer at a sale barn. The gift shop is targeted toward kids. In the interactive area, kids can prepare imaginary dinners in the kitchen or dress up like cowboys.

Alabama Shakespeare Festival

One Festival Drive, Montgomery; (800) 841-4ASF or (334) 271-5353
www.asf.net

Hours: Midweek shows generally begin at 7:30 p.m., Friday evenings at
8 p.m., and Saturday at 2 p.m. and 8 p.m.

Admission: $21–30 (depending on performance) for adults, $15 for
children ages 6–12, children ages 5 and younger not permitted

Appeal by Age Group:

Pre-school	Grade School	Teens	Young Adults	Over 30	Seniors
N/A	★★★★	★★★★	★★★★★	★★★★★	★★★★★

Average Touring Time: 3 hours; depends on performance

Minimum Touring Time: 2 hours; depends on performance

Rainy Day Touring: Recommended

Author's Rating: ★★★★★   Age-group appeal depends upon the particular performance

Services and Facilities:

Restaurants No	Lockers No
Alcoholic beverages No	Pet kennels No
Disabled access Yes	Rain check N/A
Wheelchair rental No	Private tours Yes
Baby stroller rental No	

Description and Comments   One of the top five major Shakespeare companies in the world, this Festival is actually a permanent attraction with world-class theater productions and educational programs year-round. The best plan of action is to call ahead for a schedule and then plan your trip accordingly. We also recommend taking a picnic lunch or dinner, as the English-style grounds surrounding the theater are magnificent; they are planted with trees and flowers mentioned throughout the performances of Shakespeare's plays.

There is one slight drawback: Children ages five and under are not permitted, so if you have young children, you'll need to make other arrangements. However, depending on the time of your vacation, there are special activities for children. Most of these are targeted for school field trips, but families can join in on the activity if desired. The holiday performance in December is also a family favorite.

Alabama State Capitol

Bainbridge Street and Dexter Avenue, Montgomery; (334) 242-3935

Hours: Monday–Friday from 8 a.m.–5 p.m., Saturday from
9 a.m.–4 p.m.

Admission: Free

Appeal by Age Group:

Pre-school	Grade School	Teens	Young Adults	Over 30	Seniors
★	★★★	★★★	★★★	★★★	★★★

Average Touring Time: 45 minutes

Minimum Touring Time: 30 minutes

Rainy Day Touring: Okay for indoors

Author's Rating: ★★★

Services and Facilities:

Restaurants No	Lockers No
Alcoholic beverages No	Pet kennels No
Disabled access No	Rain check N/A
Wheelchair rental No	Private tours Yes
Baby stroller rental No	

Description and Comments   One of the few state capitols to be designated a National Historic Landmark, the capitol was rebuilt in 1850 when the first one burned after standing for only two years. The wings on either side of the main building were added in later years.

Today, visitors can visit the original governor's suite, the house chamber where the Alabama Legislature decided to secede from the Union, and the senate chamber, all restored to authentically replicate the original construction's look. Because it is a working capitol, it's not unusual to bump into constitutional officers; you might even call ahead and see if the governor is in town and has time for you to stop by. There are self-guided tour maps for the interior.

Outside, pay special attention to the Avenue of Flags, where every state flag and a rock from each state is displayed. Look for the bronze star marking the spot where Jefferson Davis stood to take the oath of office as President of the Confederate States of America. Also make note that it was in 1965 when participants of the Selma-to-Montgomery Civil Rights March led by Dr. Martin Luther King, Jr., culminated their march on these same capitol steps. The grounds are fully shaded, making this a cool spot for a picnic.

Civil Rights Memorial

400 Washington Avenue, Montgomery; (334) 264-0286
  www.splcenter.org/centerinfo/ci-index.html

Hours: Daily, 24 hours

Admission: Free

Appeal by Age Group:

Pre-school	Grade School	Teens	Young Adults	Over 30	Seniors
★★	★★	★★★	★★★★	★★★★	★★★★

Average Touring Time: 30 minutes

Minimum Touring Time: 10 minutes

Rainy Day Touring: Not recommended

Author's Rating: ★★★★

Services and Facilities:

Restaurants No	Lockers No
Alcoholic beverages No	Pet kennels No
Disabled access Yes	Rain check No
Wheelchair rental No	Private tours No
Baby stroller rental No	

Description and Comments History is heavy, especially when it is brought to life by the stories of real people who fought for social change. Children who have studied the Civil Rights movement may be able to understand this monument's significance; otherwise, kids can run their hands along the monument and feel the water as it trickles over the names of 40 men, women, and children who died for the cause from 1955–68. For small ones, it's a chance to get down and walk around. Designed by Maya Lin, the monument sits in front of the Southern Poverty Law Center and adjoins the existing sidewalk, so it's not conducive to picnicking or hanging around.

The Montgomery Zoo

Off North Boulevard, Montgomery; (334) 240-4900
www.montgomery.al.us/zoo

Hours: Daily, from 9 a.m.–5 p.m.

Admission: $4.50 adults, $2.50 children ages 4–12, $2 seniors, free for children ages 3 and younger

Appeal by Age Group:

Pre-school	Grade School	Teens	Young Adults	Over 30	Seniors
★★★★	★★★★	★★★★	★★★	★★★	★★★

Average Touring Time: 2½ hours

Minimum Touring Time: 1 hour

Rainy Day Touring: Not recommended

Author's Rating: ★★★

Services and Facilities:

Restaurants Yes

Alcoholic beverages No

Disabled access Yes

Wheelchair rental Yes

Baby stroller rental Yes

Lockers Yes

Pet kennels No

Rain check No

Private tours No

Description and Comments Barrier-free exhibits make this 40-acre zoo a special place for both children and animals. The exhibits are divided into five "continents," each with lush vegetation and exotic wildlife in their natural surroundings. In all, there are 500 animals representing over 150 species on display. A popular exhibit features white tigers. Once you tire of walking through the zoo, hop aboard the miniature locomotive and take in the exhibits from there.

A good option is to plan lunch at the zoo. The Overlook Cafe does exactly that—allows visitors to look over the zoo as they eat. The Holiday Lights Festival presents the zoo in a different light. Families can visit at night from Thanksgiving to New Year's Day weekend while the zoo is aglow with holiday lights, many in the shape of animals and toys.

White House of the Confederacy

644 Washington Avenue, Montgomery; (334) 242-1861
  www.moc.org/whitehouse

Hours: Monday–Friday from 8 a.m.–4:30 p.m.

Admission: Free

Appeal by Age Group:

Pre-school	Grade School	Teens	Young Adults	Over 30	Seniors
★	★★	★★	★★★	★★★	★★★

Average Touring Time: 45 minutes

Minimum Touring Time: 30 minutes

Rainy Day Touring: Recommended

Author's Rating: ★★★

Services and Facilities:

Restaurants No

Alcoholic beverages No

Disabled access Yes

Wheelchair rental No

Baby stroller rental No

Lockers No

Pet kennels No

Rain check No

Private tours Possibly

Description and Comments   This was the home of Jefferson Davis and his family when Montgomery was capital of the Confederacy. There are the same sorts of things you would find in other house museums, but kids seem to enjoy the relic room on the second floor, where personal and military items of Davis and his family are on display—swords, pistols, uniforms, and letters, to name a few. Downstairs, the period furnishings reflect the lifestyle of 1861 when Montgomery was the capital.

W.A. Gayle Planetarium

1010 Forest Avenue, Oak Park; (334) 241-4798 or (334) 241-4799
www.tsum.edu/planet

Hours: School shows held Monday– Thursday from 3 p.m., Friday from 7:30 a.m.–Noon; Public shows Monday–Friday at 3 p.m., Sunday at 2 p.m.

Admission: $2

Appeal by Age Group:

Pre-school	Grade School	Teens	Young Adults	Over 30	Seniors
★★★★	★★★★	★★★★	★★★★	★★★★	★★★★

Average Touring Time: 1 hour

Minimum Touring Time: 30 minutes

Rainy Day Touring: Recommended

Author's Rating: ★★★★

Services and Facilities:

Restaurants No		Lockers No	
Alcoholic beverages No		Pet kennels No	
Disabled access Yes		Rain check No	
Wheelchair rental No		Private tours No	
Baby stroller rental No			

Description and Comments   The auditorium in this planetarium—considered one of the major planetariums in the United States—is specially designed to simulate the natural sky by projecting images of the planets, moon, stars, and other celestial objects onto a 50-foot domed ceiling. Using a versatile Spitz Space Transit instrument, over 5,000 stars and the Milky Way can be projected as they would have appeared from Earth at any time or place. The images move so that it appears as if you are actually the one in motion.

   OK, so it's a lot of scientific talk for kids to comprehend, but the point of it all is that the planetarium brings the night sky to life. Afterwards, spend some time in Oak Park, where the planetarium is located. There is a large picnic area with playgrounds and covered shelters for daytime use.

Side Trips

The Governor's Mansion   Each administration decides whether to open the Alabama Governor's Mansion for public viewing; the word is still out for the newest administration. If you do get a chance to visit, note the Southern Colonial architecture with its Greek Revival influence. And don't miss the hall of mirrors, where mirrors on each side of one room reflect off the other, creating the illusion of a "hallway of mirrors." Located at 1142 South Perry Street, Montgomery; (334) 261-1100.

Tuskegee Institute, Tuskegee   Now a respected university with students from all over the world, the Tuskegee Institute National Historic Site preserves The Oaks, the home of Booker T. Washington; the George Washington Carver Museum; and some of the original brick buildings that were constructed when the institute opened in 1881. A ranger leads the house tour; the museum tour is self-guided. What sets this museum experience apart is the vibrant location and the fascinating subject matter. Kids get to mingle in the hustle-bustle of a college campus (don't worry—it's manageable to keep up with them), plus they have the opportunity to see some the unique products that Carver concocted from sweet potatoes and peanuts— over 300 in all. The institute is also home to Moton Field and the new Tuskegee Airmen National Historic Site, where African American airmen trained during World War II. Located 45 minutes from Montgomery at Tuskegee University; (334) 727-3200.

Jasmine Hill Gardens and Outdoor Museum, Wetumpka   Advertised as "Alabama's Little Corner of Greece," this attraction features 20 acres of botanical gardens and classical sculpture honoring Olympic heroes and mythical gods. Kids, of course, won't be inclined to tour yet another garden, but they will warm to the variety of Greek statuary found throughout the grounds, along with memorabilia displays of past Olympic games. Another favorite are the Temple of Hera ruins, where the Olympic flame is lit in Greece. This replica is the only full-size re-creation of its kind in the world. Located 20 minutes north of Montgomery off U.S. 231 on Jasmine Hill Road; (334) 567-6466; www.jasminehill.org.

Family-Friendly Restaurants

BOB BAUMHOWER'S WINGS SPORTS GRILL

2232 Eastern Boulevard, Montgomery; (334) 271-1831

Meals served: Lunch and dinner
Cuisine: American

Entrée range: $4.99 and up for lunch; $7.99 and up for dinner
Kids menu: Yes
Reservations: No
Payment: All major credit cards accepted

This is first and foremost a sports bar, and while the dining area does have televisions with various sporting events on, it is located away from the bar. Plus it's loud and boisterous—kids will feel completely comfortable and you won't have to worry about keeping them quiet. Wings are the obvious specialty here, and you can get six different flavors, from mild all the way up to 911. Salads, soups, and Cajun entrées are also found on the menu. For kids, there are hamburgers, wings, chicken tenders, fish, spaghetti, and hot dogs.

While waiting for dinner to arrive, you can play NTN trivia games at the table for free, where you compete against other people in the restaurant as well as restaurants around the country.

CHAPPY'S DELI

1611 Perryhill Road, Montgomery; (334) 279-7477

Meals served: Breakfast, lunch, and dinner
Cuisine: American
Entrée range: $4 and up
Kids menu: Yes
Reservations: No
Payment: All major credit cards accepted

This local deli features New York pastrami sandwiches, and reubens as the house specials; for kids, look for the chicken strip meal, ham-and-cheese sandwiches, hamburgers, and grilled cheese sandwiches.

CHRIS'S HOTDOGS

138 Dexter Avenue, Montgomery; (334) 265-6850

Meals served: Lunch and dinner
Cuisine: American
Entrée range: $1.45 and up
Kids menu: No
Reservations: Not accepted
Payment: Cash and checks only

Old-fashioned hamburgers and hot dogs with the works are Chris's specialty, and you don't have to pay an arm and a leg to get one. They also offer chicken salad sandwiches and three-piece chicken dinners. Chris's has been around since the early 1900s, and is conveniently located downtown.

Part Two

Georgia

Georgia has become the shining star of the New South, a place where both urban and rural lifestyles thrive and provide balance for one another. This atmosphere affords families a unique vacation opportunity that weaves in and out of different geographic and cultural boundaries. One day you might find yourself in downtown Savannah, lunching along the new river-walk or strolling through an eighteenth-century graveyard; the next, you might be touring open-pit marble quarries or sampling the world's largest peach cobbler at a country festival. In other words, you can plan a strictly urban or rural experience, or you can take in a little of both.

Atlanta, of course, rules supreme—not only here in this state, but also in the entire Southeastern region. Among the offerings for active families: professional football, baseball, hockey, and basketball games; world-class museums; exhaustive shopping; theme parks; and outdoor recreation like biking, hiking, and water-skiing, to name a few.

Smaller cities also offer plenty to do. **Macon** hosts a magnificent cherry blossom festival each year. **Savannah** is known for its Old South, historical attractions. **Columbus** is an up-and-coming destination undergoing many renovations, like the new riverwalk and downtown revitalization. **Augusta** is king of golf, though you're more likely to shake hands with former president Carter in **Plains** than to garner playing time on Augusta's famous golf course.

Connecting these cities are well maintained state roads and interstates, with small towns like **Thomasville, Helen,** and **Plains** dotted along them. State parks abound, and lakes and rivers are abundant and open for recreational use.

Georgia was the last of the original 13 colonies, but its history stretches back much farther than that, to the time when Creek and Cherokee Native Americans inhabited the area. It wasn't until 1730 that the colony was settled and named after King George II. Georgia thrived up until the Civil

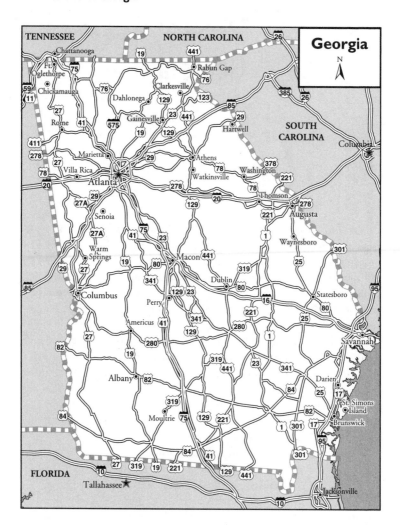

War but was then burned and pilfered like much of the South. The latter part of the nineteenth century and beginning of the twentieth century were devoted to industrial and business growth, a trend that continues today.

If you fly into the state, Atlanta will most likely be the origination point of your trip, but it also makes a good beginning for an automobile vacation. The MARTA (Atlanta's metro rail system) is efficient and extends to many suburbs, but that's not to say that Atlanta is a city you can take in by

Kids' Beat

- The state butterfly is the eastern tiger swallowtail; the state tree is the live oak; the state fish is the largemouth bass; and the state flower is the Cherokee rose.

- Georgia's nickname, the Peach State, was adopted long before the peach was named the state fruit.

- Georgia is the largest state east of the Mississippi and is larger than any other state in the southeastern region of the United States. It is 315 miles long from north to south.

- Georgia has two sweet claims to holiday fame: The Claxton Bakery in Claxton, which bakes 6 million pounds of fruitcake each year, and Bob's Candy Canes in Albany, which produces 461,049,616 candy canes annually.

- Georgia has 159 counties—more than any other state in the country.

- Gainesville, the Poultry Capital of the World, has a city ordinance against eating fried chicken with a fork.

- Ashburn is home to the world's largest peanut monument, a tribute to the state's profitable peanut crop.

foot. You'll still need a car to get around—and an automobile is essential if you plan trips to other cities and towns in the state.

If you plan to see only Atlanta, a long weekend is the minimum amount of time you'll need to catch all the sights and attractions. The same goes for a beach trip to **Jekyll Island, Tybee Island,** or other coastal destinations along the eastern side of the state.

For a lengthier exploration of Georgia, plan at least a week. Spend the first two or three days in Atlanta, then leisurely drive south, stopping at points of interest along the way. Wind up your trip with two or three days at the beaches along the Atlantic coast. If you visit during the winter, vary this itinerary and head to the mountains around **Helen** for shopping in a quaint Bavarian village. Still another option would be to plan your trip according to the state's nine travel regions: The Historic High Country, the Northeast Georgia Mountains, the Atlanta metro area, the Classic South, Presidential Pathways, Plantation Trace, Magnolia Midlands, Colonial Coast, and the Historic Heartland—all outlined in the state's promotional

Georgia's Not-to-Be-Missed Attractions	
Around the State	Dahlonega Gold Panning Rock City Gardens Okefenokee Swamp Alpine Helen Whitewater rafting Appalachian Trail Cheahaw Park Georgia islands

Atlanta	Atlanta Cyclorama
	Fernbank Museum of Natural
	    History
	Fernbank Museum of Science
	Martin Luther King Jr. National
	    Historic Site
	Stone Mountain Park
	Zoo Atlanta
	Centennial Olympic Park

Columbus	Callaway Gardens
	Franklin D. Roosevelt State Park
	Little White House State
	    Historic Site
	National Infantry Museum,
	    Fort Benning

Macon	Georgia Music Hall of Fame Georgia Sports Hall of Fame Museum of Arts and Sciences/Mark Smith Planetarium
Savannah	Juliette Gordon Low's Birthplace Savannah National Wildlife Refuge

materials. If time permits, take in a classic Georgia festival. Practically every small town and city has one.

Note: The Alabama/Georgia border marks the change from Central Standard Time to Eastern Standard Time.

GETTING THERE

By Plane. Frequent air travelers often joke that if you want to go to heaven, you'll have to go through the Atlanta airport. Atlanta's Hartsfield International Airport is the busiest airport in the world. Interstates 85 and 285 provide direct access to airport parking, and interstates 75 and 20 also provide access. The airport is about 20 minutes from downtown (when traffic is flowing smoothly, that is); there is also a MARTA station (Atlanta's metro rail system) inside that can easily transport your family downtown and to other out-lying areas. Hartsfield Airport does not page passengers; instead, it refers travelers to the individual airlines for information. For general information, call (404) 530-6830 or log on to www.atlanta-airport.com for information about everything from airport parking to the lost and found.

Other airports include: Savannah International Airport, at 400 Airways Avenue, (phone (912) 964-0514), www.savapt.com; Macon Airport, (phone (912) 788-6310); Bush Field Airport in Augusta, (phone (706) 798-3236); and Columbus Metropolitan Airport, (phone (706) 324-2449).

By Train. Passenger trains serve Atlanta, Gainesville, and Toccoa on a limited basis. Information on train schedules is available at (800) 872-7245 or (404) 881-3061, or log on to www.amtrak.com.

By Car. Many of the roads in Atlanta and its suburban areas were refurbished for the 1996 Olympic games and remain in good condition. State highways and back roads vary in condition but are better than those in other southern states. Interstate 75 divides the state in half from north to south; I-16 provides passage from Macon to the east toward Savannah; I-85 runs southwest to northeast through Atlanta; and I-20 bisects the north-central part of the state, crossing through Atlanta from west to east. Atlanta has 78 miles of High Occupancy Vehicle (HOV) lanes to the far left of each side of the interstate. They are designed to increase traffic flow and reduce air pollution. At least two or more occupants must be in the vehicle in order to use the HOV lanes.

For updates on road construction, slated projects, and real-time videos of current traffic conditions, log on the Georgia Department of Transportation's Web site, www.dot.state.ga.us. Georgia law requires all front-seat occupants to buckle up, and children younger than age four must be restrained in federally approved safety restraints. Check out the Georgia Department of Public Safety at www.georgianet.org for details about state laws.

How To Get Information before You Go

State

Georgia Department of Industry, Trade, & Tourism, P.O. Box 1776, Atlanta 30301; (404) 656-3590 or (800) VISIT-GA; www.gomm.com or www.georgia.org

Georgia Hospitality and Travel Association, 600 West Peachtree Street, Suite 1500, Atlanta 30308; (404) 873-4482

Georgia State Parks & Historic Sites, 205 Butler Street, Suite 1354, Floyd Tower East, Atlanta 30334; (800) 864-7275 or (404) 656-0559; www.gastateparks.org

Great Inns of Georgia, 541 Londonberry Road NW, Atlanta 30327; (404) 843-0471; www.bbonline.com/ga/greatinns

Regional

Northeast Georgia Mountain Travel Association, P.O. Box 464, Gainesville 30528; (404) 231-1820

Bed & Breakfast Atlanta, 1608 Briarcliff Road, Suite 5, Atlanta 30306; (404) 875-0525 or (800) 967-3224; www.bedandbreakfastatlanta.com

Historic Heartland Travel Association, P.O. Box 1619, Perry 31069; (912) 988-8000; www.perryga.com

Pine Mountain Tourism Association & Welcome Center, 101 East Broad Street, Pine Mountain 31822; (706) 663-4000 or (800) 441-3502

Warm Springs Area Tourism Association, 30 Broad Street, Warm Springs 31830; (706) 655-3322 or (800) FDR-1927

Local

Albany Convention & Visitors Bureau, 225 West Broad Avenue, Albany 31701; (912) 434-8700 or (800) 475-8700; www.albanyga.com

Alpharetta Convention & Visitors Bureau, 3060 Royal Boulevard South, Suite 145, Alpharetta 30022; (678) 297-2811 or (800) 294-0923; www.alpharettacvb.com

Alpine Helen/White County Convention & Visitors Bureau, 726 Brucken Strasse, Helen 30545; (706) 878-2181 or (800) 858-8027; www.helenga.org

Americus-Sumter Tourism Council Office, 400 West Lamar Street, Americus 31709; (912) 924-2646; www.americustourism.com

Athens Convention & Visitors Bureau, 300 North Thomas Street, Athens 30601; (706) 357-4430 or (800) 653-0603; www.visitathensga.com

Atlanta Convention & Visitors Bureau, 233 Peachtree Street, #2000, Atlanta 30043; (404) 521-6634 or (800) 285-2682; www.acvb.com

Augusta Metropolitan Convention & Visitors Bureau, 32 8th Street, Augusta 30903; (706) 823-6600 or (800) 726-0243; www.augustaga.org

Brunswick & The Golden Isles Visitors Bureau, 4 Glynn Avenue, Brunswick 31520; (800) 933-COAST or (912) 265-0620; www.bgivb.com

Carrollton Area Convention & Visitors Bureau, 118 South White Street, Carrollton 30117; (800) 292-0871 or (770) 214-9746

Cartersville Bartow County Convention & Visitors Bureau, P.O. Box 200397, Cartersville 30120; (800) 733-2280 or (770) 387-1357; www.notatlanta.org

Cobb County Convention & Visitors Bureau, 1 Galleria Parkway, Atlanta 30339; (770) 933-7228 or (800) 451-3480; www.cobbcvb.com

Columbus Convention & Visitors Bureau, 1000 Bay Avenue, Columbus 31902; (706) 322-1613 or (800) 999-1613; www.columbusga.com/ccvb

Covington-Newton County Convention & Visitors Bureau, 2101 Clark Street, Covington 30014; (800) 616-8626 or (770) 787-3868; www.citybreeze.com

Cumming Forsyth Chamber of Commerce, 110 Old Buford Road, Suite 120, Cumming 30040; (770) 887-6461

Dalton Convention & Visitors Bureau, 2211 Dug Gap Battle Road, Dalton 30722-2046; (706) 272-7676 or (800) 331-3258; www.nwgeorgia.com/daltoncvb

DeKalb Convention & Visitors Bureau, 750 Commerce Drive, #200, Decatur 30030; (800) 999-6055 or (404) 378-2525; www.dcvb.org

Gwinnett Convention and Visitors Bureau, 1505 Lakes Parkway, Suite 110, Lawrenceville 30043; (770) 277-6212 or (888) GWINNETT; www.gcvb.org

Jekyll Island Convention & Visitors Bureau, 381 Riverview Drive, Jekyll Island 31527; (877) 4-JEKYLL or (912) 635-4080; www.jekyllisland.com

Macon Convention/Visitors Bureau & Welcome Center, P.O. Box 6354, Macon 31208-6354; (912) 743-3401; www.maconga.org

Marietta Welcome Center & Visitors Bureau, No. 4 Depot Street, Marietta 30060; (770) 429-1115 or (800) 835-0445; www.mariettasquare.com

Pine Mountain Tourism Association, 111 Broad Street, Pine Mountain 31822; (706) 663-4000 or (800) 441-3502

Historic Roswell Convention & Visitors Bureau, 617 Atlanta Street, Roswell 30075; (770) 640-3253 or (800) 776-7935; www.cvb.roswell.ga.us

Savannah Convention & Visitors Bureau, P.O. Box 1628, Savannah 31402-1628; (912) 944-0456; www.savcvb.com

Thomasville Tourism Authority, 135 North Broad Street, Thomasville 31799; (800) 704-2350 or (912) 227-7099; www.thomasvillega.com

Valdosta-Lowndes County Convention & Visitors Bureau, 1703 Norman Drive, Valdosta 31601; (912) 245-0513 or (800) 569-8687; www.datasys.net/valdtourism

Warner Robins Convention & Visitors Bureau, 99 North First Street, Warner Robins 31099; (888) 288-WRGA or (912) 922-5100

Waycross/Ware County Tourism and Conference Bureau, 200 Lee Avenue, Waycross 31501; (912) 283-3742; www.gacoast.com/navigator/waycross.html

---

More Georgia Websites

Georgia Symbols   www.geobop.com/world/na/us/ga
Georgia Coloring Page   www.georgia.org/tourism/kids_color.html
Martin Luther King, Jr.   seattletimes.nwsource.com/mlk
Gardening for Kids
www.accessatlanta.com/community/groups/extension/gardening_for_kids.html
Peachtree City for Kids Only   peachtreecity.zipcities.com/forkidsonlylinx.htm

---

Family Outdoor Adventures

▲ - Camping
♥ - Author's favorite

♥ - *Alpine Helen*   Until 1969, Helen was just another North Georgia lumber town. When the industry went under, town fathers came up with a creative way to generate business—turn the town into a Bavarian village. Corny as it sounds, it worked. Today, almost a half-million people visit the village each year for a taste of Germany. The buildings sport gingerbread and gabled roofs, and merchants dress in traditional Bavarian garb. It won't cost you anything to stroll the streets and enjoy the street entertainers and scenery, and most restaurants (which also serve German fare) are reasonable. If you plan to spend the day, consider visiting the Alpine Amusement Park, with rides like bumper boats, a 40-foot Ferris wheel, putt-putt golf, an arcade, and a tilt-a-whirl (phone (706) 878-2306). Charlemagne's Kingdom (phone (706) 878-2200) is another interesting attraction that features Germany in miniature, complete with railroads, trains, towns, and music. For information about the town, call (706) 878-2181 or (800) 858-8027, or visit the website at www.helenga.org.

Appalachian Trail The Appalachian Trail, the most hiked trail in the United States, begins at Springer Mountain in North Georgia and traverses 14 states and seven national parks before winding up in Maine. In all, Georgia has 78 miles of rugged terrain, all of which lie in the Chattahoochee National Forest. The trail is well marked and maintained, with sections appropriate for any age hiker. It is busiest from March through May, but the Georgia sections can be hiked at any time of the year. Information about short hikes can be found at the Amicalola State Park Visitors Center, (706) 265-4703.

♥ - *Blue Ridge Scenic Railway, Blue Ridge* Hobos young and old alike will jump at the chance to ride the rails on a historic locomotive. The Blue Ridge Scenic Railway, complete with steam engine and vintage passenger cars, travels from Murphy Junction in Blue Ridge along the Toccoa River to McCaysville. The views along the way will keep youngsters occupied, as will the concessions on the train. It's a 26-mile ride one-way, with time to get out and stretch your legs in McCaysville and Copperhill, Tennessee. The railroad was built over 100 years ago and is now the only mainline railroad excursion service based in Georgia. The entire trip lasts around three hours. The Railway maintains a regular schedule with morning and afternoon departures daily. Call ahead for a schedule and reservations. The cost is $22 for adults, $20 for seniors, $12 for children ages 3–12, and free for ages 2 and under. Blue Ridge is in north central Georgia on Highway 515, 90 miles from Atlanta; (800) 934-1989; www.brscenic.com.

♥ - *Dahlonega Gold Panning, Dahlonega* "Thar's gold in them thar hills." In 1828, one of the largest gold deposits east of the Mississippi was discovered in Dahlonega, creating America's first major gold rush and coining the now-famous phrase. Today, families can explore two underground mines. The Consolidated Gold Mine on 125 Consolidated Road, (706) 864-8473, offers walking tours with expert miners through 250 feet of underground tunnels and gives you the opportunity to pan for gold. Crisson's Gold Mine, (706) 864-6363, first operated in 1847 and now run by a fourth generation of gold miners, also has tours and gold panning opportunities, including indoor mining in the winter. Downtown, the Dahlonega Courthouse Gold Museum tells the story of the gold rush through exhibits of mining equipment, gold from the mines, and a short film. Call (706) 864-2257 for information or log on to www.dahlonega.org.

Lake Lanier Islands Resort, Lake Lanier Islands   Located 45 minutes from Atlanta, Lake Lanier came into existence in 1957 when the Army Corp of Engineers created the lake to capture water from the Chattahoochee River. The peaks of several mountains remained above the water line to form islands that have become popular vacation destinations. The islands offer the best of both vacation options: A place to wind down after an active schedule and a place to keep busy with the plethora of outdoor activities. Boating, swimming, and horseback riding are favorites, but you can also catch some downtime by simply sitting along the edge of the 38,000-acre lake. It's a good compromise for families with children of different ages; the younger ones can hang out at the pool, while the older ones can play on the lake. For a wet-and-wild family outing, head to Lake Lanier Beach and Water Park, a good place to escape the Georgia heat. Your kids will have fun choosing which attraction to try out first: One of the ten water slides, the wave pool that simulates nine different types of waves, paddle boats, sailboats, canoes, Wave Runners, or the kiddie lagoon, to name a few. When your gang tires of the water, they can scale the rock-climbing wall, play volleyball, lie on the beach, or get in a game of putt-putt. In the summer, the park has evening concerts; call ahead for a schedule. It's open Memorial Day to Labor Day 10 a.m.–6 p.m., weekends from 10 a.m.–7 p.m. Cost is $6 per car, plus $18.95 for adults and $13.95 for children. Contact them at 6950 Holiday Road, Lake Lanier Islands; (770) 932-7275 or (800) 840-LAKE; www.lakelanierislands.com.

Finally, there are several places to stay in a variety of price ranges, but one of the best deals is at the Hilton. The Hilton Vacation Station, a program designed to make children feel like VIPs, operates during the summer. Upon arrival, each child receives a colorful backpack (infants get a reusable plastic bib), and parents get a Welcome Key Packet that highlights family services, activities, and attractions. Plus, there is a Vacation Station Lending Desk stocked with toys and games appropriate for each age group. Rates start at $129. The Hilton is at 6950 Holiday Road; (770) 932-7200; www.lakelanierislands.com.

♥ - *Okefenokee Swamp, Waycross*   The name itself (pronounced Oak-E-fin-oak-E) is enough to make kids want to stop and explore. In the early days, its location at the headwaters of the Suwannee and St. Mary's Rivers made it a prime location for hunting and fishing for Indians and early settlers; today the swamp offers families the chance to experience a different kind of outdoors. Here, the black waters—stained by the tannins from cypress trees—create an eerie backdrop for the wildlife and unusual plants that lurk in the shadows. It has been designated both a National Wildlife Refuge and part of the National Wilderness System.

There are several entrances into the Swamp, but three in particular are the most convenient. To the east is the Suwannee Canal Recreation Area, 11 miles southwest in Folkston with a visitors' center and a restored homestead. You'll also find a nine-mile Swamp Island Drive and a Swamp Walk over a 4,000-foot boardwalk extending into the swamp and leading to a 50-foot-high observation tower. State Route 121/23, Folkston; (912) 496-3331.

To the west, the Stephen C. Foster State Park, 17 miles northeast of Fargo, is one of the few state parks inside a National Wildlife Refuge. Guided boat tours, picnic areas, motorboat and canoe rentals, and an interpretive center are offered, along with campsites and nine cabins for rent. State Route 177, Fargo; (800) 864-7275, (912) 637-5274.

Okefenokee Swamp Park sits to the north, 13 miles from Waycross, and is an easy way to experience the natural wilderness. Guided boat tours take guests through the black waters of the largest freshwater swamp in the country. Afterwards, visit the Swamp Creation Center with a living swamp display of plants and animals. A nature center, wildlife observatory, and replica of a swamp homestead are also found in the park. A more recent addition is the Pioneer Island Express, with a 36-inch-gauge replica steam engine. Climb aboard for a train ride through the swamp to see an authentic turpentine site, a honey bee farm, a moonshine still, and an Indian village. The journey also lets you get off and explore Pioneer Island for an up-close look at how the swamp's early settlers once lived. Lodging is nearby. 5700 Okefenokee Swamp Park Road, Waycross; (912) 283-0583; www.okeswamp.com.

Rock City Gardens, Lookout Mountain   "See Rock City" has become such a part of Southern culture that you might have doubted such a place really existed. Wonder no more. Located on Lookout Mountain, Rock City has plenty of natural sites to see, and over the years they have expanded the park to include amenities that make this an easy place for families to spend the day.

The highlights are definitely the views and the unusual rock formations. Among the photo opportunities: A 1,000-ton rock balanced on an extremely small base; the Grand Corridor with its sheer rock walls rising hundreds of feet to the sky; and Needle's Eye passage, so narrow the wind whistles when it passes through. To give you a sense of how magnificent these formations are, saunter across Swing-Along Bridge, which stretches 180 feet between the chasm of two high outcroppings.

Kids, however, will probably be just as interested in the trivia gleaned from their visit. From Eagle's Nest and Lover's Leap, seven states are in view: Alabama, Georgia, Kentucky, North Carolina, South Carolina, Tennessee, and Virginia. Lover's Leap is also the speculated site of tragedy for two Indian lovers. They ran away together, but when caught, the brave was thrown from the end of Lover's Leap; his beautiful lover leaped over the edge after him. And then there's the tale about gnomes who once held seasonal gatherings in a clearing on the far side of Fat Man's Squeeze. When they realized humans could make it through the narrow passage, they moved their meetings deeper into the forest.

Rock City has several activities going on throughout the year. Call ahead for a schedule and reservations. Parking is free; admission is $9.95 for adults, $5.50 for children ages 3–12, and free for ages 2 and younger. 1400 Patten Road on Lookout Mountain in northeast Georgia; (706) 820-2531; www.seerockcity.com.

Sky Valley Resort, Dillard   Skiing in Georgia? That's right. Though the season is obviously limited, the advantages of heading to the slopes in the Peach State—which has elevations of 3,500 feet—are affordability and convenience. Plus, if your brood has never tried skiing, practicing and learning here adds value to subsequent trips out West. In all, there are five trails and a bunny slope, and night-skiing is available. Slopes are open from December to March, and when summer arrives, the resort has other outdoor options. Hiking, swimming, tennis, and golf are among the activities to take up your time. There is a restaurant at the resort and nearby homes for rent range from one to five bedrooms. 1 Sky Valley, 7 miles from Highlands, North Carolina, and four miles from Dillard; (800) 437-2416 for automated ski information, (800) 262-8259 for accommodations, (706) 746-5302 for general information; www.skyvalley.com.

Sporting Events, Atlanta   Sporting families will be disappointed when visiting Atlanta—only because there are so many events to choose from that, ultimately, something will have to be passed by. The most famous team is probably the Atlanta Braves, a contender for the last several years in the World Series. Games are held at Turner Stadium; the stadium is also open for tours daily. The Atlanta Thrashers are the city's National Hockey League expansion team, playing in the new Philips Arena, also home to the Atlanta Hawks NBA team. The pro football team, the Atlanta Falcons, play in the Georgia Dome. For ticket information, call (404) 521-6634, (800) 285-2682; www.acvb.com.

♥ - *Tallulah Gorge State Park, Tallulah*   Even youngsters who prefer amusement parks and arcades will be entertained at Tallulah Gorge State Park in the northeastern corner of the state. For starters, there's Tallulah Gorge, a two-mile-long chasm that's almost 1,000 feet deep—second in depth only to the Grand Canyon. Circus Star Karl Wallenda once walked a tightrope across the expanse. Then there are the waterfalls, three in all, with the highest falling 700 feet. The scenery alone is worth the trip, but when you've had enough of hiking the trails to the overlooks, you can picnic, explore the interesting plant life along the nature trails, bike, fish, swim in the 63-acre lake, lay out on the adjacent manmade beach, or play tennis in the park. Whitewater paddling is an option the first two weekends in April and the first three weekends in November. There is also an interpretive center with exhibits and a video about the area. Be forewarned, however, that because of the heights and the rugged terrain in the gorge, experiencing this park on foot is better suited for older kids. There are RV sites but no campgrounds. U.S. Highway 441 in Tallulah; (800) 864-7275 or (770) 754-8257; www.gastateparks.org.

▲ - *Unicoi State Park, Helen*   Home of the annual Children's Fishing Rodeo, Unicoi State Park is one of the most visited parks in the state. Its location is one reason, as the park is situated close to Helen's Alpine Village, Babyland General Hospital in Cleveland (home of the Cabbage Patch dolls), and the Appalachian Trail. Other reasons it's so popular are that in addition to all the usual activities available at state parks, like hiking, swimming, and biking, Unicoi also has a craft shop with regional crafts on-site, and it hosts an annual music festival, art show, and a variety of environmental and cultural programs. Pedal boats, a restaurant, a man-made beach, tennis, and fishing are available. There are 85 campsites for tents and RVs; cost is $22 per night. The park also features 30 family cottages that cost from $125–145 and a 100-room lodge that costs $89 per night. The park is located two miles northeast of Helen on Highway 356. Admission is charged for state park access. Call (706) 878-3982 or (800) 573-9659 for reservations, or log on to www.gastateparks.org.

Whitewater Rafting   Georgia's abundance of wild-water rivers make for a wet and woolly adventure in the state's back country. The Chattooga River, where the movie *Deliverance* was filmed, has some of the most hazardous Class II–V white-water rapids in the country. Other rivers, such as the Chattahoochee, Ogeechee, Altamaha, Suwannee, and Alapaha, are calmer and better suited for innertubing and canoeing, especially if you have small children. There are plenty of guided tours available for half-day, full-day, and overnight excursions, but the least expensive and perhaps the most enjoyable way to ride the waves is to rent a canoe and take your time paddling through the state's national forests and parks. Wear your bathing suit and pack a picnic so you can stop along the way for an impromptu lunch.

If you prefer a guided ride, there are several outfitters to choose from. Appalachian Wildwaters/USA Raft, an outfitter in nearby Benton, Tennessee, offers rafting on nine rivers including the Ocoee, Pigeon, Nantahala, Nolichucky, and French Broad; (800) USA-RAFT;. Wild Water Rafting braves the Chattooga, Nantahala, Ocoee, and Pigeon rivers; (800) 451-9972; www.wildwaterrafting.com.

Calendar of Festivals and Events

March

Georgia's Cherry Blossom Festival, Macon   Featuring the best of Southern traditions and contemporary entertainment, Macon's International Cherry Blossom Festival celebrates the blossoming of 224,000 Yoshino cherry trees with more than 500 spectacular events including concerts, tours, parades, arts and crafts, a hot-air balloon festival, sports, and international cuisine; (800) 768-3401.

April

Baxley Tree Fest, Baxley   This annual celebration of trees and tree products is unlike any other. Focused on the forestry industry, it features logging and loader competitions, chain-saw carving, a forestry tour, arts and crafts, a street dance, fireworks, softball and tennis tournaments, a cake baking competition, a motorcycle show, the Tree Trek road race, a bike ride, concerts, air events and sky divers, a carnival, and a petting zoo; (912) 367-7731; www.applingdacoc.com.

Georgia Renaissance Festival, Fairburn   A medieval atmosphere sets the stage for this Renaissance Festival, complete with jousting knights, comedic jugglers, Shakespearean parodies, and high-flying Birds of Prey. Ten stages feature more than 100 shows daily, and there is an Artist Marketplace with thousands of handcrafted items. Food also reflects the Renaissance period, with items such as giant roaster turkey legs. The Festival takes place for several weekends beginning at the end of April, then again in October and November; (770) 964-8575.

Mossy Creek Barnyard Festival, Perry   Billed as a Top 100 Event in North America, this festival has arts and crafts, demonstrations, music, storytelling, farm animals, wagon hayrides, and country cooking; (912) 922-8265.

Riverfest Weekend/Salisbury Fair, Columbus   One of the South's largest outdoor festivals occurs each year along Columbus' Riverwalk. Expect a midway carnival, folk-life village, folk-art and fine-art booths, a children's art show and interactive area, a parade, and live entertainment on six stages; (706) 576-4760.

Vidalia Onion Festival, Vidalia   World-famous for its sweet onions, this city's annual event includes a street dance, a rodeo, arts and crafts, an air show and exhibitions, a two-mile fun run and 10K road race, a softball tournament, an onion-eating contest, and cooking school; (912) 538-8687.

May

Andersonville Historic Fair, Andersonville   Confederate and Union encampments, mock Civil War battles, live entertainment, old-time craftsmen at work, and more than 200 booths of arts, crafts, antiques and collectibles await visitors. This event is held annually in May and October; (912) 924-2558.

June

Georgia Peach Festival, Byron   What makes this Southern festival unique is the chance for a free taste of the World's Largest Peach Cobbler. Adding to the fun are craftspeople, a parade, live entertainment, peach bin races, and tours of the peach shed where the peaches are stored; (912) 825-4002; www.mindspring.com/~gapeachfest.

Jekyll Island Music Festivals, Jekyll Island   Music showcased on the seashore is the highlight of this twice-yearly event. June and August are the usual months for the festival; (800) 841-6586.

Watermelon Days Festival, Cordele   Known as the Watermelon Capital of the World, Cordele's annual festival is family-oriented, with street dances, gospel singing, a parade, arts and crafts, and live entertainment. The festival stretches over several weeks in mid-summer; (912) 273-1668.

July

Fantastic 4th Celebration, Stone Mountain   One of the premier Fourth of July celebrations in the state, Stone Mountain's event features spectacular fireworks, a lasershow, and daytime attractions and activities for families; (770) 498-5702; www.stonemountainpark.org.

September

Kingsland's Labor Day Catfish Festival, Kingsland   Historic downtown Kingsland is the setting for this fun family festival. A variety of events are flavored with Southern hospitality, including arts and crafts, a parade, a golf tournament, a children's area, and festival foods with the main dish being "King Catfish." Nationally known entertainment is free to the public with festival seating; (800) 433-0225; www.georgiacoast.com/navigator/kingsland.html.

Plains Peanut Festival, Plains   Peanuts are the obvious headliner for this attraction, but it's also your chance to shake hands with former president Carter and his wife. Other activities include a folk play, road races, arts and crafts, a peanut-trailer-backing contest, a parade, a peanut museum, peanut education, displays of peanut-farming equipment, and live entertainment on two stages; (912) 824-5445.

October

Big Pig Jig, Vienna   The annual Georgia Barbecue Cooking Championship is the main draw for this weekend of activities, with a "People's Choice" tasting tent for BBQ aficionados. There is also a children's area, a parade, arts and crafts booths, pageants, a golf tournament, carnival rides and games, a 5K race, and stage shows each of the three nights of the celebration. The winner of the Cooking Championship receives a large cash prize; (912) 268-8275; www.bigpigjig.com.

Chattahoochee Heritage Festival, Columbus   Held at Flat Rock Park, this three-day event includes activities such as Native American dancing demonstrations, black-powder shooting, buckskinners, heritage demonstrations, an antique car show, Civil War camps and battle reenactments, arts and crafts, and a children's activity area with clowns and art projects; (706) 324-1546.

Chiaha Harvest Fair, Rome   Billed as a "toe-tappin', cider-sippin', fun-for-everyone arts festival," the main attraction at this fair is the juried showcase of southeastern artists and craftspeople. Complimentary hot apple cider, continuous live entertainment, 14 unique food booths, children's activities, and river boat rides are also part of the festivities; (706) 235-4542.

Georgia Marble Festival, Jasper   Tours of open-pit marble quarries—open to the public only during this festival—make this one of the most unique events in Georgia. Additionally, there are marble sculpture and fine-art competitions, crafts, music, an auto show, and a theatrical production; (706) 692-5600.

Oktoberfest, Helen   North Georgia celebrates this German holiday in style, with more than 300,000 people attending each year's bash to dance, eat, sing, and, of course, drink plenty of German beer. A two-month-long festival, Okterberfest kicks off the Thursday after Labor Day and continues through the last weekend in October; (706) 878-2181 or (800) 858-8027; www.helenga.org.

November

Mule Day, Calvary   Held at the Fairgrounds, this event attracts more than 75,000 visitors annually. There are 500 arts and crafts booths, a mule parade, concessions, cane grinding, and syrup making, along with contests for tobacco spitting, plowing, and greased-pig racing. The event is almost always the first Saturday in November; (912) 377-6853.

December

The Holiday Celebration, Stone Mountain.   Holiday lights and music, a holiday-themed lasershow, a magic train ride, and, of course, Santa Claus himself, are part of the festivities of this holiday celebration. The event kicks off the day after Thanksgiving and continues through December 31; (770) 498-5702; www.stonemountainpark.org

Atlanta

Like its symbol, the legendary phoenix of Egyptian mythology, Atlanta rose from the ashes of the Civil War by attracting business and state government to the city. By the twentieth century, Atlanta had emerged as the capital of the New South and was the site of the 1996 Summer Olympic Games. Its numerous accolades include being voted the top city with the highest quality of life in the United States (Corporate Resources Group, 1997); the nation's most friendly city (Roper Starch Worldwide, 1996); and the number one city for African Americans (*Ebony,* 1997). More than 700 Fortune 1,000 companies have operations in Atlanta, and 23 are headquartered here. All these statistics mean only one thing for families: An array of cultural attractions, activities, and entertainment unsurpassed elsewhere in the South.

Situated in the foothills of the Appalachian and Blue Ridge mountains, Atlanta is a good home base for any Georgia vacation. For one thing, flying into the city will save you money, as Atlanta is the largest, and therefore the most competitive, airport in the Southeast. It's also a good place to explore if your vacation time is limited. The weather is usually cooperative year round, with the biggest weather threat being sporadic rainfall.

Probably the biggest complaint you'll have about this southern city is the traffic. The interstate system is comprehensive, but if you travel during peak hours in the morning or afternoon, expect traffic to move slowly and sometimes to stop altogether.

Family Lodging

Evergreen Resort and Conference Center

You get what you pay for, and at Evergreen what you're paying for is a convenient, easy location and great service. Located within the grounds of Stone Mountain Park, this AAA four-star, four-diamond hotel is accessible to all park attractions, making it easy to slip back to the room between activities for a quick nap or snack. The resort sits on the waterfront, providing unobstructed views of the lake from your room's balcony; on the side, you get vistas of the woods and natural surroundings. There are both indoor and outdoor pools, tennis courts, jogging trails, a spa, and the Waterside Restaurant. Rates start at $69 for weekend seasonal specials. 1 Lakeside Drive, 16 miles east of Atlanta off Highway 78; (770) 469-2250 or (800) 722-1000; www.evergreenresort.com.

Hilton Atlanta & Towers

The downtown location of this large hotel makes it an ideal hub for families interested in taking in metro Atlanta's sights. Plus there are traditional guest rooms and suites to choose from, so you can pick the space that best suits your family's needs. During our stay, we took advantage of the basketball courts, pool tables, and tennis courts; other on-site recreational facilities include a pool, jogging track, and fitness center. This hotel is a Hilton Vacation Station during the summer months, a program designed to make children feel like VIPs. Upon arrival, each child received a colorful backpack (infants get a reusable plastic bib) and parents get a Welcome Key Packet highlighting family services, activities, and attractions. Plus, there is a Vacation Station Lending Desk stocked with toys and games appropriate for each age group. Rates begin at $125. 255 Courtland Street NE, Atlanta; (404) 659-2000 or (800) 774-1500; www.hilton.com

Holiday Inn Select Perimeter Dunwoody

Located a mile east of Perimeter Mall, this hotel has 250 guestrooms and two suites, all with Nintendo availability and in-room coffee makers, hairdryers, and voice mail. Room service is available, and there is also the Bristol Bar & Grill with buffets for breakfast, lunch, and dinner. An outdoor swimming pool and a fitness room are other amenities available to families. Rates begin at $119. 4386 Chamblee Dunwoody Road; (770) 457-6363; www.basshotels.com/holiday-inn.

Twin Oaks B&B and Farm Vacations, Villa Rica

Conveniently situated near several Atlanta attractions, Twin Oaks is the kind of place that makes families feel at home on the road. The owner is an animal lover—geese, peacocks, Canada geese, cats, dogs, an African gray parrot, and a Moluccan cockatoo are among her menagerie. There are three cottages with full-size refrigerators, microwaves, and toasters, and a two-bedroom suite off the main house. Rates start at $100; 9565 East Liberty Road; (770) 459-4374; www.bbonline.com/ga/twinoaks.

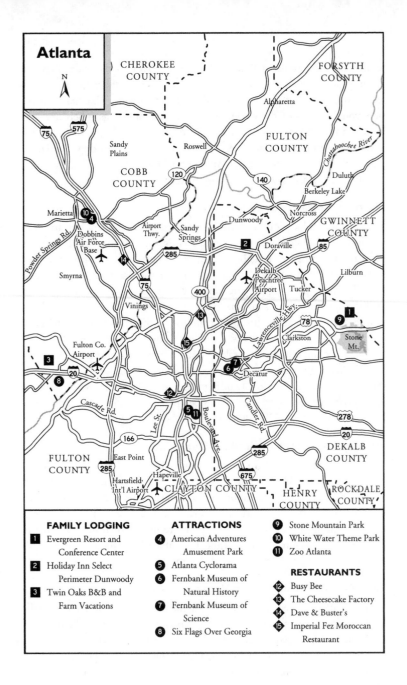

Atlanta

N

CHEROKEE COUNTY

FORSYTH COUNTY

Alpharetta

Chattahoochee River

FULTON COUNTY

75 575

Sandy Plains

Roswell

Duluth

120 140

Berkeley Lake

COBB COUNTY

Marietta

Dobbins Air Force Base

Airport Thwy.

Sandy Springs

Dunwoody

Norcross

GWINNETT COUNTY

10 **4**

2 Doraville

85

Lilburn

Powder Springs Rd.

285

14

Dekalb Peachtree Airport

Tucker

Smyrna

75

400

Vinings

13

Lawrenceville Hwy.

78

9 **1**

15

Clarkston

Stone Mt.

Fulton Co. Airport

3

20

8

7
6 Decatur

12

Candler Rd.

Cascade Rd.

Lee St.

5
11

Boulevard Ave.

278

20

166

FULTON COUNTY

East Point

285

Hartsfield Int'l Airport

Hapeville

DEKALB COUNTY

285

675

CLAYTON COUNTY

HENRY COUNTY

ROCKDALE COUNTY

FAMILY LODGING

1 Evergreen Resort and Conference Center

2 Holiday Inn Select Perimeter Dunwoody

3 Twin Oaks B&B and Farm Vacations

ATTRACTIONS

4 American Adventures Amusement Park

5 Atlanta Cyclorama

6 Fernbank Museum of Natural History

7 Fernbank Museum of Science

8 Six Flags Over Georgia

9 Stone Mountain Park

10 White Water Theme Park

11 Zoo Atlanta

RESTAURANTS

12 Busy Bee

13 The Cheesecake Factory

14 Dave & Buster's

15 Imperial Fez Moroccan Restaurant

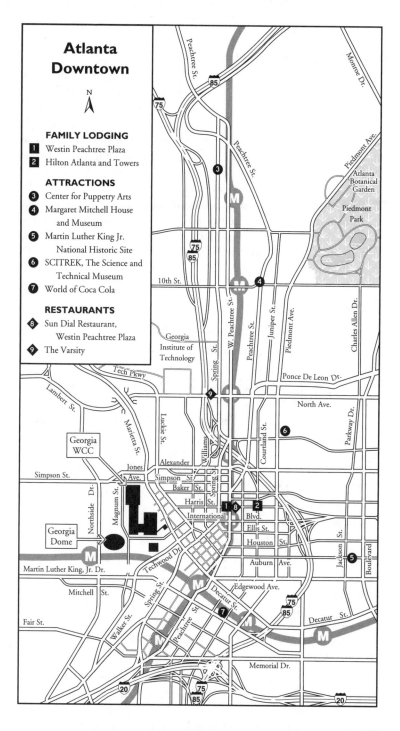

Atlanta Downtown

N

FAMILY LODGING

1 Westin Peachtree Plaza
2 Hilton Atlanta and Towers

ATTRACTIONS

3 Center for Puppetry Arts
4 Margaret Mitchell House
   and Museum
5 Martin Luther King Jr.
   National Historic Site
6 SCITREK, The Science and
   Technical Museum
7 World of Coca Cola

RESTAURANTS

8 Sun Dial Restaurant,
   Westin Peachtree Plaza
9 The Varsity

The Westin Peachtree Plaza

While this hotel doesn't feature kitchenettes in guest rooms, it does have an appealing location within walking distance of Centennial Olympic Park, CNN Center, the World of Coca-Cola, Turner Stadium, and the Georgia Dome. And kids will love the fact that, with 73 stories, The Westin is the tallest hotel in the western hemisphere. Obviously, the views are spectacular; the building is circular in design, meaning that all rooms, especially those on the higher floors, have vistas of the city. There are three restaurants, an indoor/outdoor swimming pool, a fitness center, and 24-hour room service. The Westin Kids Club caters to the young set, with sports bottles upon arrival that are filled free of charge at dinner, coloring books, bath toys, and safety kits complete with bandages, ID bracelets, and outlet covers. Rates start at $109. 210 Peachtree Street NW; (800) WESTIN-1, www.westin.com.

Attractions

American Adventures Amusement Park

250 North Cobb Parkway, Atlanta; (770) 424-9283
  www.whitewaterpark.com

Hours: Memorial Day–Labor Day, daily 10 a.m.–8 p.m., school holidays and weekends remainder of year, 10 a.m.–6 p.m.

Admission: $4 adults, $15 children ages 4–17; $4 ages 3 and younger

Appeal by Age Group:

Pre-school	Grade School	Teens	Young Adults	Over 30	Seniors
★★★★	★★★★	★★★★	★★	★	★

Average Touring Time: 2–3 hours

Minimum Touring Time: 1 hour

Rainy Day Touring: Recommended

Author's Rating: ★★★   A good place to go on rainy days

Services and Facilities:

Restaurants Yes		Lockers Yes	
Alcoholic beverages No		Pet kennels No	
Disabled access Yes		Rain check No	
Wheelchair rental Yes		Private tours No	
Baby stroller rental No			

Description and Comments   When you've been museum-hopping or driving all day, your kids need a creative outlet for all that pent-up energy. American Adventures is a good solution. This amusement center, a sophisticated version of the traveling fairs that visit small towns and cities, has all the traditional rides like Tilt-a-Whirl, Scrambler, bumper cars, swings, a Ferris wheel, and go-carts. Pint-sized versions are available for the younger ones. Another cool play area is the Foam Factory, a multilevel fun house with more than 50,000 foam balls that are positioned and dumped onto the folks below. The Factory also has interactive activities like a basketball arena and a foamball table.

Atlanta Cyclorama

800-C Cherokee Avenue SE, Atlanta; (404) 658-7625

Hours: Daily 9:20 a.m.–4:30 p.m.; until 5:30 p.m. Labor Day–May 31

Admission: $5 adults, $4 seniors, $3 children ages 6–12, free for children ages 5 and younger

Appeal by Age Group:

Pre-school	Grade School	Teens	Young Adults	Over 30	Seniors
★★	★★★	★★★	★★★★	★★★★	★★★★

Average Touring Time: 1 hour

Minimum Touring Time: 1 hour

Rainy Day Touring: Recommended

Author's Rating: ★★★★ A different kind of experience that the entire family will enjoy

Services and Facilities:

Restaurants No	Lockers No
Alcoholic beverages No	Pet kennels No
Disabled access Yes	Rain check N/A
Wheelchair rental No	Private tours N/A
Baby stroller rental No	

Description and Comments Some places never go out of style. A case in point is the Cyclorama. Finished in 1885, this diorama painting—the largest in the world—depicts the 1864 Civil War Battle of Atlanta on a circular screen. It doesn't sound particularly high tech, but believe it or not, your kids will get a thrill out of sitting in the revolving seats in the center of the theater. The presentation is accompanied by sound effects and dramatic lighting—enough to keep them entertained for the 35 minutes of the film.

Center for Puppetry Arts

1404 Spring Street NW, Atlanta; (404) 873-3391
   www.puppet.org

Hours: Performances at 10 a.m. and 11:30 a.m. weekdays during school year

Admission: $5 adults, $4 children

Appeal by Age Group:

Pre-school	Grade School	Teens	Young Adults	Over 30	Seniors
★★★	★★★★★	★★★★★	★★★★	★★★★	★★★★

Average Touring Time: 2 hours

Minimum Touring Time: 1 hour

Rainy Day Touring: Recommended

Author's Rating: ★★★★

Services and Facilities:

Restaurants No	Lockers No
Alcoholic beverages No	Pet kennels No
Disabled access Yes	Rain check No
Wheelchair rental No	Private tours No
Baby stroller rental No	

Description and Comments   Atlanta seems like an odd place for the largest collection of puppets in the world, yet it was here that Vincent Anthony founded the Vagabond Marionettes in 1966. The company performed for schools, churches, and community organizations for 11 years before the Center for Puppetry Arts opened. Today, kids can visit the center and watch performances, view puppets from all over the world, and attend workshops where they can make their own. The puppet arcade, where you can use controls to make puppets move, and Jim Henson's puppet characters from the movie *Pigs in Space* are two of the most visited exhibits.

Fernbank Museum of Natural History

767 Clifton Road NE, Atlanta; (404) 378-0127
    www.fernbank.edu/museum

Hours: Monday–Saturday 10 a.m.–5 p.m., Sunday noon–5 p.m.;
    IMAX Theater, Friday until 10 p.m.

Admission: $8.95 adults, $7.95 students and seniors, $4.95 ages 12 and
    younger

Appeal by Age Group:

Pre-school	Grade School	Teens	Young Adults	Over 30	Seniors
★★★★	★★★★★	★★★★★	★★★★	★★★★	★★★★

Average Touring Time: 3 hours

Minimum Touring Time: 1 hour

Rainy Day Touring: Recommended

Author's Rating: ★★★★   Something for everybody

Services and Facilities:

Restaurants Yes	Lockers Yes
Alcoholic beverages No	Pet kennels No
Disabled access Yes	Rain check N/A
Wheelchair rental Yes	Private tours No
Baby stroller rental No	

Description and Comments   Using Georgia as a microcosm, this museum focuses on the history of the world, human culture, and the environment. Some exhibits are suited for particular age groups, such as the Fantasy Forest geared toward ages three to five, but undoubtedly all age groups will find something of interest in each display. Fernbank's permanent exhibits include A Walk Through Time in Georgia, a chronological story about the development of life on earth; Spectrum of the Senses, a gallery filled with hands-on interactive learning stations that demonstrate the physical properties of light and sound; Cultures of the World, a display of decorative objects from around the world; and First Georgians, focusing on the state's prehistoric human inhabitants.

Fernbank Museum of Science

156 Heaton Park Drive NE, Atlanta; (404) 378-4311
  www.fernbank.edu

Hours: Exhibit Hall: Monday 8:30 a.m.–5 p.m., Tuesday–Thursday
  8:30 a.m.–10 p.m., Saturday 10 a.m.–5 p.m., Sunday 1–5 p.m.;
  Observatory: Thursday–Friday 8–10:30 p.m. clear evenings only

Admission: Free, except for planetarium: $2 adults, $1 children

Appeal by Age Group:

Pre-school	Grade School	Teens	Young Adults	Over 30	Seniors
★★★★	★★★★★	★★★★★	★★★★	★★★★	★★★★

Average Touring Time: 2 hours

Minimum Touring Time: 1 hour

Rainy Day Touring: Recommended

Author's Rating: ★★★★   Something for everybody

Services and Facilities:

Restaurants No	Lockers No
Alcoholic beverages No	Pet kennels No
Disabled access Yes	Rain check N/A
Wheelchair rental Yes	Private tours Yes
Baby stroller rental Yes	

Description and Comments   More than a museum, Fernbank Museum of Science is a combination of exhibits, interactive programs, and workshops designed to enhance science programs in the Dekalb County schools. Luckily for families, the programs are also open to the public free of charge. The exhibit area in the science center includes displays of animal and plant life in the Okefenockee Swamp, a look at prehistoric Atlanta during the dinosaur era, a simulated cave with all its critters, and the crown jewel—the original Apollo 6 space capsule from the last unmanned space flight. You'll also find an observatory with a 36-inch telescope, a planetarium that is open nightly during the week and afternoons on the weekends, and a 65-acre virgin hardwood forest behind the facility with paved hiking and biking trails. If you call ahead, you can get a schedule of workshops that your family can participate in—everything from seismology and ornithology to geology and astronomy.

Margaret Mitchell House and Museum

990 Peachtree Street, Atlanta; (404) 249-7012

Hours: Daily, 9 a.m.–4 p.m.

Admission: $7 adults, $6 seniors and children ages 7–17, free for children ages 6 and younger

Appeal by Age Group:

Pre- school	Grade School	Teens	Young Adults	Over 30	Seniors
★	★★	★★★	★★★★	★★★★	★★★★

Average Touring Time: 30 minutes

Minimum Touring Time: 15 minutes

Rainy Day Touring: Not recommended

Author's Rating: ★★★★

Services and Facilities:

Restaurants No	Lockers No
Alcoholic beverages No	Pet kennels No
Disabled access Yes	Rain check No
Wheelchair rental No	Private tours No
Baby stroller rental No	

Description and Comments   One of Atlanta's newest attractions, the Margaret Mitchell House & Museum in Midtown is a shrine to *Gone with the Wind* and its author. Part of the museum is housed in the three-story Tudor Revival mansion where Mitchell wrote the Pulitzer Prize–winning novel. This section focuses on her life, with exhibits telling the story of her years as a journalist. A former bank building across the street houses collections that tell the story of the movie, from costumes, movie scripts, photos, set sketches, and seats from the Loew's Grand Theatre where the movie premiered. Kids are entertained here as long as their parents don't get caught up in looking at and reading each exhibit.

Martin Luther King, Jr. National Historic Site

450 Auburn Avenue NE, Atlanta; (404) 524-1956

Hours: Daily 9 a.m.–5:30 p.m. (until 8 p.m. during Daylight Savings Time)

Admission: Free

Appeal by Age Group:

Pre-school	Grade School	Teens	Young Adults	Over 30	Seniors
★	★★★	★★★	★★★★	★★★★	★★★★

Average Touring Time: 3 hours

Minimum Touring Time: 1 hour

Rainy Day Touring: Recommended

Author's Rating: ★★★★ A moving experience

Services and Facilities:

Restaurants No	Lockers No
Alcoholic beverages No	Pet kennels No
Disabled access Yes	Rain check N/A
Wheelchair rental Yes	Private tours Yes
Baby stroller rental No	

Description and Comments One of Atlanta's most famous sons is remembered at the Martin Luther King, Jr. National Historic Site. The site covers about ten blocks and encompasses King's birthplace, grave, and the Ebenezer Baptist Church where he preached. Admission is free, and a free brochure for a self-guided tour can be picked up at the new visitors center across from the King Center. Begin at Exhibition Hall, where photos and memorabilia of Dr. King are on display. Take your time strolling the grounds and getting a sense of this man's accomplishments. If you can read about King before your visit, this stop will be all the more relevant.

SciTrek, The Science & Technology Museum of Atlanta

395 Piedmont Avenue, Atlanta; (404) 522-5500, (800) 522-3955
www.scitrek.org

Hours: Monday–Saturday 10 a.m.–5 p.m.; Sunday noon–5 p.m.

Admission: $7.50 adults, $5 seniors, college students, military personnel with ID, and children ages 3–17, free for children ages 2 and younger

Appeal by Age Group:

Pre-school	Grade School	Teens	Young Adults	Over 30	Seniors
★★★★	★★★★	★★★★★	★★★★	★★★★	★★★★

Average Touring Time: 2 hours

Minimum Touring Time: 1 hour

Rainy Day Touring: Recommended

Author's Rating: ★★★★ A great way to turn your kids on to science

Services and Facilities:

Restaurants No	Lockers Yes
Alcoholic beverages No	Pet kennels No
Disabled access Yes	Rain check N/A
Wheelchair rental Yes	Private tours No
Baby stroller rental No	

Description and Comments One of the top ten science museums in the country, SciTrek is loud, interactive, and fun—with exhibits that will hold your children's attention for hours. All displays are based on the basic principles of science, making this seemingly tough subject easy to understand. One of our favorites is the Electro Magnetic Junction, where you can close a circuit with your body, watch magnetic forces hurl a metal ring 22 feet into the air, and witness a lightning storm in a jar. Other exhibits include Perceptions and Illusion, an exhibit on optical illusions that "enables" you to lift a race car with one hand; the Color Factory, where primary colors of light can be mixed to produce an array of color hues; and KidSpace, a permanent exhibit exclusively for 2- to 7-year-olds with musical instruments, computers for drawing, and an experiment with water flow on a kid-sized dam. In all, there are over 150 science experiments to play with.

Six Flags Over Georgia

7661 Six Flags Parkway, Atlanta; (770) 948-9290
  www.sixflags.com

Hours: Memorial Day through Labor Day, daily 10 a.m.–9 p.m., Friday through Saturday until midnight; weekends only from mid-March through Memorial Day and September through October

Admission: $35 adults, $25 seniors and children

Appeal by Age Group:

Pre-school	Grade School	Teens	Young Adults	Over 30	Seniors
★★★	★★★★	★★★★	★★★	★★★	★★★

Average Touring Time: 2 days

Minimum Touring Time: 1 day

Rainy Day Touring: Not recommended

Author's Rating: ★★★

Services and Facilities:

Restaurants Yes	Lockers Yes
Alcoholic beverages No	Pet kennels Yes
Disabled access Yes	Rain check Yes
Wheelchair rental Yes	Private tours No
Baby stroller rental Yes	

Description and Comments With heart-pounding rides and live Broadway–style shows, Six Flags Over Georgia can keep your group busy for a couple of days. Areas throughout the park are themed, such as Bugs Bunny World (for children up to 54 inches tall). The newest and most popular ride is the Georgia Scorcher, a stand-up roller coaster. Batman: the Ride, at 105 feet in height and reaching speeds of 50 miles per hour, is also a favorite.

Stone Mountain Park

U.S. Highway 78, Stone Mountain; (770) 498-5690 or (800) 317-2006
www.stonemountainpark.com

Hours: June–August, 6 a.m–midnight; remainder of year, 10 a.m.–5:30 p.m.

Admission: $6 parking; $16.05 adults, $12.85 children, $10.70 GA residents; tickets can also be purchased for individual attractions

Appeal by Age Group:

Pre-school	Grade School	Teens	Young Adults	Over 30	Seniors
★★★	★★★★	★★★★	★★★★	★★★★	★★★★

Average Touring Time: 1 day

Minimum Touring Time: 1 day

Rainy Day Touring: Not recommended

Author's Rating: ★★★★ A fabulous getaway to the great outdoors

Services and Facilities:

Restaurants Yes	Lockers No
Alcoholic beverages No	Pet kennels No
Disabled access Yes	Rain check Yes
Wheelchair rental Yes	Private tours No
Baby stroller rental Yes	

Description and Comments The largest mass of exposed granite in the world, Stone Mountain attracts families who enjoy kicking about in the great outdoors. Besides the exhaustive activities list—including an antique car museum, Civil War museum, antebellum plantation, petting zoo, tennis complex, water slide, batting cages, putt-putt golf, steam locomotive train rides, and an 18-hole golf course—this 3,200-acre park has a plethora of outside activities. Hiking trails, boating, bike rentals and trails, and camping facilities will satisfy any outdoorsman, and to top it off, there's a skylift to the top of the mountain that affords you a magnificent view of the area. Another wonder is the gigantic carving of General Robert E. Lee, Stonewall Jackson, and President Jefferson Davis. Covering three acres, this Confederate tribute is so big it is considered the largest bas-relief sculpture in the world. There are guided tours on top of the mountain and at the plantation, and special presentations at the zoo. One more reason to visit: The laser light show held nightly during the summer months.

White Water Theme Park

250 Cobb Parkway North, Atlanta; (770) 424-WAVE
   www.whitewaterpark.com

Hours: Memorial Day–Labor Day, daily 10 a.m.–8 p.m.; weekends in
   May, 10 a.m.–6 p.m.

Admission: $24 adults, $16 children 3–4 feet tall

Appeal by Age Group:

Pre- school	Grade School	Teens	Young Adults	Over 30	Seniors
★★★★	★★★★	★★★★	★★★★	★★★	★★★

Average Touring Time: 1 day

Minimum Touring Time: 1 day

Rainy Day Touring: Not recommended

Author's Rating: ★★★

Services and Facilities:

Restaurants Yes	Lockers Yes
Alcoholic beverages No	Pet kennels No
Disabled access Yes	Rain check Yes
Wheelchair rental Yes	Private tours N/A
Baby stroller rental Yes	

Description and Comments If you don't have time to brave Georgia's rivers, White Water Theme Park gives you the same wet-and-wild experience in a controlled environment. Plus, there are attractions for all ages, from water playgrounds and the Bahama Bob-Slide family raft ride for toddlers to the Tree House Island, Atlanta Ocean wave pool, and lazy rivers for older kids. Take advantage of the park's shady areas, and make sure you reapply sunscreen often, as Atlanta's summer sun can be quite intense.

World of Coca-Cola

55 Martin Luther King Jr. Drive, Atlanta; (404) 676-5151
  www.coke.com

Hours: Monday–Saturday 9 a.m.–5 p.m., Sunday Noon–6 p.m.

Admission: $6 adults, $4 seniors, $3 children ages 6–11, free for children ages 5 and younger

Appeal by Age Group:

Pre-school	Grade School	Teens	Young Adults	Over 30	Seniors
★★★	★★★	★★★	★★★	★★★	★★★

Average Touring Time: 1 hour

Minimum Touring Time: 45 minutes

Rainy Day Touring: Recommended

Author's Rating: ★★★

Services and Facilities:

Restaurants No	Lockers No
Alcoholic beverages No	Pet kennels No
Disabled access Yes	Rain check N/A
Wheelchair rental Yes	Private tours No
Baby stroller rental No	

Description and Comments It seems that all major corporations have a museum these days, and attached to the museum is a nice, large gift shop where you can buy all sorts of merchandise. This is exactly what you'll find at the World of Coca-Cola, though we have to admit that the museum exhibits present an interesting chronicle not only of the 100-year history of Coca-Cola but also of our culture. Old radio and television ads, a demonstration of the bottling process, a never-ending collection of memorabilia, and a futuristic soda fountain are among the highlights. Of course, you also get to sample Coca-Cola products, including those made specifically for certain parts of the world that are not available in the United States.

Zoo Atlanta

800 Cherokee Avenue SE, Atlanta; (404) 624-5600
  www.zooatlanta.org

Hours: Monday–Sunday, 9:30 a.m.–5:30 p.m.

Admission: $12 adults, $10 seniors, $8 children ages 3–11, free for children ages 2 and younger

Appeal by Age Group:

Pre-school	Grade School	Teens	Young Adults	Over 30	Seniors
★★★★★	★★★★★	★★★★★	★★★★★	★★★★★	★★★★★

Average Touring Time: 3 hours

Minimum Touring Time: 2 hours

Rainy Day Touring: Recommended

Author's Rating: ★★★★★   An animal-friendly zoo

Services and Facilities:

Restaurants Yes	Lockers No
Alcoholic beverages No	Pet kennels No
Disabled access Yes	Rain check N/A
Wheelchair rental Yes	Private tours No
Baby stroller rental Yes	

Description and Comments   If only every zoo would follow in the foot-steps of Zoo Atlanta and create a natural, nurturing environment for the animals that live there. This is one of the best examples, with gorillas, tigers, lions, giraffes, elephants, birds, and orangutans living in naturalistic habitats with no cages. Gorillas Willie B., Kudzoo, and Olympia are among the most popular animals who live here, and don't forget the new giant panda exhibit. In all, there are more than 1,000 animals to watch during your visit. There is also a slithery reptile collection, a petting zoo, a railroad to cart you around the grounds, and a favorite for both kids and kids at heart—the Greatest Baby Elephant Show on Earth. If you make a day of it, there are two McDonald's locations as well as other food vendors located on zoo grounds.

Side Trips

Centennial Olympic Park   Centennial Olympic Park is one of those places you have to stop by just to say you visited. Located in the heart of downtown Atlanta, this 21-acre green space is the legacy of Atlanta's 1996 Centennial Olympics. The centerpiece is the worlds' largest fountain, the Fountain of Rings, inspired by the Olympics' five interconnecting rings. Water jets in the rings go off four times a day, at 12:30, 3:30, 6:30, and 9:30 p.m. Located at International Boulevard and Techwood Drive, Atlanta; (404) 222-7275.

Wren's Nest House Museum   The Wren's Nest House Museum, home of Joel Chandler Harris, is a good way to introduce your child to this famous Georgia author—and a good place to spend a rainy afternoon. Harris is famous for his Uncle Remus tales, many of which are told in the storytelling programs and guided tours of his Victorian-era home. There is a bookstore on the premises that sells his books and lots of Uncle Remus Memorabilia. 1050 Ralph David Abernathy Boulevard SW, Atlanta; (404) 753-7735.

Yellow River Game Ranch, Lilburn   The Yellow River Game Ranch is home to over 600 animals, from black bears and bunnies to kid goats and buffalo, all of which are free to roam the 24-acre park. Be sure to take your camera, as kids can walk up to any of the animals and pet and feed them. There are even newborn animals on exhibit. 4525 Highway 78 in Lilburn, 2 miles past Stone Mountain; (770) 972-6643 or www.yellowrivergame-ranch.com.

Reynolds Plantation, Greensboro   On the banks of Lake Oconee, Reynolds Plantation is an all-inclusive resort community with both residential homes and hotel accommodations. The Plantation is known for its three championship golf courses, all designed by golfing greats and host to several major tournaments. Other pastimes for families include swimming at the resort pool or at Plantation Point Lake Park, which has its own sandy beach, a sporting clays course, tennis, and walking the trails that wind through the resort. A Ritz-Carlton hotel will open in 2001. Rates for a two-bedroom cottage with breakfast begin at $330 per night. 100 Linger Longer Road, Greensboro; (800) 852-5885; www.reynoldsgolf.com.

Georgia Museum of Art, Athens   Housing the state's official art collection of over 8,000 works, this free public museum is located on the campus of the University of Georgia in Athens. Much of the collection came from Alfred H. Holbrook, a retired attorney from New York, but the state has added to this initial gift to create an impressive collection. There are monthly participatory tours and family days for children on Saturdays; call ahead for a complete schedule. Athens is about one hour from Atlanta. Open Tuesday, Thursday, Saturday 10 a.m.–5 p.m., Wednesday 10 a.m.–9 p.m., and Sunday 10 a.m.–5 p.m.; (706) 542-GMOA.

Babyland General, Cleveland   Xavier Roberts is one clever fellow. Rather than create an ordinary baby doll, he came up with the concept of "adopting" individual dolls. Babyland General, housed in an actual 1919 clinic, is where these Cabbage Patch Kids are delivered. Watch the labor and delivery in the hospital's fantasy "cabbage patch," then take home one of your own, complete with birth certificate and adoption papers. Open Monday–Saturday 9 a.m.–5 p.m., Sunday 10 a.m.–5 p.m.; 73 West Underwood Street; (706) 865-5505; www.cabbagepatchkids.com.

Amicalola Falls State Park, Dawsonville   Many visitors come to Amicalola to begin their hike of the Appalachian Trail, which officially begins at Springer Mountain just outside the park. You will be remiss if you don't take at least an introductory tour of the 1,210 acres of Amicalola.

Among the finds: Amicalola Falls, a 729-foot waterfall that is three times the height of Niagara Falls. The park also has good facilities for overnight stays. One of the most interesting is the Hike Inn, where you hike five miles to the inn, spend the night in a comfortable room, then hike out again the next morning. This option is a fun one if your children are older, but it can be a long trek for little ones. There is also the Amicalola Falls Lodge, with fabulous panoramic views of the Blue Ridge mountains, nearby cottages with fireplaces, and camping and RV sites with water hookups and power. If you stay for a couple of days, book a canoe trip at the Amicalola River Rafting Outpost and canoe, tube, kayak, or raft down the Amicalola River. The park is two hours from Atlanta. Open daily, 7 a.m.–10 p.m.; $2 for parking; State Road 52; (706) 265-8888, (800) 864-7275; www.gastateparks.org.

Family-Friendly Restaurants

BUSY BEE CAFE

810 Martin Luther King Jr. Drive, Atlanta; (404) 525-9212

Meals served: Lunch and dinner
Cuisine: Southern
Entrée range: $4.99 and up
Kids menu: Yes
Reservations: No
Payment: V, MC, AMEX

Famous for cooking up soul food for over 50 years, The Busy Bee's most popular menu item is chitlins, but they also serve just about every other kind of Southern fare you can think of. Be sure to leave room for cobbler—there's peach, apple, and blackberry to choose from.

THE CHEESECAKE FACTORY

3024 Peachtree Road NW, Atlanta; (404) 816-2555

Meals served: Lunch and dinner
Cuisine: American
Entrée range: $4.95 and up
Kids menu: No
Reservations: No
Payment: All major credit cards accepted

Steaks, pizza, salads, and appetizers can all be found on the Cheesecake Factory's menu, but it's the 40 cheesecakes that attract customers and keep them coming back for more. Centrally located, this is a good stop for an afternoon lunch or an after-dinner treat.

DAVE & BUSTER'S

2215 D&B Drive, Atlanta; (770) 951-5554
www.daveandbusters.com

Meals served: Lunch and dinner
Cuisine: American
Entrée range: $5.95 and up
Kids menu: Yes
Reservations: Yes
Payment: All major credit cards accepted

Dave & Buster's is a chain, and it's spreading like wildfire across the country for good reason. At last, there's a Discovery Zone for both children and grown-ups, where kids can play wild and crazy games to their hearts content. Shuffleboard, home-run derby, billiards, basketball, and the Dave & Buster speedway are a few of the activities available. Plus, Dave & Buster's serves hearty helpings of all-American foods—pizzas and pastas, burgers and seafood, and steaks and ribs are among the offerings.

IMPERIAL FEZ MOROCCAN RESTAURANT

2285 Peachtree Road NE, Atlanta; (404) 351-0850
www.imperialfez.com

Meals served: Dinner
Cuisine: North African/Moroccan
Entrée range: $16.99 and up
Kids menu: Yes
Reservations: Yes
Payment: All major credit cards accepted

For a dining experience your family won't soon forget, visit the Imperial Fez for dinner. Sample traditional dishes like lamb couscous, lamb shank with shitake mushrooms, prawns, Cornish hens with artichoke hearts, and kabobs. The food is great, but it's the atmosphere that kids remember. Sit on low benches or deep pillows on the floor while belly dancers weave around the dining room. A six-course menu is served nightly for $45 per person and à la carte dishes are offered Sunday through Thursday. All menu items can be halved for kids.

SUN DIAL RESTAURANT, BAR AND VIEW

Westin Peachtree Plaza, Atlanta; (404) 589-7506
www.sundialrestaurant.com

Meals served: Lunch and dinner
Cuisine: Steakhouse
Entrée range: $8 and up
Kids menu: Yes
Reservations: No
Payment: All major credit cards accepted

After a day of exploring in downtown Atlanta, relax at the Sun Dial, the revolving restaurant at the top of the Westin Peachtree. It's more of an adult place for dinner, but you and the kids can enjoy Shirley Temples and appetizers in the bar while taking in the panoramic view of the city. A scenic glass elevator whisks you up to the restaurant, and telescopes are available to hone in on specific sites. If you don't order anything, it costs $5 for adults and $2.50 for children and seniors to get in.

THE VARSITY

61 North Avenue NW, Atlanta; (404) 881-1706
www.thevarsity.com

Meals served: Lunch and dinner
Cuisine: Fast food
Entrée range: $2 and up
Kids menu: No
Reservations: No
Payment: Cash and travelers checks

Billed as the World's Largest Drive-in, this hot dog stand serves 12,000 to 15,000 people daily, and more Coca-Cola than any other single place in the world. Try to go before or after the lunch rush, because sometimes you just can't find a parking spot or get in the restaurant at all. It opened in 1928 and today still serves the same greasy hot dogs that made it famous. The chili cheese dogs and onion rings, washed down by chocolate shakes, were hits at our table, but you can also order chicken wings, hamburgers, ice cream, and fried pies.

Columbus

Though Columbus is rarely considered a tourist town, Georgia's second-largest city is both a destination for families interested in history and out-door activities, and a departure point for those who want to explore the small towns in central and southwest Georgia. Founded in 1827, it sits on the bank of the **Chattahoochee River** along Georgia's western border, just across the river from Phenix City, Alabama.

In 1865, one of the last battles of the Civil War was fought in Columbus, and now, over 100 years later, the city's rich military history is show-cased in two world-class museums. The **National Infantry Museum** is located on the Main Post of Fort Benning, and the **Woodruff Museum of Civil War Naval History** is the only one of its kind in the United States.

Both museums, along with many other interesting Columbus sites, are grouped together in five tours outlined in the Convention and Visitors Bureau's Passport to Columbus. Pick one up at the Visitors Center to help you chart your course.

Columbus is also the birthplace of Coca-Cola. Dr. John Stith Pemberton, a pharmacist, concocted the drink and called it "French-wine d'coca" as it was a derivative of the coca plant. When he moved to Atlanta, Pemberton sold his formula, and the rest is history.

North of Columbus are the vacation favorites **Callaway Gardens,** one of Georgia's most popular attractions, and the **Little White House,** a retreat for Franklin Delano Roosevelt. To the south is Plains, the **Andersonville National Historic Site and Cemetery,** several state parks, and Albany, Valdosta, and Thomasville, all of which make easy day trips for stir-crazy kids.

Family Lodging

Callaway Gardens Resort

Callaway Gardens has a variety of family-friendly accommodations, including typical hotel rooms and suites, and two- to four-bedroom villas with

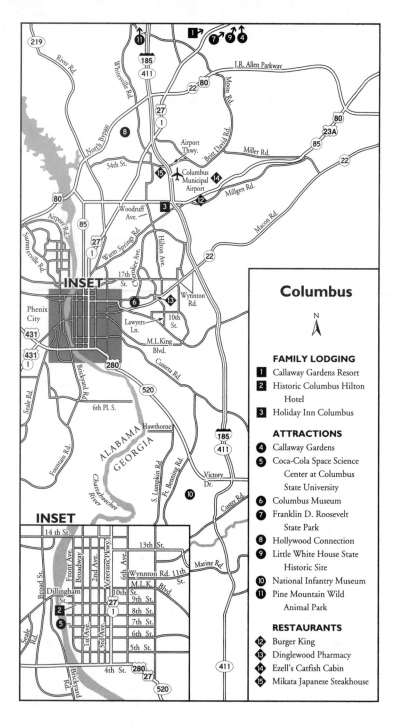

Columbus

N↑

FAMILY LODGING

1 Callaway Gardens Resort
2 Historic Columbus Hilton Hotel
3 Holiday Inn Columbus

ATTRACTIONS

4 Callaway Gardens
5 Coca-Cola Space Science Center at Columbus State University
6 Columbus Museum
7 Franklin D. Roosevelt State Park
8 Hollywood Connection
9 Little White House State Historic Site
10 National Infantry Museum
11 Pine Mountain Wild Animal Park

RESTAURANTS

12 Burger King
13 Dinglewood Pharmacy
14 Ezell's Catfish Cabin
15 Mikata Japanese Steakhouse

full-sized kitchens and living areas. Except for the hotel rooms, where you can sometimes hear noise coming from the courtyard areas, all of the accommodations are secluded. Furthermore, none are what we consider luxurious, which means you don't have to worry about what your child might break or damage. Besides, you won't be in your room for extended lengths of time. The resort and surrounding gardens have several family-friendly restaurants and plenty of day- and nighttime activities, from the Day Butterfly Center to the Discovery Bicycle Trail. There are also 63 holes of golf, and a man-made beach at Robin Lake. In summer, the resort offers weeklong family "camps," where kids and parents alike can spend time either together or separately in educational workshops and fun-filled activities sessions. Rates begin at $114. Off Highway 27, an hour from Atlanta and 30 minutes from Columbus; (800) CALLAWAY; www.callawaygardens.com.

Historic Columbus Hilton Hotel

This national landmark is built around a 100-year-old Empire Woodruff gristmill in downtown Columbus near several kid-friendly attractions. The accommodations are predictable but comfortable; you can choose from standard rooms or suites. There is a fine-dining restaurant and bar-and-grill on site, and access to a fitness center. Rates begin at $99. 800 Front Avenue, Columbus; (800) 524-4020 or (706) 324-1800; www.hilton.com.

Holiday Inn Columbus, North I-85

Located off North I-85 at Peachtree Mall and only 1½ miles from the airport, the Holiday Inn is convenient and affordable. One advantage for families with tots—the hotel is only two stories high, so you don't have to trek 20 stories to your room. There are no suites, and the rooms offer the standard hotel amenities: Cable TV, ironing board and iron, in-room coffee maker, and voice mail. For kids on the go, there is an outdoor pool and an in-house exercise facility. The Terrace Cafe restaurant and the Lobby Lounge are on-site, and room service is available. Rates begin at $89. 2800 Manchester Expressway, Columbus; (706) 324-0231 or (800) HOLIDAY.

Attractions

Callaway Gardens

P.O. Box 2000, Pine Mountain; (800) 225-5292

www.callawaygardens.com

Hours: Daily; schedule varies according to activity

Admission: $10 adults, $5 children ages 6–12, free for children ages 5 and younger

Appeal by Age Group:

Pre-school	Grade School	Teens	Young Adults	Over 30	Seniors
★★★★	★★★★	★★★★	★★★★★	★★★★★	★★★★★

Average Touring Time: 2 days for all activities

Minimum Touring Time: 1 day

Rainy Day Touring: Not recommended

Author's Rating: ★★★★★

Services and Facilities:

Restaurants Yes	Lockers No
Alcoholic beverages Yes	Pet kennels No
Disabled access Yes	Rain check No
Wheelchair rental Yes	Private tours Yes
Baby stroller rental No	

Description and Comments   Created by the Callaway family in 1952, the 14,000 acres of this natural attraction are more like a family retreat. That's not to say that there's nothing to do; rather, the plethora of activities in which you can participate are all set in laid-back, wooded surroundings. The gardens were the first attraction and continue to fascinate visitors with or without a green thumb. Either walk, drive, or bicycle through the thousands of hollies, azaleas, and wildflowers. Mr. Cason's Vegetable Garden, with more than 400 varieties of vegetables, fruits, and herbs, and the John A. Sibley Horticultural Center, a five-acre garden in one of the world's most advanced greenhouses, are other horticultural attractions. If you're staying at the resort, pace yourself by mixing tours of the gardens with energy-burning breaks in between—fishing, swimming at Robin Lake Beach, tennis, or golfing are all options. A family favorite is the Cecil B. Day Butterfly Center. As the largest glass-enclosed, tropical conservatory for living butterflies in North America, the center has 1,000 free-flying butterflies and hummingbirds on display. And the newest attraction is the Virginia Hand Callaway Discovery Center. An auditorium, exhibit wing, educational wing, and restaurant can be found inside the facility, which is also the launching point for several new activities in the gardens, including horseback riding, camping, and biking paths. One more note: If you go during the holiday season, be sure to call ahead and get tickets to the Fantasy In Lights, a gigantic holiday light display throughout the gardens.

Coca-Cola Space Science Center at Columbus State University

701 Front Avenue, Columbus; (706) 649-1470

www.ccssc.org

Hours: Tuesday–Friday, 10 a.m.–4 p.m.; Saturday, 1:30–9 p.m.; Sunday, 1:30–4 p.m.

Admission: Free, shows $3–6

Appeal by Age Group:

Pre-school	Grade School	Teens	Young Adults	Over 30	Seniors
★★★	★★★★	★★★★	★★★	★★★	★★★

Average Touring Time: 2 hours

Minimum Touring Time: 1 hour

Rainy Day Touring: Recommended

Author's Rating: ★★★

Services and Facilities:

Restaurants No	Lockers No
Alcoholic beverages No	Pet kennels No
Disabled access Yes	Rain check No
Wheelchair rental No	Private tours No
Baby stroller rental No	

Description and Comments The Coca-Cola Space Science Center is one of 31 centers throughout the United States designed to make science, math, and technology interesting and fun. Probably the most popular attraction is the interactive Challenger Learning Center, where you can fly simulated missions to the moon. Another hit for kids of all ages is the Omnisphere Theater, where the audience participates in three-dimensional time travel complete with laser lights. More conventional but just as intriguing is the Mead Observatory, where highly detailed images of celestial objects and live shots of the sun are captured for group viewing. Throughout the year, the observatory opens at night for special astronomical events; call ahead for a schedule.

Columbus Museum

1251 Wynnton Road; (706) 649-0713
www.columbusmuseum.com

Hours: Tuesday–Saturday, 10 a.m.–5 p.m.; Sunday, 1–5 p.m.

Admission: Free

Appeal by Age Group:

Pre-school	Grade School	Teens	Young Adults	Over 30	Seniors
★★★★	★★★★	★★★	★★★	★★★	★★★

Average Touring Time: 2 hours

Minimum Touring Time: 30 minutes

Rainy Day Touring: Recommended

Author's Rating: ★★★   Interactive room piques interest in art

Services and Facilities:

Restaurants Yes	Lockers No
Alcoholic beverages No	Pet kennels No
Disabled access Yes	Rain check No
Wheelchair rental Yes	Private tours Yes
Baby stroller rental Yes	

Description and Comments   The second-largest museum in Georgia and one of the largest in the Southeast, the Columbus Museum should be applauded for its efforts to make exhibitions of American art and regional history kid-friendly. The Transformations gallery is hands-on, where kids can investigate the colors and textures of various types of artwork, while the *Chattahoochee Legacy*, an award-winning film, traces the history of the Chattahoochee Valley area so that kids can follow the storyline.

Franklin D. Roosevelt State Park

2970 State Highway 190, Pine Mountain; (706) 663-4858
   www.gastateparks.org

Hours: Daily, 7 a.m.–10 p.m.

Admission: $2 per vehicle

Appeal by Age Group:

Pre-school	Grade School	Teens	Young Adults	Over 30	Seniors
★★	★★	★★★	★★★	★★★	★★★

Average Touring Time: 2 hours

Minimum Touring Time: 1 hour

Rainy Day Touring: Not recommended

Author's Rating: ★★★

Services and Facilities:

Restaurants No	Lockers No
Alcoholic beverages No	Pet kennels No
Disabled access Yes	Rain check No
Wheelchair rental No	Private tours No
Baby stroller rental No	

Description and Comments   Franklin D. Roosevelt State Park is Georgia's largest, and each year more than 300,000 people enjoy the many activities available. There are 40 miles of hiking trails with plenty of loops and turnarounds that allow you to lengthen or shorten your hike to a suitable distance for your family. The park's two lakes offer fishing and flatboat rentals, and there are stables at the foot of Pine Mountain with horses for rent either by the hour or overnight. One of the more unique features of the park is the rock pool, where rock mined from the mountain and the roadbeds was used to build a huge swimming hole. Interestingly, the pool was built by Roosevelt's Civilian Conservation Corps during the Depression. If you want to stay a couple of days, there are 21 cottages and 140 campsites. Rates begin at $13 for camping, and cottages begin at $65; (800) 864-7275.

Hollywood Connection

1683 Whittlesey Road, Columbus; (706) 571-3456

Hours: Monday–Thursday, 3:30—10:30 p.m.; Friday, 3:30 p.m.–midnight; Saturday, 11:30 a.m.–midnight; Sunday, 11:30 a.m.–10 p.m.

Admission: $1–5 for various rides

Appeal by Age Group:

Pre-school	Grade School	Teens	Young Adults	Over 30	Seniors
★	★★	★★★	★★★	★★★	★★★

Average Touring Time: 2 hours

Minimum Touring Time: 1 hour

Rainy Day Touring: Recommended

Author's Rating: ★★

Services and Facilities:

Restaurants Yes	Lockers No
Alcoholic beverages No	Pet kennels No
Disabled access Yes	Rain check No
Wheelchair rental No	Private tours N/A
Baby stroller rental No	

Description and Comments   Now located in several major cities across the country, the Hollywood Connection started in Columbus as an extension of the popular movie theater chain. The point was probably to keep kids of all ages entertained before and after the movie, but there are so many things to do that we skipped the movie entirely and took advantage of the rides and activities. A sophisticated putt-putt golf course, skating rink, carousel, arcade, and lots of rides for toddlers are a few of the offerings. Several food vendors are on-site, including the classic Dinglewood's, serving its famous Columbus hot dogs.

Little White House State Historic Site

401 Little White House Road on Highway 95 West, Warm Springs;
(706) 655-5870; www.gastateparks.org

Hours: Daily, from 9 a.m.–5 p.m.; last tour at 4 p.m.

Admission: $5 adults, $4 seniors, $2 children ages 6–18, free for children ages 5 and younger

Appeal by Age Group:

Pre-school	Grade School	Teens	Young Adults	Over 30	Seniors
★	★★	★★★	★★★	★★★	★★★

Average Touring Time: 1 hour

Minimum Touring Time: 30 minutes

Rainy Day Touring: Recommended

Author's Rating: ★★

Services and Facilities:

Restaurants No	Lockers No
Alcoholic beverages No	Pet kennels No
Disabled access Yes	Rain check Yes
Wheelchair rental Yes	Private tours No
Baby stroller rental No	

Description and Comments   If you've got a car full of rambunctious kids, a house tour won't be the most popular option on your agenda, but there are some interesting observations to be made at the Little White House. Franklin Delano Roosevelt built the three-bedroom cottage in 1932 before he became president, in the hope that the nearby springs could cure his polio. It was here that he died in 1945. A highlight of the tour is the unfinished portrait that was being painted at the time of his death. An adjacent museum, connected to the cottage by a path lined with rocks from each state, takes a look at his life. You can also tour the guesthouse, servants' quarters, and garage, where Roosevelt's 1938 roadster is on display.

National Infantry Museum, Fort Benning

Baltzell Avenue, Fort Benning; (706)545-2958

Hours: Monday–Friday, 8 a.m.–4:30 p.m.; Saturday–Sunday, 12:30–4:30 p.m.

Admission: Free

Appeal by Age Group:

Pre-school	Grade School	Teens	Young Adults	Over 30	Seniors
★★	★★★	★★★	★★★	★★★★	★★★★★

Average Touring Time: 1½ hours
Minimum Touring Time: 1 hour
Rainy Day Touring: Recommended
Author's Rating: ★★★
Services and Facilities:

Restaurants No	Lockers No
Alcoholic beverages No	Pet kennels No
Disabled access Yes	Rain check No
Wheelchair rental Yes	Private tours No
Baby stroller rental No	

Description and Comments   Columbus is known for its military museums, and the National Infantry Museum at Fort Benning is arguably the best. Stationed at the world's largest and most modern military training center, the museum preserves the history and tradition of the infantry with collections of military art and artifacts. Weapons carried by allies and enemies are on display, accompanied by uniforms, documents, and equipment used in wars dating to the American Revolution. The most fascinating exhibit is the Axis Power Exhibit of captured military paraphernalia, including flags and weapons from Nazi Germany, Imperial Japan, and Fascist Italy. The museum visit is all the more educational if an older relative who served in a war can tag along and tell their personal story.

Pine Mountain Wild Animal Park

1300 Oak Grove Road; (706) 663-8744 or (800) 367-2751
   www.animalsafari.com

Hours: Opens daily at 10 a.m; closing time varies
Admission: $12.95 adults, $11.95 seniors, $9.95 children ages 3–9, free for children ages 2 and younger
Appeal by Age Group:

Pre-school	Grade School	Teens	Young Adults	Over 30	Seniors
★★★★★	★★★★★	★★★★★	★★★★	★★★★	★★★★

Average Touring Time: 4 hours
Minimum Touring Time: 3 hours
Rainy Day Touring: Recommended
Author's Rating: ★★★★
Services and Facilities:

Restaurants Yes	Wheelchair rental Yes
Alcoholic beverages No	Baby stroller rental Yes
Disabled access Yes	Lockers No

Pet kennels Yes   Private tours Yes
Rain check No

Description and Comments   Take your car or hop aboard a school bus–turned–safari jeep for a ride through this 500-acre, free-roaming animal park. Hundreds of exotic animals live here, including South American black jaguars, baboons, peacocks, llamas, giraffes, camels, wild pigs, and zebras—many are tame enough to feed from the windows of the bus. Afterwards, visit Old McDonald's Farm, where youngsters can pet a variety of farm animals and get an up-close view of wolves, bears, monkeys, alligators, and tropical birds. There is also a restaurant and gift shop on the grounds, along with the Georgia Wildlife Museum. Forty-two exhibits have stuffed animals on display—a somewhat odd attraction considering the park's motto of environmental conservation, but interesting nonetheless.

Side Trips

Columbus Riverwalk   On a sunny day—and you're bound to have at least one no matter what time of year you visit—set out to explore the banks of the Chattahoochee River from the convenience of Columbus' grand Riverwalk. Historic cotton warehouses, environmental learning areas that highlight the river's ecosystem, grassy parks, and many Columbus attractions can be found here, making this an ideal stop for a family on the go. Chances are you won't make it from one end to the other, simply because the walk has extended to 12 miles over the past few years. Instead, grab lunch in one of the downtown eateries and continue your afternoon outside. You can park along the road that runs parallel to the Riverwalk, so pack a couple of quilts to spread out under the sky for quiet time or a lazy afternoon nap.

Westville, Lumpkin   If you think traveling with children is a challenge, imagine what it must have been like 100 years ago. At Westville, you'll get the chance to see what life was like for Georgia's pioneers in the 1800s. Craftsmen in period dress are at work in various stores and workshops much as they would have been in yesteryear. Soap, candles, syrup, gingerbread, and biscuits are some of the items produced, and there is even a blacksmith who fashions horseshoes and other necessities from iron. Kids can participate in a number of these old-fashioned activities. Open Tuesday–Saturday 10 a.m.–5 p.m., Sunday 1–5 p.m. Five miles south of Lumpkin Square on Martin Luther King Drive; (912) 838-6310 or (888) 733-1850.

Plains   Surrounded by peanut fields and with little more than a strip of shops downtown, Plains is the epitome of a small Southern town—with the exception of its famous son, the 39th president of the United States, Jimmy Carter. Carter was born and raised in Plains, and when he launched his presidential campaign, he did so from the old Plains depot. The depot is now the Visitors Center (phone (912) 824-4104) for the 77-acre Jimmy Carter National Historic District. Stop by for an audiotape tour that locates points of interest for Carter buffs—a museum and his former high school, home, and hang-outs. Downtown has several souvenir shops, including the Plains Trading Post, with antiques, Indian crafts, and collectibles. If you visit on Sunday, attend Marantha Baptist Church, where Carter teaches Sunday school.

Andersonville National Historic Site, Andersonville In 1864–65, Andersonville was home of the Andersonville Civil War Prison, where 13,000 Northern soldiers died—more are buried here than at any other prison camp in the North or South. Today, what remains is a grim reminder of the tragedies of war. A National Prisoner of War Museum traces camp conditions from the Revolutionary War to those of modern day, and the visitors center features diaries and photographs of prisoners. The National Cemetery features rows of solemn white grave markers. If you visit in the spring and fall during one of the many festivals and fairs, re-enactors tell the story of what life was like for soldiers in the prison camp. Andersonville is 50 miles south of Macon on Highway 49; (912) 924-0343 or (800) C-COTTON; www.c-cotton.org.

Chehaw Park, Albany Situated on the banks of the Flint River, 700-acre Chehaw Park attracts families with a love of the great outdoors. There are eight parks in the complex, with trails for jogging and biking, a BMX track, picnic areas, miniature train rides, creek-side hiking, and RV and tent campgrounds. The crown jewel of Chehaw is the Wild Animal Park. Designed by Jim Fowler of *Wild Kingdom,* the park is a natural preserve for a number of exotic animals, including deer, zebras, elephants, and ostriches. Elevated boardwalks and pathways give the smallest child a good view of the animals. Open daily from 9:30 a.m.–5 p.m.; 105 Chehaw Park Road, Albany; (912) 430-5275.

Birdsong Nature Center, Thomasville The 565 acres of lush fields, wooded forests, and swamp in this nature preserve offer a pristine haven for birds and other native wildlife. Betty and Ed Komarek, both dedicated naturalists, purchased the land in 1938 and used controlled burning and other land-management techniques to transform this Georgia farm into a haven for wildlife. They began Birdsong in 1981 and it is now a nonprofit preserve. While visiting, hike the Bluebird Trail, where a series of 30 nest boxes are maintained and monitored throughout the year for activity and nesting success. Take time to look through the Bird Window, where you can identify and observe the center's feathered friends, and visit the Listening Place, where you can hear birdcalls, frogs, and alligators. There are nature trails and a wildlife and butterfly garden, plus nature programs are offered year round. Open Wednesday–Friday from 9 a.m.–noon, Saturday from 9 a.m.–2 p.m., and Sunday from 1–5 p.m.; $5 adults, $2.50 children; 2106 Meridian Road, Thomasville; (912) 377-4408.

Pebble Hill Plantation, Thomasville Although children younger than six are not permitted into the house, the grounds at Pebble Hill will keep them occupied for a couple of hours. Pebble Hill was once the winter home of the Hannas from Cleveland, a wealthy and influential family who supposedly financed *Gone with the Wind.* With over 65,000 square feet in the main house and an overflow cottage for additional guests, the Hannas could easily entertain their friends and family, as well as business associates, politicians, and royalty such as the Duke and Duchess of Windsor. Stables, kennels, a schoolhouse, servants' quarters, a carpenter shop, and a dog hospital were some of the other structures located on the property. Elisabeth Ireland Poe, better known as Miss Pansy, was the last of the Hanna heirs and an avid sportswoman. Throughout the house, the collection of Audubon prints and carvings and sculptures of her dogs and horses command as much attention as the prime antiques, crystal, and porcelain. When Miss Pansy died, she willed the house be opened to the public and provided ample funding to ensure her wishes were followed. Open Tuesday–Saturday, 10 a.m.–5 p.m.; Sunday 1–5 p.m. Cost is $3 adults and $1.50 children for grounds, $7 adults and $3.50 children for house tour. Off U.S. Highway 319 South between Thomasville and Tallahassee; (912) 226-2344.

Family-Friendly Restaurants

BURGER KING

3101 Gentian Boulevard, Columbus; (706) 565-7525

Meals served: Breakfast, lunch, and dinner
Cuisine: American
Entrée range: $1 and up
Kids menu: Yes
Reservations: No
Payment: All major credit cards accepted

It's part of the national chain, but this Burger King is housed in the old train depot. The dining room resembles an old-fashioned trolley, and there is an indoor playground. A favorite for local kids.

DINGLEWOOD PHARMACY

1939 Wynnton Road, Columbus; (706) 322-0616

Meals served: Lunch and dinner
Cuisine: Hot dogs
Entrée range: $1.50 and up
Kids menu: No
Reservations: No
Payment: All major credit cards accepted

This hot dog joint is a Columbus tradition. While you can get almost any topping you desire for your wiener, the hands-down favorite is the scrambled dog, a hot dog cut into pieces and topped with onions, cheese, chili sauce, and oyster crackers.

EZELL'S CATFISH CABIN

4001 Warm Springs Rd., Columbus; (706) 568-1149

Meals served: Dinner
Cuisine: Catfish; Southern
Entrée range: $6.89 and up
Kids menu: Yes
Reservations: No
Payment: V, MC, D

When you're tired of fast food and pasta, Ezell's is a good, healthy alternative. Ezell's serves piping-hot fried catfish along with other seafood entrées. The restaurant opens for dinner nightly and also for lunch from Friday to Sunday.

MIKATA JAPANESE STEAKHOUSE

5300 Sidney Simons Boulevard; (706) 327-5100

Meals served: Dinner
Cuisine: Japanese
Entrée range: $13 and up
Kids menu: Yes
Reservations: Yes
Payment: All major credit cards accepted

Who says you can't play with your food? Kids love this place, and they're prone to cleaning their plate, especially when the entrée du jour has been flipped onto their plate. The seafood is especially good.

Macon

Eighty miles south of Atlanta, Macon is a quaint city overflowing with rich architecture, a wealth of natural beauty, and genuine Southern hospitality. This preserved pocket of antebellum history lies deep in the heart of Georgia, and it narrowly escaped the widespread destruction of the Civil War. As a result, almost all of its antebellum homes remain intact, and many have been restored to their original nineteenth-century Greek Revival glory.

Macon also has an incredible African-American history. The **Pleasant Hill Historic District** is one of the first black neighborhoods listed on the National Register of Historic Places, and more recently, the city's uncanny ability to produce musical talent has provided the world with the likes of Otis Redding and James Brown.

Because of its size and location, Macon is an ideal weekend getaway for Southern travelers. One of the best times to visit is in the spring during the annual **Cherry Blossom Festival,** when the 100,000 cherry trees throughout the city are in full bloom. If time permits, take a two-hour guided driving tour with **Sidney's Old South Tours** for the best introduction to the sites and secrets of Macon—the $10 fee includes entry into many of the city's historic sites. Macon is accessible from the interstate, but surrounded by many small towns, each with its own offbeat and interesting attractions.

Family Lodging

Crowne Plaza Macon
The downtown location of this Crowne Plaza makes it convenient for families combining business with a mini-getaway. Accommodation choices include standard rooms, junior suites, and executive suites. There is an exercise room, pool, sauna, and sun deck for leisure occupations; room service and babysitting services are also available. Rates begin at $79. 108 First Street, Macon; (912) 746-1461; www.crowneplaza.com.

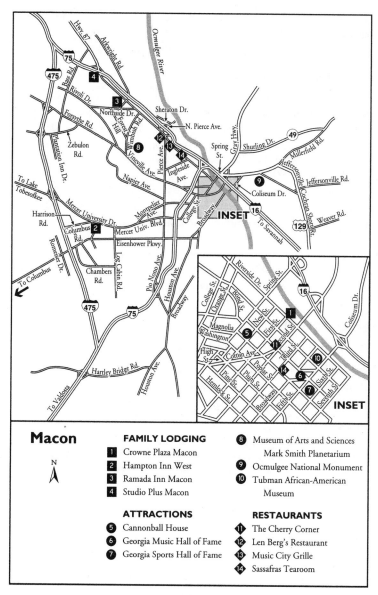

Macon

N

FAMILY LODGING
1. Crowne Plaza Macon
2. Hampton Inn West
3. Ramada Inn Macon
4. Studio Plus Macon

ATTRACTIONS
5. Cannonball House
6. Georgia Music Hall of Fame
7. Georgia Sports Hall of Fame

8. Museum of Arts and Sciences
   Mark Smith Planetarium
9. Ocmulgee National Monument
10. Tubman African-American
    Museum

RESTAURANTS
11. The Cherry Corner
12. Len Berg's Restaurant
13. Music City Grille
14. Sassafras Tearoom

Ramada Inn Macon

Recently renovated, Ramada Inn Macon offers a fitness center and pool, restaurant with room service, free continental breakfast, guest laundry, and refrigerators and microwaves in each room. The hotel is close to local restaurants and attractions. Rates begin at $49.50. 3850 Riverside Drive, Macon; (912) 474-9902 or (888) 298-2054; www.ramada.com.

Studio Plus Macon, I-75

Also on Riverside Drive, Studio Plus is an all-suite hotel where each room has a fully equipped kitchen. There is a swimming pool on the property. Convenient to downtown. Rates begin at $59. 4000 Riverside Drive, Macon; (912) 474-2805 or (800) 646-8000; www.studioplus.com.

Hampton Inn West

Convenient to both downtown and the interstate, Hampton Inn West is located on the outer perimeter of Macon. Both standard rooms and Jacuzzi suites are available. A swimming pool, free deluxe continental breakfast, free local calls, free in-room movie channel, and a microwave and refrigerator in each room round out the amenities. Another plus: Children under age 18 stay free. Rates begin at $49. 5010 Eisenhower Parkway, off I-75; (912) 757-9711 or (800) HAMPTON; www.hamptoninn.com.

Attractions

The Cannonball House and Confederate Museum

856 Mulberry Street, Macon; (912) 745-5982

Hours: Monday–Saturday, 10 a.m.– 4 p.m.

Admission: $4 adults, $3 seniors, $1 children 12 and younger

Appeal by Age Group:

Pre-school	Grade School	Teens	Young Adults	Over 30	Seniors
★	★★	★★★	★★★	★★★	★★★

Average Touring Time: 30 minutes

Minimum Touring Time: 20 minutes

Rainy Day Touring: Recommended

Author's Rating: ★★★

Services and Facilities:

Restaurants No	Lockers No
Alcoholic beverages No	Pet kennels No
Disabled access Yes (partial)	Rain check N/A
Wheelchair rental No	Private tours Yes
Baby stroller rental No	

Description and Comments   Maintained by the United Daughters of the Confederacy, this house and museum depict life as it was during the 1800s.

There are servants' quarters to tour, and the museum is housed in the old kitchen, a separate building in the back yard. Uniforms, swords, and other memorabilia dating to the 1800s are on display. The main draw, however, is the hallway. Weaving its way into the front parlor window, a stray cannonball fired from federal artillery across the Ocmulgee River bounced into the hall without exploding, and today it sits on the same spot where it landed back in 1864.

Georgia Music Hall of Fame

200 Martin Luther King Jr. Boulevard, Macon; (888) GA-ROCKS or (912) 750-8555; www.gamusichall.com

Hours:　Monday–Saturday, 9 a.m.–5 p.m.; Sunday, 1–5 p.m.

Admission:　$7.50 adults, $5.50 seniors and college students, $3.50 children ages 6–16, free for children ages 5 and younger

Appeal by Age Group:

Pre-school	Grade School	Teens	Young Adults	Over 30	Seniors
★★★	★★★★★	★★★★★	★★★★★	★★★★★	★★★★★

Average Touring Time:　1½ hours

Minimum Touring Time:　1 hour

Rainy Day Touring:　Recommended

Author's Rating:　★★★★★　Fosters a love of music

Services and Facilities:

Restaurants No	Lockers No
Alcoholic beverages No	Pet kennels No
Disabled access Yes	Rain check No
Wheelchair rental Yes	Private tours No
Baby stroller rental No	

Description and Comments　Put on your dancing shoes and get ready to groove to the tunes of Little Richard, Odis Redding, Lena Horne, REM, and Trisha Yearwood—only a few of the many musical talents from the Peach State highlighted in the Georgia Music Hall of Fame. Macon was an obvious choice for the museum because the city has spawned an amazing number of musical legends, including the Allman Brothers Band and James Brown. The museum resembles a make-believe Tune Town, with various "clubs" along city streets featuring different styles of music, memorabilia, instruments, photos, costumes, lights and laser videos, and CD-listening stations. The Children's Wing has interactive and interpretive displays. Record a song and listen to it in the recording booth, watch yourself dance on video, or beat drums to the beat of a particular song.

Georgia Sports Hall of Fame

301 Cherry Street, Macon; (912) 752-1585;
  www.gshf.org

Hours: Monday–Saturday, 9 a.m.–5 p.m.; Sunday, 1–5 p.m.

Admission: $6 adults, $5 seniors, $3.50 ages 6–16; family package $15

Appeal by Age Group:

Pre-school	Grade School	Teens	Young Adults	Over 30	Seniors
★	★★	★★★	★★★	★★★	★★★

Average Touring Time: 2½ hours

Minimum Touring Time: 1½ hours

Rainy Day Touring: Recommended

Author's Rating: ★★★

Services and Facilities:

Restaurants No	Lockers No
Alcoholic beverages No	Pet kennels No
Disabled access Yes	Rain check No
Wheelchair rental No	Private tours Yes
Baby stroller rental No	

Description and Comments Even if you aren't a sports fan, you'll enjoy the Georgia Sports Hall of Fame. Besides the many exhibits honoring Georgia athletes like Hershel Walker, Jackie Robinson, and Bill Elliott, there are lots of interactive games to keep your children entertained. Take a spin in the NASCAR simulator, practice your field goal kicking, and see what it's like to compete as a wheelchair paralympian. There is also a theater designed to resemble an old-fashioned ballpark. Most people watch the 16-minute film before the tour to get a sense of Georgia's sporting legacy.

Museum of Arts and Sciences/Mark Smith Planetarium

4182 Forsyth Road, Macon; (912) 477-3232;
  www.masmacon.com

Hours: Monday–Thursday and Saturday, 9 a.m.–5 p.m.; Friday, 9 a.m.–9 p.m; Sunday, 1–5 p.m.; Planetary presentations daily at 4 p.m. and Fridays at 4 and 7 p.m.

Admission: $5 adults, $4 seniors, $3 ages 12 and older, $2 ages 2–11

Appeal by Age Group:

Pre-school	Grade School	Teens	Young Adults	Over 30	Seniors
★★	★★★	★★★	★★★	★★★	★★★

Average Touring Time: 1½ hours
Minimum Touring Time: 1 hour
Rainy Day Touring: Recommended
Author's Rating: ★★★
Services and Facilities:

Restaurants No	Lockers No
Alcoholic beverages No	Pet kennels No
Disabled access Yes	Rain check N/A
Wheelchair rental Yes	Private tours No
Baby stroller rental No	

Description and Comments A planetarium, hands-on science and nature discovery room, and art galleries emphasizing innovative contemporary works are reasons to visit the Museum of Arts and Sciences. Exhibits focus on the world at large, with Macon as a microcosm. Don't miss the 40-million-year-old whale fossils that were discovered near Macon and are now on display. You'll also find an artist's garret, scientist's workshop, and an enclosed backyard animal habitat where animals from tamarinds to alligators make their home around a giant manmade banyan tree. The museum offers several programs and live animal shows throughout the week; call ahead for a schedule.

Ocmulgee National Monument

1207 Emery Highway, Macon; (912) 752-8257
   www.nps.gov/ocmu
Hours: Daily, 9 a.m.–5 p.m.
Admission: Free
Appeal by Age Group:

Pre-school	Grade School	Teens	Young Adults	Over 30	Seniors
★★	★★	★★★	★★★	★★★	★★★

Average Touring Time: 4 hours
Minimum Touring Time: 1½ hours
Rainy Day Touring: Not recommended
Author's Rating: ★★★
Services and Facilities:

Restaurants No	Lockers No
Alcoholic beverages No	Pet kennels No
Disabled access Yes	Rain check N/A
Wheelchair rental Yes	Private tours No
Baby stroller rental No	

Description and Comments For reasons unknown to modern archaeologists, Mississippian Indians constructed, one basketful of dirt at a time, the massive earthen mounds that are now preserved in this park. Several mounds are found on the grounds, and most are the length of a football field and as high as a three-story building. Nature trails zigzag through the park, and there is a reconstruction of a ceremonial earth lodge only steps from the visitors center. Many school groups visit Ocmulgee on field trips, but unless you corner a park ranger to explain the significance of the site, your children might think this is little more than an open expanse ideal for outdoor cavorting.

Tubman African-American Museum

340 Walnut Street, Macon; (912) 743-8544
  www.tubman.com

Hours: Monday–Saturday, 10 a.m.–5 p.m.; Sunday, 2–5 p.m.

Admission: $3

Appeal by Age Group:

Pre-school	Grade School	Teens	Young Adults	Over 30	Seniors
★★	★★★	★★★	★★★	★★★	★★★

Average Touring Time: 1½ hours

Minimum Touring Time: 1 hour

Rainy Day Touring: Recommended

Author's Rating: ★★★

Services and Facilities:

Restaurants No	Lockers No
Alcoholic beverages No	Pet kennels No
Disabled access Yes	Rain check N/A
Wheelchair rental No	Private tours No
Baby stroller rental No	

Description and Comments Small but important, the Tubman African-American Museum showcases the art, history, and culture of African Americans. The largest of its kind in Georgia, this museum features a mural documenting the journey "From Africa to America" and houses 14 galleries, including one on local black history and inventions by African Americans (the super soaker is but one example). The museum is named for Harriet Tubman, whose Underground Railroad supposedly ran through Macon.

Side Trips

Pleasant Hill Historic District Macon has a rich African-American history, and nowhere is this more apparent than in the Pleasant Hill Historic District. The community was one of the first black neighborhoods listed on the National Register of Historic Places. Many of the clapboard Victorian houses that line the streets are private residences or offices, but you can walk or drive by them. The childhood homes of Little Richard and Lena Horne are found in this area, along with Linwood Cemetery, where some of Macon's influential black community leaders were laid to rest.

Uncle Remus Museum, Eatonton   The birthplace of Joel Chandler Harris houses a museum named after his famous storytelling character, but this is also the site where Harris met the slaves who gave him the stories and the dialect for his writing. The museum is reconstructed from two original slave log cabins and is similar to the one where Uncle Remus lived in Harris' stories. Shadow boxes, wood carvings, first editions of Harris' works, and newspaper clippings tell the story of Harris and his characters. Open Monday–Saturday, 10 a.m.–5 p.m.; Sunday, 2–5 p.m.; closed Tuesdays from September–May. Highway 441, Eatonton; (706) 485-6856.

Museum of Aviation, Warner Robins   A short drive from Macon, the Museum of Aviation in Warner Robins is the fourth-largest aviation museum in the United States. Besides an extensive display of memorabilia dating to WWI and the largest collection on the Tuskegee airmen, there are over 70 historic aircraft to view and many interactive exhibits that explore aviation history. Participate in a rocket launch, climb inside a C-130 cargo plane, "fly" a Cessna 150 in the Black Eagles exhibit, and explore the cockpit of a RF4C simulator. The museum has a gift shop with cool aviation souvenirs, a canteen where you can watch planes from Robins Air Force Base land and take off, and a theater showing Smithsonian films. Open daily, 9 a.m.–5 p.m.; admission is free. Highway 247, Warner Robins; (912) 752-1585 or (912) 926-6870, Ext. 22.

Family-Friendly Restaurants

THE CHERRY CORNER

502 Cherry Street, Macon; (912) 741-9525

Cuisine: American
Meals served: Lunch and dinner
Entrée range: $1.50 and up
Kids menu: No
Reservations: No
Payment: All major credit cards accepted

This is an Italian cafe with sandwiches, pizzas, salads, soups, fresh Italian gelato ice cream, Italian sodas, and a bakery. Cherry Corner also has outdoor seating and is close to local attractions.

LEN BERG'S RESTAURANT

Old Post Office Alley, Macon; (912) 742-9255

Meals served: Lunch
Cuisine: Southern
Entrée range: $4.10 and up
Kids menu: Yes
Reservations: No
Payment: Cash only

Southern–style fixin's are the house specialty, from fried chicken to butter biscuits. But even if you don't eat at Len Berg's, be sure to stop by for a scoop of homemade peach ice cream.

MUSIC CITY GRILLE

2440 Riverside Drive, Macon; (912) 741-1144

Meals served: Lunch and dinner
Cuisine: American
Entrée range: $5 and up
Kids menu: Yes
Reservations: No
Payment: All major credit cards accepted

Pasta, pizza, sandwiches, steaks, and seafood round out the Music City menu. This place is like a local Hard Rock Cafe, with memorabilia and displays about Macon's music scene. Outdoor seating is available.

S&S CAFETERIA

2626 Riverside Drive, Macon; (912) 746-9406

Meals served: Lunch and dinner
Cuisine: Southern
Entrée range: $2.29 and up
Kids menu: Yes
Reservations: No
Payment: All major credit cards accepted

You can't beat the kids' meal for $1.59—that's a meat and two veggies, jello, bread, and tea. The atmosphere is diner style—just right for families who don't want to worry about minding their manners as they might have to in fancier restaurants. And the Riverside location makes this an easy place to stop for dinner.

Savannah and Tybee Island

While Savannah is world famous for its architecture and historic preservation, the city will be much of a bore to children (and adults as well) if your time is spent touring one museum or historic building after another. Instead, look for creative ways to explore this European–style city.

As one of the South's easiest cities to navigate on foot, strolling or jogging from **Forsyth Park** to the river is the best way to see the sights. This 20-block jaunt is just as enjoyable when divided into smaller areas for walking. Visit one of the quaint bookstores and purchase a book on the city's history, then spread a blanket underneath one of the massive oaks in a city square and hang out for an afternoon. Plan an impromptu picnic or better yet, if you visit in the summer, dine outdoors for breakfast instead of bearing the heat of midday. The Visitors Center provides cassette tapes for both walking and driving tours.

If you plan to stay overnight, look into one of the inns or bed and breakfasts reminiscent of European pensiones. Many allow children to stay.

Eating in Savannah is more than dining out—it has been elevated to an art form. Comfort food was created here, and if you don't believe it, sit down to a creamy bowl of she-crab soup. Another kid-pleasing dish is a low country boil, full of fresh corn on the cob, shrimp, onion, new potatoes, sausage, and celery—they can pick out whatever they don't like and still have more than enough to eat. In restaurants, it's served swimming in simmering juices by heaping bowlfuls, but if you're lucky enough to secure an invitation to a plantation party, the entire meal is turned out on newspapers, where guests dig in with their fingers.

If you have sand in your shoes, spend the day at nearby **Tybee Island**, where beach bums frolic in the frothy waves of the Atlantic. Fishing buffs can schedule deep-sea charters, or if you're up for a walk on the wild side, embark on an afternoon excursion through lush Savannah low country.

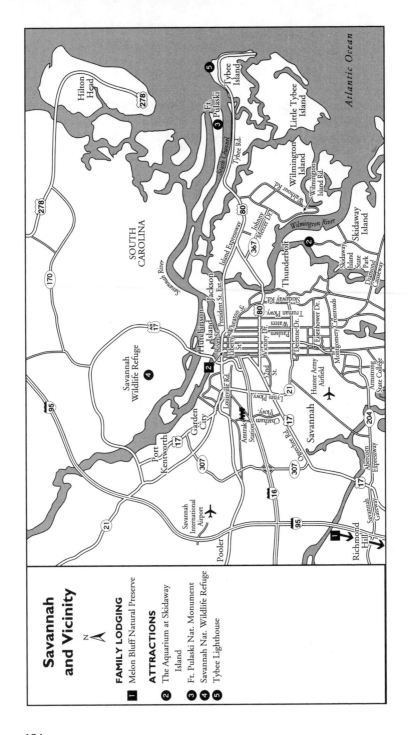

Savannah and Vicinity

N

FAMILY LODGING
1 Melon Bluff Natural Preserve

ATTRACTIONS
2 The Aquarium at Skidaway Island
3 Ft. Pulaski Nat. Monument
4 Savannah Nat. Wildlife Refuge
5 Tybee Lighthouse

154

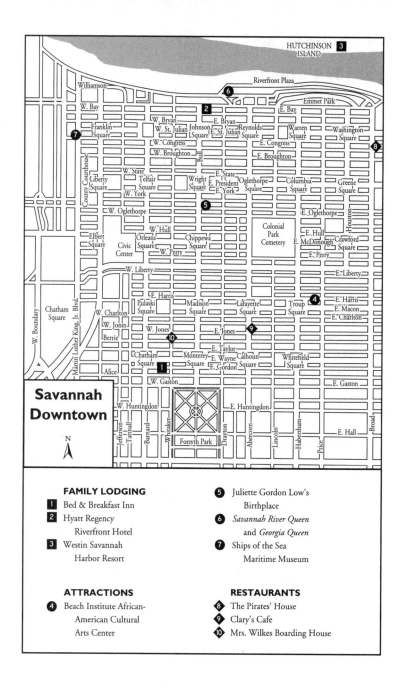

HUTCHINSON
ISLAND **3**

Riverfront Plaza

Williamson

6

Emmet Park

W. Bay **2** E. Bay

W. Bryan E. Bryan

Franklin
Square **7** W. St. Julian Johnson E. St. Julian Reynolds Warren Washington
Square Square Square Square Square

W. Congress E. Congress

W. Broughton E. Broughton

W. State E. State

Liberty Telfair Wright E. President Oglethorpe Columbia Greene
Square Square Square Square Square Square Square

W. York E. York

W. Oglethorpe **5** E. Oglethorpe

Colonial
Park E. Hull
W. Hull Cemetery

Elbert Orleans Chippewa E. McDonough Crawford
Square Civic Square Square E. Perry Square
Center W. Perry

W. Liberty E. Liberty

Chatham E. Harris
Square Pulaski Madison Lafayette Troup **4** E. Macon
W. Charlton Square Square Square Square E. Charlton

W. Jones Berrie W. Jones E. Jones **9**

10

E. Taylor
Chatham Monterey E. Wayne Calhoun Whitefield
Square Square E. Gordon Square Square **1**

W. Gaston E. Gaston

**Savannah
Downtown** W. Huntingdon E. Huntingdon

N Forsyth Park E. Hall

Chatham
Square

FAMILY LODGING

1 Bed & Breakfast Inn

2 Hyatt Regency
Riverfront Hotel

3 Westin Savannah
Harbor Resort

ATTRACTIONS

4 Beach Institute African-
American Cultural
Arts Center

5 Juliette Gordon Low's
Birthplace

6 *Savannah River Queen*
and *Georgia Queen*

7 Ships of the Sea
Maritime Museum

RESTAURANTS

8 The Pirates' House

9 Clary's Cafe

10 Mrs. Wilkes Boarding House

Family Lodging

Bed and Breakfast Inn Services

No trip to Savannah would be complete without a stay at one of the restored, century-old bed and breakfasts. Most are located downtown, offering prime locations for tourists afoot. They all have unique amenities, so be sure to ask what is included with your stay, especially when the price seems inflated. Two services for finding a bed and breakfast in Savannah are RSVP Savannah, (800) 729-7787, and Savannah Historic Inns and Guest Houses, (912) 233-7666.

Bed & Breakfast Inn

This downtown nineteenth-century townhouse overlooking Chatham Square has 15 guest rooms, a garden suite, and cottages with cooking facilities. And the biggie—it's kid-friendly. Rates start at $85 and include breakfast. 117 and 119 West Gordon Street, Savannah; (912) 238-0518.

Hyatt Regency Riverfront Hotel

Right in the middle of the riverfront hustle and bustle, the Hyatt is a full-service hotel with guest rooms that offer views of the water. Amenities include an indoor, heated swimming pool, an exercise room, a full-service restaurant, and nearby golf, tennis, a spa, and beaches. Rates begin at $189. 2 West Bay Street, Savannah; (912) 238 1234 or (800) 633-7313.

Melon Bluff Natural Preserve

Take a break from citified activities and prop up your feet at Melon Bluff, a 3,000-acre nature preserve that was once a former timberland and rice plantation. Located 35 mintues from Savannah, the preserve's accommodations are family-style in a bed and breakfast that offers three historic buildings, including a restored barn. Guided tours in a wagon drawn by a pair of mules make it easy for families to explore the outdoors. River kayaking, mountain biking, hiking, bird watching, and horseback riding are activities for the more energetic. Children ages 8 and older only. Rates start at $85. 2999 Islands Highway, Midway; (888) 246-8188; www.melonbluff.com.

Westin Savannah Harbor Resort

Across the Savannah River on Hutchinson Island, the new Westin fronts Savannah's historic district. You'll find an 18-hole championship golf course, a deep-water marina with sailing and fishing excursions, and a Greenbrier Spa on site. The restaurant, the Riverview, specializes in local seafood. Rates begin at $149. 1 Resort Drive, Savannah; (912) 201-2000 or (800) WESTIN1; www.westin.com.

Attractions

The Aquarium at Skidaway Island

30 Ocean Science Circle, Savannah; (912) 598-2496

Hours: Monday–Friday, 9 a.m.– 4 p.m.; Saturday, noon– 5 p.m.

Admission: $1, free for children ages 6 and younger

Appeal by Age Group:

Pre-school	Grade School	Teens	Young Adults	Over 30	Seniors
★★★	★★★	★★★	★★★	★★★	★★★

Average Touring Time: 2 hours

Minimum Touring Time: 1 hour

Rainy Day Touring: Recommended

Author's Rating: ★★★

Services and Facilities:

Restaurants No	Lockers No
Alcoholic beverages No	Pet kennels No
Disabled access Yes	Rain check No
Wheelchair rental No	Private tours No
Baby stroller rental No	

Description and Comments   Part of the University of Georgia Marine Extension Service, the aquarium is a public facility designed to teach visitors about the native marine and estuarine animals. Sharks, turtles, and fish of all colors, shapes, and sizes are on display, and all exhibits have plaques providing more information and step-up platforms so little ones can get a closer look at the animals. Outdoors, a nature trail with interpretive signage points out native plants and trees, and there is a shady picnic area overlooking the marsh and river.

Beach Institute African-American Cultural Arts Center

502 East Harris Street, Savannah; (912) 234-8000

Hours: Tuesday–Saturday, noon– 5 p.m.

Admission: $3

Appeal by Age Group:

Pre-school	Grade School	Teens	Young Adults	Over 30	Seniors
★★	★★★	★★★	★★★	★★★	★★★

Average Touring Time: 1 hour

Minimum Touring Time: 30 minutes

Rainy Day Touring: Recommended

Author's Rating: ★★★

Services and Facilities:

Restaurants No	Lockers No
Alcoholic beverages No	Pet kennels No
Disabled access Yes	Rain check No
Wheelchair rental No	Private tours Yes
Baby stroller rental No	

Description and Comments Any children who think modern-day school is strict are sure to change their minds after a visit to the Beach Institute. Built in 1867 as a school for freed African-American children, the restored building is stark and bare, reminiscent of schools a century ago. Besides the classroom, there are changing exhibits and the permanent Ulysses Davis woodcarving collection. Davis, a barber who whittled between clients, created more than 200 works and is nationally recognized for his contributions to folk art.

Fort Pulaski National Monument

Cockspur Island; (912) 786-5787

Hours: Daily, 8:30 a.m.–5:30 p.m.

Admission: $2 adults, free for children ages 16 and younger

Appeal by Age Group:

Pre-school	Grade School	Teens	Young Adults	Over 30	Seniors
★★★	★★★★	★★★★	★★★★	★★★★	★★★★

Average Touring Time: 4 hours

Minimum Touring Time: 1½ hours

Rainy Day Touring: Not recommended

Author's Rating: ★★★★ A different kind of monument experience

Services and Facilities:

Restaurants No	Lockers No
Alcoholic beverages No	Pet kennels No
Disabled access Yes	Rain check No
Wheelchair rental No	Private tours No
Baby stroller rental No	

Description and Comments What sets this place apart from other forts and historic monuments is its castle-like appearance, complete with drawbridges and a moat. It has an underground tunnel system and two levels that feature displays of soldiers' quarters, cannons, and a prison. The grounds also include a hiking trail with interpretive signs, a picnic area, and a visitors center with a gift shop and a 15-minute introductory video.

Juliette Gordon Low's Birthplace

142 Bull Street, Savannah; (912) 233-4501

Hours: Monday, Tuesday, Thursday–Saturday, 10 a.m.– 4 p.m.; Sunday, 12:30– 4:30 p.m.

Admission: $5 adults, $4 children ages 6–18, free for children ages 5 and younger

Appeal by Age Group:

Pre-school	Grade School	Teens	Young Adults	Over 30	Seniors
★	★★★	★★★	★★★	★★★	★★★

Average Touring Time: 1 hour

Minimum Touring Time: 45 minutes

Rainy Day Touring: Recommended

Author's Rating: ★★★

Services and Facilities:

Restaurants No	Lockers No
Alcoholic beverages No	Pet kennels No
Disabled access Yes (partial)	Rain check No
Wheelchair rental No	Private tours Yes
Baby stroller rental No	

Description and Comments Thousands of girls visit Savannah each year to tour the home of Girl Scouts of America founder Juliette Gordon Low. Born in 1860, Low grew up in the house. Many of the original furnishings remain, along with family portraits and art that she painted. There are also two dollhouses on display. Girl Scouts can earn a merit badge by touring the home.

Savannah National Wildlife Refuge

100 Business Center Parkway, Savannah; (912) 652-4415

Hours: Daily during daylight

Admission: Free

Appeal by Age Group:

Pre-school	Grade School	Teens	Young Adults	Over 30	Seniors
★★★	★★★★	★★★★	★★★	★★★	★★★

Average Touring Time: 2 hours

Minimum Touring Time: 1 hour

Rainy Day Touring: Not recommended

Author's Rating: ★★★

Services and Facilities:

Restaurants No	Lockers No
Alcoholic beverages No	Pet kennels No
Disabled access Yes	Rain check No
Wheelchair rental No	Private tours Yes
Baby stroller rental No	

Description and Comments   Established in 1927, the Savannah National Wildlife Refuge is home to a variety of native wildlife, from birds and alligators to snakes and otters. The 25,608 acres of the refuge include freshwater marshland, bottomland hardwood swamps, creeks, and tidal rivers. You can drive through the refuge for a quick, overall tour, or call ahead and schedule a guided tour with a ranger or volunteer.

Savannah River Queen and the Georgia Queen

9 East River Street, Savannah; (912) 232-6404 or (800) 786-6404
www.savannah-riverboat.com

Hours: Sightseeing, dinner, brunch, and moonlight cruises; schedule varies

Admission: Dinner cruise: $34.95 adults, $21.95 children; Sightseeing cruise: $13.50 adults, $8.50 children ages 12 and younger

Appeal by Age Group:

Pre-school	Grade School	Teens	Young Adults	Over 30	Seniors
★★★	★★★★	★★★★	★★★★	★★★★	★★★★

Average Touring Time: 2 hours

Minimum Touring Time: N/A

Rainy Day Touring: Recommended

Author's Rating: ★★★★   An interesting way to see Savannah

Services and Facilities:

Restaurants Yes	Lockers No
Alcoholic beverages Yes	Pet kennels No
Disabled access Yes (partial)	Rain check No
Wheelchair rental No	Private tours No
Baby stroller rental No	

Description and Comments   Ply the waters of the Savannah River in an old-fashioned paddle wheeler and see Savannah the way General James Oglethorpe saw it in 1733. The sightseeing cruise features a narration of the Savannah River's history by the captain. The dinner cruise has live entertainment and a full dinner menu.

Ships of the Sea Maritime Museum

41 Martin Luther King Jr. Boulevard, Savannah; (912) 232-1511

Hours: Daily, 10 a.m.–5 p.m.

Admission: $3 adults, $1.50 children ages 7–12, free for children ages 6 and younger

Appeal by Age Group:

Pre- school	Grade School	Teens	Young Adults	Over 30	Seniors
★★	★★★	★★★	★★★	★★★	★★★

Average Touring Time: 1½ hours

Minimum Touring Time: 1 hour

Rainy Day Touring: Recommended

Author's Rating: ★★★

Services and Facilities:

Restaurants No	Lockers No
Alcoholic beverages No	Pet kennels No
Disabled access Yes (partial)	Rain check No
Wheelchair rental No	Private tours No
Baby stroller rental No	

Description and Comments Housed in 200-year-old Scarbrough House, the Ships of the Sea Maritime Museum has a fascinating collection of 75 ships-in-a-bottle, including models of the *Mayflower*, the *SS Savannah*, viking ships, and more. Marine artifacts are on display, and upstairs you can get a panoramic view of the Savannah River.

Side Trips

Walking Savannah Unlike many Southern cities, Savannah is best seen on foot. The town layout follows the original 1732 European design based on grids, with large squares in the middle for use as parks and public green space. There are 21 in all, and each has a different feel. The best way to decide which your family should visit is to pick up a free walking tour map or rent an audiotape from the Savannah Visitors Center at 301 Martin Luther King Jr. Boulevard, (912) 944-0455. Housed in a restored railroad station, the center has brochures on all local attractions and informative employees who can steer you in the right direction. This is also where you can catch a trolley or bus tour.

On the Waterfront The Savannah River waterfront has long shaped the character of Savannah, first as a means of economy and transportation and now as an entertainment district for locals and visitors alike. More than 75 restaurants line River Street, along with nightclubs, boutiques, and souvenir shops. The street is also the site of many city festivals and street parties. Allow time to visit the Train Museum at 315 River Street for a look at a model train track and displays of antique toy trains (phone (912) 233-6175). Ships of the Sea maritime museum is also found here. Factors Walk is lined with restored cotton warehouses turned eateries and shops.

City Market   After a morning of exploration, work your way towards City Market, a restored downtown area of shops and restaurants. You can eat lunch and then browse through boutiques filled with one-of-a-kind art, clothing, souvenirs, specialty foods, and regional crafts. There are also studios where working artists demonstrate their skills.

Family-Friendly Restaurants

THE PIRATES' HOUSE

20 East Broad Street, Savannah; (912) 233-5757

Meals served: Lunch and dinner
Cuisine: Seafood
Entrée range: $15 and up
Kids menu: Yes
Reservations: No
Payment: All major credit cards accepted

Once a hangout for pirates and sailors, this restaurant has been a Savannah mainstay since 1753. The seafood menu is unremarkable, but the way the staff caters to kids will make you want to come back. The maitre d' seats your party wearing a pirate's mask that is also the menu. And while you're waiting, the kids can push a button on the wall to hear and see Jolly George, the life-sized robot, talk and move.

CLARY'S CAFE

404 Abercorn, Savannah; (912) 233-0402

Meals served: Breakfast and lunch
Cuisine: American
Entrée range: $2 and up
Kids menu: Yes
Reservations: No
Payment: All major credit cards accepted

While the southern fare at Clary's is certainly authentic and tasty, don't pass up ordering from the breakfast menu. The inside of the restaurant resembles an old drugstore, and there are a few tables outside if you're lucky enough to snag one. The restaurant is a downtown hangout for locals and visitors who want an authentic Savannah experience.

MRS. WILKES BOARDING HOUSE

107 Jones Street, Savannah; (912) 232-5997

Meals served: Breakfast and lunch
Cuisine: Southern
Entrée range: $5–8
Kids menu: No
Reservations: No
Payment: Cash only

Mrs. Wilkes Dining Room is where to go for southern soul food. Fried chicken, sweet potato soufflé, black eyed peas, turnip greens, and cornbread are but a few of the dishes passed around the boarding house–style dining room. Its also convenient to local attractions and B&Bs.

Tybee Island

This northern-most island along Georgia's coast is so close to Savannah that it is often called "Savannah Beach." It is about 30 minutes outside the city and accessible by car. There are a few hotels, but most accommodations are condominiums and rental homes. Overall, the island is low-key—a place where regular folks go to take a dip in the Atlantic. Downtown has several souvenir shops and a beach where the local surfers go to hit the waves. On the outer edges, the island is more secluded, where families sometimes have the entire beach to themselves.

FAMILY LODGING

A variety of daily or weekly condominium and beach house rentals are available on the island—some of which even allow pets. Summer reservations can be limited so call and make reservations as soon as you confirm your travel plans. Rates begin at $200 per night. Tybee Beach Rentals, (800) 755-8562 or (912) 786-8805; Tybee Island Rentals, (800) 476-0807 or (912) 786-4034.

ATTRACTION

Tybee Lighthouse

30 Meddin Drive, Tybee Island; (912) 786-4077

Hours: April–Labor Day, daily, 10 a.m.–6 p.m.; Rest of year,
   Monday–Friday, noon–4 p.m.; weekends, 10 a.m.–4 p.m.
Admission: $3 adults, $2 seniors, $1 children

Appeal by Age Group:

Pre-school	Grade School	Teens	Young Adults	Over 30	Seniors
★	★★	★★★	★★★	★★★	★★★

Average Touring Time: 1 hour

Minimum Touring Time: 30 minutes

Rainy Day Touring: Not recommended

Author's Rating: ★★

Services and Facilities:

Restaurants No	Lockers No
Alcoholic beverages No	Pet kennels No
Disabled access No	Rain check No
Wheelchair rental No	Private tours No
Baby stroller rental No	

Description and Comments   Since 1736, Tybee Lighthouse has stood in this same spot in one form or another and has weathered two major wars: The Revolutionary War and the Civil War. The first 60-foot section was built in 1773; the top 94-foot section was constructed in 1867. Climb to the top of the 154-foot tower—178 steps in all—for a great view of the island and the ocean. There are six historical buildings around the base of the lighthouse, including the lighthouse keeper's cottage.

Georgia's Islands

There are 13 islands in the chain of barrier islands skirting Georgia's coastline, but only eight are open to the public, and three of these have restricted access. Those that are inhabited were first settled by Native Americans, and later developed by wealthy plantation owners who used the land to grow cotton. At the turn of the twentieth century, northern industrialists recognized the area's potential as a playground for the rich and famous and built upscale resorts that are still in operation. Over the years, each island has developed its own personality, but overall the area is rich in wildlife and natural beauty.

For information on Tybee Island, see the previous section on Savannah.

Sapelo Island

With limited access, Sapelo Island affords visitors the chance to explore and learn about the island's protected beaches and salt marsh ecosystem through the Sapelo Island Natural Estuarine Research Reserve. Take a guided bus tour that rolls by the ruins of a nineteenth-century antebellum cotton and sugar plantation, Hog Hammock; a "Gullah," an African-American community that has its own language; and the Georgia Marine Research Institute, once the mansion of R.J. Reynolds. You can also take a mule-drawn wagon tour around the island. Excursions to the reserve vary according to season; call ahead for specific days and times. Cost is $10 for adults and $6 for children ages 6–18; (912) 437-3224 or (912) 437-2251; www.inlet.geol.sc.edu/SAP/home.html.

Little St. Simons Island

Accessible only by private ferry from the north end of St. Simons Island, Little Saint Simons is Georgia's last family-owned barrier island. Overnight

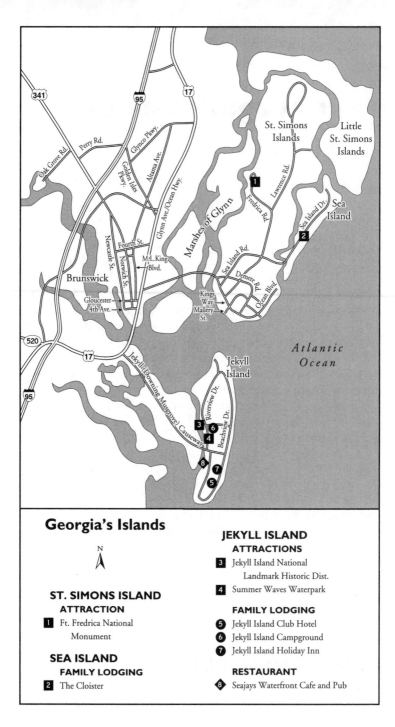

Georgia's Islands

N

ST. SIMONS ISLAND
ATTRACTION
1 Ft. Fredrica National
Monument

SEA ISLAND
FAMILY LODGING
2 The Cloister

JEKYLL ISLAND
ATTRACTIONS
3 Jekyll Island National
Landmark Historic Dist.
4 Summer Waves Waterpark

FAMILY LODGING
5 Jekyll Island Club Hotel
6 Jekyll Island Campground
7 Jekyll Island Holiday Inn

RESTAURANT
8 Seajays Waterfront Cafe and Pub

accommodations are available in the inn or one of the two cottages from March through May and October and November. In the summer, the entire island, which has lodging for 24, must be booked. The family reserves the island as a retreat for the winter. Another catch: Children under age six are not permitted. Call for rates and schedules; (912) 638-7472.

St. Simons Island

Georgia's first military outpost was established here in 1736 when General James Oglethorpe built Fort Frederica. Later, oaks from the island were used in the construction of the Revolutionary War battleship *USS Constitution,* better known as Old Ironsides. Another historical bit of trivia is that downtown Neptune Park is named after a slave who carried his master's body home from the Civil War. As a reward, he was given the plot of land that is now the park. St. Simons has several miles of public beaches at Massengale Park, with picnic and bathroom facilities. A visitors center on the island has information on what to see and do. The toll over the F.J. Torras/St. Simons Causeway is $0.35.

FAMILY LODGING

The most convenient accommodations for families on the island are the condominiums and cottages for rent. Full-size kitchens, living areas, and bedrooms make it seem like home away from home. Rates start at $200 and up. Call (888) STSIMONS.

ATTRACTION

Fort Frederica National Monument

Route 9, Box 286C, St. Simons Island; (912) 638-3639
  www.nps.gov/fofr

Hours: Daily, 8 a.m.–5 p.m.; museum, daily, 9 a.m.–5 p.m.

Admission: $4 per vehicle

Appeal by Age Group:

Pre-school	Grade School	Teens	Young Adults	Over 30	Seniors
★★	★★★	★★★	★★★	★★★	★★★

Average Touring Time: 3 hours

Minimum Touring Time: 2 hours

Rainy Day Touring: Recommended

Author's Rating: ★★★

Services and Facilities:

Restaurants No	Lockers No
Alcoholic beverages No	Pet kennels No
Disabled access Yes	Rain check N/A
Wheelchair rental Yes	Private tours Yes
Baby stroller rental No	

Description and Comments   Fort Frederica was built by General James Oglethorpe in 1736, when he laid claim to the Georgia territory for England. Frederica soon grew to over 500 people, but was disbanded in 1749 as the coastline became a target for military threats. All that is left now are ruins of the fortification, but you can watch a 30-minute film about the site or take a ranger-led tour. In the summer, interpretative soldier-and colonial-life programs are underway.

Sea Island

This five-mile-long island is home to several upscale residential neighborhoods as well as the tony Cloisters, a resort visited by the rich and famous since 1928. It is accessible from St. Simons Island by a bridge that crosses the marsh.

FAMILY LODGING

The Cloisters

This four-star resort has something for everyone: Championship golfing at the Sea Island Golf Club, a full-service spa, and a killer kids club. In the summer, daily playtime is provided without charge for children ages 3–12 and includes activities like jeep train tours, sea turtle nest patrols, spa and sporting events for teens, and nature programs. Likewise, afternoon golf and tennis are complimentary for younger guests. Nighttime activities like hamburger suppers and dinner-and-a-movie are available for an additional charge, and babysitters are available any time for infants. Entertainment for the whole family includes horseback beach rides, tennis, ballroom dancing lessons, plantation suppers, and instruction on shooting sporting clays at the Sea Island Shooting School. And don't forget the beach and pools—perfect for taking advantage of hot summer days. One note: Jackets are required for men and boys at dinner, so make sure you pack accordingly. All rates are based on a full American plan, meaning that all meals are included in the price of your stay. Rates start at $358. (912) 638-3611; www.cloister.com. Private condominiums on the island are also for rent. Call (800) SEA-ISLAND.

Jekyll Island

Like other Georgia islands, Jekyll Island was developed as a private retreat for the rich and famous. In fact, it is said that before World War II, its summer residents controlled one-sixth of the world's wealth. Jekyll played an important role in the slave trade, with the last major shipment of slaves arriving here on the *Wanderer* in 1858. Today, the island is owned by the state, which means that all ten miles of beaches are accessible to the public. There are several chain hotels located along the beach and a handful of attractions, all of which are family-friendly. The beach, however, is the highlight of the island, with action-packed fun from parasailing and jet-skiing to simply playing in the waves along the shore. Jekyll is accessible via the Jekyll Island Causeway, and there is an island parking fee of $3.

FAMILY LODGING

Jekyll Island Club Hotel

A grand dame of historic hotels, Jekyll Island Club was built in 1887 in true Victorian style, complete with turrets and wrap-around porches. Other hints of its glorious past include a well-maintained croquet greensward and indoor tennis courts. Both standard hotel rooms and suites are available in this Radisson property, and there are plenty of in-house options to keep families entertained. The cottages surrounding the hotel were where wealthy guests wintered, but today they are occupied by small boutiques and artists' workshops. Rates start at $119; 371 Riverview Drive, Jekyll Island; (800) 535-9547 or (912) 635-2600; www.jekyllclub.com

Jekyll Island Campground

Just one mile from the beach, this 18-acre campground offers primitive and RV campsites, a camp store, laundry facilities, and bike rentals. Rates start at $18.02 per night with electric and water hook-ups. North Beachview Drive, Jekyll Island; (912) 635-3021.

Jekyll Island Holiday Inn Beach Resort

On the Atlantic side of the island, the Holiday Inn Beach Resort has both standard and deluxe rooms, the latter equipped with a mini-refrigerator and microwave. On-site amenities include tennis courts, bike rentals, a swimming pool, playground, and full-service restaurant. All kids stay and eat free. Rates start at $79. 200 South Beachview Drive, Jekyll Island; (912) 635-3311.

ATTRACTIONS

Jekyll Island Club National Landmark Historic District

Stable Road, Jekyll Island; (912) 635-4036 or (912) 635-2762

Hours: N/A

Admission: N/A

Appeal by Age Group:

Pre-school	Grade School	Teens	Young Adults	Over 30	Seniors
★	★★	★★★	★★★★	★★★★	★★★★

Average Touring Time: 4 hours

Minimum Touring Time: 2 hours

Rainy Day Touring: Not recommended

Author's Rating: ★★★

Services and Facilities:

Restaurants Yes	Lockers No
Alcoholic beverages Yes	Pet kennels No
Disabled access Yes	Rain check N/A
Wheelchair rental No	Private tours Yes
Baby stroller rental No	

Description and Comments   One of the largest restoration projects in the Southeast, the Jekyll Island National Historic Landmark District features 33 homes and buildings, including several mansions and the Jekyll Island Clubhouse. The Museum Visitors Center, located in the Old Stables, has artifacts and displays about historic preservation and offers behind-the-scenes tours upon request. To make touring more enjoyable for kids, take a guided tram tour. The tram departs daily on the hour from 10 a.m.–3 p.m. and costs $10 for adults and $6 for children ages 6–18.

Summer Waves Waterpark

Off I-95 at Exit 6, Jekyll Island; (912) 635-2074 or (912) 635-3636
www.summerwaveswaterpark.com

Hours: Summer hours: Sunday–Friday, 10 a.m.–6 p.m.; Saturday, 10 a.m.–8 p.m.; hours vary in other seasons

Admission: $14.95 adults, $8 seniors, $12.95 children under 48 inches tall, free for children ages 3 and younger; $7.50 after 4 p.m.

Appeal by Age Group:

Pre-school	Grade School	Teens	Young Adults	Over 30	Seniors
★★★★★	★★★★★	★★★★★	★★★	★★★	★★★

Average Touring Time: 1 day

Minimum Touring Time: 4 hours

Rainy Day Touring: No

Author's Rating: ★★★

Services and Facilities:

Restaurants Yes	Lockers Yes
Alcoholic beverages No	Pet kennels No
Disabled access Yes	Rain check No
Wheelchair rental No	Private tours N/A
Baby stroller rental No	

Description and Comments Open Memorial Day to Labor Day and on selected weekends throughout the year, Southeast Georgia's largest water playground is a fun way to cool off on a hot summer day. There are 11 acres of water rides, from an endless river and kiddie pool to a five-story enclosed flume and water slides. There are three McDonald's locations inside. Coolers are not allowed, but there are picnic tables outside the park where you can lunch.

SIDE TRIPS

Wildlife on Jekyll Island   Jekyll Island's rich coastal environment provides a unique opportunity to learn about salt marshes, maritime forests, and the beach's pristine dune system. The island is also teeming with wildlife, including deer, wild turkeys, raccoons, egrets, herons, and alligators. Guided nature walks led by wildlife experts are available (phone (912) 635-9102), or you can explore on your own by hiking, biking, or riding a horse through the miles of nature trails traversing the island. (For horseback rides, phone (912) 635-9500). Nightly sea turtle walks are also offered during the nesting season from June through August, providing visitors the opportunity to witness endangered loggerhead turtles as they lay their eggs (phone (912) 635-2284). And if you're captivated by the gentle nature of dolphins, hop aboard for a Dolphin Watch (phone (912) 635-3137 or (912) 635-3152).

The Jekyll Island Club   Golf has been a tradition on Jekyll Island since 1899, when the first course was built for the winter residents. Today, you don't have to be wealthy to hit the greens; the course has been state-owned and open to the public since 1947. There are three 18-hole courses: Oleander, Indian Mound, and Pine Lakes. Cost is $29 for adults for daily unlimited greens fees and $14.50 for juniors. Reservations can be made up to six months in advance, (912) 635-2368. The nine-hole course, Great Dunes, costs $17 for daily unlimited greens fees and is available on a first-come, first-served basis, (912) 635-2170.

FAMILY-FRIENDLY RESTAURANT

SEAJAY'S WATERFRONT CAFE AND PUB

1 Harbor Road, Jekyll Island; (912) 635-3200
www.seajays.com

Meals served: Breakfast and lunch
Cuisine: American
Entrée range: $6.25 and up
Kids menu: Yes
Reservations: No
Payment: All major credit cards accepted

Seajay's specialty is low country boil, a traditional dish with shrimp, fish, corn on the cob, smoked sausage, and potatoes simmered in a seasoned broth. They also serve a killer Brunswick stew. For kids, they have chicken tenders, nacho chips and dip, and a variety of sandwiches and soups.

Cumberland Island

The largest and southernmost of Georgia's barrier islands, Cumberland Island was once home to Sea Island cotton plantations. In the early twentieth century, a resort community popped up that included several members of the Carnegie clan. Today, their heirs operate Greyfield, one of the original family houses and now an exclusive inn that's the only lodging on the island (JFK Jr. was married here). As a day guest, you can explore the miles of hiking trails weaving throughout this pristine environment, visit the historic ruins of the Dungeness Mansion and the homes of the Carnegie Estate, and, if you call ahead, arrange a guided ranger tour along the Cumberland Island National Seashore. There are no cars, bikes, or pets allowed on the island, and make sure you pack food and drinks or pick up box lunches in downtown St. Mary's, as you can't buy any on the island. The island is accessible by twice-daily passenger ferry service from downtown St. Mary's, and only 300 visitors are allowed per day. Primitive camping is allowed. Cost is $10.17 adults, $8.03 seniors, $6.05 children 12 and younger; (912) 882-4335 or (912) 882-4336.

Part Three

Kentucky

Stephen Foster waxed poetic about "My Old Kentucky Home," and after a visit to the Bluegrass State, you, too, might take a liking to Kentucky. The state was named for a Cherokee Indian word, "Kaintuckee," which historians believe means "meadowland." Kentucky separated from the Commonwealth of Virginia in 1792 to become America's 15th state. It retained its commonwealth status, meaning that the government is based on the common consent of the people, an idea that dates to the 1600s with Oliver Cromwell in England. Other commonwealths include Virginia, Massachusetts, and Pennsylvania.

Kentucky was a border state during the Civil War, and although many Kentuckians enlisted in the Confederacy, the state officially remained in the Union. Ironically, both Abraham Lincoln and Jefferson Davis were born in Kentucky.

We like Kentucky for a couple of reasons, the main one being the richness of natural resources, which in turns means diversity of outdoor attractions. A number of rivers cut across the state, including the Ohio, the Mississippi, and the Kentucky. Along with manmade lakes—there are no natural lakes in the state—there are a plentitude of water activities, from swimming and water-skiing to fishing and canoeing.

And let's not forget horses. Stables offering guided horseback rides, museums devoted to all things equestrian, and horse farms showcasing the crème de la crème of the racing world can all be found in Kentucky.

Another reason Kentucky is a good vacation spot is the climate. Summers are not as hot and humid as in other southern states. That's not to say that the heat can't be miserable at times, but it's less likely to last as long. Plus, the winters are still milder than other northern locales. The best time to visit, climate-wise, is in late spring when the state is its greenest. However, May is also the month of the **Kentucky Derby**, and if you're anywhere near

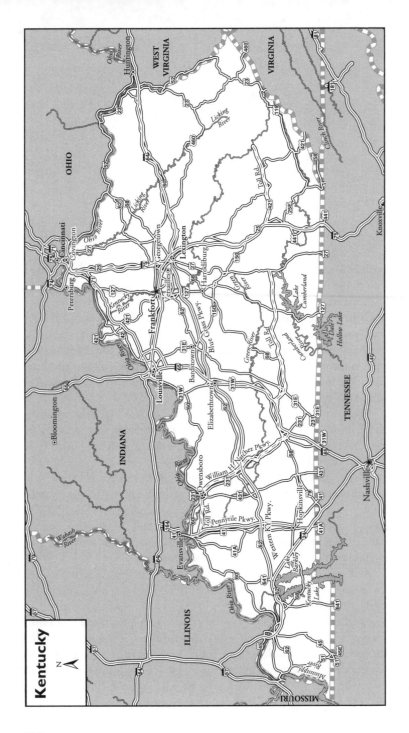

Kentucky

Kids' Beat

- Unlike other states, Kentucky was never a territory. Instead, it was part of Virginia until it became its own state in 1792.

- The state butterfly is the viceroy; the state tree is the tulip tree; the state fish is the Kentucky bass; and the state flower is the goldenrod.

- Kentucky's nickname is the Bluegrass State, so-named because of the "blue" grass that grows profusely throughout the state. If you look closely, however, the grass is really green. Its bluish-purple buds give it a rich blue cast.

- Louisvillian John Colgan invented chewing gum in 1873. He called it "Taffy Julie."

- The legendary fight between the Hatfields and McCoys took place in Pike County in the mid-1800s over Civil War sentiments, inter-family romance, land ownership, and mountain pride.

Louisville, expect crowds and a hard time finding a hotel room. Early fall is another good time to visit, as the leaves are in full color.

Louisville and **Lexington** are the places to visit if you're after citified experiences. Louisville, the state's largest city, has museums, restaurants, and the perennial favorite, **Six Flags Kentucky Kingdom.** Lexington is horse country and also home to the **University of Kentucky.**

If you want to see the outskirts of any major Kentucky city or hit the back roads, a car is essential. You can book hotels in cities along the way, and spend your days exploring points of interest in-between. One place that's a must for any itinerary: **Mammoth Cave National Park,** the longest cave system in the world.

Note: Kentucky has two time zones. The western part of the state is within the Central Standard Time zone (CST), while the eastern portion is within the Eastern Standard Time zone (EST). The line dividing the two zones falls between Bowling Green and Louisville.

Note: Telephone area codes have changed for several regions. They are noted with specific cities; for smaller towns, call (800) 225-TRIP to verify an area code.

GETTING THERE

By Plane.   Louisville International Airport, 15 minutes south of downtown on I-65, is the state's largest airport. American, Comair, Continental,

Kentucky's Not-to-Be-Missed Attractions	
Around the State	Churchill Downs The Kentucky Derby Mammoth Cave National Park Shaker Village of Pleasant Hill Vent Haven Museum

Louisville	Abraham Lincoln Birthplace
	    National Historic Site,
	    Hodgenville
	Churchill Downs
	Hillerich & Bradsby Louisville
	    Slugger Museum and Bat Factory
	Louisville Zoo

Lexington	Keeneland Race Course
	Kentucky Horse Park and
	    International Museum of the
	    Horse
	Lexington Children's Museum

Frankfort	Kentucky Military History Museum Salato Wildlife Education Center & Game Farm

Bowling Green	Barren River Imaginative Museum
	    of Science
	National Corvette Museum and
	    Production Facility

Northern Kentucky	Big Bone Lick State Park
	Cincinnati Zoo & Botanical
	    Garden, Cincinnati
	Cinergy Children's Museum,
	    Cincinnati
	Newport Aquarium
	Vent Haven Museum

Delta, Northwest, Southwest, TWA, United, and USAirways all fly into Louisville (phone (502) 367-4636). Lexington Bluegrass Airport, at 400 Versailles Road is four miles west of downtown, and has service from Delta,

USAir, ASA, ComAir, Continental Express, Northwest Airlink, TWA Express, and United Express (phone (606) 254-9336). Other alternatives include the Nashville International Airport (an hour from the Kentucky border) for access to the southwestern part of the state, and Cincinnati (one-and-a-half hours from Lexington) for access to the northeastern part of Kentucky.

By Train. Passenger trains serve Louisville, Ashland, Fulton, and Maysville, as well as Jeffersonville, Indiana, and Cincinnati, Ohio, on a limited basis. Information on train schedules is available at (800) 872-7245 or www.amtrak.com.

By Car: Kentucky is well connected with a network of interstates and state highways. Interstates 75, 65, and 24 travel north to south, I-64 traverses the eastern part of the state, and I-24 connects Western Kentucky with Illinois. Other heavily traveled roads include the Bluegrass, Western Kentucky, Daniel Boone, and Cumberland Parkways. As expected, the back roads vary in condition. Still, driving is one of the best ways to enjoy the Bluegrass State.

For updates on current road construction, slated projects, and traffic conditions, call for a Kentucky Road Report at (800) 459-7623 or log on to www.kytc.state.ky.us/roadcond/roadcond.htm. For printable maps and real-time videos of current traffic conditions, log on to Kentucky Traffic Center at www.kytc.state.ky.us/traffic_center. If you are involved in an accident, call (800) 222-5555. The speed limit on interstates and the parkways is 65 miles per hour. Kentucky law requires that children less than 40 inches tall must be restrained in federally approved safety restraints.

HOW TO GET INFORMATION BEFORE YOU GO

State

Kentucky Department of Travel, 500 Mero Street, Suite 22, Frankfort 40601; (800) 225-8747; www.kentuckytourism.com

Kentucky Travel Guide, 812 South Third Street, Louisville 40203; (502) 584-2720; www.kytravel.com

Kentucky State Parks, 500 Mero Street, Suite 10, Frankfort 40601; (800) 255-7275; www.kystateparks.com

Regional

Kentucky Homes B&B, 1219 South Fourth Avenue, Louisville 40203; (502) 635-7341

Local

Ashland Area Convention & Visitors Bureau, P.O. Box 987, 728 Greenup

Avenue, Ashland 41105; (800) 377-6249 or (606) 329-1007; www.visit-ashlandky.com

Bardstown-Nelson County Tourist & Convention Commission, 107 East Stephen Foster, Bardstown 40004; (800) 638-4877 or (502) 348-4877

Bell County Tourism Commission, P.O. Box 788, Middlesboro 40965; (800) 988-1075 or (606) 248-1075

Berea Recreation Tourist & Convention Commission, P.O. Box 556, 201 North Broadway, Berea 40403; (606) 986-2540; www.berea.com

Bowling Green–Warren County Tourist Commission, 352 Three Springs Road, Bowling Green 42104; (800) 326-7465 or (270) 782-0800; bowlinggreen.ky.net/tourism

Burkesville Tourism Commission, P.O. Box 821, Burkesville 42717; (502) 864-2234

Cadiz-Trigg County Chamber of Commerce, P.O. Box 735, 22 Main Street, Cadiz 42211; (270) 522-3892; www.barkleylake.com

Campbellsville-Taylor County Tourist Commission, P.O. Box 4021, Broadway and Court, Campbellsville 42719; (800) 738-4719 or (270) 465-3786

Cave City Tourist & Convention Commission, P.O. Box 518, Cave City 42127; (800) 346-8908 or (270) 773-3131; www.cavecity.com

Columbia-Adair County Tourist Commission, 1115 Jamestown Street #3, Columbia 42728; (502) 384-4401

Carrollton-Carroll County Tourist Commission, P.O. Box 293, Old Stone Jail, Court Street, Carrollton 41008; (800) 325-4290 or (502) 732-7036

Corbin Tourist & Convention Commission. 101 North Depot Street, Corbin 40701; (800) 528-7123 or (606) 528-6390

Cumberland-Benham-Lynch Tourist Commission, P.O. Box D, 104 Freeman Street, Cumberland 40823; (606) 848-1530

Danville-Boyle County Convention & Visitors Bureau, McClure-Barbee House, 304 South Fourth #201, Danville 40422; (800) 755-0076 or (606) 236-7794; www.danville-ky.com

Edmonson County Tourist & Convention Commisssion, P.O. Box 628, Brownsville 42210; (800) 624-8687; www.cavesandlakes.com

Elizabethtown Tourism & Convention Bureau, 1030 North Mulberry Street, Elizabethtown 42701; (800) 437-0092 or (502) 765-2175; www.ltadd.org/etowntourism

Franklin-Simpson County Tourism Commission, P.O. Box 737, Franklin 42134; (502) 586-3040

Frankfort-Franklin County Tourism & Convention Commission, 100 Capital Avenue, Frankfort 40601; (800) 960-7200 or (502) 875-8687; www.frankfortky.org

Fulton Tourist Commission, 1010 West State Line, Fulton 42041; (502) 472-3893

Georgetown-Scott County Tourist Commission, 399 Outlet Center Drive, Georgetown 40324; (888) 863-8600 or (502) 863-2547; www.georgetown-ky.com

Grant County Tourist Commission, 214 South Main #1, Williamstown 41097; (800) 382-7117 or (606) 824-3451

Grayson Tourism & Convention Commission, P.O. Box 296, Grayson 41143; (606) 475-5128

Harlan Tourist & Convention Commission, P.O. Box 489, Harlan 40831; (606) 573-4156; www.seky.net/harlantourism

Hazard-Perry County Tourist Commission, 601 Main Street #3, Hazard 41701; (606) 439-2659; www.kentucky.net/hazard

Harrodsburg-Mercer County Tourist Commission, P.O. Box 283, 103 South Main, Harrodsburg 40330; (800) 355-9192 or (606) 734-2364; www.harrodsburgky.com

Henderson County Tourist Commission, 2961 U.S. 41 North, Henderson 42420; (502) 826-3128; www.go-henderson.com

Hopkinsville-Christian County Tourist Commission, P.O. Box 1382, 1209 South Virginia, Hopkinsville 42241; (800) 842-9959 or (502) 885-9096

Lebanon-Marion County Chamber of Commerce, 21 Court Street, Lebanon 40033; (502) 692-9594; www.hamdays.com

Leitchfield-Grayson County Tourist Commission, 10 Court Street, Leitchfield 42755; (502) 259-5587; www.ltadd.org/leitchfield

Leslie County Tourism Commission, P.O. Box 948, Hyden 41749; (606) 672-2344

Letcher County Tourist Commission, 306 Madison Street, Whitesburg 41858; (606) 633-0108

Lexington Convention & Visitors Bureau, 301 East Vine, Lexington 40507; (800) 845-3959, (859) 244-7712; www.visitlex.com

Livingston County Tourist Commission, 721 Complex Drive, Grand Rivers 42045; (502) 928-4411

London–Laurel County Tourism Commission, 140 West Daniel Boone Parkway, London 40741; (800) 348-0095 or (606) 878-6900; www.tourky.com/london

Louisa Tourist & Convention Commission, P.O. Box 808, Louisa 41230; (606) 638-0244

Louisville Convention & Visitors Bureau, 400 South First, Louisville 40202; (800) 626-5646 or (502) 584-2121; www.gotolouisville.com

Lyon County Tourist Commission, P.O. Box 1030, Eddyville 42038; (502) 388-4104 or (800) 355-3885; www.lakebarkely.com

Marshall County Tourist Commission, P.O. Box 129, Benton 42025; (800) 467-7145 or (502) 362-4128; www.kentuckylake.org

Maysville–Mason County Tourist Commission, 216 Bridge Street, Maysville 41056; (606) 564-9411

McCreary County Tourist Commission, P.O. Box 72, Whitley City 42653; (606) 376-3008

Morehead Tourism Commission, 150 East First Street, Morehead 40351; (606) 784-6221

Mount Sterling Tourism Commission, 51 North Maysville Street, Mount Sterling 40353; (606) 498-5343; www.mountsterlingky.com/tourism/tourism.htm

Mount Vernon–Rockcastle County Tourism Commission, P.O. Box 1261, Mount Vernon 40456; (800) 252-6685 or (606) 256-9814

Murray Tourist Commission, 805 North 12th, Murray 42071; (800) 651-1603 or (502) 753-5171

Northern Kentucky Convention & Visitors Bureau, 605 Philadelphia, Covington 41011; (800) 447-8489 or (606) 655-4155; www.nkycvb.com

Oldham County Tourist & Convention Commission, 108 East Main Street, LaGrange 40031; (800) 813-9953 or (502) 222-0056

Owensboro-Daviess County Tourist Commission, 212 East Second, Owensboro 42301; (800) 489-1131 or (502) 926-1100; www.visitorowensboro.com

Paducah-McCracken County Convention & Visitors Bureau, 128 Broadway, Paducah 42001; (800) PADUCAH or (502) 443-8783

Paintsville Tourism Commission, P.O. Box 809, 304 Main Street, Paintsville 41240; (800) 542-5790 or (606) 789-1469

Paris–Bourbon County Tourism Commission, 2011 Averson Drive, Paris 40361; (606) 987-0779

Pike County Tourism Commission, P.O. Box 1497, Pikeville 41502; (800) 844-7453 or (606) 432-5063; www.kymtnnet.org/pikef1.html

Powell County Tourism Commission, P.O. Box 1028, Stanton 40380; (606) 663-1161

Prestonsburg Tourist Commission, One Hal Rogers Drive, Highway 114, Prestonsburg 41653; (606) 886-1341; www.prestonsburgky.com

Princeton Tourist Commission, 206 Jefferson Street, Princeton 42445; (502) 365-7801

Radcliff-Fort Knox Tourist Commission, P.O. Box 845, 306 North Wilson, Radcliff 40159; (800) 334-7540 or (502) 352-1204; www.ltadd.org/radcliff

Richmond Tourist Commission, 354 Lancaster Avenue, Richmond 40475; (800) 866-3705 or (606) 626-8474; www.richmond-ky.com

Russell County Tourist Commission, P.O. Box 64, U.S. 127 South Russell Springs 42642; (502) 866-4333

Shelbyville–Shelby County Tourism Commission, P.O. Box 622, 316 Main Street, Shelbyville 40065; (502) 633-6388

Shepherdsville–Bullitt County Tourist Commission, 445 Highway 44 East, Shepherdsville Square #5, Shepherdsville 40165; (800) 526-2068 or (502) 543-8687

Somerset–Pulaski County Tourist Commission, P.O. Box 622, 522 Ogden, Somerset 42502; (800) 642-6287 or (606) 679-6394

Williamsburg Tourist & Convention Commission, P.O. Box 2, Williamsburg 40769; (800) 552-0530 or (606) 549-0530

Winchester–Clark County Tourist Commission, 2 South Maple, Suite A, Winchester 40391; (606) 744-0556

Woodford County Tourist Commission, 110 North Main, Versailles 40383; (606) 873-5122

<table>
<tr><td colspan="2">More Kentucky Websites</td></tr>
</table>

University of Kentucky Department of Entomology	www.uky. edu/agriculture/entomology/ythfacts/bugfood/bugfood.htm
Kentucky Derby Virtual Postcards	horseracing.mining co.com/sports/horseracing/library/derby/blpost.htm
Abraham Lincoln's Home	www.nps.gov/liho/index.htm
Bluegrass Amateur Astronomy Club	www.ms.uky.edu/~bgaac
Kentucky Geological Survey	www.uky.edu/kgs/home.htm
Kentucky Paleontological Society	www.uky.edu/otherorgs/kps
Kentucky Symbols	www.geobop.com/world/na/us/ky

Family Outdoor Adventures

▲ - Camping
♥ - Author's favorite

Berea   Berea College was founded in 1855 to provide higher education to those who could not afford it. The tradition continues today as students work on campus in lieu of paying tuition. Many students understudy local artisans and learn traditional crafts. As a result, these skills pass down to other generations instead of becoming lost. Woodworking, pottery, jewelry-making, weaving, furniture-making, and quilting are some of the skills taught.

You can picnic and tour the campus, but the main reasons for families to visit are the exceptional arts and crafts festivals held here. The Kentucky Guild of Artists and Craftsmen Festival is held each May and October, and the Berea Craft Festival takes place in July; (606) 985-3000; www. berea.edu.

Bike Riding   Serious bikers take note: Kentucky has over 1,000 miles of lightly traveled back roads just right for bicycle touring. Wind through horse farm country past old rock fences, historic homes, and shady streams—scenery that makes even the most avid cycler slow down and take in the view. Around Lexington, you'll find two scenic roads perfect for amblers. Old Frankfort Pike from Lexington to U.S. 60 is part of the Scenic Byway, and Pisgah Pike, north of U.S. 60 to KY 1681 is the largest listed rural historic district in Kentucky—and a Kentucky Scenic Byway. If you're a serious cyclist, the Kentucky section of the TransAmerica Bike Trail is more than 600 miles long, running from mountainous Pike County in the east of rural Crittenden County across the Ohio River from Illinois. Call (888) 225-TRIP for a free state guide to bicycle tours.

▲ – *Cumberland Gap, Middlesboro* The mighty Appalachian Mountains kept many early American pioneers from migrating west—that is, until the Cumberland Gap was discovered. This natural break in the mountain chain was carved by wind and water millions of years ago. Large animals used it for their migratory journeys, and Native Americans trekked through the Gap as a shortcut.

Today, visitors come here for the breathtaking scenery and the variety of outdoor activities. Some specific points of interest that you shouldn't miss include Hensley Settlement, Pinnacle Outlook, and White Rocks.

Sand Cave At Pinnacle Overlook, take in a sweeping view of Kentucky, Virginia, and Tennessee from 2,440 feet. Hensley Settlement is a restored mountain community on Brush Mountain. See log cabins and learn about the lifestyles of the Hensleys and Gibbons, two families who settled here. The Settlement can be reach by horseback, hiking, or park shuttle. White Rocks, a massive limestone formation, provides a magnificent view of Virginia. Sand Cave, a 75-foot overhang of sandstone, has at least seven different colors of sand in its formation. Both of these places are also reached on horseback or by hiking.

In all, there are over 50 miles of hiking trails throughout 20,000 acres of forest, ranging in length from a ¼-mile loop trail to the 21-mile Ridge Trail. The ranger-guided tours are excellent and range from walks along the Wilderness Road to the Hensley Settlement to programs on longhunter and pioneer encampments. The visitors center has information on all the various hikes, along with a museum that highlights the Gap's history as a transportation corridor. Admission is free; camping is $10 per night. P.O. Box 1848, Middlesboro 40965; (606) 248-2817; www.nps.gov/cuga.

Horsing Around Kentucky is the place for equestrian enthusiasts. For starters, there are plenty of stables in the Bluegrass State offering horseback rides and guided or self-guided rides. A few to try: Deer Run Stables in Richmond, (606) 527-6339; Big Red Stables in Harrodsburg, (606) 734-3118; Wildwood Stables at Sugar Creek Resort in Nicholasville, (606) 885-9359; and Buffalo Springs Horse Park in Cumberland, (606) 561-6661. You can also log on to www.state.ky.us/tour/index3.htm for a complete list of stables.

Then consider that Kentucky, world-famous for it horses, has more than 400 horse farms in the Bluegrass area alone—some swankier than houses we've been in. Calumet Farm, producer of nine Kentucky Derby winners, can be toured by appointment (phone (859) 231-8272 or www.calumet-farm.com), along with Spendthrift Farm on Ironworks Pike, (606) 299-5271. Most are in the Lexington area and are accessible only through organized tours. Call Bluegrass Tours, (606) 252-5744, or the Historic and Horse Farm Tours, (606) 268-2906.

Several museums in the state are devoted to horses. The International Museum of the Horse at the Kentucky Horse Park in Lexington, (606) 233-4303), is perhaps the most comprehensive museum in the world devoted to horses. The American Saddle Horse Museum, (800) 829-4438 or (606) 259-2746, also in Lexington, highlights the history of the American Saddlebreed, Kentucky's only native breed. Churchill Downs in Louisville, (502) 636-4400, has a museum featuring all things Derby. And don't forget about the state's legendary race courses, including the Red Mile in Lexington, (606) 255-0752, so-named for the color of the clay on the track.

Kentucky Bourbon   It's your call on whether to take your children on a distillery tour, but even though they won't be able to sample the merchandise, they will find it interesting to see how American's only native spirit is produced. About 95 percent of all bourbon is made in the Bluegrass State—an amount that earns it, if unofficially, the distinction of state drink. In fact, the famous Kentucky Derby drink, a mint julep, is made with bourbon, sugar, and mint. Take a tour and see what ingredients are used to make a mash, learn about fermentation in old cypress barrels, and discover what terms like "white dog" and "angel's share" mean.

Several Kentucky distilleries have guided tours. Labrot & Graham makes bourbon in copper-pot stills housed in an early 1800s limestone building (7855 McCracken Pike off U.S. 60 in Lexington; (606) 879-1812). Wild Turkey Distillery, a larger production facility, explains both traditional and modern mass production, including a look at the mechanized bottling line (U.S. 62 West near Lawrenceburg; (502) 839-4544. At the Ancient Age/Leestown Company, you'll hear the story of Benjamin Blanton, who began making whiskey at this location in the late 1860s (U.S. 421 north of Frankfort; (502) 223-7641). Heaven Hill, the largest family-owned distillery in the United States, has a tourmobile with stops at the distillery, Stephen Foster's Old Kentucky Home, and other Bardstown attractions (Highway 49; (502) 348-4877). The Jim Beam American Outpost in Clearmont has exhibits like the art of barrel making and what is thought to be the oldest moonshine still in America (phone (502) 542-9877). In addition to a tour, The Maker's Mark Distillery lets you seal a purchased bottle with a unique seal (Highway 52 East near Loretto; (502) 865-2099). And if you're interested in seeing the other side of the barrel, ride by the stone house where Carrie Nation, America's most famous temperance leader, was born. The home is in Lexington on Fisherford Road.

♥ - *Kentucky Crafts*   Kentucky was one of the first Southern states to elevate everyday crafts to art. From quilting and weaving to woodworking and pottery, the state has become famous for its skilled artisans and craftspeople. As a result, it's easy to find museums and galleries with provocative exhibits and studios where you can watch artists in action.

- If you like quilts, visit Paducah's Museum of the American Quilter's Society. With three galleries full of antique and contemporary quilt exhibits, it's the only national museum dedicated to quilters; (270) 442-8856.

- The Kentucky Art and Craft Gallery in Lexington specializes in unique arts and crafts handmade by Kentucky artists. Carved gourds, raku pottery from Kentucky clay, blown glass, and jewelry are among the items for sale; 609 West Main Street, Lexington; (502) 589-0102.

- Lexington is also home to the Artists' Attic, where you can watch artists and craftspeople at work; Victorian Square, 401 West Main Street, Lexington; (606) 254-5501.

- If you have an interest in folk art, you'll be in heaven at the Kentucky Folk Art Center. The permanent collection of more than 650 works by Kentucky folk artists includes walking sticks, paintings, woodcarvings, historical figures, and painted furniture; 102 West First Street, Morehead; (606) 783-2204.

- In Waco, you'll find Bybee Pottery, the oldest pottery business west of the Alleghenies. The Cornelison family began making pottery here in 1845; today, they continue to use local clay to make their trademark solid-color and speckled bowls, mugs, and plates; Highway 52 East, Waco; (606) 369-5350.

For more information about Kentucky crafts, contact the Kentucky Craft Marketing Council at (888) KY-CRAFT.

The Kentucky Derby, Louisville   Billed as the "most exciting two minutes in sports," the Kentucky Derby began in 1875 and has remained the oldest consecutively held thoroughbred race in America. That doesn't mean much if you haven't attended a Derby, but if you've been lucky enough to finagle tickets, you'll agree that little compares to the excitement and electricity of Derby Day. Kids, of course, are not allowed to bet, but they can attend the Derby.

The Derby is open to three-year-old thoroughbred horses and is the first part of the Triple Crown. (The remaining two are the Belmont Stakes and the Preakness.) More than 150,000 people attend the 1.25-mile race, and celebrating begins a month before, heating up the week of the race. A gigantic fireworks show kicks off the celebration, followed by helium balloon races, balls, festivals, and the Great Steamboat Race, where the *Belle of Louisville* races against Cincinnati's *Delta Queen*. Contact Churchill Downs at (502) 636-4460; www.kentuckyderby.com. For festival information, call (800) 928-FEST; www.kdf.org.

▲ ♥ - *Mammoth Cave National Park, Mammoth Cave*   Think of this as a two-layer park. On the top, a host of family-friendly activities await.

Old-growth forests—52,000 acres in all—are crisscrossed with trails for hiking, biking, and horseback riding. Pristine lakes set the stage for fishing and swimming. The Green and Nolin rivers wind their way through the park, creating some of the best canoe runs in the state. And campsites and park lodging are sprinkled throughout. But these diversions are hardly the only reasons people visit this park.

The main attraction lies underground. More than 350 miles of explored chambers and passageways make up the longest cave system known in the world. Its origins stretch back to 280 million years ago, when a shallow sea resided and left layers of mud, shells, and sand that eventually turned into limestone. Rainwater seeped through cracks in the ground, dissolving some of the stone. Over millions of years, the cracks widened and a system of underground streams began to hollow out caves.

What all this geo-talk means is that you can go underground and walk through magnificent chambers or slide on your belly through narrow passageways. Either way, it's an experience you won't soon forget. And while the caves themselves are unbelievable, the formations created by mineral deposits are just as fantastic. Many have been given names for objects and places they resemble. Fat Man's Misery, Bottomless Pit, Bridal Altar, and Solomon's Temple are just a few.

There are several different ways to explore Mammoth Cave. The Frozen Niagara Tour extends ¾ mile down 280 stairs. See impressive pits and domes, stalactites and stalagmites, and visit Grand Central Station. The Travertine Tour is a good choice if you have small children. At ¼ mile, it's less strenuous and passes by a variety of formations, including the Frozen Niagara. The shortest tour, the Discovery Tour, is another good option. The Violet City Lantern Tour, offered only in spring and summer, is three miles of exploration with lantern light. The shadows cast on the cave walls are fascinating but can be scary for young kids. The Making of Mammoth Tour, 2½ miles, explains the geology of the cave and its formations. The Historic Tour explores two miles of caves, including the Rotunda Room and the historic graffiti area where ancient humans have left their mark. And the Wild Cave Tour, a must for older spelunkers, lets you crawl, climb, and squeeze your way through passages off the beaten path. There is a special ½ mile tour for visitors in wheelchairs.

The visitors center will help you figure out which tour is best for your family. You can also pick up information about other park attractions.

If you go, be sure to wear comfortable shoes and take a light jacket, as the caves can be chilly. All tours are guided and vary in length. Reservations are strongly recommended; make them at least a week in advance; (800) 967-2283 or (502) 758-2225.

A hotel, a motor lodge, and 40 cottages within the grounds are open from June through October. Rates begin at $53 for cottages that sleep four. For accommodations, call (502) 758-2328. The park has four main entrances, and entry into the park is free. Tour costs vary; call ahead for prices. Mammoth Cave National Park, Mammoth Cave ; (502) 758-2328; www.nps.gov/maca.

Shaker Village of Pleasant Hill   Take a walk back in time at Shaker Village, a living history park in Pleasant Hill. The Shakers, a religious sect so nicknamed for their ritualistic dance, settled here in the early 1800s, and their legacy remains in the simple buildings restored on this 2,700-acre site. Innovative and practical, the Shakers invented items such as the flat broom, the clothespin, and the circular saw. Their fame, however, grew for the excellence of their simple but well-made furniture.

There are 33 buildings in all at this National Historic Landmark. Many of the buildings serve as workshops for artisans dressed in period costumes. The tour is basically self-guided, but as you walk around watching demonstrations of traditional skills, such as blacksmithing, candle-making, and yarn-dying, costumed interpreters tell stories about the Shaker life. Make sure to take in the Farm Deacon's Shop, where the use of herbs as medicinal cures is explained. The historic farm has heirloom farm breeds like draft horses and shorthorn milking cows. The Centre Family home has an exhibit of original Shaker furniture. If you're up to it, you can board the Dixie Belle sternwheeler for a look at the area's limestone cliffs.

What makes this village different from other interpretive towns is the restaurant and guest accommodations that actually let you experience the Shaker lifestyle. Fifteen of the buildings are now guest accommodations complete with Shaker furniture and textiles. At the Trustees' Office Inn, sit down to an old-fashioned Kentucky breakfast of grits, eggs, sausage, and biscuits; other Shaker specialties are served family-style at lunch and dinner.

The village is open April through October daily from 9:30 a.m. to 5 p.m. Winter hours vary. Shaker Village is seven miles from Harrodsburg on Highway 68; 3501 Lexington Road, Harrodsburg 40330; (800) 734-5611 or (606) 734-5411; www.lexinfo.com/historic/pleasanthill.html.

Calendar of Festivals and Events

January

Native American Weekend, Jamestown   A weekend event portraying various aspects of Native American Culture through lectures and demonstrations by Native Americans. A buffalo dinner is also provided; (800) 325-1709.

April

Chocolate Festival, Washington   Rivers of dark sweet chocolate flow through this 1700s village. Fill your Easter Basket with homemade goodies; an Easter Egg hunt for adults only, fudge contests, chocolate cuisine, chocolate trivia, and cooking contests are part of the fun; (606) 759-7423; www.washingtonky.com.

American Quilter's Society National Quilt Show, Paducah   Named one of the top 100 events in North America by the American Bus Association, the Quilt Show is a mecca for quilting enthusiasts, with over 400 quilts on display; (270) 575-9958.

May

Fort Smith Civil War Re-enactment & Narrated Heritage Tour, Smithland   Civil War period encampment skirmishes are reenacted, along with a Grand Ball on Saturday night. There are also narrated walking tours of numerous pre-Civil War buildings; (270) 928-2446.

Derby Tractor and Truck Pull, Edmonton   This event is held on Derby Saturday; (270) 432-3883.

Second Annual Ghost Roads Homecoming , Bedford   This is a Civil-War-era event with an emphasis on the Underground Railroad; (502) 268-5858; www.geocities.com/prestonplantation.

June

Great American Brass Band Festival, Danville   Called the "most prominent and most unusual music festival in the country," this world-class show brings bands from across the country together in an unprecedented weekend of free music and entertainment. Continuous music both days; (800) 755-0076; www.danville-ky.com.

Riverwalk Arts and Crafts Festival, Maysville   Juried arts and crafts show on riverfront, along with a food court and big band music round out the celebration; (606) 564-9411; www.cityofmaysville.com.

July

Owensboro Summer Festival, Owensboro   Carnival rides, dog shows and musical entertainment for all to enjoy. The festival is concluded with the Owensboro Symphony pops concert and fireworks; (800) 489-1131.

September

Col. John Floyd Excursion, Prestonsburg   The *John Floyd,* a historic flatboat, rediscovers the Big Sandy and Ohio Rivers with explorers John Floyd, Daniel Boone, George R. Clark, Simon Kenton, Isaac Shelby, and Mary Ingles. Inland community groups transport water samples to the *Floyd* for relay to Paducah for display; (800) 844-4704; www.prestonsburgky.org.

KWW 25th Annual Arts and Crafts Festival, Golden Pond   Hand-crafted items, food and drinks, and live music are part of the festival. The 200 booths include craftspeople and artisans from several states; (800) 448-1069.

Cave Run Storytelling Festival, Morehead   This annual storytelling festival at Cave Run Lake offers nationally known storytellers plus state and local talent; (800) 654-1944.

Berea Spoonbread Festival, Berea   A citywide festival featuring hot air balloon, live music, spoonbread contest, with hot spoonbread being served from Boone Tavern, a crafts festival, parade, live auction, and children's activities; (606) 986-9760.

Poppy Mountain Bluegrass Festival, Morehead   The largest traditional Bluegrass festival in the country features local, regional, and national talents. Activities for the whole family are included, from horseback riding to free train rides, shuttle and taxi service in classic old cars to children's activities and pig roast. A car is given away each year, among other prizes; www.poppymountainbluegrass.com.

World Chicken Festival, London   Ranked as one of the top 20 events for 1999 by the Southeast Tourism Society, the World Chicken Festival draws crowds of 200,000. There are 200 booths, carnival rides, and the world's-largest known stainless steel skillet service for serving up fried chicken; (606) 878-6900; www.chickenfestival.com.

Anderson County Burgoo Festival, Lawrenceburg   Features food, crafts, and entertainment with Main Street closed for the duration of event. Burgoo is sold by the committee; (502) 839-6959.

Appalachian Harvest Festival, Renfro Valley   An old-fashioned celebration of the fall harvest including molasses made by mule-drawn press, authentic covered wagon train, antique farm machinery and steam engine show, clogging, mountain music, children's activities, country talent roundup and craft demonstrations featuring blacksmithing, basket weaving and much more; (800) 765-7464; www.renfrovalley.com.

October

Halloween Walk with the Animals, Frankfort   Ever wonder what happens at the wildlife center after dark? Find out during the Game Farm's annual after-hours "Walk with the Animals." This kid friendly, trick-or-treat event raises money for future exhibits. There is also a campfire, hay maze, and nightly costume contest with prizes for the winner; (800) 858-1549.

December

Christmas in Paducah, Paducah   Christmas parade, candlelit Christmas trail, jinglebell run, horsedrawn carriage rides, and holiday concerts are part of the festivities; www.paducah-tourism.org.

Louisville

Kentucky's largest city is a goldmine for families who like to do something different every day. It's a no-brainer to start with a horse, of course, and here you can tour both the **Kentucky Derby Museum** and **Churchill Downs**—if you're lucky (and rich), you might even snag a ticket to horse racing's premier event. Later, batter up to **Hillerich & Bradsby's Louisville Slugger Museum and Bat Factory,** or follow in the footsteps of Mark Twain and cruise down the Ohio on an authentic sternwheeler.

General George Rogers Clark, a Revolutionary War hero, founded Louisville in 1778 on the bend of the Ohio River. Clark named the city in honor of King Louis XVI for France's assistance during the war.

Today, "Loo-uh-vul," as natives call it, is within a day's drive for over half of the people in the United States. The metropolitan area includes Jefferson, Bullitt, and Oldham counties in Kentucky and Clark, Floyd, Harrison, and Scott counties in Indiana.

If you're planning a Louisville vacation, you'll be glad to know that any time of year makes for a pleasant visit. Summers average 75 degrees; winters are on the chilly side at 35 degrees.

Family Lodging

Hyatt Regency Louisville

This hotel's downtown location is a good place for families who plan to spend a couple of days in Louisville and want to be near the action. There are two restaurants on site, an indoor pool, an exercise room, and a gigantic atrium that rises 18 stories. Rates start at $169. 320 West Jefferson Street, Louisville; (502) 587-3434 or (800) 633-7313; www.hyatt.com.

Seelbach Hilton

First opened in 1905, this hotel was featured in F. Scott Fitzgerald's *The Great Gatsby.* It is Louisville's only four-star, four-diamond hotel, and it features

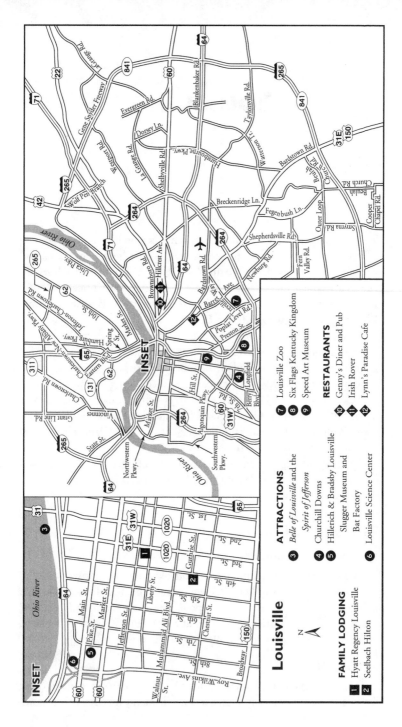

Louisville

N

FAMILY LODGING

1 Hyatt Regency Louisville
2 Seelbach Hilton

ATTRACTIONS

3 Belle of Louisville and the Spirit of Jefferson
4 Churchill Downs
5 Hillerich & Bradsby Louisville Slugger Museum and Bat Factory
6 Louisville Science Center
7 Louisville Zoo
8 Six Flags Kentucky Kingdom
9 Speed Art Museum

RESTAURANTS

10 Genny's Diner and Pub
11 Irish Rover
12 Lynn's Paradise Cafe

Kentucky's first and only five-diamond restaurant. The rooms have four-poster beds and marble baths, and there is a pool on property. Though it might be a bit upscale for families with rowdy toddlers, the Seelbach is the place to stay in Louisville—and it has a convenient downtown location. Rates begin at $139. 500 Fourth Street, Louisville; (502) 585-3200 or (800) 774-1500, www.hilton.com.

Attractions

Belle of Louisville and the Spirit of Jefferson

Fourth Street Wharf, Louisville; (502) 574-2992
www.belleoflouisville.com

Hours: Daily in summer at 1 p.m.; days for spring and fall cruises vary

Admission: $10 adults, $9 seniors, $6 children, free ages 2 and younger

Appeal by Age Group:

Pre-school	Grade School	Teens	Young Adults	Over 30	Seniors
★★	★★★	★★★	★★★	★★★	★★★

Average Touring Time: 3 hours

Minimum Touring Time: 3 hours

Rainy Day Touring: Not recommended

Author's Rating: ★★★

Services and Facilities:

Restaurants Yes	Lockers No
Alcoholic beverages No	Pet kennels No
Disabled access Yes	Rain check No
Wheelchair rental No	Private tours No
Baby stroller rental No	

Description and Comments   Louisville offers river cruises aboard two different steamboats. At 85 years old, the *Belle of Louisville* is the nation's oldest operating steamboat, and as such, designated a National Historic Landmark. The *Spirit of Jefferson* also plies the waters of the Ohio River in Mark Twain–style. Cruises are available from late spring through fall; specialty cruises are offered for certain holidays and events. The most popular cruise, the sightseeing cruise, includes narration about the history of the river and the city. It lasts two hours. Other cruises include a sunset cruise, a riverside cruise, and a Saturday-night party cruise. While this may seem like a good activity for families, we found that younger children get bored about halfway through the cruise. Take along books or something to keep them occupied until the end of the cruise.

Churchill Downs

700 Central Avenue, Louisville; (502) 636-4400
www.churchilldowns.com

Hours: May–July and November weekdays: gates open at 1:30 p.m.,
races at 3 p.m.; weekends: gates open at 11:30 a.m., races at 1 p.m.;
closed December–March; museum: daily 9 a.m.–5 p.m.

Admission: General admission, $2 adults, $1 seniors, free for children
ages 12 and younger; clubhouse reserved seating, $2

Appeal by Age Group:

Pre-school	Grade School	Teens	Young Adults	Over 30	Seniors
★★★	★★★	★★★	★★★★	★★★★	★★★★

Average Touring Time: 2½ hours

Minimum Touring Time: 1 hour

Rainy Day Touring: Not recommended

Author's Rating: ★★★   Thrilling to watch the races

Services and Facilities:

Restaurants Yes	Lockers No
Alcoholic beverages Yes	Pet kennels No
Disabled access Yes	Rain check No
Wheelchair rental No	Private tours Yes
Baby stroller rental No	

Description and Comments   Opened in 1875, Churchill Downs is known
throughout the world as the home of the Kentucky Derby, the first jewel
of the Triple Crown. On Derby Day, which falls the first Saturday in May,
seats are impossible to finagle, and if you do happen to find tickets, expect
to pay a pretty penny. We suggest visiting at another time when you can
take in the course and the museum. If you are early risers, check out Dawn
at the Downs, when the horses are out for exercise during the early morning hours (for information call (502) 636-3351; cost is $10.95).

The Kentucky Derby Museum at Churchill Downs (phone (502) 637-
1111; cost $6) offers hourly tours. Learn about the history of the Derby, test
your Derby trivia, watch a 360-degree slide presentation, tour the Downs,
and demystify the intricacies of parimutuel betting. Additionally, you can see
memorabilia and photos of some of its famous champions, including jockey
clothing, Kentucky Derby trophy sketches, collectable Kentucky Derby
glass, exhibits on the history of Derby dress and the mint julep.

Hillerich & Bradsby Louisville Slugger Museum and Bat Factory

800 West Main Street, Louisville; (502) 588-7227
www.slugger.com

Hours: Monday–Saturday, 9 a.m.–5 p.m.

Admission: $5 adults, $4.50 seniors, $3 children ages 6–12, free for children ages 5 and younger

Appeal by Age Group:

Pre-school	Grade School	Teens	Young Adults	Over 30	Seniors
★★★	★★★★	★★★★	★★★★	★★★★	★★★★★

Average Touring Time: 1½ hours

Minimum Touring Time: 1 hour

Rainy Day Touring: Recommended

Author's Rating: ★★★

Services and Facilities:

Restaurants No	Lockers No
Alcoholic beverages No	Pet kennels No
Disabled access Yes	Rain check N/A
Wheelchair rental Yes	Private tours Yes
Baby stroller rental No	

Description and Comments   There's no way you can miss this museum. Outside, a 120-foot, 68,000-pound baseball bat modeled after Babe Ruth's Louisville Slugger sits at the entrance. Inside is everything you want to know and more about the world of baseball and bat making. Hillerich and Bradsby began making bats over 100 years ago, and the likes of Babe Ruth, Yogi Berra, and Joe DiMaggio used Louisville Sluggers. The tour includes displays of historic World Series bats; interactive exhibits such as a pitching machine, full-size dugout, and a museum playing field; and a replica of a white ash forest, the wood used to make the bats. You'll also see how the bats are made, and kids get a 16-inch bat as a souvenir. If you are so inclined, you can order a bat at the beginning of the tour and pick up your own personalized slugger at the end.

Louisville Science Center

727 West Main Street, Louisville; (502) 561-6100
www.lsclouienet.org

Hours: Monday–Thursday, 10 a.m.–5 p.m., Friday–Saturday, 10 a.m.–
9 p.m.; Sunday, noon–6 p.m.

Admission: Exhibit only: $5.50 adults, $4.50 seniors and children ages 2–
12; exhibit and IMAX: $7.50 adults, $6 seniors and children ages 2–12

Appeal by Age Group:

Pre-school	Grade School	Teens	Young Adults	Over 30	Seniors
★★★★★	★★★★★	★★★★★	★★★★	★★★★	★★★★

Average Touring Time: ½ day

Minimum Touring Time: 2 hours

Rainy Day Touring: Recommended

Author's Rating: ★★★★   Stimulating visit

Services and Facilities:

Restaurants Yes	Lockers Yes
Alcoholic beverages No	Pet kennels No
Disabled access Yes	Rain check No
Wheelchair rental Yes	Private tours No
Baby stroller rental Yes	

Description and Comments   This science center strives to bring out the
"little scientist in all of us," and we have to agree that it does. The exhibits
are engaging, from the interactive displays that stretch the brains of
teenagers to the plenty of objects for little hands to touch and feel. Permanent exhibits include The World We Create, a tribute to man's inventions with 50 areas for kids to investigate and invent things of their own.
The Mummy's Tomb allows you to examine a 3,400-year-old mummy and
compare customs of ancient Egypt to those of our own. In Natural Selections, explore rocks, minerals, fossils, and other artifacts in order to learn
about a century's worth of natural history. And in the Permanent Tooth,
discover everything you need to know about your teeth, from structure and
development to good nutrition and brushing techniques. There is also an
IMAX theater with changing shows.

Louisville Zoo

1100 Trevilian Way, Louisville; (502) 459-2181
www.louisvillezoo.com

Hours: Daily, 10 a.m.–5 p.m.; closes at 4 p.m. September through-
March; stays open until 8 p.m. Wednesday–Friday from June–August

Admission: $7.95 adults, $5.95 seniors, $4.95 children, free ages 2 and
younger; train: $1.75; tram: $1.50

Appeal by Age Group:

Pre-school	Grade School	Teens	Young Adults	Over 30	Seniors
★★★★★	★★★★★	★★★★★	★★★★	★★★★	★★★★

Average Touring Time: ½ day

Minimum Touring Time: 2 hours

Rainy Day Touring: Not recommended

Author's Rating: ★★★★★ A pleasure to visit

Services and Facilities:

Restaurants Yes	Lockers No
Alcoholic beverages No	Pet kennels No
Disabled access Yes	Rain check No
Wheelchair rental Yes	Private tours No
Baby stroller rental Yes	

Description and Comments   More than 1,300 animals are on display at this 75-acre naturalistic zoo. The Herp-Aquarium, a simulated rain forest, is a favorite exhibit, with smoky jungle frogs as the newest resident. Another popular place for kids is Boma, an African petting zoo. Rather than have the same old American farm animals, this village-style petting zoo features those of Africa. The entire African Outpost section resembles turn-of-the-century Africa, where "remote villages" provide food and supplies to travelers. A new concept, the Islands exhibit, has several different species rotating though the same exhibit area—an idea that simulates a natural habitat.

Six Flags Kentucky Kingdom

937 Phillips Lane, Louisville; (502) 366-2231
   www.sixflags.com/kentuckykingdom

Hours: June–August, weekdays 10 a.m.–9 p.m., weekends until 10 p.m.;
   May, September–October open weekends; closed November–April

Admission: $29.99 adults, $15 seniors and children; parking: $3

Appeal by Age Group:

Pre-school	Grade School	Teens	Young Adults	Over 30	Seniors
★★★★	★★★★★	★★★★★	★★★	★★★	★★★

Average Touring Time: 1 day

Minimum Touring Time: ½ day

Rainy Day Touring: Not recommended

Author's Rating: ★★★ A real kid-pleaser

Services and Facilities:

Restaurants Yes	Lockers Yes
Alcoholic beverages No	Pet kennels No
Disabled access Yes	Rain check No
Wheelchair rental Yes	Private tours No
Baby stroller rental Yes	

Description and Comments   Another amusement park in the Six Flags family, Kentucky Kingdom has a good variety of rides and shows for both teenagers and toddlers. Two of the most thrilling rides are the Hellevator, a 15-story, free-fall ride, and Chang, a stand-up roller coaster over 4,000 feet long. For younger kids, the rides and shows are named after Warner Brothers characters. The Road Runner Express has cars that travel separately along the track instead of being hooked together. The Looney Tunes ACME Prop Warehouse is an interactive tree house with foam balls, and A'Wound the World in 80 Seconds lets kids become the pilot of a hot-air balloon.

Speed Art Museum

2035 South Third Street, Louisville; (502) 634-2700
   www.speedmuseum.org

Hours: Tuesday, Wednesday, Friday 10:30 a.m.–4 p.m., Thursday
   10:30 a.m.–8 p.m., Saturday 10:30 a.m.–5 p.m., Sunday noon–5 p.m.

Admission: Free; Art Sparks is $3.50

Appeal by Age Group:

Pre-school	Grade School	Teens	Young Adults	Over 30	Seniors
★★★★	★★★★★	★★★★★	★★★★★	★★★★★	★★★★★

Average Touring Time: ½ day

Minimum Touring Time: 2 hours

Rainy Day Touring: Recommended

Author's Rating: ★★★★★   Exceptional art learning center

Services and Facilities:

Restaurants Yes	Lockers Yes
Alcoholic beverages No	Pet kennels No
Disabled access Yes	Rain check No
Wheelchair rental Yes	Private tours No
Baby stroller rental Yes	

Description and Comments   Kentucky's oldest art museum has an impressive collection, with works by Rembrandt, Rubens, Monet, and Thomas Moore, to name a few. But what really impressed us was the new Art Sparks, an interactive art learning center with funky workshops and activities to help kids and families connect with art. Some examples include dancing inside a moving video artwork, creating digital art with a computer, video-taping your opinion about a particular piece, and trying on a Dutch collar and cape. For preschoolers, Planet Preschool brings art to a level they can understand and enjoy.

Side Trips

A Day in the Park   Louisville's city park system is the work of famed designer Frederick Law Olmsted, the same designer of New York City's Central Park. Cherokee, Iroquois, and Shawnee parks are part of his original plans and reflect his philosophy that each park should be consistent with its natural topographic attributes as well as its social function within the community. Because of Olmsted's foresight, Louisville and Jefferson County currently have 9,375 acres of parkland, making it one of the nation's top cities in the ratio of parkland per citizen. For park information, call (502) 456-8130.

Abraham Lincoln Birthplace National Historic Site, Hodgenville   This 116-acre park—a third of the size of the Lincoln's original farm—serves as a memorial to Abraham Lincoln. Lincoln was born here in 1809 in a one-room log cabin almost identical to the one preserved in the Memorial Building. Other objects also tell the story of Lincoln's childhood, including tools and utensils representative of the period and the Lincoln family Bible.

The cross-section of a large oak that once stood as a boundary marker for the Lincoln Farm is one of the most interesting objects we found in the park. On display in the visitors center, the growth rings on the wood are labeled with a chronology of events of Lincoln's life.

Also of interest to families are the two miles of hiking trails, a film on Lincoln's life in Kentucky, and programs and talks about Lincoln in the Memorial Building.

The park is open November through March, daily 8 a.m.–4:45 p.m.; April, May, September, October, daily 8 a.m.–5:45 p.m.; and June through August daily 8 a.m.–5:45 p.m. Admission is free. 2995 Lincoln Farm Road, U.S. 31 East to Route 61, three miles south of Hodgenville; (502) 358-3137; www.www.nps.gov/abli.

Family-Friendly Restaurants

GENNY'S DINER AND PUB

2227 Frankfort Avenue, Louisville; (502) 893-0923

Meals served: Breakfast, lunch, and dinner
Cuisine: American

Entrée range: $6 and up
Kids menu: Yes
Reservations: Yes
Payment: Cash only

Genny's is known for its "frickle pickles," but good hamburgers and friendly service are also customary. A family fun place close to Louisville attractions.

IRISH ROVER

2319 Frankfort Avenue, Louisville; (502) 899-3544

Meals served: Lunch and dinner
Cuisine: Irish
Entrée range: $4.95 and up
Kids menu: Yes
Reservations: Yes
Payment: All major credit cards accepted

Irish Rover is the place to go for comfort food, especially when fast food has been your family's primary vacation fare. House specialties are fish 'n' chips and cottage pie (similar to shepherd's pie). The atmosphere is that of a relaxed and casual Irish pub.

LYNN'S PARADISE CAFE

984 Barret Avenue, Louisville; (502) 583-EGGS

Meals served: Breakfast, lunch, and dinner
Cuisine: American
Entrée range: $4.95 and up
Kids menu: Yes
Reservations: Yes
Payment: All major credit cards accepted

This funky eatery serves Louisville's favorite home cooking.

Lexington

Its sounds cliché to call a city picture-perfect, but with its rolling hills, meandering rock fences, network of streams, and manicured horse farms, Lexington is just that. Known as the heart of bluegrass country, the city was founded in 1775. By the early 1800s, it was one of the largest and wealthiest towns west of the Allegheny Mountains—so cultured that it was nicknamed the "Athens of the West." Today, the Lexington area includes parts of Fayette, Bourbon, Clark, Jessamine, Madison, Scott, and Woodford counties.

It's hard to simply pass through Lexington because there are so many family-friendly attractions to visit. Not surprisingly, many of them have something to do with our four-footed friends. There's the **Kentucky Horse Park,** the **American Saddle Horse Museum,** tours at **Keeneland** and the **Red Mile Harness Track,** horse farm visits, and riding stables.

Yet that's not to say that this is a one-horse town. Lexington is also a university town, a fact that gives the city a lively, young feel. The campus is ideal for impromptu picnics, and there is plenty of free or low-cost entertainment to be found, including catching a Kentucky Wildcats basketball game—one of the most successful programs in collegiate basketball.

If you have only a day to spend in the city, plan an equestrian itinerary. Visit museums in the morning to learn about the city's rich horse history then head to the stables for an afternoon of horsing around.

Note: The area code for the Lexington area has changed from 606 to 859.

Family Lodging

B&B at Halifax Lane Farm

Who's sleeping downstairs? A horse, of course! The upstairs of the old foaling barn at Halifax Lane Farm has been renovated into luxurious guest accommodations, complete with a panoramic view of horse farms and the stonewall-lined Yarnallton Road. Downstairs, it's still a horse barn, with stalls outfitted with tile walls and wooden floors. Halifax Lane Farm is outside the

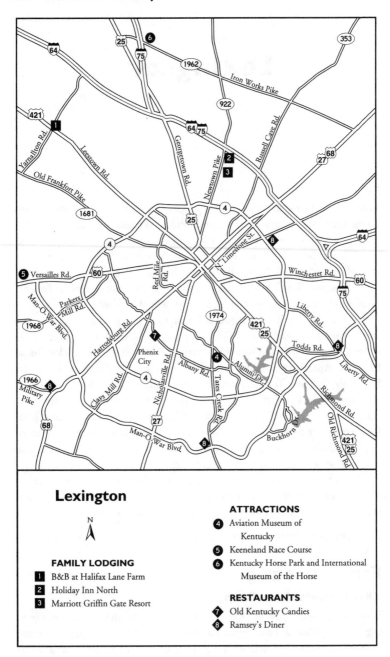

Lexington

N
Λ

FAMILY LODGING

1 B&B at Halifax Lane Farm
2 Holiday Inn North
3 Marriott Griffin Gate Resort

ATTRACTIONS

4 Aviation Museum of
   Kentucky
5 Keeneland Race Course
6 Kentucky Horse Park and International
   Museum of the Horse

RESTAURANTS

7 Old Kentucky Candies
8 Ramsey's Diner

city, but the grounds are perfect for kids—and parents—who are tired of hotel stays. 1201 North Yarnallton Road, Lexington; (859) 225-5485.

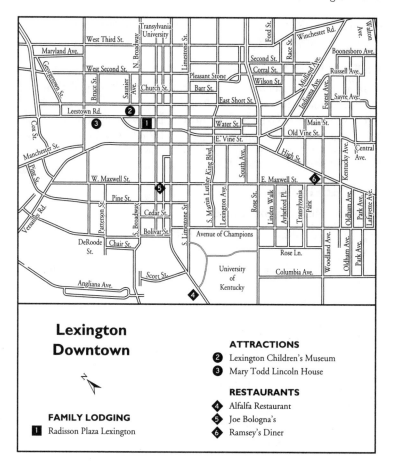

Lexington Downtown

N

FAMILY LODGING

1 Radisson Plaza Lexington

ATTRACTIONS

2 Lexington Children's Museum
3 Mary Todd Lincoln House

RESTAURANTS

4 Alfalfa Restaurant
5 Joe Bologna's
6 Ramsey's Diner

Holiday Inn North

One of the first properties in the nation to have a "fun-tronics" center with video and virtual-reality games, this Holiday Inn also has a Holidome with an indoor amusement arcade, indoor pool, basketball court, and health facilities. The property is near the Kentucky Horse Park and the Kentucky Horse Center. Rates begin at $69. Newtown Pike at I-75/I-64, Lexington; (800) HOLIDAY or (859) 233-0512.

Marriott Griffin Gate Resort

One of Lexington's nicest resorts, the Marriott has all the amenities of a full-service hotel plus an 18-hole golf course, tennis courts, indoor/outdoor pools, a sauna, a fitness center, children's programs, and a sand volleyball court. The resort is close to the Kentucky Horse Park and the Mary Todd

Lincoln house. Rates begin at $129. 1800 Newtown Pike (Exit 115, I-75), Lexington; (800) 228-9290 or (859) 231-5100; www.marriotthotels.com.

Radisson Plaza Lexington

Centrally located to all downtown attractions, the University of Kentucky, and Victorian Square Shoppes, the Radisson has a pool and health club and a combination of standard hotel rooms and suites with in-room whirlpools. Pets are allowed. Rates begin at $79. 369 West Vine Street, Lexington; (800) 333-3333 or (859) 231-9000; www.radisson.com.

Attractions

Aviation Museum of Kentucky

Hangar Drive, Lexington; (859) 231-1219
   www.aviationky.org

Hours: Tuesday, Thursday, Friday, Saturday, 10 a.m.–5 p.m.; Sunday,
   1–5 p.m.

Admission: $3 adults, $2 seniors, $1.50 children

Appeal by Age Group:

Pre-school	Grade School	Teens	Young Adults	Over 30	Seniors
★★★★	★★★★	★★★	★★★	★★★★	★★★★★

Average Touring Time: 1 hour

Minimum Touring Time: 45 minutes

Rainy Day Touring: Recommended

Author's Rating: ★★★

Services and Facilities:

Restaurants No	Lockers No
Alcoholic beverages No	Pet kennels No
Disabled access Yes	Rain check N/A
Wheelchair rental Yes	Private tours Yes
Baby stroller rental No	

Description and Comments   If you can't fly the friendly skies, you can at least get up close to aircraft that do. Located at Blue Grass Airport, this museum has a variety of air-worthy and restored aircraft on display, along with memorabilia and exhibits about the history and legends of aviation. Some of the planes you'll see include an A-4F Skyhawk II from the Blue Angels Navy Flight Demonstration Squadron, a Stearman Model 75, and a Cessna UC-78 Bobcat used in WWII. There is also a replica of a quadra-plane, a fabric and bamboo contraption that was the first powered flying machine flown in Kentucky. For kids, the Augusta Bell, a 206B observer helicopter, is one of the highlights because you can sit inside and fiddle with the gauges, levers, and buttons. Many of the volunteers are aviation buffs or war veterans who can tell you about the history of each aircraft, along with personal stories about flying.

Keeneland Race Course

4201 Versailles Road, Lexington; (800) 456-3412 or (859) 254-3412
  www.keeneland.com

Hours: Daily 6:30 a.m.–5 p.m.; races in April and October

Admission: $2.50 adults, free for children ages 12 and younger

Appeal by Age Group:

Pre-school	Grade School	Teens	Young Adults	Over 30	Seniors
★★★★★	★★★★★	★★★★★	★★★★★	★★★★★	★★★★★

Average Touring Time: 1 hour

Minimum Touring Time: 30 minutes

Rainy Day Touring: Not recommended

Author's Rating: ★★★★★   Breakfast with the Works is a unique opportunity to meet jockeys and learn about the horses

Services and Facilities:

Restaurants Yes	Lockers No
Alcoholic beverages Yes	Pet kennels No
Disabled access Yes	Rain check N/A
Wheelchair rental Yes	Private tours Yes
Baby stroller rental No	

Description and Comments   Designated as a National Historic Landmark, Keeneland is home of the Blue Grass Stakes, a popular horse race that measures an eighth of a mile shorter than the Derby's one-and-one-fourth miles. Racing occurs in April and October, and on Saturday's during these months, you can participate in Breakfast with the Works, where you eat breakfast with jockeys, horse owners, and trainers in the equestrian dining room from 7–8:30 a.m. Afterwards, watch as the horses work out around the track, get photos made in the pint-sized jockey outfits, rub on Keeneland tattoos, and take in a horseshoe toss. A 30-minute program is also held trackside, featuring expert speakers in the field, from vets to jockeys. The full buffet breakfast is $4 and free for ages 3 and younger. Other activities are free, and reservations are not required. Mid-March to late November provides another unique experience of viewing public workouts. These are scheduled daily from 6–10 a.m. on the main track. Additionally, there is a thoroughbred sale five times a year. Fusaichi Pegasus, the 2000 Derby winner, was purchased at one of these sales.

Kentucky Horse Park and International Museum of the Horse

4089 Iron Works Pike, off I-75, Lexington; (800) 678-8813 or (859) 233-4303; www.imh.org

Hours: April 1–October 31, daily 9 a.m.–5 p.m.

Admission: $16 adults, $11 for children ages 7–12

Appeal by Age Group:

Pre-school	Grade School	Teens	Young Adults	Over 30	Seniors
★★★★★	★★★★★	★★★★★	★★★★★	★★★★★	★★★★★

Average Touring Time: 4 hours

Minimum Touring Time: 2 hours

Rainy Day Touring: Museum recommended; horse park not recommended

Author's Rating: ★★★★★   Everything you want to know about the horse and more

Services and Facilities:

Restaurants Yes	Lockers Yes
Alcoholic beverages No	Pet kennels No
Disabled access Yes	Rain check Yes
Wheelchair rental Yes	Private tours No
Baby stroller rental Yes	

Description and Comments   The only disadvantage to visiting this park is deciding where to start. The International Museum of the Horse leaves nothing to guesswork in tracing the 58-million-year history of the horse, beginning with eophippus, the tiny first horse, to the variety of horse breeds in modern times. Interactive exhibits include collections of carriages and racing vehicles, trophies won at various race courses, equine art, information about more than 85 breeds of horses from around the world, and displays about owners and breeders. One of the most interesting sections is "Calumet Farm: Five Decades of Champions," an exhibit that highlights the racing legacy of Lexington's most famous farm. An hour will only skim the surface of what this museum has to offer; if you or your kids are equestrian buffs, plan to spend at least a couple of hours. If that's not enough, the American Saddle Horse Museum, also on the grounds, highlights the history of the American Saddlebreed, Kentucky's only native breed. For information on the museum, phone (800) 829-4438 or (606) 259-2746.

Once you work your way through the museum, head for the working horse farm. From April to October, a Parade of Breeds is held twice daily to showcase the farm's 45 breeds of horses and their unique characteristics.

Afterwards, you can pet the horses and ask owners and riders questions. The Hall of Champions presentation gives you a chance to get up close to the farm's retired race horses, and again, it's a good time to ask questions. These sessions are held three times daily—at 10:15 a.m., 1 p.m., and 3:30 p.m.

The farm also has daily presentations on the thoroughbred, standard-bred, and quarter horses. Depending on the time of year you visit, you can take in a horse event—the park hosts over 60 horse shows and events each year in the indoor arena, steeple-chase course, polo fields, and dressage and show rings.

Your visit to the park won't be complete without a ride on a horse. Horse-back rides, carriage rides, and horse-drawn streetcar rides are all options.

Lexington Children's Museum

440 West Short Street, Lexington; (859) 258-3256
www.lfucg.com/childrensmuseum

Hours: Tuesday–Friday, 10 a.m.–6 p.m.; Saturday, 10 a.m.–5 p.m.; Sunday, 1–5 p.m.

Admission: $3, free for children ages 1 and younger

Appeal by Age Group:

Pre-school	Grade School	Teens	Young Adults	Over 30	Seniors
★★★★★	★★★★★	★★★★★	★★★★★	★★★★★	★★★★★

Average Touring Time: 1½ hours

Minimum Touring Time: 1 hour

Rainy Day Touring: Recommended

Author's Rating: ★★★ Good presentation of science

Services and Facilities:

Restaurants No	Lockers No
Alcoholic beverages No	Pet kennels No
Disabled access Yes	Rain check N/A
Wheelchair rental No	Private tours Yes
Baby stroller rental No	

Description and Comments Learning is fun at this hands-on museum—so fun that kids won't realize its educational bent. There are seven galleries in all ranging in scope from nature, history, and science to geography and archaeology. At Brainzilla, touch a giant brain and then see the real thing. Natural Wonders features a tyrannosaurus rex skull, dinosaur eggs, hands-on fossils, and a mountain climbing wall. The Home exhibit, with its Samoan dinner and camel-powered mobile home, explains how children live around the world. In Heartscape, walk through a giant heart and lungs.

And while the Bubble Factory is certainly not the most sophisticated exhibit at the museum, it's a hands-down kids' favorite. They just love to play with bubbles, and here they can find out what it feels like to be inside a giant bubble. The museum is attached to the Lexington Children's Theatre.

Mary Todd Lincoln House

578 West Main Street, Lexington; (859) 233-9999

Hours: Tuesday–Saturday, 10 a.m.– 4 p.m.; closed December–mid-March

Admission: $6 adults, $3 ages 5 and younger

Appeal by Age Group:

Pre-school	Grade School	Teens	Young Adults	Over 30	Seniors
★	★★	★★★	★★★	★★★	★★★

Average Touring Time: 45 minutes

Minimum Touring Time: 30 minutes

Rainy Day Touring: Recommended

Author's Rating: ★★★

Services and Facilities:

Restaurants No	Lockers No
Alcoholic beverages No	Pet kennels No
Disabled access No	Rain check N/A
Wheelchair rental No	Private tours Yes
Baby stroller rental No	

Description and Comments   This stop won't win any points for being exciting and fun, but it does carry great historical significance. Born in to one of Lexington's most influential families, Mary Todd married Abraham Lincoln and became one of America's most controversial first ladies. Mary lived in this house until she was 21, and she and Lincoln visited several times after they married. Today, you'll see family furniture and heirlooms, and a few of Mary's personal items. One other area of note about this Georgian-style brick house is the backyard herb and perennial garden, designed in the fashion of gardens of the mid-1800s.

Side Trips

Llama Trekking   Hiking may have been your family's favorite pastime before you visited Kentucky, but after a llama trek in Woodford County, you can bet that it's likely to change. The trek at Seldom Scene Farm follows a scenic, wooded trail near the Kentucky River, with you leading a llama that carries your gear. The two-to-three mile hike includes a gourmet lunch and a tour of the farm, which is home to about 20 llamas, 30 alpacas, a yak, miniature donkeys, goats, and reindeer. 1710 Watts Ferry Road; (859) 873-1622.

Fort Boonesborough State Park, Richmond It doesn't take a rocket scientist to guess who this park is named after. Daniel Boone, along with Richard Henderson, scouted this area for the Transylvania Company in 1775. The log cabins, fort, and stockade they built established a settlement that would remain a stopping point and trade center on the Kentucky River for the next 50 years. However, by 1820, Boonesborough had become a ghost town. Today, reconstruction of the early settlement lets visitors experience pioneer life and learn about the travels of Daniel Boone.

If the park is on your itinerary, there are several ways you can occupy your time. One of our favorites is the Kentucky Riverwalk Trail, a self-guided nature trail with information about native plants, animals, historic and geologic sites posted along the trail.

Another personal favorite is the pool complex. A junior Olympic-size swimming pool with a water slide, misty fountain, and special children's area is a good way to beat the heat. There is also a sand beach perfect for sunbathing.

If you are more interested in history, the park offers a combination guided tour of the fort and White Hall State Historic Site, the home of abolitionist Cassius Clay. Tours are offered daily from 9 a.m.–5:30 p.m. from April 1 through October 31.

Other diversions include fishing, boating, a putt-putt golf course, two gift shops with a selection of Kentucky crafts, and 167 campsites with water and electrical hookups. The campground also features daily planned activities for both adults and children from Memorial Day through Labor Day. The park is open April through September daily from 9 a.m.–5:30 p.m., and Wednesday through Sunday from Labor Day through October 31. Off U.S. Highway 25 at 4375 Boonesboro Road, Richmond; (800) 255-7275 or (859) 527-3131; www.state.ky.us/agencies/parks/ftboones.htm.

Hummel Planetarium & Space Theatre, Richmond This attraction will have you seeing stars. Located at Eastern Kentucky University, the Hummel is one of the largest and most sophisticated planetariums in the United States. There are no telescopes here; instead, programs are projected onto a dome screen. The topics change throughout the year, so call ahead for a program schedule. The planetarium is open year-round, with a children's show at 5 p.m. and a main feature at 7 p.m. on Thursday and Friday. On Saturday, the children's features are at 2 and 6 p.m., the main features at 3:30 and 7:30 p.m.. Admission is $4 adults, $3.50 seniors and students, and $3 for children ages 12 and younger. Kit Carson Drive, Lexington; (859) 622-1547; www.planetarium.eku.edu.

Family-Friendly Restaurants

ALFALFA RESTAURANT

557 South Limestone Street, Lexington; (859) 253-0014

Meals served: Lunch and dinner
Cuisine: Italian/Greek
Entrée range: $5.25 and up
Kids menu: No
Reservations: Yes
Payment: All major credit cards accepted

Italian and Greek dishes are served at this old-fashioned restaurant. A different cuisine is highlighted each Wednesday night, giving you the opportunity to try a variety of ethnic foods.

JOE BOLOGNA'S

120 Maxwell Street, Lexington; (859) 252-4933

Meals served: Lunch and dinner
Cuisine: Italian/American
Entrée range: $4.95 and up
Kids menu: Yes
Reservations: No
Payment: All major credit cards accepted

Close to downtown and the University of Kentucky campus, Joe Bologna's has long been a family favorite. You could say the food here is blessed, as the restaurant is housed in an old synagogue. Pastas and pizzas are the house specialties.

OLD KENTUCKY CANDIES

450 Southland Drive, Lexington; (800) 786-0579 and (606) 278-4444
www.oldkycandy.com

Meals served: N/A
Cuisine: N/A
Entrée range: N/A
Kids menu: N/A
Reservations: N/A
Payment: All major credit cards accepted

This is the place to go for bourbon chocolates and cherries, both made with 100-proof Jim Beam Kentucky bourbon. Kids will be just as happy with the handmade chocolates sans the liquor. The store also gives free tours of their facility.

RAMSEYS DINER

496 East High Street, Lexington; (859) 259-2708

4053 Tates Creek Center, Lexington; (859) 271-2638

1660 Bryan Station Road, Lexington; (859) 299-9669

4391 Harrodsburg Road, Lexington; (859) 219-1626

3090 Helmsdale Drive, Lexington; (859) 264-9396

Meals served: Lunch and dinner
Cuisine: American
Entrée range: $3.50
Kids menu: Yes
Reservations: No
Payment: All major credit cards accepted

There aren't too many places you can go to get a peanut butter and jelly sandwich. Ramseys also serves home-cooked meals and is known for sandwiches like the "hot brown," an open-faced turkey sandwich smothered with gravy. The original location is downtown on High Street, and there are four others in the city.

Frankfort

Founded as a frontier outpost, Frankfort is capital of the Commonwealth, a designation it received in 1792 as a compromise between the largest cities of Louisville and Lexington. History in Frankfort is alive and well, evident in the number of historic homes available for tour, the grand architecture of government buildings, and at the **Kentucky History Center,** a repository with interactive exhibits about the state's past.

One of the most unique stops in Frankfort is the huge floral clock outside of the capitol. One of the most moving is the **Vietnam Veteran's Memorial.** The memorial is a giant sundial inscribed with the names of all Kentuckians who lost their lives in the war. The sundial casts a shadow on each name on the anniversary of that veteran's death.

For travelers flying in to the capital city, the Lexington Bluegrass Airport is 25 minutes away and the Louisville International Airport is about 1½ hours away.

Family Lodging

Hampton Inn
Located near the intersection of I-64 and U.S. Highway 127, the Hampton has an outdoor swimming pool, exercise facilities, and a complementary continental breakfast buffet. There are free local calls, free in-room movie channels, and a microwave and refrigerator in each room to round out the amenities. Children under 18 stay free. Rates begin at $49. 1310 U.S. 127 South; (502) 223-7600, or (800) HAMPTON; www.hamptoninn.com.

Holiday Inn – Capital Plaza
Close to the Kentucky History Center, this Holiday Inn has an atrium lobby with a waterfall fountain, indoor pool, whirlpool, sauna, exercise, room, and covered parking. It adjoins the Fountain Place Shops and the Civic Center.

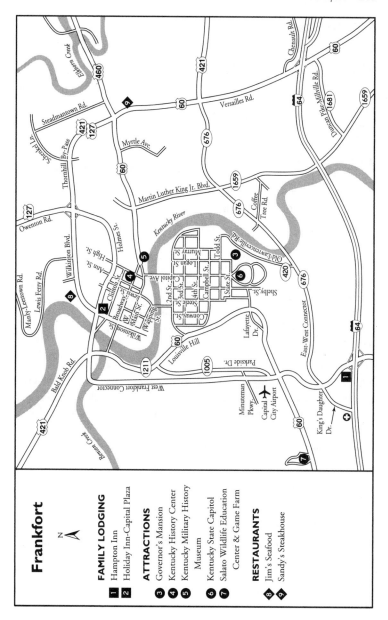

Frankfort

N

FAMILY LODGING
1 Hampton Inn
2 Holiday Inn–Capital Plaza

ATTRACTIONS
3 Governor's Mansion
4 Kentucky History Center
5 Kentucky Military History Museum
6 Kentucky State Capitol
7 Salato Wildlife Education Center & Game Farm

RESTAURANTS
8 Jim's Seafood
9 Sandy's Steakhouse

Rates begin at $69. 405 Wilkinson Boulevard; (502) 227-5100; (800) HOLI-DAY; www.holidayinnfrankfort.com.

Attractions

Governor's Mansion

Capital Avenue, Frankfort; (502) 564-3449

Hours: Tuesday and Thursday, 9–11 a.m.

Admission: Free

Appeal by Age Group:

Pre-school	Grade School	Teens	Young Adults	Over 30	Seniors
★	★★	★★★	★★★	★★★	★★★

Average Touring Time: ½ hour

Minimum Touring Time: ½ hour

Rainy Day Touring: Not recommended

Author's Rating: ★★★

Services and Facilities:

Restaurants No	Lockers No
Alcoholic beverages No	Pet kennels No
Disabled access Yes	Rain check N/A
Wheelchair rental No	Private tours No
Baby stroller rental No	

Descriptsion and Comments   For about two seconds, kids will enjoy touring the Governor's Mansion. After that, it's going to seem like just another big house. The tour is downstairs only and includes the ballroom, hall, parlor, formal salon, and state dining room. The mansion, constructed from native limestone, is in the Beaux Arts style and was patterned after Petit Trianon, Marie Antoinette's villa at Versailles. The mansion is located next to the capitol.

Kentucky History Center

West Broadway, Frankfort; (877) 4-HISTORY, (502) 564-1792
   www.kyhistory.org

Hours: Tuesday–Saturday, 10 a.m.–5 p.m.; Thursday, until 8 p.m.;
   Sunday, 1–5 p.m.

Admission: Free

Appeal by Age Group:

Pre-school	Grade School	Teens	Young Adults	Over 30	Seniors
★	★★	★★★	★★★	★★★	★★★

Average Touring Time: 1½ hours

Minimum Touring Time: 45 minutes

Rainy Day Touring: Recommended

Author's Rating: ★★★

Services and Facilities:

Restaurants No	Lockers No
Alcoholic beverages No	Pet kennels No
Disabled access Yes	Rain check No
Wheelchair rental Yes	Private tours No
Baby stroller rental Yes	

Description and Comments   It's not that Kentucky has more history than other places. It's just that its residents seem to value their history more than other states. This center is testimony to Kentuckians' dedication. A genealogical research library, museum store, and the Kentucky History Museum are found here. Families will be most interested in the museum, which includes exhibits on 12,000 years of Kentucky history, from the survey notes penned by pioneer Daniel Boone to the state's World War II heroes. There are also changing exhibits on all things Kentucky. The most recent was "Saving Kentucky Treasures," a display of old Kentucky treasures that were taken out of storage for public viewing.

Kentucky Military History Museum

East Main Street, Frankfort; (502) 564-3265

www.state.ky.us/agencies/khs/museums/military/military_index.htm

Hours: Tuesday–Saturday, 10 a.m.–5 p.m.; Sunday, 1–5 p.m.

Admission: Free

Appeal by Age Group:

Pre-school	Grade School	Teens	Young Adults	Over 30	Seniors
★★	★★★	★★★	★★★	★★★	★★★★

Average Touring Time: 2 hours

Minimum Touring Time: 1 hour

Rainy Day Touring: Recommended

Author's Rating: ★★★

Services and Facilities:

Restaurants No	Lockers No
Alcoholic beverages No	Pet kennels No
Disabled access Yes	Rain check N/A
Wheelchair rental Yes	Private tours No
Baby stroller rental No	

Description and Comments   Trace the history of Kentucky's military heritage, including the service of the Kentucky Militia, State Guard, and other volunteer military organizations. For starters, the building itself is part of the story. It's an 1850 Old State Arsenal. Inside, weapons, uniforms, flags, photographs, stories from Kentucky veterans, and other memorabilia high-lighting Kentucky's part in various wars are on view. Check out the Civil War flags and Scud missile pieces.

Kentucky State Capitol

Capitol Avenue, Frankfort; (502) 564-3449

Hours: Monday–Saturday, 8:30 a.m.–4 pm.; Sunday, 1–4:30 p.m.; tours daily until 4 p.m.

Admission: Free

Appeal by Age Group:

Pre-school	Grade School	Teens	Young Adults	Over 30	Seniors
★★	★★★	★★★	★★★	★★★	★★★

Average Touring Time: 1 hour

Minimum Touring Time: 30 minutes

Rainy Day Touring: Not recommended

Author's Rating: ★★★

Services and Facilities:

Restaurants No	Lockers No
Alcoholic beverages No	Pet kennels No
Disabled access Yes	Rain check N/A
Wheelchair rental No	Private tours Yes
Baby stroller rental No	

Description and Comments   Completed in 1910, the capitol was designed in the Beaux Arts style and features 70 columns in all. Throughout the building there are murals and sculptures of important Kentuckians, and you can also see the First Lady doll collection. The first floor has changing history and cultural exhibits. That said and done, the most interesting part of the capitol to us is the working floral clock. The face of this outdoor timepiece is composed of thousands of flowers—and the large minute hand and smaller hour hand actually work.

Salato Wildlife Education Center & Game Farm

1 Game Farm Road (off U.S. 60); (502) 564-7863
www.state.ky.us/agencies/fw/wincal.htm

Hours: Game Farm grounds: daily from sunrise to sunset; Wildlife Center: November 1–April 30, Tuesday–Friday, 10 a.m.–4:30 p.m.; Saturday, until 5 p.m.; Sunday, 1 p.m.–5 p.m.; May 1–October 31, Tuesday–Friday, 9 a.m.–5 p.m.; Saturday until 6 p.m., Sunday, 1–6 p.m.

Admission: Game Farm grounds: free; Wildlife Center: $2 adults, $1 children

Appeal by Age Group:

Pre-school	Grade School	Teens	Young Adults	Over 30	Seniors
★★★★★	★★★★★	★★★★★	★★★★★	★★★★★	★★★★★

Average Touring Time: 3 hours

Minimum Touring Time: 2 hours

Rainy Day Touring: Not recommended

Author's Rating: ★★★★★

Services and Facilities:

Restaurants No	Lockers No
Alcoholic beverages No	Pet kennels No
Disabled access Yes	Rain check No
Wheelchair rental No	Private tours No
Baby stroller rental No	

Description and Comments Located three miles west of Frankfort, Salato teaches kids about the state's rich plant and animal life. The outdoor animal exhibits are no doubt the favorites among kids. See an American bald eagle, white-tailed deer, wild turkey, bison, and elk, and learn about their role in Kentucky history. Inside, there are life-size replicas of record-size fish caught in Kentucky, a diorama of a Kentucky forest, live Kentucky fish in a giant aquarium, and lots of live venomous native snakes. Call ahead and you can also participate in the center's scheduled educational programs for both adults and children. The center has public fishing lakes, designated points for watching wildlife, and a picnic area. Pack a lunch, your binoculars, and hiking shoes, and plan to spend time outdoors.

Side Trips

Frankfort Cemetery Kentucky's most famous pioneer, Daniel Boone, died in Missouri, but his remains were returned to Kentucky. He and his wife, Rebecca, now rest in peace at the Frankfort Cemetery overlooking the city. Other notables also buried here include artist Paul Sawyier, former vice president Richard M. Johnson, and 17 Kentucky governors. The cemetery is at 215 East Main Street and is open daily from 7 a.m.–4 p.m.; (502) 227-2403; www.findagrave.com/pictures/109.html.

Canoe Kentucky If you're looking for an outdoor activity away from the hustle and bustle of museums and amusement parks, slip on your swimsuit and grab a paddle. Kentucky has more running water than any state except Alaska. The state is blessed with recreational streams perfect for canoeing, and Frankfort in particular is noted for this pastime on the Kentucky River (Class I), Elkhorn Creek, and Benson Creek (Class I–II). Still Waters Canoe

Trails, (502) 223-8896, rents canoes on the Kentucky and Elkhorn and has guided moonlight tours available at certain times of the year. Canoe Kentucky offers guided and self-guided canoe and raft trips on the Elkhorn and Benson creeks and also has rentals available. Contact Canoe Kentucky at (800) KCANOE or (502) 227-4492; www.canoeky.com.

Family-Friendly Restaurants

JIM'S SEAFOOD

950 Wilkinson Boulevard, Frankfort; (502) 223-7448

Meals served: Lunch and dinner
Cuisine: Seafood
Entrée range: $9.25 and up
Kids menu: Yes
Reservations: No
Payment: All major credit cards accepted

Good seafood is hard to find, especially in Kentucky. But you'll be pleasantly surprised by the quality and the portions at Jim's. Another plus: Jim's is downtown, making it a good place to stop after touring the state buildings.

SANDY'S STEAKHOUSE

194 Versailles Road, Frankfort; (502) 695-3030

Meals served: Lunch and dinner
Cuisine: American
Entrée range: $5 and up
Kids menu: Yes
Reservations: No
Payment: All major credit cards accepted

Steaks, sandwiches, and salads are offered at Sandy's, one of the favorites among locals. The atmosphere is casual, and the location is convenient to Frankfort attractions.

Bowling Green

Situated in the south central part of Kentucky, Bowling Green is the fifth-largest city in the state. It is 60 miles from Nashville, making that city's airport the most affordable point of arrival for families flying in for a visit. During the Civil War, this central city was chosen as the Confederate capital of Kentucky. Today, walking tours highlight six historic areas, all listed on the National Register, and there is a **Bowling Green Civil War Driving Tour** that features visits to four forts. Tour information is available at the Visitors Center off I-65 at Exit 22.

Bowling Green is a good in-between stop for families traversing the state. There are several unique attractions, a variety of hotels, and over 300 restaurants in the area.

Note: The area code in western Kentucky has changed to 270. Bowling Green, like other parts of western Kentucky, is on Central Standard Time (CST).

Family Lodging

Best Western Motor Inn

The name is a throwback to the '50s, but the Best Western Motor Inn is actually one of the better places for families to stay in Bowling Green. There are indoor and outdoor swimming pools on the property, along with a playground, tennis courts, a whirlpool, a fitness center, and a game room. Suites are available, and all local calls are free. Rates begin at $65. I-65 at Exit 22 and U.S. Highway 231 South; (800) 343-2937 or (270) 782-3800; www.bestwestern.com.

University Plaza Hotel

The University Plaza Hotel is in downtown Bowling Green and close to local attractions. All rooms have a refrigerator and microwave, small pets

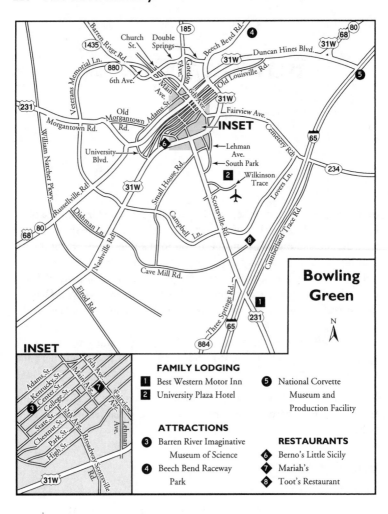

Bowling Green

N

INSET

FAMILY LODGING

1 Best Western Motor Inn
2 University Plaza Hotel

5 National Corvette
  Museum and
  Production Facility

ATTRACTIONS

3 Barren River Imaginative
  Museum of Science
4 Beech Bend Raceway
  Park

RESTAURANTS

6 Berno's Little Sicily
7 Mariah's
8 Toot's Restaurant

are accepted, and there is an indoor pool. Suites are available. Rates begin at $99. I-65 at Exit 22; (270) 745-0088, (800) 801-1777.

Attractions

Barren River Imaginative Museum of Science

1229 Center Street, Bowling Green; (270) 843-9779

Hours: Thursday–Saturday, 10 a.m.–3 p.m.; Sunday, 1–4 p.m.

Admission: $3.50 adults, $2.50 children

Appeal by Age Group:

Pre-school	Grade School	Teens	Young Adults	Over 30	Seniors
★★★★	★★★★	★★★★	★★★	★★★	★★★

Average Touring Time: 1½ hours

Minimum Touring Time: 1 hour

Rainy Day Touring: Recommended

Author's Rating: ★★★ Imaginative exhibits

Services and Facilities:

Restaurants No	Lockers No
Alcoholic beverages No	Pet kennels No
Disabled access Yes	Rain check N/A
Wheelchair rental No	Private tours Yes
Baby stroller rental No	

Description and Comments Kids can never get enough of the hands-on exhibits usually found at science museums, and this one is no exception. One of our favorites is the Van de Graaf Electrostatic Generator, an experiment that makes your hair stand on end. The Magic Mirrors creates the illusion of suspending your body, while the BRIMS Blaster lets you feel what it's like to be in the midst of a mini-twister tornado.

Beech Bend Raceway Park

798 Beech Bend Road, Bowling Green; (270) 781-7634
www.beechbend.com

Hours: Memorial Day–Labor Day: Friday–Saturday, 10 a.m.–10 p.m.; Sunday–Thursday, 10 a.m.–8 p.m.; September and May: weekends only; closed remainder of year

Admission: $1 at gate; rides start at $1; $15 for armband for all rides except go-cart and games

Appeal by Age Group:

Pre-school	Grade School	Teens	Young Adults	Over 30	Seniors
★★★★	★★★★	★★★★	★★★	★★★	★★★

Average Touring Time: ½ day

Minimum Touring Time: 2 hours

Rainy Day Touring: Not recommended

Author's Rating: ★★★

Services and Facilities:

Restaurants Yes	Lockers No
Alcoholic beverages No	Pet kennels No
Disabled access Partial	Rain check No
Wheelchair rental No	Private tours N/A
Baby stroller rental No	

Description and Comments Beech Bend is a drag strip, amusement park, and recreation center all rolled in to one. The drag strip is one of the oldest and most prestigious quarter-mile runs in the country. Stock car races in a variety of classes are held at night, while drag races, also in a variety of classes, are held on Saturday and Sunday.

The amusement park has everything from go-carts and bumper cars to a Tilt-A-Whirl and Ferris wheel. Throw in a swimming pool and giant water slide, and you have enough to keep your brood occupied for the better part of a day. Conveniently, Beech Bend also has a riverside campground open year-round, complete with full hookups, bathhouses, and laundry facilities.

National Corvette Museum and Production Facility

350 Corvette Drive, Bowling Green; (800) 53-VETTE, (270) 781-7973; production facility: (502) 745-8419; www.corvettemuseum.com

Hours: April 1–September 30, daily 8 a.m.–6 p.m.; October 1–March 31, daily 8 a.m.–5 p.m.

Admission: Free

Appeal by Age Group:

Pre-school	Grade School	Teens	Young Adults	Over 30	Seniors
★★	★★★★	★★★★	★★★★	★★★★	★★★★★

Average Touring Time: 4 hours

Minimum Touring Time: 1½ hours

Rainy Day Touring: Recommended

Author's Rating: ★★★ The plant tour is fascinating

Services and Facilities:

Restaurants No	Lockers No
Alcoholic beverages No	Pet kennels No
Disabled access Yes	Rain check No
Wheelchair rental Yes	Private tours Yes
Baby stroller rental No	

Description and Comments Car-crazy kids will get a kick out of this museum. Cars, cars, and more cars are on display, showcasing the evolution of one of America's most popular sports cars. See a replica of a 1950s gas station, watch films about the making of the Corvette, and get a peek at types of cars that never made it into production. As a souvenir, climb into the car on display and get your picture made. As expected, you can stop at the Corvette Store on your way out to purchase a variety of apparel, collectibles, and gift items. Call ahead to schedule a guided tour.

If you have a true car buff along, be sure to tour the production facility about ¼-mile from the museum. Here you'll have the opportunity to view the noisy production area, where the cars are actually put together step-by-step by both robots and workers.

Family-Friendly Restaurants

BERNO'S LITTLE SICILY

1423 U.S. Highway 31 West Bypass, Bowling Green; (270) 781-7680

Meals served: Lunch and dinner
Cuisine: Italian
Entrée range: $5.50 and up
Kids menu: Yes
Reservations: Yes
Payment: All major credit cards accepted

Berno's serves up a good Chicago-style pizza pie, along with salads, sandwiches, and traditional Italian entrées like spaghetti and lasagna. The atmosphere is low key, so families feel welcome.

MARIAH'S

801 State Street, Bowling Green; (270) 842-6878

Meals served: Lunch and dinner
Cuisine: American
Entrée range: $7.50 and up
Kids menu: Yes
Reservations: No
Payment: All major credit cards accepted

Convenient to downtown attractions, Mariah's is in Bowling Green's oldest brick house, now listed on the National Register of Historic Homes. Anything with chicken is considered the house specialty, but salads, sandwiches, pasta, steaks, and seafood are also on the menu.

TOOT'S RESTAURANT

2500 Scottsville Road, Bowling Green; (270) 843-2335

Meals served: Lunch and dinner
Cuisine: American
Entrée range: $2.50 and up
Kids menu: Yes
Reservations: No
Payment: All major credit cards accepted

With old-time rock and roll blaring in the background, Toot's has a comfortable, loud dining room perfect for talkative youngsters. And the food is pretty good, too, with entrées like Danish baby back ribs, chicken wings, and seafood. They also serve fried dill pickles, a tasty appetizer if you can get your kids to try them.

Northern Kentucky

Touted as the "southern side of Cincinnati" both in geography and feel, Northern Kentucky, the compilation of Kenton, Campbell, and Boone counties, is coming into its own as a vacation destination. Tourism officials like to say the area offers the convenience of Cincinnati without the headache, and it's true. Virtually a suburb of Cincinnati, Northern Kentucky has lower hotel and car rates, less traffic, and more parking.

The riverfront is the current hot spot, with cruises, entertainment, restaurants, and the popular **Newport Aquarium.** Another favorite is **Main-Strasse Village,** a German neighborhood with ethnic shops and restaurants, and, of course, one of the biggest Oktoberfest celebrations in the state. There are a variety of sites to take in, and one of the best ways to do so is to hop aboard the Southbank Shuttle. Operating daily, the shuttle stops at designated points near area attractions, including attractions in Cincinnati. At $0.25, it's the cheapest ride around—and you don't have to worry about parking your car at various points of interest.

Summers can be humid along the riverfront; early spring and late fall can be breezy.

Note: The area code for Covington has changed from 606 to 859.

Family Lodging

Clarion Riverview

The Clarion is on the riverfront, with 236 rooms close to shopping, sports, and entertainment. There is a complimentary shuttle to and from the airport as well as to downtown Cincinnati. The rooftop pool is indoors during the winter; in warmer months, the roof opens to let in the sun. A fitness center, tanning salon, and restaurants are located on the property. Rates begin at $93.60. I-75 and Fifth Street Exit, Covington; (800) 292-2079 or (859) 491-1200; www.clarion.com.

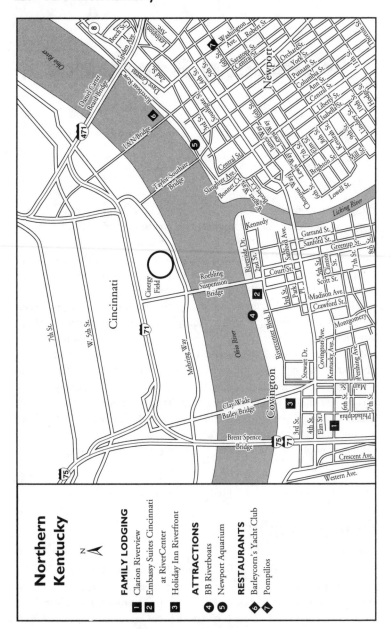

Northern Kentucky

N

FAMILY LODGING

1. Clarion Riverview
2. Embassy Suites Cincinnati at RiverCenter
3. Holiday Inn Riverfront

ATTRACTIONS

4. BB Riverboats
5. Newport Aquarium

RESTAURANTS

6. Barleycorn's Yacht Club
7. Pompilios

Embassy Suites Cincinnati at RiverCenter

The name is deceiving since this hotel is on the Kentucky side of the Ohio River, but it sits only a half-mile across the water from downtown Cincinnati. The roomy accommodations, complete with a private bedroom, separate living area for watching television, and refrigerator and wet bar for quick snacks, work well for families. You also get a complimentary, cooked-to-order breakfast. Kids 18 and younger stay free. Rates start at $109 in both summer and winter. 10 East RiverCenter Boulevard, Covington; (800) EMBASSY or (859) 261-8400; www.embassy-suites.com.

Holiday Inn Riverfront

A Holidome property, this hotel features indoor and outdoor swimming pools, a sauna, a fitness center, a whirlpool, and free games. Pets are allowed in guest rooms, room service is available, and there is airport transportation. Rates begin at $99. Located off I-75 at 600 West Third Street, Covington; (800) HOLIDAY, (859) 491-2331; www.basshotels.com/holiday-inn.

Attractions

BB Riverboats

One Madison Avenue, Covington; (800) 261-8586 or (859) 261-8500
www.bbriverboats.com

Hours: Cruises leave daily but time changes; call ahead for information.

Admission: Daytime cruise: $9 adults, $8 seniors, $5 children ages 4–12; Lock & Dam cruise: $64.95 adults, $60.95 seniors, $40 children ages 4–12

Appeal by Age Group:

Pre-school	Grade School	Teens	Young Adults	Over 30	Seniors
★★	★★★	★★★	★★★	★★★	★★★

Average Touring Time: 1 hour

Minimum Touring Time: 1 hour

Rainy Day Touring: Not recommended

Author's Rating: ★★★

Services and Facilities:

Restaurants Yes	Lockers No
Alcoholic beverages Yes	Pet kennels No
Disabled access Yes	Rain check No
Wheelchair rental No	Private tours N/A
Baby stroller rental No	

Description and Comments Seeing a city from the water always offers a unique perspective, and BB Riverboat cruises are no different. A variety of cruises set sail daily on the Ohio River from Covington Landing. If you have small children, the daytime harbor cruise is a good choice. This cruise lasts one hour and features captain's commentary. The Lock & Dam tour lasts a full day. Covering 64 miles and including lunch and dinner, this trip sails upriver and through the Meldahl Lock & Dam. Entertainment, games, and river lore are part of the package. Cruises are limited from November through April so call ahead before making plans.

Newport Aquarium

One Aquarium Way; (800) 406-FISH; (859) 491-FINS
   www.newportaquarium.com

Hours: Memorial Day–Labor Day, daily 10 a.m.–9 p.m.; Labor Day–
   Memorial Day, daily 10 a.m.–6 p.m.

Admission: $13.95 adults, $11.95 seniors, $8.95 children ages 3–12

Appeal by Age Group:

Pre-school	Grade School	Teens	Young Adults	Over 30	Seniors
★★★★★	★★★★★	★★★★★	★★★★★	★★★★★	★★★★★

Average Touring Time: 2½ hours

Minimum Touring Time: 2 hours

Rainy Day Touring: Recommended

Author's Rating: ★★★★★

Services and Facilities:

Restaurants Yes	Lockers No
Alcoholic beverages Yes	Pet kennels No
Disabled access Yes	Rain check N/A
Wheelchair rental No	Private tours No
Baby stroller rental No	

Description and Comments   Modern aquariums have become works of art. There's no doubt that the aquarium's main priority is to maintain quality of life for the marine animals, but consideration has also been given to the least invasive ways for humans to view this marine life in their simulated natural habitats.

At this aquarium, walk through acrylic tunnels underneath and around aquariums filled with one million gallons of water. In all, there are 11,000 marine animals representing 6,000 species. There are four themed areas, each exhibiting native animals.

Practically every exhibit is a favorite, but there are several here that we couldn't get out of our minds. In Surrounded by Sharks, only the acrylic tunnel separates you from the 25 nurse, sand tiger, and sandbar sharks, some of which are as long as 8½ feet. There is an open-air viewing area where you can watch them being fed. At Gator Bayou, walk across a small bridge over the swampland swarming with American alligators. The Bizarre & the Beautiful showcases some of the weirdest animals we've ever seen, including a longhorn cowfish, a giant Pacific octopus that changes colors, and a flashlight fish. And the Dangerous & Deadly exhibit has deadly electric eels, cuttlefish, poison frogs, piranhas, and stingrays waiting for their next victim.

This attraction is not something to rush through. Make sure you set aside at least a morning or afternoon for your visit. There are markers posted at each aquarium, so you can take as much time as you like to learn about the marine life on display.

Side Trips

Vent Haven Museum, Fort Mitchell   Talk about hanging out with a bunch of dummies! This museum houses the world's largest collection of ventriloquists' dummies. Figures representing 20 countries are on display, along with hundreds of photographs and collectibles all related to ventriloquism. While the museum is open by appointment only, the one-hour guided tour gives you inside information about this fascinating hobby. Cost is $2 for adults, $1 for children ages 8–12. Open May through September; call ahead for an appointment. (859) 341-0461.

Big Bone Lick State Park, Union   The name is enough to make you want to stop at this state park, and once you do, be prepared to spend the better part of a day. Big Bone Lick is where herds of prehistoric mammals like bison, mastodons, ground sloths, and giant mammoths came for salt at the end of the last ice age. Many of these prehistoric creatures were trapped and perished in the sulfur springs swamps. Their fossilized remains were discovered in the 1700s, spawning a new scientific field of study and garnering Big Bone Lick the designation as the preeminent archaeological site in the United States and the Birthplace for American Vertebrate Paleontology.

A small museum on site displays fossilized bones and a video about the animals that once roamed the park. Outside, the Discovery Trail, with its re-created grasslands, wetlands, and wooded savannas, simulates what it must have been like for the animals who became trapped in the springs. A boardwalk leads through the various ecosystems. The Big Bone Creek Trail wanders through original swampland and leads to the last remaining salt-sulphur spring. Its final loop, the Bison Trace, is where you can view the resident herd of buffalo.

Big Bone Lick has a campground with utility hookups, grills, a swimming pool, and a playground. The 7.5-acre lake offers fishing for largemouth bass, bluegill, and catfish, and there is a 3.5-mile hiking trail along the banks. Putt-putt golf, tennis, volleyball and basketball courts, softball fields, and horseshow pits are also available on site. Camping rates are $16.

3380 Beaver Road, Union; (800) 255-PARK or (859) 384-3522; www.ky-stateparks.com.

Cincinnati Zoo & Botanical Garden, Cincinnati   World-famous, the Cincinnati Zoo & Botanical Garden is just across the river from Covington. The zoo is best known for its white Bengal tigers, Komodo dragons, and lowland gorillas, but the new Jungle Trails exhibit, an African and Asian rain forest with trails and tropic animals, is also garnering attention. Orangutans and Bonobo chimpanzees, along with a variety of nighttime creatures, live in this lush, natural setting. Other interesting exhibits are the World of Insects, where you can walk through a butterfly garden, and the Wings of the World, with interactive activities about birds. The Zoo is the second oldest in the country and one of the best in terms of providing animals with realistic natural habitats in which to live. The Zoo is open daily from 9 a.m.–5 p.m. and until 6 p.m. from Memorial Day through Labor Day. Admission is $11 for adults, $8.50 for seniors, $5.50 for children ages 2–12. 3400 Vine Street, Cincinnati; (800) 94-HIPPO, (513) 559-7742; www.cincyzoo.org.

Cinergy Children's Museum, Cincinnati   Part of the complex of museums at the Cincinnati Museum Center, the Cinergy Children's Museum is designed specifically with children in mind. By climbing, crawling, exploring, and imagining, children learn about themselves, their world, and the relationship between the two. There are nine exhibits in all, and though you can expect to spend the good part of an afternoon at the museum, we doubt you'll have one minute of boredom. A big plus to this museum is that exhibits are interactive, with developmentally appropriate for all ages, including infants.

One of our favorites is The Woods exhibit, a two-story exploration of the natural world. Kids are encouraged to imagine what it would be like to play in a forest. They can hunt for fossils, look for animals, and hunt for treasure. Another exhibit, Kids Town, lets children learn about how a community works together. Through role playing, they can shop at a grocery store, cook food in the diner, repair a car in the car shop, and take an animal to the vet. There are nine exhibit areas in all.

The museum is open Wednesday, Thursday, and Sunday from noon–5 p.m.; Friday from noon–8 p.m., and Saturday from 10 a.m.–5 p.m. Admission for the children's museum only is $6.50 for adults, $4.50 for children ages 3–12. 1301 Western Avenue, Cincinnati; (800) 733-7071 or (513) 287-7071; www.cincymuseum.org.

Family-Friendly Restaurants

BARLEYCORN'S YACHT CLUB

201 Riverboat Row, Newport; (859) 292-2978

Meals served: Lunch and dinner
Cuisine: American
Entrée range: $9 and up
Kids menu: Yes
Reservations: No
Payment: All major credit cards accepted

Located on Riverboat Row, Barleycorn's serves the best burgers in town, along with homemade soup, Texas-style chili, and seafood. The restaurant sits just behind the aquarium and offers an excellent riverfront view.

POMPILIOS

600 Washington Street, Newport; (859) 581-3065

Meals served: Lunch and dinner
Cuisine: Italian/American
Entrée range: $4 and up
Kids menu: No
Reservations: No
Payment: All major credit cards accepted

Only a few blocks form the river in the heart of downtown, Pompilios is a nice, affordable restaurant that caters to families. From pasta and pizza to steaks and seafood, no entrées cost over ten bucks. There is no kids' menu but smaller portions can be requested.

Part Four

Louisiana

The folks in Louisiana have a saying for everything, but one you should remember while traveling in the state is: "Laissez les bons temps rouler." Translated, this phrase means, "Let the good times roll," and it is practically the Louisiana state motto, as it nicely sums up the state's unique heritage and lifestyle. You should also familiarize yourself with several other words and phrases before setting off on your journey to Louisiana, because once you get there, you will realize that this place is unlike any other in the country.

The first words you need to know before visiting Louisiana are "Cajun" and "Creole." Many Louisianans are descendants of Acadians, or Cajuns, who were French settlers exiled from Nova Scotia by the English in the 1760s. The word Creole can refer to Cajuns and any other descendant of European, especially Spanish or French, settlers. Louisiana culture is steeped in the traditions of the Cajuns and the Creole, from language to architecture to religion to food—especially the food.

Many residents of Louisiana are of French heritage, so it is no wonder that the state is proud of its culinary heritage. Walk into a restaurant in the New Orleans' **French Quarter** or any small town on the bayou and you will encounter a myriad of food choices: gumbo, jambalaya, étoufée, andouille sausage, boiled crawfish, po-boys. Cajun and Creole foods have evolved over the years as an interpretation of French culinary expertise, using Caribbean and African-inspired spices and Bayou bounty. In fact, the food of Louisiana is the only cuisine to have completely originated in the "New World."

Louisiana very different than other states, and each region of Louisiana is different from the other, despite having similar histories and backgrounds. **New Orleans,** the crown jewel of the state, is where everything happens. It is the home to one of the world's biggest festivals—**Mardi Gras**—and the one of the nation's largest buildings—the **Superdome.** New Orleans is also one of the few places where you can witness proper ladies biting the heads off of crawfish; modern-day practitioners of voodoo; and funeral parades accompanied by brass bands.

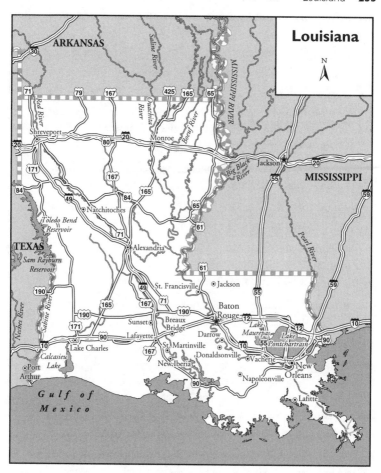

Just an hour west of New Orleans, you'll find another world in **Baton Rouge,** the site of the largest state capital in the nation and the official heart of Louisiana Plantation Country. **Lafayette,** capital of Acadiana, is home base for Cajun culture and is the place to go for a swamp tour or a zydeco show. Farther north in the middle of "Sportsman's Paradise," lies **Shreveport,** a far cry from the Bayou.

Louisiana is extremely hot during the summer and humid year round. So, if weather is a concern, consider visiting the state during the winter and early spring. During this time of year, the weather is generally mild, but the crowds are not. Mardi Gras, which usually takes place in mid-February, draws travelers from around the world to New Orleans. Many of

Kids' Beat

- Louisiana's topography is flat and low-lying. Its highest point is Driskill Mountain, at only 539 feet.

- The state bird is the brown pelican; the state dog is the Catahoula leopard dog (a.k.a., the Catahoula hound); the state flower is the magnolia blossom; the state insect is the honeybee; and the state tree is the bald cypress.

- Louisiana's state capitol building, located in Baton Rouge, is the tallest in the nation at 34 stories high.

- New Orleans is home to the longest bridge in the world, the Lake Pontchartrain Causeway, which stretches 24 miles.

- Patriots who fought in the Battle of New Orleans, one of the most famous battles of the War of 1812, were unaware that the war had ended two weeks prior to the engagement.

- President Thomas Jefferson bought the Louisiana Purchase from the French in 1803 for a mere $15 million. The 800,000-square-mile territory consisted of present-day Louisiana as well as Arkansas, Iowa, Missouri, North and South Dakota, Nebraska, Oklahoma, Wyoming, and parts of Minnesota, Kansas, Montana, and Colorado.

these vacationers choose to travel through Louisiana before or after the big event. However, no matter when you go, be it high season or the hot season, a trip to Louisiana will be rewarding.

GETTING THERE

By Plane.   The New Orleans International Airport, (504) 464-0831, is served by major carriers American, Continental, Delta, United, USAirways, Northwest, Southwest, and TWA, and a few regional airlines, such as Gulfstream and Comair. It is also a gateway for international flights from Mexico and Canada and Central America. Located 14 miles from downtown New Orleans, the airport is a short ride to the city's major attractions. In most cases, New Orleans International is the connection airport for flights to Baton Rouge, Shreveport, and other Louisiana destinations.

Louisiana's Not-to-Be-Missed Attractions	
Around the State	Atchafalaya Swamp Great River Road– "Plantation Country"
New Orleans	Audubon Zoo City Park New Orleans French Quarter New Orleans Historic Voodoo Museum Old U.S. Mint St. Louis Cathedral
Baton Rouge	Laura Plantation Louisiana Naval War Memorial Museum *(USS Kidd)* Louisiana State Capitol

Lafayette	George Rodrigue Museum
	    (Blue Dog paintings)
	McIlhenny Company Tabasco Sauce
	    Factory, Avery Island
	Vermilionville

Shreveport	Ark-La-Tex Antique and Classic Vehicle Museum Sci-Port Discovery Center

Louisiana's other airports include Baton Rouge's Metropolitan Airport, (504) 355-0333, located eight miles from downtown Baton Rouge, and Shreveport Regional Airport, (318) 673-5370, located five miles from downtown Shreveport. These airports are served by Delta, Northwest, American Eagle, and smaller, regional carriers. The cities of Alexandria, Lake Charles, Lafayette, and Monroe also have small airports.

By Train. Two Amtrak routes make stops in most Louisiana cities. In the north, Amtrak stops in Shreveport and Bossier City. Amtrak's southern route through Louisiana passes through Lake Charles, Lafayette, New

Iberia, Schriever, and New Orleans. Baton Rouge can be reached via a connection in New Orleans. For information on Amtrak routes, schedules, and reservations, call (800) 872-7245 or visit www.amtrak.com.

By Car.   Interstate 10 traverses the state in the south, from New Orleans to Lake Charles, whereas I-20 crosses the northern part of Louisiana, from Monroe to Shreveport. I-49 runs north-to-south, from Shreveport to Lafayette. Other routes include I-12 and I-55.

How To Get Information before You Go

State

Louisiana Tourism Office, P.O. Box 94291, Baton Rouge 70804; (504) 342-8100 or (800) 334-8626; www.louisianatravel.com

Louisiana State Parks Office, P.O. Box 44426, Baton Rouge 70804; (504) 342-8111 or (888) 677-1400; crt.state.la.us

Regional

Jefferson Parish Tourist Information Center, 300 Veterans Highway, I-10 and Loyola Drive, Kenner 70624; (504) 468-7527

Iberville Parish Tourist Center, 57735 Main Street, Plaquemine 70764-2564; (504) 687-7158

West Baton Rouge Tourist Information Center, U.S. Highway 61 at the state line, St. Francisville 70775; (504) 635-6962

Acadia Parish Tourist Commission, 114 East First Street, Crowley 70526-5102; (318) 783-2108

Natchitoches Parish Tourist Commission, 781 Front Street, Natchitoches 71457-4643; (318) 352-8072

Local

New Orleans Metropolitan Convention and Visitors Bureau, 1520 Sugar Bowl Drive, New Orleans 70112; (504) 566-5003 or (800) 672-6124; www.neworleanscvb.com

Baton Rouge Area Convention and Visitors Bureau, 730 North Boulevard, Baton Rouge 70802; (225) 382-3578 or (800) LA-ROUGE; www.bracvb.com

Southwest Louisiana Lake Charles Convention and Visitors Bureau, 1211 North Lakeshore Drive, Lake Charles 70601; (318) 436-9588 or (800) 456-SWLA; www.visitlakecharles.org

---

More Louisiana Websites

Encyclopedia of Cajun Culture   www.cajunculture.com

Mardi Gras Fun   www.mardigrasfun.com

Louisiana Legislature's Kids Page   www.legis.state.la.us/pubinfo/ kids.htm

Mardi G. Raccoon Kid's Activity Page   www.mardi.com

Louisiana Gumbo Kid's Links   lagumbo.com/kids

Blue Dog Art for Kids   www.bluedogart.com/kids/blue_dog_ kids.htm

French Lessons for the Family   www.louisianatravel.com/music_ fun/fr_lessons

---

Shreveport-Bossier Convention and Tourist Bureau, P.O. Box 1761, Shreveport 71166; (800) 551-8682; www.shreveport-bossier.org

Family Outdoor Adventures

▲ = Camping

♥ = Author's favorite

♥ - *Atchafalaya Swamp and River Basin, Krotz Springs*   Hang on for the ride of your life through the Atchafalaya Swamp. Sanctioned airboat excursions, available throughout the year, are the only way to see this pristine swampland. Plus, kids will be simply enthralled by the boat ride—it's loud, bumpy, and somewhat futuristic in feel as the boat skims the water top instead of being propelled by a submerged motor. One note: The very reasons older kids love the rides are the same reasons we don't recommend them for toddlers and younger children.

Much of Louisiana's lore is derived from tales originating in the swamplands. If a trip to these storied, murky wetlands is not on your itinerary, you may fail to understand the essence of Cajun culture. The Atchafalaya, which comes from the Choctaw "hacha falaia," meaning "long river," is a river and extensive network of swamps, wetlands, marshes, and bogs. In fact, the Atchafalaya Basin is the largest undeveloped wetlands area in the country.

More wildlife than people inhabit the Atchafalaya, making it a favorite haunt for anglers and hunters. The area serves as a wintering area for approximately one-half of the migratory bird species in North America, with at least 300 different types of birds in Atchafalaya at one time. Calling the waters home are catfish, bass, crawfish, shrimp, and crabs, as well as frogs, snakes, and alligators. Nutria, beavers, foxes, raccoons, and black bears also contribute to the diverse wildlife of the area; (318) 566-2251.

♥ - *Jean Lafitte National Historical Park, Southern Louisiana* If you want to explain the interesting history and culture of Louisiana to your kids, a visit to Jean Lafitte is a good way to begin. Stretching across the southern portion of Louisiana, the Jean Lafitte National Historical Park and Preserve is a sanctuary for the flora and fauna of the Mississippi River Delta region, with visitors centers throughout that highlight the area's history. Because Jean Lafitte covers such a large area of the state, the National Park Service set up six separate stations throughout the preserve, with a headquarters in New Orleans, to explain the environmental and cultural diversity found here.

The towns of Lafayette, Eunice, and Thibodaux each have a visitor center dedicated to the Acadian heritage of the region. They are: The Acadian Cultural Center in Lafayette, the Prairie Acadian Cultural Center in Eunice, and the Wetlands Acadian Cultural Center in Thibodaux. These centers interpret the history of the Acadian, or Cajun, people through displays of artifacts, short films, and exhibits.

The other three park centers are located in and around the New Orleans metropolitan area. Approximately six miles southeast of the city lies the Chalmette Battlefield and National Cemetery, site of the bloody Battle of New Orleans of 1815 and the cemetery for soldiers fallen during the Civil War, the Spanish-American War, both World War I and World War II, as well as Vietnam. During the second week of January each year, men and women throughout Louisiana come to the Chalmette Battlefield to take part in a re-enactment of the Battle of New Orleans.

The Barataria Preserve in Marrero, due southwest of New Orleans, is the place to go to learn more about the people and wildlife that have inhabited the swamps and marshlands of the region. And, the French Quarter Visitor Center in New Orleans has extensive information about the Native American, Spanish, French, and English influence on the area.

For more information about the park, contact the Jean Lafitte National Historical Park and Preserve Headquarters at 365 Canal Street, Suite 2400, New Orleans, 70130-1142; (504) 589-3882, ext. 102; www.nps.gov/jela.

▲ - *Kisatchie National Forest, Pineville* Offering a variety of outdoor opportunities, the Kisatchie is the only national forest in Louisiana. Activities include hunting, fishing, bird-watching, swimming, boating, canoeing, cycling, horseback riding, and hiking. Families can choose from developed recreational areas throughout the forest or more primitive areas for camping or generally exploring the natural bounty of the Kisatchie.

Five notable campgrounds include the Kincaid, Kisatchie Bayou, Caney Lakes, Cloud Crossing, and Valentine Lake, all of which are developed camping sites with picnic tables, drinking water, flush toilets, and RV parking. Most of these also have boat ramps, grills and small beaches for swimming. Primitive areas are exactly that and are lacking in most of the amenities available at the more popular recreation sites. However, unlike developed areas that charge a small fee of approximately $7 per family for the upkeep of the campgrounds, primitive areas are free. Usually preferred by hunters, the primitive areas such as Bucktail (near Middle Fork), Saddle Bayou (in the Catahoula District) and Coyote and Corral (in the Red Dirt Preserve) are ideal for those who wish to steer clear of crowds.

Kisatchie National Forest also has exceptional hiking trails, where you can view diverse animal and plant life. The longest trail is the Wild Azalea National Recreation Trail, which stretches 31 miles through the hardwood forest. Wild azaleas and dogwoods are in full bloom from mid-March through mid-April, offering a feast for the senses. Families can take two- to three-hour hikes along the trail, or set up tents in Valentine Lake or Evangeline Primitive Camp if they want to take a couple days to explore the natural splendor; (318) 473-7160.

New Orleans Saints Football, New Orleans   In recent years, the New Orleans Saints have caused more than one fan to have devilish thoughts about the team. In fact, one of David Letterman's suggestions in a Top Ten List of New Nicknames for New Orleans was "Where the Saints go six and ten." But, this NFL football franchise still brings in large crowds for each game. Games are played in New Orleans' massive Superdome, which is an indoor stadium big enough for a crowd of more than 60,000. Although Saints' fans do not have to endure rain or snow while they attend the games, the spectator event is still considered an outdoor activity by many. Tickets for games are available on a subscription basis, or can be purchased in person at the Superdome, Sugar Bowl Drive at Poydras Street, New Orleans; (504) 731-1700; www.nfl.com.

♥ - *Poverty Point National Monument, Epps*   Scientists continue to be baffled by the mounds and earthenworks that make up Poverty Point, one of the oldest archaeological finds of native peoples in North America. Indeed, the Native Americans of eastern North America, including the Creeks, Choctaw, and Natchez, were mound-building people. But, the mounds found in Poverty Point are larger and pre-date all others by thousands of years. Also fascinating is that the mounds form a perfect semi-circular geometrical pattern, reminding some of Stonehenge or sacred Mayan sites, leaving modern man to ponder what type of ceremonies Poverty Point was used for. This park is managed by the state of Louisiana, and brochures about the mounds can be picked up at the entrance. For more information, call (318) 926-5492.

Calendar of Festivals and Events

January

Sugar Bowl, New Orleans   One of the finest college football events in the country happens on or around New Year's Day. Tickets for the game are almost impossible to get unless you are an alumnus of one of the featured teams; (504) 587-3800.

Creole Heritage Festival, Melrose   Celebrate Creole culture with arts, crafts, zydeco music, and fireworks; (800)259-1714.

February

Mardi Gras, New Orleans   This pre-Lenten festival is known worldwide as an anything-goes type of party. But many facets of the event remain largely a family affair. Kids get to watch dozens of floats, bands, and masqueraders parading through the streets, and if they are lucky, they will be showered with strands of beads and piles of candy. Indeed, most other towns in Louisiana celebrate Fat Tuesday in some way or another, but New Orleans' party is the biggest and the best.

March

Tennessee Williams/New Orleans Literary Festival, New Orleans   Celebrities and theater buffs gather in the Crescent City each year in late March to celebrate literature, and, in particular, the works of Tennessee Williams. In addition to musical and stage performances, attendees at the festival can participate in literary walking tours of New Orleans; (504) 283-3227 or (504) 581-1144; www.tennesseewilliams.net.

April

New Orleans Jazz and Heritage Festival, New Orleans   Thousands of spectators descend on New Orleans each year to watch the finest jazz, blues, rock, and country artists perform. Past performers at the Jazz Festival include the Neville Brothers, Fats Domino, Ray Charles, Wynton Marsalis, Mahalia Jackson, Willie Nelson, Hootie and the Blowfish, and Lenny Kravitz, to name very few. The simultaneous Heritage Festival attracts more than 100 arts and crafts exhibitors, food vendors, storytellers, etc.; (504) 522-4786; www.nojazzfest.com.

Festival International de Louisiane, Lafayette   This festival unites Louisiana with the French-speaking world through food, art, and film. It is always held the third week in April; (318) 232-8086; www.fil.net-connect.net.

Louisiana State Fiddlers Championship, Natchitoches   The state's top fiddlers compete for prizes and admiration; (318) 472-6255 or (888) 677-3600.

Blessing of the Shrimp Fleet, Dulac   Shrimp boats parade through the water in colorful finery, while onlookers feast on shrimp cooked hundreds of ways; (504) 563-2325.

Crescent City Classic, New Orleans   This annual 10K and fun run starts at Jackson Square and ends with food and live music; (504) 861-8686; www.ccc10k.com.

May

Breaux Bridge Crawfish Festival, Breaux Bridge   Once you've had a taste of "poor man's lobster," you will be glad that this annual festival lasts for three days. Sample crawfish cooked in a variety of ways while you enjoy Cajun and zydeco music. Breaux Bridge also stages a parade and an arts and crafts show during this event; (318) 332-6655.

Contraband Days and Pirate Festival, Lake Charles   For approximately two weeks each May, citizens of Lake Charles celebrate the legacy of gentleman pirate Jean Lafitte, who is said to have hidden much of his booty in the waters around the town. Mock pirate invasions, nighttime boat parades, and a fireworks display are just a few of the attractions; (318) 436-5508.

June

Great French Market Tomato Festival, New Orleans   This yearly festival pays homage to the juicy red fruit. Enjoy tomato tastings, cooking demonstrations, and musical entertainment; (504) 522-2621.

Louisiana Peach Festival, Ruston   Georgia isn't the only Southern state to salute the peach. Louisiana's celebration lasts a little over a week and features recipe contests and family entertainment; (800) 392-9032.

September

Festivals Acadiens, Lafayette   Enjoy a weekend of listening and dancing to down-home, Cajun music. Craft booths, storytellers, and food demonstrations also introduce the Acadian experience to festival visitors; (800) 346-1958.

Southwest Louisiana Zydeco Music Festival, Opelousas   Zydeco music, played with scrubboards (frottoir), spoons, fiddles, triangles (ti-fers) and accordions, is the traditional music of the Louisiana Creole culture. This fun September festival celebrates the music, cuisine, and culture of the Creole people; (318) 942-2392.

October

Br'er Rabbit Folk Festival, Vacherie   Kids and adults will revel in the Br'er Rabbit Folk Festival, held each year at the Laura Plantation outside Baton

Rouge. Storytellers, puppet shows, and theatrical productions recount the tall tales of Uncle Remus and friends, and Creole and Cajun music, dance, food, and arts and crafts make the weekend festival a joyous event; (225) 265-7690; www.lauraplantation.com.

December

Christmas New Orleans Style, New Orleans   December is spent getting ready for the Big Easy's second biggest celebration: Christmas. Throughout the month, there are many yuletide events, including staged Christmas pageants, caroling, cooking and craft demonstrations, and numerous concerts. This is a great time to see the grand mansions of New Orleans dressed in Christmas finery; (504) 522-5730.

New Orleans

Most people are only familiar with the New Orleans they see on film and television. *A Streetcar Named Desire,* a play written by native son Tennessee Williams and brought to the big screen by director Elia Kazan, portrayed a hot, humid New Orleans, simmering under the shade of a balcony fringed with decorative wrought iron. *Easy Rider* and *Interview with a Vampire* introduced viewers to voodoo and New Orleans' above-ground cemeteries, dubbed the "Cities of the Dead" by Mark Twain. Of course, everyone is familiar with the wild parties and spectacular floats and parades of Mardi Gras as they are televised worldwide each year.

Many of these portrayals of "N'awlins" (not "New Or-LEENS") offer a glimpse into the realities of the Big Easy. But, there are many other sights, sounds, and flavors that make up this unique city. At the heart of it all is the **French Quarter,** or the Vieux Carré, with its gorgeous architecture, excellent restaurants, and rowdy **Bourbon Street.** You will want to stay in this area if you plan to visit traditional attractions such as the **St. Louis Cathedral,** the **Historic New Orleans Collection** museum, or the **Old U.S. Mint,** but families will probably want to find lodgings elsewhere during Mardi Gras. Less traditional and perhaps more fun sites to see in the French Quarter include the **Voodoo Museum** and the **Aquarium of the Americas.** One note: It's hard to filter out the noise of the city's boisterous celebrations at night, so if you're traveling with an infant, choose an upper-floor or courtyard-facing room at one of the larger hotels. You'll be giving up the unmatched charm of the smaller bed and breakfasts and inns, but you'll have better luck at a quieter night.

Traveling farther west, you'll find the quaint **Garden District,** which is the area where you'll find relatively quiet hotels, lovely old mansions, and **Lafayette Cemetery No. 1.** The Garden District is convenient to the streetcar line—indeed, still in operation in New Orleans, albeit on a limited basis—and kid-friendly sites such as **Storyland,** the **Botanical Gardens,** and the **Audubon Zoo.**

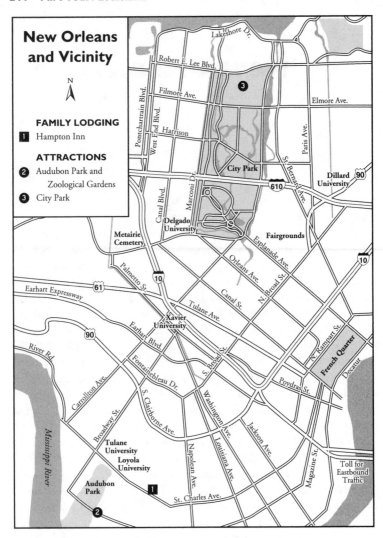

New Orleans and Vicinity

N

FAMILY LODGING
1 Hampton Inn

ATTRACTIONS
2 Audubon Park and
Zoological Gardens
3 City Park

And above all, don't forget to eat while you're in New Orleans. Coffee houses such as **Cafe du Monde** and po-boy joints like **Mother's** will give you something to write home about.

Family Lodging

French Quarter Courtyard

The quaint French Quarter Courtyard is a surprising find among the rows of high-priced inns and aesthetically sterile chain hotels in this area. The

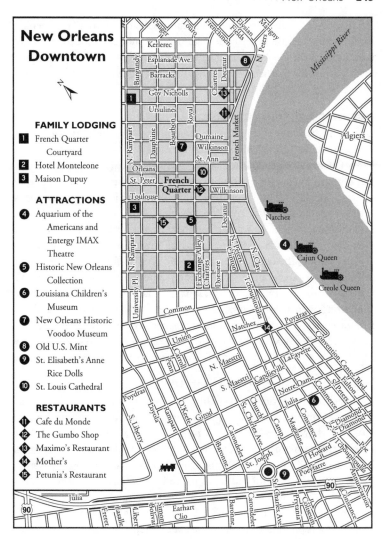

New Orleans Downtown

FAMILY LODGING

1 French Quarter Courtyard
2 Hotel Monteleone
3 Maison Dupuy

ATTRACTIONS

4 Aquarium of the Americans and Entergy IMAX Theatre
5 Historic New Orleans Collection
6 Louisiana Children's Museum
7 New Orleans Historic Voodoo Museum
8 Old U.S. Mint
9 St. Elisabeth's Anne Rice Dolls
10 St. Louis Cathedral

RESTAURANTS

11 Cafe du Monde
12 The Gumbo Shop
13 Maximo's Restaurant
14 Mother's
15 Petunia's Restaurant

51-room inn is housed in an antebellum mansion, complete with typical New Orleans wrought-iron balconies, and the surrounding grounds feature a well-manicured courtyard, sparkling fountains, and a European–style pool. Nearby attractions include the popular Aquarium of the Americas and the Children's Museum. As the name implies, the French Quarter is only steps away.

The historic mansion was converted into a hotel in the mid-1990s, and its original hardwood floors have been polished to perfection. All 42 guest rooms and 9 suites come with hand-carved four-poster beds, and many rooms have balconies that overlook the pool and courtyard. Amenities include cable television, 24-hour valet parking, and complimentary breakfast. Rates for the French Quarter Courtyard start at $69, and children under 17 stay free with parents. 1100 North Rampart Street, New Orleans; (504) 522-7333 or (800) 290-4233.

Hampton Inn, Garden District

Although this is one of the newest hotels in the Crescent City, the Hampton Inn's subtle, colonial architecture blends in well with the old mansions of St. Charles Avenue. Located in the picturesque and relatively quiet Garden District, the five-story, 100-room hotel is ideal for families who want to avoid the hustle and bustle of the French Quarter. Kid-friendly attractions, such as the Audubon Park and Zoo, are within walking distance of the inn. And the attractions of downtown and the French Quarter are just a few minutes ride on the St. Charles Streetcar, which stops just outside the hotel.

You will find the typical amenities at the Garden District Hampton Inn, including spacious rooms, cable television, an outdoor pool, and a complimentary deluxe continental breakfast bar. For families, this hotel also offers connecting rooms, cribs, and, for an extra fee, childcare services. Parking is free for guests. Room rates start at approximately $98 per night, and children under 18 stay free with parents. 3626 St. Charles Avenue, New Orleans; (504) 899-9990 or (800) 426-7866; www.hamptoninn.com.

Hotel Monteleone, French Quarter

Listed among the ritzier of New Orleans accommodations, the Hotel Monteleone is a grand hotel befitting its Royal Street address. Built in 1886, the Spanish-style Monteleone has seen people and eras come and go. Famous guests, such as Tennessee Williams and William Faulkner, have stayed the night in one of the hotel's 600 rooms or have visited the hotel's gleaming lobby, giving both legend and status to the French Quarter landmark.

Despite the hotel's glossy façade of brass, crystal, and marble, the storied Monteleone offers modern accommodations and amenities and is actually appropriate for families. Kids and parents will enjoy the rooftop swimming pool and satellite television and the hotel's proximity to shops, restaurants, and area attractions.

The Hotel Monteleone has three restaurants on-site, room service, laundry and medical services, and babysitting. Twenty-eight suites and 570 guest rooms are comfortably furnished with queen- or king-size beds and come equipped with a coffee maker, iron and ironing board, hairdryer, alarm clock, and analog dataport for laptop computers. If you need an extra bed, the hotel offers roll-aways for an extra $25 per night. Room rates start at $140, but are more expensive during Christmas, Mardi Gras, and

Jazz Fest. Children under 17 stay free with parents. 214 Rue Royale, New Orleans; (504) 523-3341; www.hotelmonteleone.com.

Maison Dupuy, French Quarter

Expect to have a comfortable stay at the Maison Dupuy, not only because the hotel's grounds and guest rooms are impeccably furnished, but also because the property is conveniently located just steps from Bourbon Street and the fun of the French Quarter. Before being renovated in 1997, the 200-room, five-story Maison Dupuy served as a Cotton Press, a blacksmith shop, and a sheet-metal works. You'll be able to tell immediately upon looking at the exterior of the hotel that she has had quite a past.

As for the interior, everything is immaculate and new. Rooms are furnished with four-poster queen- or king-size beds and a perfectly appointed sitting area with couch and desk. All guest rooms have patios or balconies that overlook the courtyard and pool. Rooms are equipped with cable TV with in-room movies, iron and ironing board, hair dryer, refreshment center, and a safe. Rates for the Maison Dupuy start at $129 per night (double occupancy) and increase dramatically around major events like Mardi Gras and Jazz Fest. However, in the off-season you may find prices as low as $89. Children 18 and under stay free with parents. 1001 Rue Toulouse, New Orleans; (504) 586-8000; www.maisondupuy.com.

Attractions

Aquarium of the Americas and Entergy IMAX Theater

1 Canal Street at the Mississippi River, New Orleans;
  (504) 581-4629 or (800) 774-7394
  www.auduboninstitute.org/html/aa_aquariumain.html

Hours: Sunday–Thursday, 9:30 a.m.–6 p.m.; Friday–Saturday until 7 p.m.; IMAX, daily 10 a.m.–6 p.m.

Admission: $13 adults, $10 seniors, $6.50 children ages 11 and younger; IMAX: $7.75 adults, $6.75 seniors, $5 children ages 11 and younger; Aquarium and IMAX: $17.25 adults, $14 seniors, $10.50 children ages 11 and younger

Appeal by Age Group:

Pre-school	Grade School	Teens	Young Adults	Over 30	Seniors
★★★★	★★★★	★★★★	★★★★	★★★★	★★★★

Average Touring Time: 3 hours

Minimum Touring Time: 2 hours

Rainy Day Touring: Recommended

Author's Rating: ★★★★ Fascinating exploration of other worlds

Services and Facilities:

Restaurants Yes

Alcoholic beverages No

Disabled access Yes

Wheelchair rental No

Baby stroller rental No

Lockers No

Pet kennels No

Rain check No

Private tours No

Description and Comments   Much of New Orleans culture is based around water. For instance, the Mississippi River, back country swamps, and the warm, gentle waves of the Gulf of Mexico have been a source of food and commerce for the region for centuries. So it is appropriate that the Aquarium of the Americas is located here. More than one million gallons of water and 15,000 fish, amphibians, birds, and mammals make up exhibits about wildlife in the Caribbean, the Amazon, the Mississippi River Basin, and the Pacific Northwest, to name a few. In these manmade aquatic habitats, you will have a chance to see everything from enormous sea turtles to tiny seahorses. The ubiquitous Louisiana alligator is also on view.

If the underwater world fascinates you, you should take the time to see a movie at the deluxe Entergy IMAX Theater. High-definition, 3D films that focus on the earth's fragile environment are usually shown at the theater, including titles that look at the Galapagos Islands, space exploration, and more. Not only are the movies educational and entertaining, but the IMAX is also one of your best options if your plans get rained out—a common occurrence in this subtropical location.

Audubon Park and Zoological Gardens

6500 Magazine Street, Audubon Park, New Orleans; (504) 581-4629 or (800) 774-7394

www.auduboninstitute.org/html/aa_zoomain.html

Hours: Winter: daily 9:30 a.m.–5 p.m.; Summer: daily 9:30 a.m.–6 p.m.; closed Mardi Gras, first Friday in May, Thanksgiving, and Christmas

Admission: $9 adults, $5 seniors, $4.75 children ages 2–12

Appeal by Age Group:

Pre-school	Grade School	Teens	Young Adults	Over 30	Seniors
★★★★★	★★★★★	★★★★★	★★★★★	★★★★★	★★★★★

Average Touring Time: 3 hours

Minimum Touring Time: 2 hours

Rainy Day Touring: Not recommended

Author's Rating: ★★★★★ One of the best zoos in the country

Services and Facilities:

Restaurants Yes	Lockers Yes
Alcoholic beverages No	Pet kennels No
Disabled access Yes	Rain check No
Wheelchair rental No	Private tours Yes
Baby stroller rental No	

Description and Comments Housing some of the most diverse wildlife, including more than 1,500 species from North and South America to Asia and Africa, the Audubon Zoo is one of the nation's largest and best zoological parks. Rare zoo attractions include white tigers, white alligators, Komodo dragons, jaguars, and golden tamarin monkeys. Also on view at the 53-acre Audubon Zoo are bears, giraffes, elephants, lions, orangutans, and countless reptile and bird species. Notable exhibits include the Louisiana Swamp Exhibit and the Embraceable Zoo. The former re-creates the cypress marsh and wilderness of the state with alligators, snakes, wetlands fowl, and raccoons, along with a replica of a Cajun cabin. The latter is the facility's answer to a petting zoo, and opportunities abound for adults and little ones to touch and interact with hedgehogs, prairie dogs, and other small animals.

The Audubon Zoo is located in the bend of the Audubon Park, the Big Easy's 400-acre stretch of green grass and enormous shade trees along the banks of the Mississippi River. Here, families can bike, ride horses, picnic, play Frisbee, or simply bask in the sun. Entrance to the park is free, and it is an ideal spot to visit either before or after your tour of the zoo.

City Park, including Storyland and Carousel Gardens

Victory Avenue, at the southern end of City Park, New Orleans;
(504) 483-9382; Carousel info, (504) 483-9356
www.neworleanscitypark.com

Hours: Sunrise–sunset

Admission: Varies according to activity

Appeal by Age Group:

Pre-school	Grade School	Teens	Young Adults	Over 30	Seniors
★★★★	★★★★	★★★★	★★★★	★★★★	★★★★

Average Touring Time: 2 hours

Minimum Touring Time: 1½ hours

Rainy Day Touring: Not recommended

Author's Rating: ★★★★ An attraction to please everyone

Services and Facilities:

Restaurants Yes, nearby	Lockers No
Alcoholic beverages No	Pet kennels No
Disabled access Yes	Rain check No
Wheelchair rental No	Private tours Yes, for some locales
Baby stroller rental No	

Description and Comments   At 1,500 acres, City Park is the fourth-largest urban park in the nation. There are a ton of activities to choose from: Golf, tennis, softball, Frisbee, fishing, picnicking, or simply relaxing. Also located here are the New Orleans Botanical Gardens, kid-friendly Storyland, and the Carousel Gardens.

Escape to the Botanical Gardens to see more than 2,000 varieties of flowers and plants as well as beautiful landscaping, including classic fountains, red brick walkways, and cozy, wooden benches. The Gardens are open Tuesday through Sunday from 10 a.m.–4:30 p.m., and guided tours are available from 10 a.m.–3 p.m. Admission is $3 for adults and $1 for children ages 5–12.

Both Storyland and Carousel Gardens are ideal if you've got young ones in tow. Storyland, built in the 1950s, is a theme park of fairy-tale fantasies. Children can play in NeverNever land, mount make-believe dragons, or climb inside the mouth of a whale. Puppet shows are also regularly featured at the small theme park. Admission is $2 for both children and adults. Carousel Gardens is a delight to toddlers, who revel in catching a ride on intricately painted horses. The Gardens' 1906 Carousel is a sight to behold for all. Rides aboard the Carousel cost $1 each, and children as young as 2 can take part under the supervision of an adult.

Historic New Orleans Collection

533 Royal Street at St. Louis Street, New Orleans; (504) 523-4662
  www.hnoc.org

Hours: Tuesday–Saturday, 10 a.m.–5 p.m.

Admission: Free; guided tours, $4 per person

Appeal by Age Group:

Pre-school	Grade School	Teens	Young Adults	Over 30	Seniors
★	★★	★★★	★★★	★★★	★★★

Average Touring Time: 1½ hours

Minimum Touring Time: 1 hour

Rainy Day Touring: Recommended

Author's Rating: ★★★   Best overview on the history of New Orleans

Services and Facilities:

Restaurants No	Lockers No
Alcoholic beverages No	Pet kennels No
Disabled access Yes	Rain check No
Wheelchair rental No	Private tours Yes
Baby stroller rental No	

Description and Comments   In order to learn more about the city of New Orleans beyond the Mardi Gras madness, consider a visit to the Historic New Orleans Collection. Here, you can browse exhibits on early Louisiana history, including portraits, old maps, documents, artifacts, and memorabilia from the French and Spanish eras, the Louisiana Purchase, the Civil War, the Jazz Age, and more. Small children will definitely be disappointed by this hands-off gallery, but teens and young adults may enjoy seeing and reading about the historical side of the Crescent City.

Louisiana Children's Museum

420 Julia Street, New Orleans; (504) 523-1357; www.lcm.org

Hours: Tuesday–Saturday 9:30 a.m.–4:30 p.m.; Sunday, noon–4:30 p.m. In summer museum also opens on Mondays with regular weekday hours.

Admission: $5; free ages 1 and younger

Appeal by Age Group:

Pre-school	Grade School	Teens	Young Adults	Over 30	Seniors
★★★★	★★★★	★★	★★	★★	★★

Average Touring Time: 2 hours

Minimum Touring Time: 1½ hours

Rainy Day Touring: Recommended

Author's Rating: ★★★   Educational and entertaining for everyone

Services and Facilities:

Restaurants No	Lockers No
Alcoholic beverages No	Pet kennels No
Disabled access Yes	Rain check No
Wheelchair rental No	Private tours No
Baby stroller rental No	

Description and Comments   The relatively new Children's Museum is a great place to bring kids on rainy or sweltering days. Hands-on exhibits let tots make their own news broadcast, explore the human body, or steer a tugboat. The First Adventures Toddler Playscape is an excellent place to let two- and three-year-olds let loose.

Plan on calling the museum or checking its website for information on upcoming workshops for kids and families. These supervised seminars include science experiments, drawing and painting how-tos, and music demonstrations.

Old U.S. Mint

400 Esplanade Avenue, New Orleans; (504) 568-6968

Hours: Tuesday–Sunday, 9 a.m.–5 p.m.

Admission: $4 adults, free ages 12 and younger

Appeal by Age Group:

Pre-school	Grade School	Teens	Young Adults	Over 30	Seniors
★★★	★★★	★★★	★★★	★★★	★★★

Average Touring Time: 2 hours

Minimum Touring Time: 1 hour

Rainy Day Touring: Recommended

Author's Rating: ★★★ Tremendous collection of jazz and Mardi Gras memorabilia

Services and Facilities:

Restaurants No	Lockers No
Alcoholic beverages No	Pet kennels No
Disabled access Yes	Rain check No
Wheelchair rental No	Private tours No
Baby stroller rental No	

Description and Comments This massive red building, across from the French Market, once served as the United States Mint, and, in fact, Confederate currency was printed here during the Civil War. Under the direction of President Andrew Jackson, the Mint was built in 1838 to make coins and bills for an expanding western frontier. The Mint closed in 1909, and it wasn't until 1981 that the building reopened as a museum dedicated to telling the story of two major influences on New Orleans history: jazz and Mardi Gras.

If you can't manage to be in New Orleans during Mardi Gras, then stroll over to the U.S. Mint to view the Mardi Gras exhibit, where you can learn about 150 years of Carnival history in Louisiana. On view are colorful costumes from a variety of krewes, masks, historical photographs, and various memorabilia. Several videos explain the history and rituals of the popular Lenten festival.

Also housed in the Old U.S. Mint is the fantastic Jazz exhibit, displaying an extensive collection of photographs, sheet music, and musical instruments from the Jazz Age to today. Not to miss here are Dizzy Gillespie's crooked trumpets and the original cornet upon which a young Louis Armstrong learned to play.

The Old U.S. Mint is part of the Louisiana State Museum, which is made up of four other historic buildings: the Cabildo, the Presbytere, the 1850 House on Jackson Square and Madame John's Legacy. Information on the museum and the artifacts exhibited within other buildings can be acquired by calling, (504) 568-6968 or visiting online at lsm.crt.state.la.us.

New Orleans Historic Voodoo Museum

724 Rue Dumaine, New Orleans; (504) 523-7685
www.voodoomuseum.com

Hours: Daily, 10 a.m. until dusk

Admission: $7 adults, $5.50 seniors, $3.50−5.50 students, free for children ages 5 and younger

Appeal by Age Group:

Pre-school	Grade School	Teens	Young Adults	Over 30	Seniors
★	★★	★★★★	★★★★	★★★	★

Average Touring Time: 1½ hours

Minimum Touring Time: 1 hour

Rainy Day Touring: Recommended (but spooky!)

Author's Rating: ★★★★ Unlike any museum you will visit

Services and Facilities:

Restaurants No	Lockers No
Alcoholic beverages No	Pet kennels No
Disabled access Yes	Rain check No
Wheelchair rental No	Private tours No
Baby stroller rental No	

Description and Comments Halloween happens every day in New Orleans, or at least it does at the Historic Voodoo Museum. Perhaps the most famous practitioner of the Afro-Caribbean rituals of voodoo, Marie Laveau, was born in New Orleans in 1794 and died in the city in 1881. Laveau's influence, and indeed the growing population of ritual-practicing Africans, Haitians, and Creoles, made New Orleans a center of voodoo culture. Continued intrigue in the quasi-religion has led the Historic Voodoo Museum to be one of the strangest and more popular museums in the French Quarter.

On display at the museum is a portrait and shrine to Laveau as well as exhibits on voodoo rituals and instruments of worship. In the Voodoo shop, you can purchase potions, salves, gris-gris bags, dolls that are said to ward off evil spirits, and customized spiritual services can be prepared for a price. The Voodoo Museum is also known for its unusual walking tours of New Orleans, including visits to a local cemetery, at which Laveau's grave is the centerpiece.

Needless to say, the Historic Voodoo Museum is not for everybody, especially young children who scare easily. But for older kids and young adults, the campy museum is no more than a haunted house. One thing is for sure—only New Orleans could be home to such a weird attraction.

St. Elisabeth's Anne Rice Dolls

1314 Napoleon Avenue and Prytania Street, New Orleans;
  (504) 899-6450

Hours: Daily tours at 11 a.m., 1 p.m., and 3 p.m.

Admission: Requested donation of $7 adults, $5 children (all proceeds
  go to the upkeep of a local school and church)

Appeal by Age Group:

Pre-school	Grade School	Teens	Young Adults	Over 30	Seniors
★★	★★★	★★★	★★★	★★★	★★★

Average Touring Time: 1½ hours

Minimum Touring Time: 1½ hours

Rainy Day Touring: Recommended

Author's Rating: ★★   Intriguing collection of old and contemporary
  dolls

Services and Facilities:

Restaurants No	Lockers No
Alcoholic beverages No	Pet kennels No
Disabled access Yes	Rain check No
Wheelchair rental No	Private tours Yes
Baby stroller rental No	

Description and Comments   Novelist Anne Rice has been perhaps the most famous resident of New Orleans for the past couple of decades. Numerous books and several feature films about vampires, voodoo, and the seedier side of New Orleans have thrust Rice and her dark views of the city into the limelight. In turn, Rice's wealth has bought her many historic properties in the city, including the old St. Elisabeth's Orphanage, which now houses her extensive doll collection. On view are more than 100 antique dolls from around the world, as well as several more macabre dolls inspired from Rice's vampire epics.

St. Louis Cathedral

725 Chartres Street (on Jackson Square), New Orleans; (504) 525-9585;
www.saintlouiscathedral.org

Hours: Daily, 7 a.m.–6:30 p.m.

Admission: Free

Appeal by Age Group:

Pre-school	Grade School	Teens	Young Adults	Over 30	Seniors
★★	★★★	★★★	★★★	★★★	★★★

Average Touring Time: 1 hour

Minimum Touring Time: 30 minutes

Rainy Day Touring: Recommended

Author's Rating: ★★★   The majestic cornerstone of New Orleans

Services and Facilities:

Restaurants No	Lockers No
Alcoholic beverages No	Pet kennels No
Disabled access Yes	Rain check No
Wheelchair rental No	Private tours Yes, every half-hour
Baby stroller rental No	

Description and Comments   If you have not seen the St. Louis Cathedral, you have not seen New Orleans. Since 1794, the Greek Revival structure has loomed like a fairy tale castle over Jackson Square. Actually, St. Louis Cathedral, erected in honor of the missionary who proclaimed the seventh Crusade, was constructed in the early eighteenth century, but was destroyed in 1722 by a hurricane and again in 1788 in a fire.

On a tour of the cathedral, you will see ornately decorated stained-glass windows depicting the life of French St. Louis as well as an enormous portrait of the man who would become King Louis IX above the altar. Small chapels and interesting art and architecture will keep you engaged for some time.

Side Trips

New Orleans Cemeteries   It was the Spanish who first decided that New Orleans' dead should be buried in above-ground tombs. Originally, French colonists had tried to bury their dead the usual way—underground. But constant rain and flooding, not to mention an abundance of swampland, kept wooden coffins from staying grounded. Although New Orleanians have since found a way to redirect water into Lake Pontchartrain and the

Mississippi River, the tradition of above-ground burial is still "alive" in the Crescent City.

You can get a glimpse of the Cities of the Dead, if you go on a walking tour with the Voodoo Museum. But, if you want to strike out on your own, check out St. Louis Cemetery No. 1 on Basin Street, or Lafayette Cemetery No. 1 on Washington Avenue. The former opens daily at 9 a.m. and closes at 3 p.m. (noon on Sundays). Voodoo master Marie Laveau is buried here, as are other notable members of early New Orleans society. Lafayette Cemetery No. 1 is best known for its role in the movie *Interview with a Vampire* and is an interesting diversion in the Garden District. Opening times for this cemetery vary.

Audubon Institute   Ornithologist and wildlife champion John James Audubon lived in Louisiana for part of his life. His legend lives on in a number of museums and refuges throughout the state. Today, New Orleans' Audubon Institute oversees the Audubon Park and Zoological Gardens, the Aquarium of the Americas, the Louisiana Nature Center, the Audubon Institute Center for Research of Endangered Species, the Freeport-McMoRan Audubon Species Survival Center, and Wilderness Park. The Audubon Living Science Museum, which will focus on the technology behind conservation efforts, is scheduled to open in 2001. For more information on the Audubon Institute's programs, call (504) 861-2537 or visit www.auduboninstitute.org.

Lake Pontchartrain Causeway and Points North   Rarely does a bridge deserve to be included in a list of attractions, but at 24 miles long, the Lake Pontchartrain Causeway is the longest bridge in the world. The lake and bridge also serve as nesting grounds for dozens of migratory bird species.

Indeed, driving across the bridge can be a rather dull experience, so planning a trip north of New Orleans will give you reason to drive on the Causeway. Head to the North Shore, where you'll find truly southern towns like Bogalusa, Hammond, and Slidell. Right across the bridge in Covington, you can visit Fancy Faces, Inc., (504) 893-2652, where artists construct and paint thousands of masks for Mardi Gras. If you want to go on an authentic swamp tour, take I-10 to Slidell. Honey Island Swamp Tours, (504)641-1769, and Swamp Monster Tours, (504) 641-5106 or (800) 245-1132, put you in touch with the Bayou's abundant natural resources. And, if you and your family enjoy looking for antiques, you are guaranteed to find vintage dolls, pottery, art, and collectibles at Ponchatoula's Antique City, (800) 542-7520.

Grand Isle   When New Orleans want to escape to the "coast," their closest option is Grand Isle. The small island at the end of Louisiana Highway No. 1 is an idyllic respite from the hustle and bustle of Crescent City life. A small community of approximately 1,500 live on the island year-round to accommodate tourism, work on the oil rigs, or haul in the daily catch from shrimp boats. During the summer, the population swells to around 12,000—certainly increasing car traffic on the island, but not hampering the beauty of Grand Isle's sunsets and beaches. Primary activities on the island are fishing, bird-watching, and miniature golf, but visitors are also welcome to wade in the warm Gulf waters. If you decide to overnight in Grand Isle, there are a few motels, bed and breakfasts, and campsites to choose from. For more information, contact the Grand Isle Tourist Commission at (504) 787-2997.

Jazzland   Just as Nashville once had its Opryland, New Orleans has its Jazzland. Opened in 2000, this 140-acre theme park located approximately 20 minutes from downtown New Orleans has water rides, roller coasters, and themed areas such as Mardi Gras, Cajun country, and more. Visitors can also catch live jazz performances as well as Creole, country, Cajun, and rock and roll concerts. Jazzland is open from May through September; (504) 242-0220; www.jazzland.com.

Family-Friendly Restaurants

CAFE DU MONDE

1039 Decatur Street; (504) 587-0835

Meals served: Open 24 hours
Cuisine: Regional
Entrée range: $3–7
Kids menu: No
Reservations: No
Payment: Cash only

If you are looking for a late-night bite or an early morning treat, stop in to Cafe du Monde, one of New Orleans' best-known and oldest cafes. Here you can indulge in cafe au lait or hot chocolate and a big plate of powdered-sugar-covered beignets (pronounced ben-YAY), the city's answer to fresh doughnuts.

THE GUMBO SHOP

630 St Peter Street; (504) 525-1486

Meals served: Lunch and dinner
Cuisine: Regional

Entrée range: $4.95–15.95
Kids menu: No
Reservations: Not necessary for groups of less than ten
Payment: All major credit cards accepted

Soup is a meal at The Gumbo Shop, where you can load up on hot, spicy bowls of seafood gumbo, andouille sausage gumbo, or jambalaya. The quaint Gumbo Shop also serves up étoufée, red beans and rice, blackened fish and chicken, and a few pasta dishes. Also worth a try are the shop's delicious desserts, including the chocolate brownie pie and the hot bread pudding with whiskey sauce. There is no special menu for kids, but prices for po-boys are reasonable at $4.95. The Gumbo Shop is just off of Jackson Square.

MAXIMO'S RESTAURANT

1117 Decatur Street; (504) 586-8883

Meals served: Lunch and dinner
Cuisine: Italian
Entrée range: $6.95–17.95
Kids menu: No
Reservations: Recommended
Payment: All major credit cards accepted

Although Creole cuisine is a must when dining in New Orleans, you don't have to have it at every meal. Consider going to Maximo's Restaurant, a traditional Italian trattoria conveniently located in the French Quarter. Instead of po-boys, crawfish, and gumbo, Maximo's serves up specialties like veal scallopine, big bowls of pasta, and crusty garlic bread. For a guaranteed tasty, yet nutritious, dinner, order the antipasto platter and spaghetti with marinara or meat sauce for hungry kids.

MOTHER'S

401 Poydras Street at Tchoupitoulas Street; (504) 523-9656

Meals served: Breakfast, lunch, and dinner
Cuisine: Regional
Entrée range: $3–12
Kids menu: No
Reservations: No
Payment: Cash only

It's always best to go to restaurants that locals frequent, and Mother's is no exception. The comfort food being served up at Mother's is New Orleans–

style po-boys, dripping with remoulade sauce and crammed with fried oysters, shrimp, or almost anything else. If you're brave, you can try the Ferdi Special, which consists of baked ham, roast beef, gravy, and "debris," better known as the blackened extras that build up while cooking the meats. Also try the jambalaya, gumbo, and turtle soup, a local favorite. Mother's has been in business for more than 50 years and still draws crowds, so be prepared to wait in line on occasion.

PETUNIA'S RESTAURANT

817 St. Louis Avenue, New Orleans; (504) 522-6440
www.petuniasrestaurant.com

Meals served: Breakfast, lunch, and dinner
Cuisine: French/Regional
Entrée range: $5.95–20.95
Kids menu: No
Reservations: Recommended
Payment: All major credit cards accepted

If you have yet to enjoy a crèpe, a thin type of pancake, stop in to Petunia's, where you can order an all-crèpe meal. Entrée crèpes are wrapped around shrimp, cheese, ratatouille, and other Creole- and French-style fillings. For dessert, try warm crèpes filled with ice cream and walnuts and topped with bananas foster or cherries. Indeed, dinners are a bit pricey, but Petunia's claims to serve the "biggest crèpes in the world," making it easy for kids and parents to share these tasty dishes. Kids will also enjoy one of a number of overstuffed po-boys, which start at $5.95.

Baton Rouge

Although its name means "red stick," Baton Rouge is hardly a standout, partly due to the city's location between chic New Orleans and Cajun capital Lafayette. But Baton Rouge avoids middle-sister syndrome, taking its place as the heart of Plantation Country, the seat of government, and the home of the state's largest university. At its very core, Baton Rouge is strictly a southern college town, but if you look closely, you'll notice that aspects of Creole and Cajun heritage have enhanced the vibe of the place. Put another way, Baton Rouge is an ideal stepping stone between two worlds.

Sites to see in Baton Rouge are of the historical variety, and they include the **Louisiana State Capitol** (both old and new); restored World War II destroyer *USS Kidd;* and various plantation homes and estates that dot the countryside along the **Great River Road.** The battleship is of special interest to kids, as are the **Louisiana Arts and Science Museum** and the **Laura Plantation,** the site where the stories of Uncle Remus and Br'er Rabbit were first brought to life.

Family Lodging

Embassy Suites Baton Rouge

You can tell by the Embassy Suites' extravagant eight-story tropical atrium garden that the hotel gives the same attention to detail to its guestrooms as it does to its public areas. The hotel's two-room, standard suites are beautifully appointed with wall-to-wall carpeting, cozy bedding and a comfortable sitting area. Amenities include an in-room coffee maker, an iron and ironing board, a microwave, a mini-refrigerator, cable television, and modem ports. Services offered at the hotel are laundry service, room service, free airport shuttle, and babysitting. Cribs are available for the very little ones. Also on the premises is a pool and Jacuzzi, and dining is easy at the award-winning, Cajun-style eatery Branberry's. The Embassy Suites is just minutes away

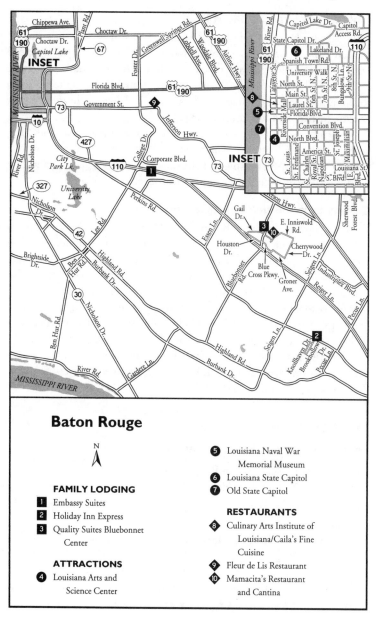

Baton Rouge

N
Λ

FAMILY LODGING

1. Embassy Suites
2. Holiday Inn Express
3. Quality Suites Bluebonnet Center

ATTRACTIONS

4. Louisiana Arts and Science Center

5. Louisiana Naval War Memorial Museum
6. Louisiana State Capitol
7. Old State Capitol

RESTAURANTS

8. Culinary Arts Institute of Louisiana/Caila's Fine Cuisine
9. Fleur de Lis Restaurant
10. Mamacita's Restaurant and Cantina

from the attractions in Baton Rouge, and rates start at $119 per night. 4914 Constitution Avenue, Baton Rouge; (800) EMBASSY or (225) 924-6566.

Holiday Inn Express Baton Rouge

Although this Holiday Inn is billed as an "Express" hotel, it is not short of creature comforts. All of the inn's 60 rooms and five suites come equipped with a mini-refrigerator, microwave, cable television with VCR, coffee maker, hair dryer, and alarm clock. You can bring in a laptop to hook-up to the room's standard dataports in case you feel like surfing the 'net or checking email, and local calls are free.

The Holiday Inn Express also features a spa and fitness center and offers laundry service. Children 19 and younger stay free with parents, but with prices starting at $64 per night, your family can also request connecting rooms; 4914 Constitution Drive, Baton Rouge; (225) 930-0600.

Quality Suites Bluebonnet Center

You can't go wrong with the Baton Rouge Quality Suites, as the 120-room hotel offers tons of amenities. On the property are an outdoor pool and exercise facility, and suites feature satellite television, irons and ironing boards, in-room phones with voicemail, and dataports. Quality Suites also adds a nice touch with its complimentary, cooked-to-order breakfasts.

This Baton Rouge hotel is ideal if you plan to visit the government buildings or the *USS Kidd*. The Mall of Louisiana and Louisiana State University are nearby, too. Rates start at $79.95, and kids younger than 19 stay free with parents or grandparents. Ask for discounts if you are a member of AAA or have a military ID. 9138 Bluebonnet Centre Boulevard, Baton Rouge; (225) 293-1199.

Attractions

Louisiana Arts and Science Center

100 South River Road, Baton Rouge; (225) 344-5272
   www.ci.baton-rouge.la.us/dept/ddd/lasc

Hours: Tuesday–Friday, 10 a.m.–3 p.m.; Saturday, 10 a.m.–4 p.m.;
   Sunday, 1–4 p.m.

Admission: $3 adults, $2 seniors and children ages 2–12

Appeal by Age Group:

Pre-school	Grade School	Teens	Young Adults	Over 30	Seniors
★★	★★★★	★★★	★★★	★★★	★★★

Average Touring Time: 2 hours

Minimum Touring Time: 1½ hours

Rainy Day Touring: Recommended

Author's Rating: ★★★   Revolving workshops and exhibits keep
   museum interesting

Services and Facilities:

Restaurants No	Lockers No
Alcoholic beverages No	Pet kennels No
Disabled access Yes	Rain check No
Wheelchair rental No	Private tours No
Baby stroller rental No	

Description and Comments No matter if your family is interested in astronomy or artworks, you'll find something fascinating at the Louisiana Art and Science Center. The Center's main attractions are its hands-on science gallery and the Challenger Center. The latter allows kids as young as age ten to participate in simulated space-flight missions. Each participant on a mini-mission (maximum crew of 16) or a full mission (maximum crew of 32) is given a job to do while aboard the "Challenger," such as navigation, communication, and maintaining life support. Such responsibility has the potential to make younger children feel on top of the world.

If art is your bag, you won't be disappointed with the featured collections at the Arts Center. Visitors will have a chance to see original works from Audubon and Ansel Adams, while traveling exhibits afford art enthusiasts a chance to see such paintings as those from Picasso and Renoir and even an original 1455 Gutenberg Bible.

Louisiana Naval War Memorial Museum

305 South River Road, Baton Rouge; (225) 342-1942

Hours: Daily, 9 a.m.–5 p.m.

Admission: $3 adults, $2 children ages 5–12; for museum and ship: $6 adults, $5 seniors, $3.50 children ages 5–12

Appeal by Age Group:

Pre-school	Grade School	Teens	Young Adults	Over 30	Seniors
★★	★★★	★★★	★★★	★★★	★★★

Average Touring Time: 2 hours

Minimum Touring Time: 1 hour

Rainy Day Touring: Not recommended

Author's Rating: ★★★

Services and Facilities:

Restaurants No	Lockers No
Alcoholic beverages No	Pet kennels No
Disabled access Yes	Rain check No
Wheelchair rental No	Private tours Yes
Baby stroller rental No	

Description and Comments   The Naval War Memorial Museum is unique because it is housed in the restored World War II destroyer ship *USS Kidd*. The massive ship has a story of its own, as it was attacked by kamikazes in the South Pacific Theater during the war. The *USS Kidd* is also the only naval ship to be allowed to fly the Jolly Roger flag, the skull and crossbones typical of pirate ships.

The museum itself is a fascinating exploration of nautical vessels from the nation's wars. It has interactive exhibits on subs, destroyers and other ships, artifacts from the wars, a Veterans Wall, and an Honor Hall. During the months when the tide is low, you can even investigate *USS Kidd* from below, as the ship rests on a number of stabilizing cement blocks. This aspect of the museum has even led it to be included in the files of Ripley's Believe it Or Not.

Louisiana State Capitol

State Capitol Drive, Baton Rouge; (225) 342-7317

Hours: Daily, 8 a.m.–4:30 p.m.; observation tower closes at 4 p.m.

Admission: Free

Appeal by Age Group:

Pre-school	Grade School	Teens	Young Adults	Over 30	Seniors
★	★★	★★★	★★★	★★★	★★★

Average Touring Time: 1 hour

Minimum Touring Time: 1 hour

Rainy Day Touring: Recommended

Author's Rating: ★★★   One of the nation's most notable capitol buildings

Services and Facilities:

Restaurants No	Lockers No
Alcoholic beverages No	Pet kennels No
Disabled access Yes	Rain check No
Wheelchair rental No	Private tours No
Baby stroller rental No	

Description and Comments   Also known as the "house that Huey built," the towering State Capitol is a testament to the ego and influence of former Louisiana governor Huey Long. Construction of the 34-story Art-Deco legislative house began in 1932, during the Great Depression, and was completed one year later in 1933. Long was assassinated in 1935 in the very building that he struggled to have built. The murder site on the first floor has become one of the capitol's main attractions, mostly because the marble floors and walls are still marked with bullet holes. Also here are original newspaper articles and photos about the incident.

You can get a great view of Baton Rouge and Plantation Country from the observation deck on the 27th floor. But make sure to take a closer look inside and outside the building. The grand marble staircase at the building's entrance has 48 steps—one for each of the states in the Union in 1933. Gleaming Memorial Hall features maps and historical documents pertaining to Louisiana and all the flags that have once flown over the territory/state, including the flags of France, Bourbon Spain, and the Republic of West Florida. Outdoors, in the Capitol Gardens, the grave of former governor Huey Long lies underneath a life-size statue of the man.

Old State Capitol

100 North Boulevard at River Road, Baton Rouge; (504) 342-0500 or (800) 488-2968

Hours: Tuesday–Saturday, 10 a.m.–4 p.m.; Sunday, noon–4 p.m.

Admission: $4 adults, $3 seniors, $2 children and students with ID, free ages 6 and younger

Appeal by Age Group:

Pre-school	Grade School	Teens	Young Adults	Over 30	Seniors
★	★	★★	★★★	★★★	★★★

Average Touring Time: 1 hour

Minimum Touring Time: 1 hour

Rainy Day Touring: Recommended

Author's Rating: ★★★   Historic building a joy to tour

Services and Facilities:

Restaurants No	Lockers No
Alcoholic beverages No	Pet kennels No
Disabled access Yes	Rain check No
Wheelchair rental No	Private tours Yes, on Mondays
Baby stroller rental No	

Description and Comments   Perched atop a hill off of Old River Road, the Old State Capitol resembles more of a medieval fortress than a legislative assembly building, with its symmetrical white towers and Spanish Bourbon–style architecture. But inside the building gives way to mahogany fixtures and marble checkerboard floors, more befitting of a southern capitol building.

Any questions that may not have been answered by the exhibits at the "new" State Capitol can certainly be answered in the old one, because here you can learn more about the Louisiana Purchase, the former governors and political figures of the state, and the assassination of Huey Long. Also housed in the Old Capitol are the state archives, including manuscripts, photographs, and sundry memorabilia dating back to the 1700s.

Side Trips

Plantation Country and the Great River Road   Just beyond Baton Rouge along the Great River Road lie numerous plantation houses, most of which are open to visitors. Two notable estates are the Oak Alley Plantation, (800)442-5539, www.oakalleyplantation.com, in Vacherie, and the Nottoway Plantation, (504) 545-2730, in White Castle. Oak Alley Plantation has been the site of many Hollywood films and is rather infamous among River Road plantations for its ghosts and other-worldly visitors. Nottoway Plantation gives name to the town in which it resides because, as the largest plantation home in the South, it is often referred to as the "white castle."

Laura Plantation, Vacherie   The French-Creole–style Laura Plantation is also on Great River Road. You will notice immediately from the architecture and the brightly painted façade that this antebellum estate is a bit different than the others. Laura Plantation, named after Southern belle Laura Locoul, is also notable because it is supposedly the place from which the beloved children's tale about Uncle Remus and Br'er Rabbit sprung. As the story goes, Joel Chandler Harris, the author of the Uncle Remus series, would visit the plantation and listen to slaves as they recounted West African folk tales. If you read the classic tales of Br'er Fox, Br'er Rabbit, and Br'er Bear, you will notice that the animal characters speak a sort of English patois—this is how Harris understood the enslaved Africans' Creole dialect, thus putting to paper a part of Louisiana's lingual heritage.

Laura Plantation is also worth a visit because of the history of Laura herself. Ms. Locoul left countless journals for her descendants so that they would know how daily life was carried out at the plantation. Visitors to the 14-acre estate can view these journals, original clothes and furnishings, the estate's gardens, and the slaves' quarters. Laura Plantation is open daily from 9 a.m.–5 p.m.; admission is $7. Phone (509) 265-7690.

Family-Friendly Restaurants

THE CULINARY ARTS INSTITUTE OF LOUISIANA/CAILA'S FINE CUISINE

427 Lafayette Street, Baton Rouge; (504) 343-6233 or (800) 927-0839

Meals served: Lunch and dinner
Cuisine: Varies
Entrée range: $5.95–10.95
Kids menu: No
Reservations: Not necessary
Payment: V, MC

Most families don't have the budget to splurge on an upscale dinner. But you can enjoy a five-star lunch or dinner at Caila's for the price you'd pay at other moderately priced restaurants. Operated by the Culinary Arts Institute of Louisiana, Caila's Fine Cuisine is a cooking school that turns out star chefs and participates in a student exchange with the famed Cordon Bleu.

The menu at Caila's is a bit tricky, as it changes daily for each meal according to the student who's running the show. Some nights you can feast on grilled shark or rack of lamb, whereas other nights feature succulent pork loin or satisfying pasta. You usually have the choice of two appetizers, which run from $2.95–4.95, and dessert. You can chow down at a lunch buffet for just $6.95 on some days.

Despite its relatively low prices, Caila's Fine Cuisine has all the trappings of an upscale dining establishment. The restaurant is probably not appropriate for young children, but older ones will probably enjoy the chance to dine on adult fare. What's more, if you choose to dine at Caila's, you can take a free tour of the cooking facilities or watch complimentary cooking demonstrations.

FLEUR DE LIS RESTAURANT

5655 Government Street, Baton Rouge; (225) 924-2904

Meals served: Lunch and dinner
Cuisine: Pizza
Entrée range: $4.95–9.95 (whole pies)
Kids menu: No
Reservations: Not necessary
Payment: Cash and checks only

The only things on the menu at Fleur de Lis Restaurant are "Roman pizza pies," but simplicity is all you need when trying to feed the family and get back on the road. Fleur de Lis offers an "Around the World" pizza with sausage, pepperoni, salami, mushrooms, onions, and anchovies, and, on the other end of the spectrum, a vegetarian pizza. Of course, families are free to choose their own toppings. Fleur de Lis is kid-friendly, but you should note that part of the restaurant serves as a bar. Nevertheless, the wait staff is considerate of families, and the pies are tasty. The restaurant is open Tuesday through Saturday from 10 a.m.–10 p.m.

MAMACITA'S RESTAURANT AND CANTINA

7524 Bluebonnet Boulevard, Baton Rouge; (225) 769-3850

Meals served: Lunch and dinner

Cuisine: Mexican
Entrée range: $6–13
Kids menu: Yes
Reservations: Not necessary
Payment: All major credit cards accepted

Enjoy delicious Mexican and Tex-Mex cuisine at Mamacita's, open until 10 p.m. every night. This family restaurant serves enchiladas, fajitas, tacos, and heaping plates of nachos with all the fixings. Healthier choices include taco salad, grilled fish, and vegetarian burritos. Mamacita's also boasts an extensive kids' menu, with items like grilled shrimp and fish, enchiladas, tacos, fajitas, and hamburgers starting at $2.95.

Lafayette

If you really want to know the meaning of the French phrase "joie de vivre" (joy of living), visit Lafayette, the heart of Cajun country and French-speaking Louisiana. Here you will find the source of Louisiana stereotypes, including alligator swamp tours, rollicking zydeco festivals, and cuisine abounding with okra, shrimp, and Tabasco sauce. Many of these portrayals of Cajun life are well founded, but they will make more sense if you visit **Vermilionville** or **Acadian Village.** These two museums allow tourists to glimpse how Acadians once lived, as well as witness how these French settlers adapted after coming to the Louisiana region. To see how far Cajuns have come, make sure you check out the **George Rodrigue Museum** at the Acadian Village. Anyone who is familiar with the famous Blue Dog paintings will enjoy seeing a large collection of original works alongside Rodrigue's series "The Saga of the Acadians."

Family Lodging

Hilton Lafayette and Towers

The largest hotel in the area with 327 guestrooms and 15 floors, the Hilton Lafayette and Towers is the obvious choice for visitors to this Cajun city. The Hilton also offers convenience to downtown attractions, shops, and restaurants, a beautiful view of the Vermilion Bayou, and plenty of amenities. Families can take advantage of the hotel's outdoor pool, fitness facilities, boat dock, and game room, take in a meal at the on-site restaurant Cafe Jardin, or simply relax in one of the well-appointed rooms.

Standard amenities at the Hilton and Towers include cable television, alarm clocks, self-adjusting thermostats, and telephones with dataports. Additional amenities, such as in-room coffee makers, hairdryers, and sofa-beds can be provided upon request. Services include 24-hour housekeeping, wake-up calls, and laundry service. The Hilton concierge will even help you

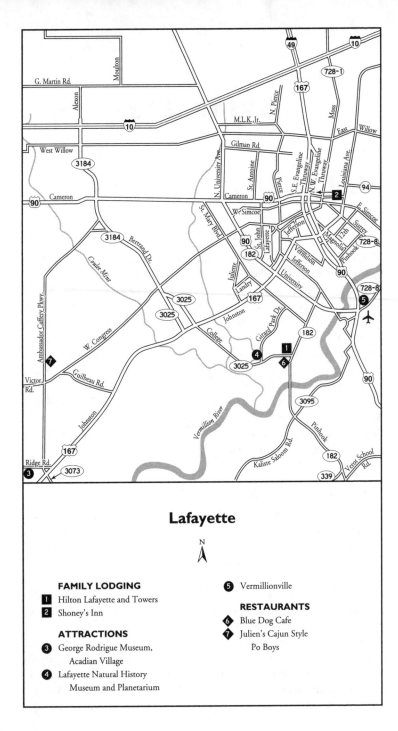

Lafayette

N

FAMILY LODGING
1 Hilton Lafayette and Towers
2 Shoney's Inn

ATTRACTIONS
3 George Rodrigue Museum,
   Acadian Village
4 Lafayette Natural History
   Museum and Planetarium

5 Vermillionville

RESTAURANTS
6 Blue Dog Cafe
7 Julien's Cajun Style
   Po Boys

arrange private tours to area attractions. Room rates at the Hilton Lafayette and Towers start at $109 per night, and children younger than 18 stay free with parents. 1521 West Pinhook Road, Lafayette; (318) 235-6111.

Shoney's Inn Lafayette

Shoney's properties are known for being family-friendly, and the Shoney's Inn Lafayette is no different. This 105-room hotel is centrally located and close to such attractions as the Lafayette Cajun Dome and Vermilionville. Accommodations at Shoney's come without any frills, but include queen- or king-size beds, irons and ironing boards, and in-room phones and televisions. Upon request, you can get a room with a small refrigerator and microwave. Breakfast is not included in the price of a room. Rates for the Shoney's Inn start at $52, and children younger than 18 stay free with parent or guardian. The Inn also offers discounts for government workers, military personnel, seniors, and members of AAA. 2216 NE Evangeline Thruway, Lafayette; (318) 234-0383.

Attractions

George Rodrigue Museum, Acadian Village

200 Green Leaf Drive, Lafayette; (337) 981-2364

Hours: Daily, 10 a.m.–5 p.m.

Admission: $6 adults, $5 seniors, $2.50 children ages 6–14

Appeal by Age Group:

Pre-school	Grade School	Teens	Young Adults	Over 30	Seniors
★★★	★★★	★★★	★★★	★★★	★★★

Average Touring Time: 2 hours

Minimum Touring Time: 1 hour

Rainy Day Touring: Recommended

Author's Rating: ★★★ Rodrigue originals are a sight to see

Services and Facilities:

Restaurants No		Lockers No
Alcoholic beverages No		Pet kennels No
Disabled access Yes		Rain check No
Wheelchair rental No		Private tours Yes
Baby stroller rental No		

Description and Comments Many Americans do not know the man behind the famous Blue Dog paintings, but a stop at the George Rodrigue Museum in the Acadian Village will change that. Louisiana native Rodrigue is the most famous of local celebrities in Lafayette, and his universally beloved Dogs are to thank for that. At the Acadian Village, visitors can view a revolving selection of the artist's own Blue Dog paintings, as well as a series of 18 paintings called the "Saga of the Acadians." The latter collection traces the history of the Cajun people from Canada to Louisiana, and is perhaps the only series of paintings ever commissioned to portray Acadian life. If you want to see further examples of Rodrigue's work, you can visit the bronze statue of Longfellow, Evangeline, and Gabriel, which the artist created in 1975. This statue, located on Kaliste-Saloom Road, is evidence that the legend of Longfellow's "Evangeline" still lives on in Cajun country.

When you are finished looking at Rodrigue's works, you can stroll around Acadian Village, which is a recreation of a Cajun community from the 1800s. Replicas and authentic Cajun buildings, including a village store, blacksmith and chapel, are open to visitors.

Lafayette Natural History Museum and Planetarium

637 Girard Park Drive, Lafayette; (318) 291-5544; www.lnhm.org

Hours: Monday–Friday, 9 a.m.–5 p.m.;, Saturday–Sunday, 1–5 p.m.

Admission: Free

Appeal by Age Group:

Pre-school	Grade School	Teens	Young Adults	Over 30	Seniors
★★	★★★	★★★	★★★	★★★	★★★

Average Touring Time: 2 hours

Minimum Touring Time: 1½ hour

Rainy Day Touring: Recommended

Author's Rating: ★★★

Services and Facilities:

Restaurants No	Lockers No
Alcoholic beverages No	Pet kennels No
Disabled access Yes	Rain check No
Wheelchair rental No	Private tours No
Baby stroller rental No	

Description and Comments   What is amazing about the Louisiana Natural History Museum is that it packs so many exhibits and displays into such a small space. There are two galleries, housing such items as Native American artifacts, rare books, photography, and even moon rocks. The Discovery Room is a small hands-on area where visitors can handle live reptiles and see a complete whale skeleton. The 58-seat planetarium offers spectacular celestial shows as well as special astronomy programs and workshops.

Vermilionville

1600 Surrey Street; (337) 233-4077 or (800) 99-BAYOU

Hours: Daily, 10 a.m. –5 p.m.

Admission: $8 adults, $6.50 seniors, $5 children ages 6–18

Appeal by Age Group:

Pre-school	Grade School	Teens	Young Adults	Over 30	Seniors
★★	★★★	★★	★★	★★★	★★★

Average Touring Time: 2 hours

Minimum Touring Time: 1 hour

Rainy Day Touring: Not recommended

Author's Rating: ★★★ Fun look at early Cajun life

Services and Facilities:

Restaurants Yes	Lockers No
Alcoholic beverages No	Pet kennels No
Disabled access Yes	Rain check No
Wheelchair rental No	Private tours Yes
Baby stroller rental No	

Description and Comments A trip to Vermilionville, the original name for the modern-day city of Lafayette, means a step back in time to early Louisiana life. Replica Acadian and Creole villages dating from the mid-1700s to the late 1800s are yours to explore, and costumed storytellers recount folk tales along the way. Vermilionville is a veritable living history museum, and visitors can attend food-and-craft demonstrations and enjoy live music.

Side Trips

McIlhenny Company, Avery Island It's hard to believe that a product known the world over is produced in such a small place. But it's true: Avery Island is the home of McIlhenny Company Tabasco Sauce Factory, (phone (800) 634-9599). Millions of bottles of the hot sauce have been produced on Avery Island since the early 1900s—first, in a small building called the "Laboratory," and since 1980 in its current location. Families can tour the Tabasco Factory and see how Capsicum peppers become one of the world's favorite condiments. Also visit the historical gallery and The Tabasco Country Store, where you can buy all things Tabasco. The Factory is open Monday through Saturday starting at 9 a.m.; admission is free.

"Rendez-vous des Cajuns" Radio Show, Eunice The oldest, continuously broadcast radio show in Louisiana can still be seen on Saturday nights in Eunice. Fans of Cajun music, humor, and heritage pack into this small town's Liberty Theatre each Saturday to hear the Cajun Country version of the Grand Ol' Opry. The show can also be heard on radio stations throughout the state, but the live show is a spectacle you'll not soon forget. Featured at the Rendez-vous are local musicians, comedians, storytellers, and various members of the Cajun community who seek their 15 minutes of fame here. Be prepared to not understand much of the show, as many of the performers still perform with a heavy French accent, or neglect to speak any English at all. 200 West Park Avenue, Eunice; (318) 457-7389.

Konriko Rice Mill and Store   Rice is as much a part of Cajun and Creole cuisine as shrimp and crawfish. Operating since 1914, Konriko is the oldest rice mill in the United States. Since 1981 it has been listed on the National Register of Historic Places. The Conrad Rice Company (Konriko) is also one of the most visited attractions in the Bayou Teche area of southern Louisiana. You can tour the rice mill and watch how rice is produced and packaged, or visit the Konriko store, where you can test rice dishes and purchase Konriko products. The Konriko Rice Mill is open Monday through Saturday, and a tour costs $2.75 for adults and $1.25 for children. A visit to the store is free. 309 Ann Street, New Iberia; (318) 367-6163, (800) 737-5667.

Family-Friendly Restaurants

BLUE DOG CAFE

1211 West Pinhook Road, Lafayette; (337) 237-0005
www.bluedogart.com/cafe

Meals served: Lunch and dinner
Cuisine: Nouveau Cajun
Entrée range: $9.95–19.95
Kids menu: No
Reservations: Recommended
Payment: All major credit cards accepted

If you don't make it to George Rodrigue's exhibition space at the Acadian Village, consider visiting the Blue Dog Cafe, where you can enjoy the art while you eat. The restaurant is owned and operated by Rodrigue, and replaces the artists' popular restaurant Cafe Tee George, which was consumed by fire in 1998. Blue Dog Cafe has many traditional Cajun items on its menu and a lot of surprises, such as crawfish enchiladas and Asian-

Cajun seafood dumplings. The foods are delectable, the atmosphere is delightful, and tables are sometimes hard to come by. There are no specific kids' menu items, however, children will do fine with most of the cafe's ample appetizers or hearty soups. Blue Dog Cafe is open Monday through Friday from 11 a.m.–2 p.m. and from 5–10 p.m. The restaurant opens Saturdays for dinner and is closed on Sundays.

JULIEN'S CAJUN STYLE PO BOYS

4400F Ambassador Caffery Parkway, Lafayette; (337) 981-8162

Meals served: Lunch and dinner
Cuisine: Cajun/American
Entrée range: $4–7.25
Kids menu: Yes
Reservations: No
Payment: All major credit cards accepted

Julien's has been serving up tasty, inexpensive po-boy sandwiches to hungry students and families since 1985. You can try a traditional Cajun po-boy with fried oysters, shrimp, or catfish topped with lettuce, tomato, and remoulade, or you can try one of Julien's specialty sandwiches like the "Rajun Cajun" or the Prime Rib po-boy. Kids under age 6 can dine on a peanut butter and jelly po-boy, a cheese-boy, or a bowl of chili and wieners for $2.29.

Shreveport

Shreveport and nearby Bossier City make up the largest metropolitan area in the region of Louisiana known as Sportsman's Paradise. These twin cities are less like the rest of Louisiana, lacking the big-city style of New Orleans and the Cajun heritage of Lafayette, and instead are more akin to Baton Rouge with its southern roots. As a sporting locale, Shreveport is ideal for fishing, hunting, canoeing, and swimming. The area also boasts Texas League AA baseball and is host to professional water-skiing competitions, golf tournaments, and the NCAA Independence Bowl game.

Attractions here are also oriented towards sports and recreation. On hot days, check out **Water Town USA** or step into the air-conditioned **Ark-La-Tex Antique and Classic Vehicle Museum.** Then, if your brain needs a little exercise, you can head over to the interactive **Sci-Port Discovery Museum,** complete with educational workshops, science and art demonstrations, and an IMAX cinema.

Family Lodging

Sheraton Shreveport Hotel

If you're looking for comfort and luxury in the middle of Sportsman's Paradise, you'll find it at the 267-room Sheraton Shreveport. Convenient to downtown as well as golfing, tennis, and fishing, the Sheraton also has an outdoor swimming pool, spa facilities, and a fitness center. On-site restaurant Rennick's serves up Cajun and American fare for lunch and dinner and is where you can enjoy your complimentary hotel breakfast.

Along with typical amenities, such as cable television, the oversized rooms at the Sheraton feature multi-line phones, dataports, in-room refrigerators, and coffee makers. Most rooms offer disabled accessibility. The Sheraton also gives you access to laundry service, room service, and a concierge, who can

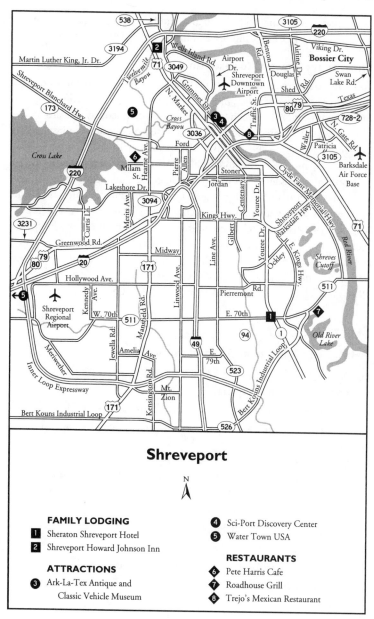

Shreveport

N

FAMILY LODGING

1. Sheraton Shreveport Hotel
2. Shreveport Howard Johnson Inn

ATTRACTIONS

3. Ark-La-Tex Antique and
   Classic Vehicle Museum

4. Sci-Port Discovery Center
5. Water Town USA

RESTAURANTS

6. Pete Harris Cafe
7. Roadhouse Grill
8. Trejo's Mexican Restaurant

plan excursions for your family to local recreational areas. A free hotel shuttle will transport you to and from the airport. Rates at the Sheraton

Shreveport range from $60–$129, and children younger than 18 stay free with parents. 1419 East 70th Street, Shreveport; (318) 797-9900.

Shreveport Howard Johnson Inn

You will be surprised at what you'll find at the Shreveport Howard Johnson. After extensive renovations, the hotel now consists of 135 finely decorated rooms, most of which overlook a spectacular courtyard garden. The HoJo is geared toward families, as it has fitness facilities, including an outdoor pool, 25-inch cable televisions in every room, and free parking for cars, trucks, and RVs. The hotel is also convenient to area attractions.

Standard rooms at the Howard Johnson come equipped with two queen-size beds, an iron and ironing board, a telephone and an alarm clock, and some rooms come with a miniature refrigerator and microwave. For families with special needs, the Howard Johnson offers a number of wheelchair-accessible rooms as well as rooms with connecting doors. Complimentary continental breakfast is served each morning. Rates at the HoJo Shreveport start at $48 per night, and children younger than 17 stay free with parents. 1906 North Market Street, Shreveport; (318) 424-6621.

Attractions

Ark-La-Tex Antique and Classic Vehicle Museum

601 Spring Street, Shreveport; (318) 222-0227
  www.softdisk.com/comp/classic

Hours: Tuesday–Saturday, 9 a.m.–5 p.m.; Sunday, 1–5 p.m.

Admission: $5 adults, $4 seniors and students, $3 children ages 6–12

Appeal by Age Group:

Pre-school	Grade School	Teens	Young Adults	Over 30	Seniors
★★	★★★	★★★	★★★	★★★	★★★

Average Touring Time: 1½ hours

Minimum Touring Time: 1 hour

Rainy Day Touring: Recommended

Author's Rating: ★★★   A fine gathering of vintage vehicles

Services and Facilities:

Restaurants No	Lockers No
Alcoholic beverages No	Pet kennels No
Disabled access Yes	Rain check No
Wheelchair rental No	Private tours No
Baby stroller rental No	

Description and Comments   The building that the Ark-La-Tex Car Museum occupies has had many incarnations. It started as a car dealership in the 1920s, turned into the Country and Western Dance Palace during the '50s and '60s, and was finally established as an antique automobile museum in 1995. On display at the Car Museum are dozens of vintage cars, trucks, and commercial vehicles, all of which are on loan from private collectors. The museum also features an automobile library and unique gift shop.

Sci-Port Discovery Center

820 Clyde Fant Parkway, Shreveport; (318) 424-3466 or (877) SCI-PORT
www.sciport.org

Hours: Monday–Friday, 9 a.m.–5 p.m.; Saturday, 10 a.m.–5 p.m.; Sunday 1–5 p.m.

Admission: $3 adults, $2.50 seniors, $2 children ages 3–17

Appeal by Age Group:

Pre-school	Grade School	Teens	Young Adults	Over 30	Seniors
★★★	★★★★	★★★	★★★	★★★	★★

Average Touring Time: 2 hours

Minimum Touring Time: 1½ hours

Rainy Day Touring: Recommended

Author's Rating: ★★★

Services and Facilities:

Restaurants No	Lockers No
Alcoholic beverages No	Pet kennels No
Disabled access Yes	Rain check No
Wheelchair rental No	Private tours No
Baby stroller rental No	

Description and Comments With its engaging, interactive exhibits about science and nature, the Sci-Port Discovery Center is a must-visit for families in Shreveport. Here you can learn about tornados, the swamp life of alligators, how rivers flow, and the functions of the human body. Sci-Port also offers special programs and camps for would-be inventors, artists, and explorers ages 5–14 years old. Kids and adults will enjoy the IMAX theater, which has featured 3-D films on swimming with dolphins, visiting the Galapagos Islands, and exploring space.

Water Town USA

7670 West 70th Street, Shreveport; (318) 938-5475
www.mardi.com/mardi_m.htm

Hours: May–September: Monday–Thursday, 10 a.m.–6 p.m.; Friday–Saturday, 10 a.m.–9 p.m.; Sunday, Noon–6 p.m.

Admission: $14.95 adults, $13.95 children less than 43 inches tall

Appeal by Age Group:

Pre-school	Grade School	Teens	Young Adults	Over 30	Seniors
★★★★	★★★★	★★★★	★★★	★★★	★★

Average Touring Time: 3 hours

Minimum Touring Time: 2 hours

Rainy Day Touring: Not recommended

Author's Rating: ★★★ Splashing good time

Services and Facilities:

Restaurants Yes	Lockers Yes
Alcoholic beverages No	Pet kennels No
Disabled access Yes	Rain check No
Wheelchair rental No	Private tours No
Baby stroller rental No	

Description and Comments How do you and your family cope with those hot and humid Louisiana days? Pack up the car and go to Water Town USA. This popular water park in Shreveport has a wave pool, slides, an Olympic-size pool, and a kiddy pool. There are also picnic areas and grassy spots set aside for Frisbee, volleyball, and other games.

Side Trip

Natchitoches This town is the oldest permanent settlement in the Louisiana Purchase Territory. Here, travelers can visit a replica of a 1732 French fort, take tours of magnificent plantation homes, including the one featured in the film *Steel Magnolias,* or tour the unique Museum of Historic Natchitoches. It is also an ideal place to hang your hat if you are planning a trip to the Kisatchie National Forest. For more information, contact the Natchitoches Parish Tourist Commission at (800) 259-1714.

Family-Friendly Restaurants

PETE HARRIS CAFE

1355 Milam, Shreveport; (318) 425-4277

Meals served: Dinner
Cuisine: American
Entrée range: $5–18
Kids menu: Yes

Reservations: Not necessary
Payment: All major credit cards accepted

The only thing that Pete Harris Cafe doesn't serve is the kitchen sink. Otherwise, you can order tons of Cajun and Creole favorites, including stuffed shrimp, beans and rice, and cups of gumbo. Or, you can indulge in any number of southern delicacies, such as pork chops, chicken livers, or fried chicken. Child's plates start at around $3 and feature chicken drumsticks, fried shrimp, or a fish filet sandwich.

ROADHOUSE GRILL

1752 East 70th Street, Shreveport; (318) 795-0540

Meals served: Lunch and dinner
Cuisine: American
Entrée range: $4.95 and up
Kids menu: Yes
Reservations: Not necessary
Payment: All major credit cards accepted

If your family has an American-sized appetite, stop into the Roadside Grill. The popular restaurant serves up all the favorites, such as hamburgers, baby back ribs, mesquite-grilled pork chops, and more. Meals for kids range from $2.29–$3.29 and include items like hamburgers, macaroni and cheese, and grilled chicken. On Tuesdays, kids eat free with parents.

TREJO'S MEXICAN RESTAURANT

9122 Mansfield Road, Shreveport; (318) 687-6192

Meals served: Lunch and dinner
Cuisine: Mexican
Entrée range: $6.95–13
Kids menu: No
Reservations: Accepted
Payment: All major credit cards accepted

A little bit of Mexico lives in Shreveport at Trejo's Mexican Restaurant. Sure, you can get your typical Tex-Mex items here, including fajitas, chimichangas, burritos, and soft- or hard-shell tacos. But, Trejo's also has authentic Mexican dishes, such as enchiladas with mole sauce and Bisteca Mexicana (Mexican-style steak). Entrée platters are extremely filling, so think twice about ordering a massive plate of Nachos del Chef as an appetizer. Trejo's does not have a kids' menu, but you can order a smaller portion of the dinner platters.

Part Five

Mississippi

M-I-double S-I-double S-I-double P-I . . . When kids think of Mississippi, this sing-song way of spelling its name comes to mind. For adults, to think of Mississippi is to think of Civil Rights struggles, the Blues, and an unparalleled legacy of American literature.

But Mississippi is also an outdoor wonderland, with the diverse natural beauty of sandy Gulf beaches, pine forests, and the rich plains of the Delta. Combined with a busy calendar of festivals and a smattering of museums, it seems that the "Hospitality State" was created especially with families in mind. As Sandy Bynum, coordinator of leisure travel for the state, says, "My mother always said you should never do anything that you couldn't take children with you. Practically every attraction in Mississippi is family-friendly."

In **Natchez,** shady streets lined with antebellum and Victorian mansions give testimony to the grandiose style of plantation life. In **Biloxi,** follow in the footsteps of Forrest Gump by taking an authentic shrimping expedition out into the Gulf of Mexico. The city also features a **Maritime and Seafood Industry Museum,** which chronicles the story of the state's vital economic relationship with the sea.

And speaking of the sea, Mississippi boasts the same clear water and white-sand beaches that have become synonymous with the Gulf Coast. After a day at the beach, stop by the **Gulf Islands National Seashore Visitors Center** in **Ocean Springs** for an interpretive look at the barrier islands, flora, and fauna found along the state's coast.

Museums are commonplace throughout Mississippi and almost every town, regardless of size, boasts at least one. The Blues, often called America's only original music, are memorialized at the **Delta Blues Museum** in **Clarksdale.** The **Checker Hall of Fame** in **Petal** exhibits memorabilia related to the history of the game of checkers. **Bay St. Louis** is home to the high tech **John C. Stennis Space Center,** where families can take guided

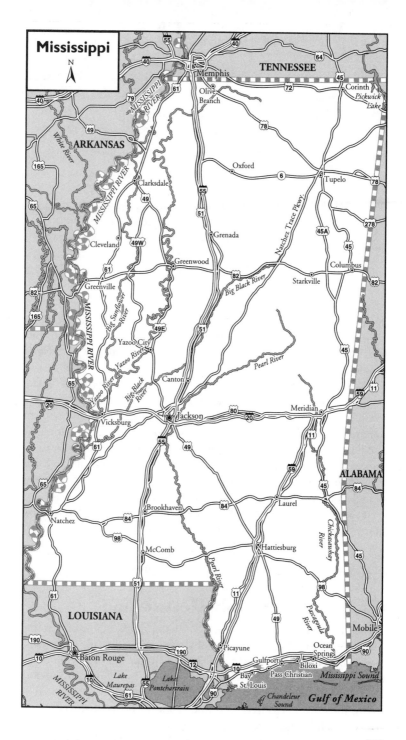

Kids' Beat

- The state bird is the mockingbird; the state flower is the magnolia blossom; the state tree is the magnolia.

- The Great Wall of China and northern Mississippi's Tennessee-Tombigbee Waterway are the only manmade objects on Earth visible to astronauts in space.

- Edward A. Barq invented root beer in Biloxi in 1898.

- The Ideal Toy Company and the "teddy bear" came into being after an incident at Onward in 1901, when Teddy Roosevelt refused to shoot a small bear cub while on an arranged hunt.

- The Mississippi Gulf Coast offers the world's longest manmade beach. It is 200 feet wide and 26 miles long.

---

tours of NASA's space shuttle main engine testing complex. And in **Vicksburg,** there are two of note: The **Biedenharn Coca-Cola Museum,** the site where Coca-Cola was first bottled in 1894, and the **Gray and Blue Naval Museum,** with a collection of over 2,500 toy soldiers. Of course, no visit would be complete without a stop at the Elvis Presley birthplace in **Tupelo.**

One major advantage to visiting the state is the weather. The climate is considered mild year-round, but unless you're accustomed to Southern summers, avoid spending too much time outdoors or in the car during the middle of the day. Spring and autumn temperatures range from 60 to 70 degrees and are the best times to visit. Winter days usually dip no lower than 45 to 50 degrees, and in the summer, expect the temperature to soar to the upper 90s accompanied by high humidity.

An automobile is essential for a Mississippi vacation, and you'll save time by using the larger cities as hubs for your activities.

Note: Mississippi is in the Central Standard Time Zone (CST). The area code in northern Mississippi has changed from 601 to 662.

Casinos as a Family Destination

The onslaught of big-time gambling is adding another dimension to the state's attractions. Tunica, Biloxi, and Gulfport have literally been transformed over the past ten years into destinations for gamblers from across the country. It seems that new hotels, restaurants, and casinos are popping up daily. And while gambling is the main attraction, many of the full-service resorts are beginning to provide an array of family-friendly programs for adults and children. Skeet shooting, swanky swimming pools, bayou excursions, golf, putt-putt, and arcades are among the offerings.

Mississippi's Not-to-Be-Missed Attractions	
Around the State	Delta Blues Museum
	Grand Village of the Natchez Indians
	Gulf Islands National Seashore
	International Checker Hall of Fame
	Mississippi Petrified Forest
	Natchez Pilgrimage
Tupelo	Elvis Presley Birthplace and Museum
	Jerry Lee Lewis Ranch
	Natchez Trace Parkway Visitors Center
Starkville	Pinedale Farms
	Rowan Oak
Jackson	City of Jackson Fire Museum and Public Fire Safety Education Center
	Jackson Zoological Park
	Mississippi Governor's Mansion
Vicksburg	Gray & Blue Naval Museum
	Vicksburg National Military Park
Mississippi's Gulf Coast	Beauvoir, Jefferson Davis Home & Presidential Library
	Buccaneer State Park
	Fort Massachusetts
	John C. Stennis Space Center
	Maritime and Seafood Industry Museum

If you are not a gambler, it's hard to ignore the casinos. They're big and flashy, and their resort-style accommodations are new and upscale. Still, each city has its own unique points of interest that can keep a family entertained, and while the resorts have a way to go in regards to the activities found in Las Vegas, new attractions and amenities are added continually as enticement for families.

Persons under age 21 are not allowed to gamble, nor are they allowed to hang around while you gamble. If you are gambling, your children have to be somewhere else. Unfortunately, the choices are limited. True, most of the hotels have nice swimming pools, but southern summer days are too hot to stay out for long. While golf and tennis are possibilities, court or greens fees are routinely charged, and you still must contend with limitations imposed by the climate.

After a short time, you will discover that the current options for your children's recreation and amusement are as follows:

1. You can simply allow your children to hang out. Given this alternative, the kids will swim a little, watch some TV, eat as much as their (or your) funds allow, and throw water balloons out of any hotel window that has not been hermetically sealed.

2. If your children are a mature age, you can turn them loose at local amusement and water parks.

3. You can hire a baby-sitter to come to your hotel room and tend your children. This works out pretty much like option 1 without the water balloons.

4. You can abandon the casino (or whatever else you had in mind) and "do things" with your kids. Swimming and eating (as always) will figure prominently into the plan, as will excursions to places that have engaged the children's curiosity.

GETTING THERE

By Plane. The largest airport in the state is Jackson International Airport at 100 International Drive, (601) 939-3713, with service from eight carriers. Other regional airports include the Biloxi/Gulfport Regional Airport, (601) 863-5951; the Tupelo Regional Airport, (662) 841-6571; the Greenville Municipal Airport (662) 334-3121; the Golden Triangle Regional airport in Columbus, (662) 327-4422; the Hattiesburg/Laurel Regional Airport, (601) 545-3111; and the Meridian Municipal Airport, (601) 482-0364. Depending on your destination, you might also opt to fly into Memphis International Airport or the New Orleans National Airport.

By Train. Amtrak has stops in Yazoo City, Bay St. Louis, Biloxi, Brookhaven, Greenwood, Gulfport, Hattiesburg, Hazlehurst, Jackson, Meridian, McComb, Pascagoula, Picayune, and Laurel. Information on train schedules is available at (800) 872-7245 or www.amtrak.com.

By Car. Mississippi's interstates include I-55, which runs from Memphis to New Orleans; I-20, which travels west to east; and I-59, which cuts across the southeastern corner of the state. The Natchez Trace parkway crosses the state from the northeastern corner to the southwestern corner.

U.S. 78 stretches from Birmingham to Memphis, U.S. 90 parallels the Gulf Coast from Alabama to New Orleans, and U.S. 49 leads from Yazoo City to Gulfport. For the latest road conditions in the state, log on to www.mdot.state.ms.us/road/road.htm.

The speed limit is 65 miles per hour throughout the state except for the Natchez Trace Parkway, which caps speed at 50 miles per hour. Mississippi law requires all front-seat occupants to buckle up, and children under two must be restrained in federally approved safety restraints.

HOW TO GET INFORMATION BEFORE YOU GO

State

Mississippi Department of Economic and Community Development, Division of Tourism Development, P.O. Box 849, Jackson 39205; (800)-WARMEST or (601) 359-3297; www.visitmississippi.org

Bed and Breakfast Association of Mississippi, 2430 Drummond Street, Vicksburg 39180; (601) 638-8893; www.missbab.com

Mississippi State Parks, P.O. Box 451, Jackson 39205-0451; (601) 364-2222 or (800) GO-PARKS; www.mdwfp.com

Regional

Area III Tourism Council (East Mississippi); (800) 327-2686; www.go-east.org

Local

Aberdeen Visitors Bureau, P.O. Box 288, Aberdeen 39730; (800) 634-3538 or (662) 369-9440

Bay St. Louis, Hancock County Tourism Development Bureau, P.O. Box 3002, Bay St. Louis 39521-3002; (800) 466-9048 or (228) 463-9222; www.hancockcountyms.org

Biloxi, Mississippi Gulf Coast Convention and Visitors Bureau, P.O. Box 6128, Biloxi 39506-6128; (888) 467-4853 or (228) 896-6699; www.gulf-coast.org

Brookhaven/Lincoln County Chamber of Commerce, P.O. Box 978, Brookhaven 39602-0978; (800) 613-4667 or (601) 833-1411; www.brook-havenms.com

Clarksdale, Coahoma County Tourism Commission, 1540 Desoto Avenue, Clarksdale 39614-0160; (800) 626-3764 or (662) 627-7337; www.clarks-dale.com

Cleveland-Bolivar County Chamber of Commerce/Tourism, P.O. Box 490, Cleveland 38732-0490; (800) 295-7473 or (662) 843-2712; www.ci.cleveland.ms.us

Columbus-Lowndes Convention and Visitors Bureau, P.O. 789, Columbus 39703; (800) 327-2686 or (601) 329-1191; www.columbus-ms.org

Corinth Area Tourism Promotion, P.O. Box 1089, Corinth 38835-1089; (800) 748-9048 or (601) 287-5269; www.corinth.net

Greenville, Washington County Convention and Visitors Bureau, 410 Washington Avenue, Greenville 38701; (800) 467-3582 or (662) 334-2711; www.thedelta.org

Greenwood Convention and Visitors Bureau, P.O. Drawer 739, Greenwood 38935-0739; (800) 748-9064 or (662) 453-9197; www.gcvb.com

Gulfport, Mississippi Gulf Coast Convention and Visitors Bureau, P.O. Box 6128; Gulfport 39506-6128; (888) 467-4853 or (228) 896-6699; www.gulfcoast.org

Hattiesburg Convention and Visitors Bureau, P.O. Box 16122, Hattiesburg 39404; (800) 638-6877 or (601) 268-3220; www.hattiesburg.org

Holly Springs Chamber of Commerce, 154 South Memphis Street, Holly Springs 38635; (662) 252-2943

Iuka, Tishomingo County Tourism Council, 203 East Quitman, Iuka 38852; (800) 386-4373 or (662) 423-0051; www.moad.com/tcdf

Metro Jackson Convention and Visitors Bureau, P.O. Box 1450, Jackson 39215-1450; (800) 354-7695 or (601) 960-1891; www.visitjackson.com

Meridian, Lauderdale County Tourism Bureau, P.O. Box 5313, Meridian 39302; (888) 868-7720 or (601) 482-8001

Mississippi Gulf Coast Convention and Visitors Bureau, P.O. Box 6128, Gulfport 39506-6128; (888) 467-4853 or (228) 896-6796; www.gulfcoast.org

Natchez Convention and Visitors Bureau, 640 South Canal Street, Box C; Natchez 39120; (800) 647-6724 or (601) 446-6345; www.natchez.ms.us

Ocean Springs Chamber of Commerce, P.O. Box 187, Ocean Springs 39566; (228) 875-4424; www.lillpr.com/oschamber

Oxford Tourism Council, P.O. Box 965, Oxford 38655; (800) 758-9177 or (662) 234-4680

Pascagoula, Jackson County Chamber of Commerce, P.O. Drawer 480, Pascagoula 39568-0480; (228) 762-3391; www.jcchamber.com

Philadelphia, Neshoba County Chamber of Commerce, P.O. Box 51, Philadelphia 39350; (601) 656-1742; www.neshoba.org

Starkville Visitors and Convention Council, 322 University Drive, Starkville 39759; (800) 649-TOUR or (662) 323-3322; www.starkville.org

Tunica County Convention and Visitors Bureau, P.O. Box 2739, Tunica 38676-2739; (888) 488-6422 or (662) 363-3800; www.tunicamiss.org

Tupelo Convention and Visitors Bureau, P.O. Drawer 47, Tupelo 38802; (800) 533-0611 or (662) 841-6521; www.tupelo.net

Vicksburg Convention and Visitors Bureau, P.O. Box 110, Vicksburg 39181-0110; (800) 221-3536 or (601) 636-9421; www.vicksburgcvb.org

---

More Mississippi Websites

The Adventures of Modern Day Tom Sawyers www.greatriver.com/freedom/report.html.

Student Resource Page www.visitmississippi.org/studentspage/studentspage.html

Mississippi River www.greatriver.com

State of Mississippi www.state.ms.us

Mississippi Counties www.mscounties.com

Cybercam of the Gulf Coast www.gulfcoast.org/cybercam

Family Outdoor Adventures

Δ = Camping
♥ = Author's favorite

♥ - *Blues Highway* It's no wonder that the Mississippi Delta has produced so many talented musicians. Here, the flat landscape with few trees—cleared more than a century ago for the area's rich cotton fields—leaves little more than imagination for entertainment. And it is in the imagination that America's blues were born. Its roots lie in African music and its heartbeat in the hard lives lived under the Delta sun. If you have aspiring musicians tagging along, this visit should drive home the notion that the best musicians don't rely on modern musical accoutrements to produce quality music. Rather, it is creativity and skill honed from hard work that turns amateurs into masters of the craft.

Meandering through the Delta and leading to Memphis is famous Highway 61. Legend has it that at the intersection of Highway 61 and

U.S. Highway 49, Robert Johnson, the "King of the Delta Blues Singers," sold his soul to the devil in order to become a famous bluesman. True or not, other native sons have followed in Johnson's footsteps, including B.B. King and Muddy Waters.

You'll find bits and pieces of Blues history throughout the Delta—a tombstone in one town, a record store in another, a plaque beside the road commemorating a person or event. The Delta Blues Museum in Clarksdale will piece together missing information, and if you're really bent on understanding and experiencing the music and culture of this region, plan your trip around one of the three major blues festivals held annually. The Sunflower River Blues Festival is held in Clarksdale the first weekend in August. The Mississippi Delta Blues Festival in Greenville occurs the third weekend in September, and Helena's King Biscuit Blues Festival is schedules the second weekend in October.

Civil War Sites Mississippi played an important but tragic role in the Civil War for both Confederate and Union forces. Many bloody battles were fought here, and it was the surrender of Vicksburg that finally severed Texas, Arkansas, and Louisiana from the rest of the Confederacy and gave the Union complete control of the Mississippi River.

Today, the battlefields, monuments, and cemeteries throughout the state stand in tribute to those who fought and are solemn reminders about the devastation of war. Many of the exhibits and displays in the parks are mild in nature, sidestepping the gruesome details of war, so most children won't be upset upon viewing them. And if your children have studied the Civil War in school, the exhibits simply reinforce and provide in-depth information about what they have already learned. Plus, many of the sites have ample outdoor space—ideal as play sites for kids who have been cooped up in the car.

For a complete Civil War tour, begin in Corinth, 20 miles south of the infamous Shiloh, Tennessee. As the junction for four railroads, the town was the site of the bloodiest battle in Mississippi history. Stop in at the Corinth Civil War Interpretive Center for a detailed look at Corinth's participation.

Brice's Cross Roads in Baldwyn was the site of a major Confederate victory; nearby in Tupelo, visit the National Battlefield. Also in northern Mississippi is Columbus. In 1866 local ladies decorated the graves of Confederate and Union soldiers in Friendship Cemetery. This "Decoration Day" led to the creation of a national Memorial Day.

Centrally located, Jackson was known as Chimneyville because it was burned on three different occasions. The Old Capitol Museum and the Governor's Mansion are points of interest.

Further east in Vicksburg, the Vicksburg National Military Park explains the surrender of the city to the Union, and there is also a Union ironclad ship, the *USS Cairo,* on display.

Finally, stop in Beauvoir in Gulfport to tour the last home of Confederate President Jefferson Davis. Davis lived in the home after the war and wrote his memoirs there.

You can plan your trip around one of the many re-enactments that occur annually. These skirmishes bring the war to life, from period campsites to soldiers dressed in authentic uniforms and carrying vintage weapons.

Fishing Fun, affordable fishing can be found at just about any of the lakes and rivers in the state as well as along the Gulf coast. For freshwater fishing, no less than 175 different species thrive in Mississippi's waters. The most popular game species include large- and small-mouth bass, striped bass, bream, white and black crappie, catfish, walleye, and sauger. Big River Guide Service, (662) 332-3341; and Muddy Water Anglers, (662) 332-9004, are two outfitters equipped for family excursions.

Fishing along the Gulf is just as plentiful. Crab, redfish, and speckled trout are easily caught off piers, estuaries and barrier islands, while shark, sea trout, cobia, red snapper, and Spanish and king mackerel provide sport offshore in the sound or the Gulf. Miss Lisa Sportfishing Charters, (228) 466-5757, carries families marsh-fishing, while the Tuna Sea Charter Boat, (228) 388-1120 or (228) 388-9333, specializes in half- and full-day trips offshore. And if you have a Forrest Gump in your group, try a shrimping expedition on the Gulf. Miss Marissa Charter Boat, (228) 832-6895, has daily shrimp tours. For a complete list of outfitters, go towww.visitmississippi.org/hunt&fish/outfitter.html.

▲ - *Gulf Islands National Seashore* Encroaching development along the Gulf of Mexico's pristine shoreline prompted Congress to create the Gulf Islands National Seashore in 1971. The seashore spans a total of 150 miles, which includes portions of islands and keys from West Ship Island in Gulfport to Okaloosa Island near Destin, Florida. Barrier islands make up most of the protected area, but it also has salt marshes, historic structures, dazzling white-sand beaches, archeological sites, and forests. With 5.5 million visitors each year, the Seashore is one of America's most popular national parks.

The Mississippi portion of the Seashore consists largely of barrier islands located ten miles offshore and accessible only by boat. East Ship, Deer, Horn, and Petit Bois islands are pristine and isolated. The islands form a natural buffer for the mainland from hurricanes and other storms; Ship Island was even split in two by one hurricane. During the 1930s, the islands served as inspiration for local artist Walter Anderson, who spent weeks at a time on the islands. The islands are now nationally designated wilderness areas and have primitive campsites but no restrooms or concessions. Call the park visitors center for more information.

West Ship Island is the most visited of the barrier islands and is where the Gulf of Mexico meets the Mississippi Sound. Boat excursions leave from the Gulfport Yacht Harbor daily March through October (phone (800) 388-3290 or (228) 864-1014), and private boats often dock near the island's Fort Massachusetts, a former Confederate POW camp. A boardwalk leads to the Gulf side of the island.

West Ship has limited food and water service, a park ranger station, and guided tours of Fort Massachusetts during the summer months. Divide your day between the beach and time spent exploring the fort. Boat excursions cost $14 for adults, $7 for children. For more information, call (228) 864-1014; www.gcww.com/shipisland.

The mainland portion of the Seashore is Davis Bayou in Ocean Springs. Davis Bayou has the typical offerings of a campground: Both electric and nonelectric sites, water hookups, picnic shelters, a nature trail, a boat launch, and The Gulf Islands National Seashore Visitor Center with an information desk and films about the Seashore. There is no beach at Davis Bayou. Park admission is free. Campsites for tents cost $14; RV sites cost $16. 3500 Park Road, Ocean Springs; (228) 875-0821; www.nps.gov/guis.

Natchez Pilgrimage   Yankees who travel south looking for antebellum homes and pretty women in hoop skirts should look no farther than Natchez and its spring and fall pilgrimages. The pilgrimages began in 1931 when a late frost thwarted blossoms for a weekend garden tour. Rather than call the event off, the organizers enlisted Natchez homeowners to open their wonderful antebellum homes to the public. The event was so successful that they scrapped the gardens altogether and have been showing homes ever since. Other historic towns like Vicksburg also have pilgrimages, but Natchez was the first and is considered to be the best.

The pilgrimage features about 30 homes in Natchez, and each has hostesses dressed in period costumes to explain the furnishings and history of each home. Refreshments are served, and music is provided at certain houses during the tour.

The event lasts five weeks each spring, and other businesses in town get in on the act as well, providing themed entertainment and specials related to the pilgrimage. Homes are shown each morning and afternoon, with the selection rotating each day. The fall event is an abbreviated version that lasts one day.

The tour requires a lot of walking, so if you are traveling with toddlers and seniors, you should plan accordingly. Also keep in mind that babies, toddlers, and even grade-school children will need special attention on the tour as many rooms contain pricey breakables. Kids can also get bored with the homes really fast, so break up your activities to allow time before or afterward for playing. However, if your child is fascinated with history and has a decent attention span, he should enjoy hearing the stories and legends about the homes and their prior occupants.

Half-day tour passes cost $24 for adults and $12 for children ages 17 and younger; (800) 221-3536; www.natchezpilgrimage.com.

Natchez Trace Parkway No one knows for certain how long people have been traveling the Natchez Trace, but as early as 1733, this worn Indian trail was included on French maps of America. In all likelihood, the path was created by Natchez, Chickasaw, and Choctaw Indians who hunted from the Mississippi River to the valleys of Tennessee. Later, as farmers began transporting crops and products on the rivers to New Orleans, they used the path as a direct return home. Wagons soon followed, but by the early 1800s, the slow pace of the trail gave way to the faster, smoother sails of steamboat travel. Today, the trace is a scenic, modern parkway that closely follows the course of the original trail. It is one of America's unique national parks.

The speed limit along the parkway is 50 miles per hour, so plan to slow down and enjoy the view. If you begin at the northeastern end, stop at the Natchez Trace Parkway Visitors Center in Tupelo, where you can get information, look at numerous displays, and watch a 12-minute film about the Trace.

The Trace is a long, thin park connecting Nashville to Natchez, and it winds through or close to several state parks. Historic markers detail the path's history, no commercial vehicles are allowed, and there are no billboards to detract from the scenery. You can drive the parkway in a day, but you'll barely have time to enjoy the scenery and stops along the way—and you're likely to end up with a carload of grumpy kids. We suggest getting out along the way at your leisure, with stops at places like the Cypress Swamp north of Jackson and the Meriwether Lewis gravesite at Grinder's Inn.

The Natchez Trace Scenic Trail lies parallel to the parkway and is also maintained by the National Park Service. There are three main segments near Nashville, Jackson, and Natchez. A small portion of the original trace is three miles from the Visitors Center in Tupelo and leads to the graves of 13 unknown Confederate soldiers. Trace State Park, between Pontotoc and Tupelo, has camping and cabins. Camping is $12 for primitive sites; $14 for sites with electricity. Cabins begin at $31.03. 2680 Natchez Trace Parkway, Tupelo 38801-8718; (662) 489-2958, (800) 305-7417, or (601) 680-4025; www.nps.gov/natr or www.nps.gov/natt.

Tennessee-Tombigbee Waterway Opened in 1985, the Tennessee-Tombigbee Waterway unites 12 rivers into a single, navigable system, shortening the barge route distance between numerous inland points and the Gulf Coast. The Waterway has three sections: River, Canal, and Divide, and ten locks and dams have been built to raise vessels the 341 feet required to travel the 234 miles from Demopolis, Alabama, to the Tennessee River.

The majority of activities involve the water. Boat ramps are conveniently located along the waterway, and if you don't have a boat of your own, you can rent one at the Aqua Yacht Harbor, one mile from the mouth of the Tenn-Tom Waterway in Iuka, (662) 423-2222. Manmade beaches were added to several lakes and are perfect points for swimming and water-skiing, while fishing—especially for small-mouth bass—lures folks from across the region.

To better understand the waterway, visit the Bay Springs Lake Visitor Center in Dennis, (662) 454-3481, or the Jamie L. Whitten Historical Center in Fulton, (662) 862-5414. Exhibits and films about the waterway provide insight into how it was built and how the series of locks and dams work. There are also displays from NASA, Appalachian Regional Commission, the National Park Service, the U.S. Forestry Service, and the USDA Soil and Conservation Service. The center has playgrounds, nature trails, picnic areas, and a fishing pier. Cost for campsites with electricity is $14 and $16 for waterfront sites. 100 Campground Road, Fulton; (662) 862-5414.

For campers, there are seven campgrounds on the waterway. Our hands-down favorite is at Bay Springs Lake, where you can set up camp on an island accessible only by boat (phone (662) 327-2142). In Mississippi, the waterway stretches from the Alabama state line southeast of Columbus north to the Tennessee River. For information, contact (662) 327-2142; www.sam.usace.army.mil/op/rec/tenn-tom.

Calendar of Festivals and Events

January

Eleventh Moon Storytelling Festival, Natchez Native Americans swap stories at this unique storytelling festival; (800) 647-6724 or (601) 446-6345.

Elks Mardi Gras Parade, Ocean Springs The celebration begins for the wildest party of all—Mardi Gras; (228) 875-7046.

February

Dixie National Rodeo and Livestock Show, Jackson The second-largest livestock show in the nation and the largest rodeo east of the Mississippi River. Lasts three weeks; (601) 961-4000.

Bassmaster Invitational Tournament, Jackson One of eight annual fishing tournaments conducted by B.A.S.S.; (334) 272-9530.

March

Natchez Spring Pilgrimage Costumed guides conduct tours of over 30 antebellum homes and mansions; (800) 647-6743 or (601) 446-6631.

Oyster Festival, Biloxi Live entertainment, Gulf seafood, and contests are part of this annual event; (228) 374-2330.

Vicksburg Spring Pilgrimage   Antebellum and Victorian homes and gardens are open for tours; (800) 221-3536 or (601) 636-9421.

Civil War Re-enactment at Florewood River Plantation, Greenwood   Relive the Civil War through re-enactments of battles and skirmishes each year at Florewood River Plantation State Park; (601) 843-8224.

Natchez Powwow at Grand Village of the Natchez Indians, Natchez   Native Americans gather each spring for two days of dance competitions, music, and craft demonstrations at the Grand Village of the Natchez Indians; (601) 446-6502.

April

Columbus Spring Pilgrimage   Tour antebellum homes with costumed guides. Also evening candlelight tours; (800) 327-2686 or (601) 329-1191.

World Catfish Festival, Belzoni   Billed as the world's largest fish fry, this festival features a catfish queen, live entertainment, and arts and crafts; (800) 408-4838 or (601) 247-4838; www.capital2.com/catfish.html.

Ralph Morgan Professional Rodeo, Lauderdale   This semiannual event features the best in professional rodeo performances; (601) 679-8861.

Riverfest, Vicksburg   A weekend of street dances, food, and arts and crafts exhibitors; (601) 636-1012.

Crosstie Arts Festival, Cleveland   More than 30 years old, this juried arts festival also has entertainment, food, vendors, and a children's area; (601) 846-4087.

Confederate Memorial Day, Biloxi   Period music, dramatic readings, and wreaths laid at the tomb of the Unknown Confederate Soldier round out activities. Held at Beauvoir, the home of Jefferson Davis; (228) 388-9074.

Natchez Trace Festival and Fiddler's Jamboree, Koscuisko   This annual festival showcases fiddler's of all skill levels and ages. Arts and crafts, food, auto display, and running and walking competitions are part of the festivities; (601) 924-3684.

May

Jimmie Rodgers Festival, Meridian   A tribute to the "Father of Country Music," this week-long celebration has performances by country stars, a street dance, and talent competition; (800) 396-5882 or (601) 483-5763.

Delta Democrat Times Grand Prix Catfish Race, Greenville   Pond-raised catfish speed along Plexiglas lanes at this unusual race. Held on the Washington County Courthouse lawn; (800) 844-1618 or (601) 335-1155.

The Squirrel on the Pearl Festival, Columbia   This festival is a tribute to former Governor Hugh White's cherished white squirrels. He introduced the squirrels on Keys Hill estate more than 60 years ago. Arts and crafts, food, displays, and rides are part of the fun; (601) 736-6385.

June

Mississippi International Balloon Classic, Greenville   Colorful hot-air balloons compete and give rides; food, arts and crafts, and live entertainment are also part of the celebration; (800) 467-3582 or (601) 453-6397.

Indian Bayou Festival and B.B. King's Homecoming, Indianola   Blues legend B.B. King returns to his hometown each year to perform at this outdoor music event. A barbecue cook-off and other activities are part of the fun; (601) 887-4454.

Steamboat Jubilee and Floozie Day, Natchez   The *Delta Queen* and *Mississippi Queen* re-enact the famous 1870 steamboat race between the *Robert E. Lee* and the *Natchez;* (800) 647-6724 or (601) 446-6345.

July

Civil War Living History, Vicksburg   Confederate and Union encampments set up on the grounds of the historic McRaven Home. Period demonstrations in textiles, cooking, fashion, and music round out the event; (601) 636-1663.

Choctaw Indian Fair, Philadelphia   Traditional Indian dancing, world series stickball, blowgun, bow and arrow, and drum-beating contests are the main events at this one-of-a-kind festival; (601) 650-1685.

Neshoba County Fair   Founded in 1889 and listed on the National Register of Historic Places, this fairground is home to what is known as "Mississippi's giant house party." Live entertainment, dancing, folk singing, and harness racing bring people from across the South to this seven-day fair; (601) 656-1742.

Faulkner and Yoknapatawpha Conference, Jackson   This literary event includes six days of lectures and discussions by scholars and dramatic readings from the works of William Faulkner; (601) 232-7282.

August

Sunflower River Blues and Gospel Festival, Clarksdale   Focusing on Mississippi's musical heritage, this festival features entertainment by local and nationally know blues and gospel artists; (601) 627-2209.

September

Mississippi Gulf Coast Blues Festival, Biloxi   Musical entertainment by top performers is provided under massive oak trees overlooking the Gulf; (800) 726-2781 or (228) 388-8010.

Mississippi Delta Blues and Heritage Festival, Greenville   One of the largest music festivals in the South, this event brings in leading blues artists from across the country; (800) 467-3582.

Sun Herald Sand Sculpture Contest, Biloxi   The world's largest sand-sculpture contest; (228) 896-2434.

Possum Town Pigfest, Columbus   One of the state's most popular events has music, midway rides, and storytellers; (601) 328-4532.

Natchez Fall Pilgrimage   Costumed guides conduct tours of over 30 antebellum homes and mansions; (800) 647-6743 or (601) 446-6631.

Yazoo County Fair, Yazoo City   The second-oldest fair in the state has arts and crafts, cake-decorating contests, amusement rides, and youth exhibits; (800) 381-0662 or (601) 746-3211.

October

Tennessee Williams Festival, Clarksdale   A literary festival honoring the Pulitzer Prize–winning playwright, this event has plays, walking tours, music, food, and literary discussions; (800) 626-3764 or (601) 627-7337.

Great Oaks Storytelling Festival, Ocean Springs   Set under a canopy of oaks, this festival highlights the best of Southern storytelling; (228) 875-4424.

Vicksburg Fall Pilgrimage   Antebellum and Victorian homes and gardens are open for tours; (800) 221-3536 or (601) 636-9421.

Mississippi State Fair, Jackson   At over 140 years old, this fair is the South's largest. International entertainers, livestock shows, midway rides, and educational demonstrations round out the events; (601) 961-4000.

Beauvoir Fall Muster, Biloxi   Set at the last home of Confederate President Jefferson Davis, the fall muster features camp demonstrations, skirmishes, and a children's play area; (228) 388-9074.

November

Christmas at Landrum's Homestead and Village, Laurel   The two-day festival at this re-creation of a working homestead and village highlights pioneer life through demonstrations, food, and entertainment; (601) 649-2546.

December

Christmas on the Water, Biloxi   A children's parade, lighting of Town Green, and a boat parade on the Mississippi Sound are part of the fun at this holiday event; (800) 245-6942 or (228) 374-3105.

Old Jackson Christmas by Candlelight, Jackson   Three antebellum sites are dressed in their holiday finest and opened to the public for candlelight tours; (601) 359-6932.

Christmas at the Old Capitol, Jackson   The 155-year-old Greek Revival building is the setting for an 1800s-style celebration; (601) 359-6920.

Tupelo

Named for the native Tupelo gum tree, this northeastern city is closer to both the Tennessee and Alabama state lines than to Jackson, the capital of Mississippi. Travelers passing through on U.S. 78 often stop for food and lodging, but those who linger won't be disappointed. Tupelo sits along the **Natchez Trace Parkway** and its visitors center provides an introduction to this unique national park. Tupelo is also the birthplace of the King of Rock and Roll, Elvis Presley. When you travel, keep in mind that Tupelo is famous for its furniture industry. Two major shows occur in February and August, and during such times the population almost doubles and lodging is next to impossible to find.

Family Lodging

AmeriHost Inn

Whirlpool suites are the main reason to check in to AmeriHost Inn. Let the kids play in the tub, then after their bedtime, you can soak away to your heart's content. Other amenities include free continental breakfast, an indoor heated pool, a whirlpool and sauna, an exercise room, free local calls, and cable TV with HBO. The location is also a plus. The hotel is three miles from the Elvis Presley Birthplace and Museum, nine miles from the Mall at Barnes Crossing, and very close to a variety of local restaurants. Rates start at $61. 625 Spicer Drive, Tupelo; (800) 434-5800 or (601) 844-7660; www.amerihostinn.com.

Courtyard by Marriott

Convenient to downtown attractions and restaurants, the Courtyard has both executive and Jacuzzi suites. Amenities like an outdoor pool and spa, an exercise room, and a breakfast cafe and lounge are bonuses. Rates start at $75. 1320 North Gloster Street, Tupelo; (800) 321-2211 or (601) 841-9960; www.courtyard.com.

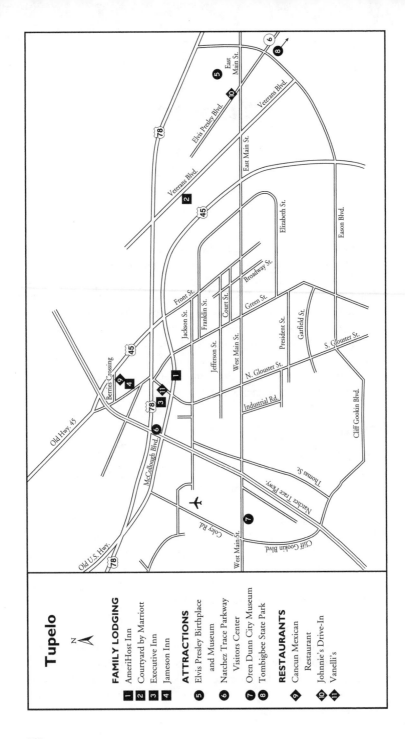

Tupelo

N

FAMILY LODGING

1 AmeriHost Inn
2 Courtyard by Marriott
3 Executive Inn
4 Jameson Inn

ATTRACTIONS

5 Elvis Presley Birthplace
   and Museum
6 Natchez Trace Parkway
   Visitors Center
7 Oren Dunn City Museum
8 Tombigbee State Park

RESTAURANTS

9 Cancun Mexican
   Restaurant
10 Johnnie's Drive-In
11 Vanelli's

Executive Inn

The Executive Inn caters to the business traveler, but families can also benefit from its spacious room layouts. If you request a suite, the bedroom connects to a separate living area, making it easy for babies to sleep in the bedroom while older children play in the living room. The inn in Tupelo has an indoor swimming pool, a hot tub and sauna, a restaurant, room service, and a mini-gym. The inn is centrally located. Rates start at $61. 1011 North Gloster Street, Tupelo; (662) 841-2222.

Jameson Inn

This colonial-style inn is nothing fancy, but you can't beat its affordable price and location next to the Mall at Barnes Crossing. The setup is traditional motel-style with doors opening up to the outside. There is also a swimming pool, fitness center and free continental breakfast. Rates average around $60 year-round. 879 Mississippi Drive, off I-45 and Gloster Street; (800) JAMESON or (662) 840-2380; www.jamesoninns.com.

Attractions

Elvis Presley Birthplace and Museum

306 Elvis Presley Drive, Tupelo; (662) 841-1245

Hours: Monday through Saturday, 9 a.m.–5:30 p.m.; Sunday, 1–5 p.m.

Admission: House tour $1, museum tour $4

Appeal by Age Group:

Pre-school	Grade School	Teens	Young Adults	Over 30	Seniors
★★	★★	★★★	★★★★	★★★★	★★★★

Average Touring Time: 1½ hours

Minimum Touring Time: 45 minutes

Rainy Day Touring: Recommended

Author's Rating: ★★★

Services and Facilities:

Restaurants No	Lockers No
Alcoholic beverages No	Pet kennels No
Disabled access Yes	Rain check No
Wheelchair rental No	Private tours Yes
Baby stroller rental No	

Description and Comments   It's hard to believe, but today's kids might have no idea who Elvis is. Here's the place to make their introduction. This modest, two-room house is where Elvis was born in 1935. His father, Vernon, built the 450-square-foot home for $180. The family, however, was eventually evicted when they couldn't pay the mortgage. Tour the home first, then visit the museum, originally a youth center built by Elvis as a gift to his former community. Inside is memorabilia collected by Janelle McComb, a lifelong friend of Presley's. There is a jumpsuit from Elvis' Las Vegas act and a pair of his motorcycle boots on display. There are guides in both the house and museum to explain exhibits and provide you with tidbits about Elvis' life.

If you can't get enough of the King of Rock and Roll, make sure you visit in January, when he was born, or August, when he died. These months attract Elvis fans from across the world. According to McComb, the get-togethers are like family reunions, with fans reliving memories of the King.

You can also stop by the Tupelo Convention and Visitors Bureau for a driving guide to other notable sites from Elvis' childhood, including his elementary and junior high schools and Tupelo Hardware where he purchased his first guitar.

Natchez Trace Parkway Visitors Center

2680 Natchez Trace Parkway, Tupelo; (800) 305-7417 or (662) 680-4025
  www.nps.gov/natr, www.nps.gov/natt

Hours: Daily, 8 a.m.–5 p.m.

Admission: Free

Appeal by Age Group:

Pre-school	Grade School	Teens	Young Adults	Over 30	Seniors
★★	★★★	★★★	★★★	★★★	★★★

Average Touring Time: 45 minutes

Minimum Touring Time: 10 minutes

Rainy Day Touring: Recommended

Author's Rating: ★★★   A good diversion from car travel

Services and Facilities:

Restaurants No	Lockers No
Alcoholic beverages No	Pet kennels No
Disabled access Yes	Rain check N/A
Wheelchair rental No	Private tours N/A
Baby stroller rental No	

Description and Comments   Maintained by the National Park Service, the Visitors Center provides a good introduction to what you can expect to see along the Trace. Begin by watching the 12-minute video about the history of the Trace, then view the exhibits throughout the center for more detailed explanations of life along the Trace. Kids gravitate toward the touch boxes, one of which is an old toy chest filled with replicas of antique toys—the kind that boys and girls traveling 100 years ago might have played with. The other has pieces of petrified objects you can touch, including tree bark, bones, and a skull. Additionally, there are displays of tools and other household objects that would have been used by early travelers of the Trace. Campsites are located down the road between Tupelo and Pontotoc. Three miles from the Visitors Center, there is a trail you can follow to 13 graves of unknown Confederate soldiers.

Oren Dunn City Museum

West Main Street at Ballard Park, Tupelo; (662) 841-6438

Hours: Monday–Friday, 8 a.m.–4 p.m.; May 15–September 15, also open Saturday and Sunday, 1–5 p.m.

Admission: $1 adults, free for children ages 4 and younger

Appeal by Age Group:

Pre-school	Grade School	Teens	Young Adults	Over 30	Seniors
★★	★★★	★★★	★★★	★★★	★★★

Average Touring Time: 1 hour

Minimum Touring Time: 45 minutes

Rainy Day Touring: Recommended

Author's Rating: ★★★

Services and Facilities:

Restaurants No	Lockers No
Alcoholic beverages No	Pet kennels No
Disabled access Yes	Rain check No
Wheelchair rental No	Private tours Yes
Baby stroller rental No	

Description and Comments Characterized as the "common man's museum," Tupelo's Oren Dunn City Museum is full of ordinary household and everyday objects that tell the story of life at the turn of the century. Dunn started the museum in 1984 with a collection of mayoral photographs, and later added other objects from more than 700 local contributors. Made up of "anything that can't be replaced," the collection includes a century-old doll, signs from former Tupelo businesses, kitchen utensils, and Civil War photographs and items. The museum is housed in restored barns, and there are other vintage buildings on the grounds, including a 1950s diner, a 1949 bookmobile, an 1870s dogtrot house, a one-room schoolhouse, a railroad depot, and a space hangar with a moon rock, space suit, and other space memorabilia.

Tombigbee State Park

264 Cabin Drive, Tupelo; (662) 842-7669; (800) GO-PARKS
www.mdwfp.com/parks.asp

Hours: Daily, 6 a.m.–10 p.m.

Admission: $2 per car, 50¢ for each person older than age 4

Appeal by Age Group:

Pre-school	Grade School	Teens	Young Adults	Over 30	Seniors
★★★	★★★	★★★	★★★	★★★	★★★

Average Touring Time: 1 day

Minimum Touring Time: ½ day

Rainy Day Touring: Not recommended

Author's Rating: ★★★

Services and Facilities:

Restaurants No	Lockers No
Alcoholic beverages No	Pet kennels No
Disabled access No	Rain check No
Wheelchair rental No	Private tours No
Baby stroller rental No	

Description and Comments Located six miles south of Tupelo, Mississippi's second-oldest state park has a variety of activities for all ages. There are three nature trails, tennis courts, horse shoes, paddle boat rentals, fishing, swimming, and an interesting 18-hole disc golf course, played the same way as regular golf except with weighted discs. If you're on the road, this is a good place to stop for a couple of hours and stretch your legs. Just be sure to pick up lunch in Tupelo or nearby Plantersville since there are no fast food restaurants nearby. The park has both cabins and campsites available for overnight stays. Primitive campsites are $9; those with electric hookups are $12. Cabins range from $41–59.

Side Trips

Brussel's Bonsai Nursery, Olive Branch Though this is a retail nursery, it's a groovy place to stop if you're in the vicinity. Brussel's is the largest importer and grower of bonsai trees in the world, and as such, has hundreds of well-groomed, miniature trees on display and for sale. The staff members are experts in this ancient art, and many have studied under Japanese masters. There are display gardens at the nursery with trees up to 50 years old. Tools, accessories, and the trees themselves are all for sale. Just south of Memphis, off Goodman Road east of Olive Branch; (800) 582-2593.

Tunica Folks around these parts like to say that the casinos sprang up overnight in what used to be the richest cotton fields in Mississippi. One look at the statistics and you'll believe it, too. In 1990, Tunica had 20 hotel rooms; today, there are 6,000, and more on the way. That makes Tunica the third-largest gaming resort destination in the United States.

Twenty minutes from Memphis International Airport, Tunica has nine big-name, world-class casinos that are open 24 hours a day. The main draw, of course, is the gaming, but like their Las Vegas counterparts, resorts are adding attractions and services to capture the family market as well. Nightly entertainment is one way the resorts cater to families, with many of the resorts featuring kid-appropriate performances by top-name performers. Another is with affordable food and lodging.

The Grand Casino Resort has additional enticements like biking and walking trails, indoor and outdoor pools, seven restaurants, an 18-hole golf course, a sporting clays course, an outlet mall, a theater with top-name performers, and Kids Quest, a special children's program. Another option for families is the Gold Strike Casino Resort. The indoor swimming pool, with its fancy rock formations, is a hit with kids, along with the nightly performances by magician Brett Daniels.

Jerry Lee Lewis Ranch, Nesbit The Killer steers clear of any tourists who drop by to tour his home, but don't let that keep you from visiting. You still get to see his piano-shaped pool and his car collection. Lewis' Ranch is in Nesbit in North Mississippi, south of Memphis and Horn Lake. $15 per person; (662) 429-1290; www.jllewis.com or www.jerryleelewis.net.

Delta Blues Museum, Clarksdale Regarded by many as the only original American music, blues music has deep roots in the rich Mississippi Delta. Its history, and its influence on other types of music, is preserved in the Delta Blues Museum. Old photos of performers and juke joints, musical instruments from famous artists, including the MuddyWood guitar from ZZ Top's guitarist, and other memorabilia like records and posters are on display. There is also a research library with periodicals and files that pertain to the history of the blues and its artists. The museum has been housed in the Clarksdale Library for the past 19 years, but will soon move downtown to the restored Illinois Central Railroad Freight Depot, complete with new exhibits. A chronological storyline about the blues is illustrated with murals, multi-media kiosks, musical listening stations, and hands-on musical instruments. Open Monday–Saturday, 9 a.m.–5 p.m.; admission is free. 114 Delta Avenue, Clarksville; (800) 626-3764 or (662) 627-6820; www.deltabluesmuseum.org.

Family-Friendly Restaurants

CANCUN MEXICAN RESTAURANT

1001 Barnes Crossing Road, Tupelo; (662) 840-0540

Meals served: Lunch and dinner
Cuisine: Mexican
Entrée range: $3.29 and up
Kids menu: Yes
Reservations: No
Payment: All major credit cards accepted

Located in the Mall at Barnes Crossing, Cancun serves everything Mexican. Kids under age ten eat for $2.95. This is a good place to go if you want to sit down and relax for dinner without having to dress up the kids. It's also close to Tupelo hotels.

JOHNNIE'S DRIVE-IN

908 East Main Street, Tupelo; (662) 842-6748

Meals served: Breakfast, lunch, and dinner
Cuisine: American
Entrée range: $4.25 and up
Kids menu: No
Reservations: No
Payment: Cash only

A Tupelo tradition, this '50s–style drive-in has both curb service and an indoor eatery. Milkshakes, hamburgers, and barbecue and among the menu items. Kids love the idea of having the food brought to the car window for back-seat banquets.

VANELLI'S

1302 North Gloster Road, Tupelo; (662) 844-4410

Meals served: Lunch and dinner
Cuisine: Greek/American
Entrée range: $7.95 and up
Kids menu: Yes
Reservations: Yes
Payment: All major credit cards accepted

Greek-style food with an American twist is served at Vanelli's. Pita sandwiches, steaks, pasta, and salads are popular menu items for kids and adults.

Starkville

Starkville is a nice change from the smaller rural towns that dot the Mississippi map. The city is home to the **Mississippi State University Bulldogs,** and as such has a vibrant college-town feel. There are a couple of sites that kids will enjoy, including several museums on campus.

Family Lodging

Best Western

Families who travel to Starkville for competitions in the nearby Sports Plex often stay at the Best Western. The Best Western has an outdoor pool, free continental breakfast, and children younger than age 12 stay free. Rates begin at $50. 119 Highway 12 West, Starkville; (800) 528-1234 or (662) 324-5555; www.bestwestern.com.

Hampton Inn

One of the newer properties in Starkville, the Hampton is close to Mississippi State University and several restaurants. There is an outdoor pool at the hotel, and continental breakfast, local calls, and in-room movies are included with your stay. Rates begin at $70. 700 Higway 12 East, Starkville; (800) HAMPTON or (662) 324-1333; www.hamptoninn.com.

Attractions

Pinedale Farms

1835 Reed Road, Starkville; (662) 323-9543
Hours: By appointment only
Admission: $15 for family groups of up to six people

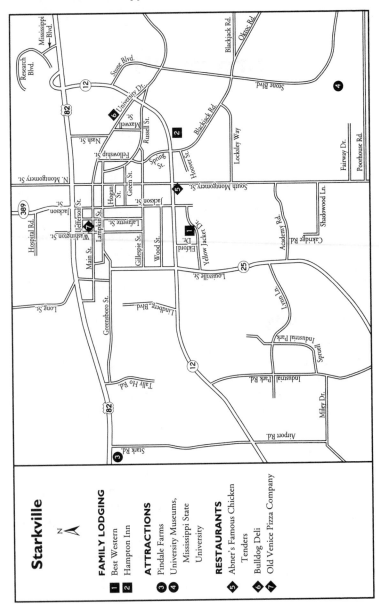

Starkville

N

FAMILY LODGING
1 Best Western
2 Hampton Inn

ATTRACTIONS
3 Pindale Farms
4 University Museums, Mississippi State University

RESTAURANTS
5 Abner's Famous Chicken Tenders
6 Bulldog Deli
7 Old Venice Pizza Company

Appeal by Age Group:

Pre-school	Grade School	Teens	Young Adults	Over 30	Seniors
★★★★★	★★★★★	★★★★	★★★★	★★★★	★★★★

Average Touring Time: 2 hours
Minimum Touring Time: 1 hour
Rainy Day Touring: Not recommended
Author's Rating: ★★★★★ An authentic farm with well-kept animals
Services and Facilities:

Restaurants No

Alcoholic beverages No

Disabled access Partial

Wheelchair rental No

Baby stroller rental No

Lockers No

Pet kennels No

Rain check N/A

Private tours N/A

Description and Comments Don't expect staged exhibits or rows of cages housing animals. Pinedale Farms is a true working farm where the animals are part of the family. The Brodnaxes raise horses and donkeys for a living, but they opened their farm to the public when friends kept insisting on its potential as a petting zoo. Meet King Tut, the resident rooster, along with goats, pigs, rabbits, chickens, emus, llamas, potbelly pigs, miniature horses, and sheep. All the larger animals are kept in pasture areas; when the tractor cranks up for a hayride, they run to their pens so they can greet the guests. Pinedale is one of the few places where children can get up close to a baby piglet or a goat. In a couple of years, the farm will be more accessible when Highway 82 is completed.

To reach the farm, go west on Highway 82 past Stark Road, turn right on County Lake Road, and right again on Reed Road.

University Museums, Mississippi State University

Mississippi State University, Starkville; (662) 325-2323
www.msstate.edu

Hours: Hours vary; call ahead for times

Admission: Free

Appeal by Age Group:

Pre-school	Grade School	Teens	Young Adults	Over 30	Seniors
★★	★★★	★★★	★★★	★★★	★★★

Average Touring Time: 1 day for all; 30 minutes for each museum

Minimum Touring Time: ½ day for half the museums

Rainy Day Touring: Not recommended

Author's Rating: ★★★★ Spend the day at school and see all the museums

Services and Facilities:

Restaurants Yes

Alcoholic beverages No

Disabled access Yes

Wheelchair rental No

Baby stroller rental No   Rain check No
Lockers No   Private tours No
Pet kennels No

Description and Comments   Besides the unique opportunity of spending
the day on a college campus, your brood can enjoy visits to the interesting
collection of eight museums housed at Mississippi State University. One in
particular is a must: The Mississippi Entomological Museum, (662) 325-
2989. The third-largest insect collection in the Southeastern United States,
this museum has over a million specimens on display. The museum is also
home to the Ross Hutchins and David Young photograph collections of
bugs, with more than 40,000 prints and slides on file.

The Dunn-Seiler Museum, (662) 325-3915, is also attractive to the
younger set, with displays of rocks, fossils, and a triceratops skull. Other
museums include the Lois Dowdle Cobb Museum of Archaeology, (662)
325-3826, filled with artifacts from the ancient Middle East and the Southeastern United States. The Department of Art Gallery, (662) 325-2790, has
exhibitions of regional and national scope. The Cully Cobb Museum in the
Forest Products Laboratory, (662) 325-2116, showcases tools and primitive
machinery. The Mitchell Memorial Library displays memorabilia and
papers from alumnus and author John Grisham. The Templeton Museum
and Archives pays tribute to America's musical history with a concentration
of musical instruments, sheet music, and memorabilia dating from the
1800s to the 1930s. And at the Engineering Research Center, (662) 325-
8278, you can experience CAVE, a virtual reality environment. Stand on
the CAVE platform, put on the special glasses, and voila!—you're whisked
away to one of the virtual environments of your choosing. Call ahead for
times as many of the museums have erratic hours.

Side Trips

Rowan Oak, Oxford   William Faulkner's antebellum home in Oxford is
on display much as he left it. His manual typewriter sits on the desk in the
study, and an outline of his last novel, The Fable, is scribbled on the wall.
Docents walk you through the home and give you the inside scoop on
Faulkner and his family, as well as information about where he got ideas for
his stories. On Old Taylor Road; open Tuesday–Saturday, 10 a.m.–12 p.m.,
2–4 p.m.; Sunday, 2–4 p.m.; (800) 758-9177 or (662) 234-4680.

Great River Road State Park, Rosedale   Located near the western border
of Mississippi, 35 miles from Greenville, the Great River Road State Park is
best known for the 30-acre Perry Martin Lake. For some of the best fishing
in the state, anglers of all ages can cast their rod for bass, perch, and white
catfish. We giggled when we saw the whiskey still created by Perry Martin, a

nationally known bootlegger during the Prohibition Era. If you are so inclined, write down his moonshine recipe—it's posted next to the still. The park has a four-level observation tower overlooking the Mississippi River. Nature trails lead to the hardwood forest and swamp on the riverbank and also to the sandbar; in low water, the sandbar becomes one of the state's largest beaches. There are campsites and picnic areas throughout. Off Mississippi 1, Rosedale; (800) GO-PARKS or (662) 759-6762; www.angelfire.com/ms/GreatRiverRoadPark/index.html.

Birthplace of the Frog, Leland   If you're interested in seeing how genius is born, stop by the Birthplace of the Frog museum in Leland. Jim Henson, creator of the Muppets, grew up here, and the museum features photos from his boyhood. Unfortunately, there are few genuine Muppets on display, but there is one scene with Kermit playing the banjo. There is also a collection of Christmas cards from Henson to his mother-in-law featuring hand-drawn Muppets. A side room is filled with Muppet memorabilia, from McDonald's Happy Meal characters to books and collectibles. A gift shop with Muppet toys is on site. Admission is free. Highway 82 in Leland. Open Monday–Saturday 10 a.m.–4 p.m.; (662) 686-2687.

Family-Friendly Restaurants

ABNER'S FAMOUS CHICKEN TENDERS

518 South Montgomery Street, Starkville; (662) 338-0098

Meals served: Lunch and dinner
Cuisine: American
Entrée range: $5 and up
Kids menu: Yes
Reservations: No
Payment: All major credit cards accepted

Conveniently located near Starkville activities, this is the place for chicken tenders the whole family will enjoy. They also have tortilla wraps, salads, and homemade desserts.

BULLDOG DELI

702 University Drive, Starkville; (662) 324-DELI
www.bulldogdeli.com

Meals served: Lunch and dinner
Cuisine: American

Entrée range: $3 and up
Kids menu: No
Reservations: No
Payment: All major credit cards accepted

Sandwiches, topped potatoes, and salads are the specialty at this deli. Order at the counter and then take a seat. Close to the University campus.

OLD VENICE PIZZA COMPANY

110 East Main Street, Starkville; (662) 320-6872

Meals served: Lunch and dinner
Cuisine: Italian
Entrée range: $6 and up
Kids menu: No
Reservations: No
Payment: All major credit cards accepted

Old Venice serves the traditional favorites but also adds its own specialty pastas to the menu. The Rasta Pasta is especially popular, with yellow peppers in a Jamaican cream sauce served over a bed of pasta. Centrally located in downtown.

Jackson

Named for Andrew Jackson, Mississippi's capital city doesn't have the hustle-bustle attitude of most capital cities. Rather, Jackson is low-key and accessible; you can get across town in a matter of 20 minutes—and that's during heavy traffic. Another incentive for families is that Jackson is affordable. Hotels and restaurants are reasonably priced, and many attractions are under $5 or free.

Speaking of attractions, the family-oriented feel of this city is reflected in its offerings for families. Museums, especially the **Jackson Fire Museum and Public Fire Safety Education Center** and the **Museum of Natural Sciences,** were designed with children in mind. Other highlights include the **Russell C. Davis Planetarium/Ronald E. McNair Space Theater** and the **Jackson Zoo.**

Jackson sits on the Pearl River and was named the capital in 1821 after legislators decided a more central location than Natchez was needed for the seat of government. It is this central location, almost dead center in the state, that makes it a good beginning for families traversing the state. Jackson is about 160 miles from the coast and 200 miles from the Tennessee border.

Spring and fall are the most pleasant times of the year to visit. The summers are hot and humid, with temperatures in the 80s and 90s. The winters, while cold to true Southerners, are mild, averaging in the 50s.

Family Lodging

Courtyard by Marriott

We chose this Courtyard because of its convenient location to Jackson attractions, the Smith Wills Stadium, and a number of chain restaurants. There are six suites; call in advance if you want to reserve one. The hotel offers express check-out service and has an outdoor swimming pool and

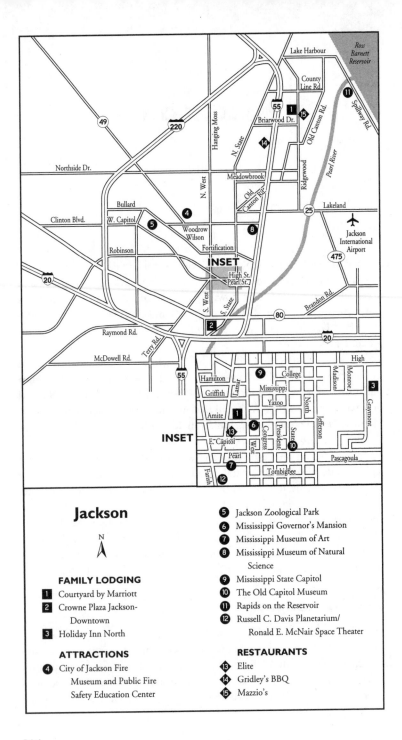

Jackson

N
^

FAMILY LODGING
1. Courtyard by Marriott
2. Crowne Plaza Jackson-
   Downtown
3. Holiday Inn North

ATTRACTIONS
4. City of Jackson Fire
   Museum and Public Fire
   Safety Education Center

5. Jackson Zoological Park
6. Mississippi Governor's Mansion
7. Mississippi Museum of Art
8. Mississippi Museum of Natural
   Science
9. Mississippi State Capitol
10. The Old Capitol Museum
11. Rapids on the Reservoir
12. Russell C. Davis Planetarium/
    Ronald E. McNair Space Theater

RESTAURANTS
13. Elite
14. Gridley's BBQ
15. Mazzio's

whirlpool. 6280 Ridgewood Court Drive, Jackson; (800) 321-3211 or (601) 956-9991; www.courtyard.com.

Crowne Plaza Jackson-Downtown

Primarily a business hotel, the Crowne Plaza has amenities suitable for families—an outdoor swimming pool, a fitness center, and voice mail, to name a few. The Bristol Bar & Grill has 24-hour room service, serves breakfast and lunch buffets, and also has a dinner menu. The hotel is ten miles from the Jackson International Airport. Rates start at $79.75. 200 East Amite Street, Jackson; (800) 2-CROWNE or (601) 353-4333; www.crowneplaza.com.

Holiday Inn North

With indoor access to rooms, this Holiday Inn has 222 rooms and 30 suites, a full-service restaurant, outdoor pool, exercise facility, and an on-site coin laundry. It is six miles to downtown Jackson and 15 miles to the airport. Rates start at $69.95. 5075 I-55 North, Jackson; (800) HOLIDAY or (601) 366-9411; www.basshotels.com.

Attractions

City of Jackson Fire Museum and Public Fire Safety Education Center

355 Woodrow Wilson, Jackson; (601) 960-2433
  www.city.jackson.ms.us/fire/pfsed_museum.html

Hours: Monday–Friday, 8 a.m.–5 p.m.; call for appointment

Admission: Free

Appeal by Age Group:

Pre-school	Grade School	Teens	Young Adults	Over 30	Seniors
★★★★	★★★★	★★★★	★★★★	★★★★	★★★★

Average Touring Time: 1½ hours

Minimum Touring Time: 1 hour

Rainy Day Touring: Recommended

Author's Rating: ★★★★★   Fabulous educational experience

Services and Facilities:

Restaurants No	Lockers No
Alcoholic beverages No	Pet kennels No
Disabled access Yes	Rain check N/A
Wheelchair rental No	Private tours Yes
Baby stroller rental No	

Description and Comments   We have yet to find a museum that does as good a job at educating its guests as Jackson's Fire Museum and Public Fire Safety Education Center. The tour begins with an educational session, and it's the kids' hands-down favorite. After a short lecture, they have to stop, drop, and roll, crawl under smoke (created by a smoke machine), and slide down a fireman's pole. In the museum, the history of Jackson's Fire Department is on display, with artifacts like an 1870 parade uniform, photos, helmets, and a 1904 horse-drawn steamer. Kids can sit on a 1936 fire engine and ring the bell. At the end of the tour, visit an operational fire station, meet the firefighters, and climb aboard a fire engine to turn on the lights and siren.

Jackson Zoological Park

2918 West Capitol Street, Jackson; (601) 352-2580
   www.teclink.net/jacksonzoo

Hours: June–August, daily 9 a.m.–6 p.m.; September–May, daily
   9 a.m.–5 p.m.

Admission: $4 adults, $2 seniors, $2 children ages 3–12, free for children ages 2 and younger

Appeal by Age Group:

Pre-school	Grade School	Teens	Young Adults	Over 30	Seniors
★★★★★	★★★★★	★★★★★	★★★★	★★★★	★★★★

Average Touring Time: 2½ hours

Minimum Touring Time: 45 minutes

Rainy Day Touring: Not recommended

Author's Rating: ★★★★

Services and Facilities:

Restaurants Yes	Lockers No
Alcoholic beverages No	Pet kennels No
Disabled access Yes	Rain check No
Wheelchair rental Yes	Private tours No
Baby stroller rental Yes	

Description and Comments   Founded in 1919, the Jackson Zoo is considered one of the best zoos for kids east of the Mississippi River. Half of the animals are still housed in traditional cages, but the other half are shown in their natural habitats. One of the favorite areas is the African rainforest, where chimps, rhinos, and other African animals can be viewed in a lush setting. The Discovery Zoo is designed with children in mind. Hands-on exhibits and interactive stations assist children in simulating what it's like to be a particular animal. In addition to the baby strollers, the zoo has wagons available for carting children around.

Mississippi Governor's Mansion

300 East Capitol Street, Jackson; (601) 359-6421

Hours: Tuesday–Friday 9:30–11 a.m.

Admission: Free

Appeal by Age Group:

Pre-school	Grade School	Teens	Young Adults	Over 30	Seniors
★	★★★	★★★	★★★	★★★	★★★

Average Touring Time: 30 minutes

Minimum Touring Time: N/A

Rainy Day Touring: Recommended

Author's Rating: ★★★

Services and Facilities:

Restaurants No	Lockers No
Alcoholic beverages No	Pet kennels No
Disabled access Yes	Rain check N/A
Wheelchair rental No	Private tours Yes
Baby stroller rental No	

Description and Comments Designated as a National Historic Landmark, this is the site of General Sherman's victory dinner following the fall of Vicksburg. It was constructed in 1842 in classic Greek Revival style and is the second-oldest continuously occupied gubernatorial residence in the United States. Tours are conducted during the week and last 30 minutes.

Mississippi Museum of Art

201 East Pascagoula Street, Jackson; (601) 960-1515
  www.msmuseumart.org

Hours: Tuesday–Saturday, 10 a.m.–5 p.m.

Admission: $5 adults, $3 seniors and children

Appeal by Age Group:

Pre-school	Grade School	Teens	Young Adults	Over 30	Seniors
★★	★★★	★★★	★★★	★★★	★★★

Average Touring Time: 2 hours

Minimum Touring Time: 1 hour

Rainy Day Touring: Recommended

Author's Rating: ★★★
Services and Facilities:

Restaurants Yes

Lockers No

Alcoholic beverages No

Pet kennels No

Disabled access Yes

Rain check N/A

Wheelchair rental Yes

Private tours Yes

Baby stroller rental No

Description and Comments Mississippi's largest art museum has the world's best collection of art by and relating to Mississippians. It is also noted for its nineteenth-and twentieth-century landscape paintings, eighteenth-century British paintings and furniture, Japanese prints, pre-Columbian ceramics, and Oceanic art. Of particular interest to those interested in Southern culture are the collections of Southern photography and the folk art. There are docent tours Monday, Wednesday, and Friday at 1 p.m., and self-guided audio tours are available at any time.

Mississippi Museum of Natural Science

2148 Riverside Drive, Jackson; (601) 354-7303
   www.mdwfp.state.ms.us/museum
Hours: Monday–Friday, 8 a.m.–5 p.m.; Saturday, 9 a.m.–5 p.m.; Sunday, 1–5 p.m.
Admission: Free
Appeal by Age Group:

Pre-school	Grade School	Teens	Young Adults	Over 30	Seniors
★★★	★★★	★★★	★★★	★★★	★★★

Average Touring Time: 2 hours
Minimum Touring Time: 1 hour
Rainy Day Touring: Recommended
Author's Rating: ★★★
Services and Facilities:

Restaurants No

Lockers No

Alcoholic beverages No

Pet kennels No

Disabled access Yes

Rain check N/A

Wheelchair rental Yes

Private tours No

Baby stroller rental No

Description and Comments Operated by the state's department of wildlife, fisheries, and parks, the Museum of Natural Sciences recently moved to a new facility and upgraded its exhibits. Now located within

LeFleur's Bluff State Park, the museum can be combined with outdoor activities that make for an indoor/outdoor outing.

The museum has the world's largest collection of specimens relating to Mississippi's natural history, all of which are displayed through interactive dioramas and exhibits. The aquarium exhibits are outstanding, especially the Mississippi Sound aquarium and the Pearl River aquarium, each with a variety of fish and other marine life indigenous to their respective waters.

When you finish inside, hike along the 2½ miles of walking trails, fish in one of the five lakes in the park, or play tennis. There is also a nine-hole golf course and driving range. The park has 30 campsites available, with a camp store and picnic area.

Mississippi State Capitol

400 High Street, Jackson; (601) 359-3114

Hours: Monday–Friday, 8 a.m.–5 p.m.

Admission: Free

Appeal by Age Group:

Pre-school	Grade School	Teens	Young Adults	Over 30	Seniors
★★	★★★	★★★	★★★	★★★	★★★

Average Touring Time: 1 hour

Minimum Touring Time: 30 minutes

Rainy Day Touring: Recommended

Author's Rating: ★★★

Services and Facilities:

Restaurants No	Lockers No
Alcoholic beverages No	Pet kennels No
Disabled access Yes	Rain check N/A
Wheelchair rental Yes	Private tours Yes
Baby stroller rental No	

Description and Comments   Patterned after the U.S. Capitol, the Mississippi Capitol has some extraordinary examples of stained glass and marble imported from around the world. See the house and senate chambers, and learn how the eagle that sits atop the dome was covered with golf leaf.

The Old Capitol Museum

100 South State Street, Jackson; (601) 359-6920; www.mdah.state.ms.us

Hours: Monday–Friday, 8 a.m.–5 p.m.; Saturday, 9:30 a.m.–4:30 p.m.; Sunday, 12:30–4:30 p.m.

Admission: Free

Appeal by Age Group:

Pre-school	Grade School	Teens	Young Adults	Over 30	Seniors
★	★★★	★★★	★★★★	★★★★	★★★★

Average Touring Time: 1½ hours

Minimum Touring Time: 1 hour

Rainy Day Touring: Recommended

Author's Rating: ★★★

Services and Facilities:

Restaurants No	Lockers No
Alcoholic beverages No	Pet kennels No
Disabled access Yes	Rain check N/A
Wheelchair rental Yes	Private tours Yes
Baby stroller rental No	

Description and Comments   Downtown tours of Jackson should start here, as this former site of state government is now a museum devoted to Mississippi history. Exhibits range from the more recent events of the Civil War and the Civil Rights Movement to a new display on the state's history from 1500 to 1800, with a focus on the life of Native Americans, Europeans, and Africans. The Indian exhibit, with ancient canoes to touch and dioramas on Indian life, is especially interesting to kids. The Old Capitol was in operation from 1839 to 1903, and was the site of historical events such as the Ordinance of Secession. It was restored in 1961.

Rapids on the Reservoir

1808 Spillway Road, Brandon; (601) 992-0500

Hours: Weekends in May and September: Saturday 10 a.m.–6 p.m., Sunday noon–6 p.m.; June–August: Monday–Friday 10 a.m.–6 p.m., Saturday 10 a.m.–9 p.m., Sunday noon–6 p.m.

Admission: $14.95 adults, $12.95 children ages 3–12, free for children ages 2 and younger

Appeal by Age Group:

Pre-school	Grade School	Teens	Young Adults	Over 30	Seniors
★★★★	★★★★★	★★★★★	★★★	★★★	★★★

Average Touring Time: 1 day

Minimum Touring Time: ½ day

Rainy Day Touring: Not recommended

Author's Rating: ★★★

Services and Facilities:

Restaurants Yes	Lockers Yes
Alcoholic beverages No	Pet kennels No
Disabled access No	Rain check Yes
Wheelchair rental No	Private tours No
Baby stroller rental No	

Description and Comments A day flies by at Rapids, with 25 acres of water attractions like typhoon speed slides, a wave pool, and a lazy river with intertubes.. Kids seem to love the slides the best. There are two five-story-high waterslides that crisscross each other, dual typhoon freefall slides, and an enclosed tube slide. A kiddie section has a replica of a pirate ship and a play area with soft foam. When you need to escape the heat, there is a "country fair" section with shade and rides.

Russell C. Davis Planetarium/Ronald E. McNair Space Theater

201 East Pascagoula Street, Jackson; (601) 960-1550
   www.city.jackson.ms.us

Hours: Schedule varies; call ahead for show times

Admission: Planetarium shows: $4 adults, $2.50 seniors and children ages 12 and younger; Laser shows: $5 adults, $3.50 seniors and children ages 12 and younger

Appeal by Age Group:

Pre-school	Grade School	Teens	Young Adults	Over 30	Seniors
★	★★★	★★★	★★★	★★★	★★★

Average Touring Time: 1 hour

Minimum Touring Time: N/A

Rainy Day Touring: Recommended

Author's Rating: ★★★

Services and Facilities:

Restaurants No	Lockers No
Alcoholic beverages No	Pet kennels No
Disabled access Yes	Rain check N/A
Wheelchair rental No	Private tours Yes
Baby stroller rental No	

Description and Comments With its high-tech wraparound screen, the largest planetarium in the Southeast is a virtual-reality trip to space. This is as close to heaven as you can get on Earth, and by the time you leave, your children will be one step closer to understanding the mysteries of the universe. Afterwards, see the exhibits on space transportation, filming in space, and the wonders of the sky. If you have time, watch a laser show on the wide-screen.

Side Trips

Mississippi Petrified Forest, Flora   What seems like a routine nature walk is actually a trip through time. In this petrified forest, signs along the path point to all things petrified and fossilized—a testimony to 36 million years of geological history. The walk itself is about six blocks (easy enough for young kids), and the museum provides you with a printed trail guide explaining each point of interest. As we searched for objects along the trail, we found the experience similar to a treasure hunt. A National Natural Landmark, the Petrified Forest is the only petrified forest in the eastern United States. There is an earth science museum at the end of the trail, with collections of petrified wood, fossils, and minerals on display. Open daily April 1 through Labor Day, 9 a.m.–6 p.m.; September 2–March 30, 9 a.m.–5 p.m. (601) 879-8189; www.mspetrifiedforest.com.

Peavey Visitors Center and Museum, Meridian   Internationally recognized as a leader in sound equipment and musical instruments, Peavey Electronics Corporation began in 1965 as a one-room shop. Today it has grown to be the third-largest company in Mississippi. People from across the world visit to tour the Meridian headquarters, and many famous musicians come to pick up and test the equipment. The tour includes a replica of Hartley Peavey's basement workshop, where he built his first amplifier, and a peek at the company's latest instruments. Open Monday–Friday 10 a.m.–4 p.m., Saturday and Sunday 1–4 p.m.; closed Thursday. Marion Russell Road in the GV Montgomery Industrial Park, Meridian; (877) 732-8391 or (601) 483-5365; www.peavey.com.

Family-Friendly Restaurants

ELITE

141 East Capitol Street, Jackson; (601) 352-5606

Meals served: Breakfast, lunch, and dinner
Cuisine: American
Entrée range: $5 and up
Kids menu: No

Reservations: No
Payment: All major credit cards accepted

A Jackson establishment for 50 years, Elite has southern-style foods from pot roast to spaghetti at unbelievably low prices. The yeast rolls are to die for. Portions are affordable but hefty, so don't expect younger kids to clean their plates. Elite is conveniently located downtown.

GRIDLEY'S BBQ

1428 Old Square Road, Jackson; (601) 362-8600

Meals served: Lunch and dinner
Cuisine: American, barbecue
Entrée range: $5 and up
Kids menu: Yes
Reservations: No
Payment: All major credit cards accepted

Serving some of the best barbecue in Jackson, Gridley's is conveniently located off I-55. There are daily blue plate specials like prime rib and mashed potatoes. A variety of other selections, such as cheese toast and hamburgers, should please picky eaters.

MAZZIO'S

1210 East County Line Road, Ridgeland; (601) 956-6797
www.mazzios.com

Meals served: Lunch and dinner
Cuisine: Italian
Entrée range: $5 and up
Kids menu: Yes
Reservations: No
Payment: All major credit cards accepted

Affordable, family–style Italian fare, like pizza, ravioli, and spaghetti—all served piping hot at this kid-friendly local chain. There are three locations in Jackson, so it should be easy to spot one near your hotel.

Vicksburg

"Vicksburg is the key," said President Abraham Lincoln. "The war can never be brought to a close until that key is in our pocket." Strategically located on the lower Mississippi River, Vicksburg was a main artery for transport during the "war of Northern aggression," and as such, a target for the Union. It was only after a 47-day battle that the Confederate flag flying over the city was lowered for the last time on July 4, 1863.

That event occurred over almost 150 years ago, but Vicksburg's temperament is still tied to the Old South, so much so that until 1945, the city refused to join the rest of the nation in celebrating Independence Day because that was the day Vicksburg was whipped.

Today, thousands of people flock to Vicksburg for a taste of the Old South. Antebellum homes turned bed-and-breakfasts each have a story to tell about the Civil War, museums throughout town provide historical and cultural insight, and the 1,800-acre **National Military Park** stands as testimony to the tragedy of a nation torn apart.

Vicksburg is a popular stop for adults and seniors traveling with tours, but if you provide some background information and plan your trip with children in mind, the younger set can enjoy the city just as much. Because nothing can be more boring for kids than house tours, choose one or two of the best, then follow up with energy-burning activities. Pick up lunch before heading to the Military Park, then break up your day with a picnic under a shady oak. And best of all, don't forget the mighty Mississippi. Any attraction involving water is bound to make a splash with kids.

Family Lodging

Battlefield Inn

While the rooms are typical hotel rooms, a free buffet breakfast, pool, putt-putt golf course, and proximity to the Vicksburg National Military Park

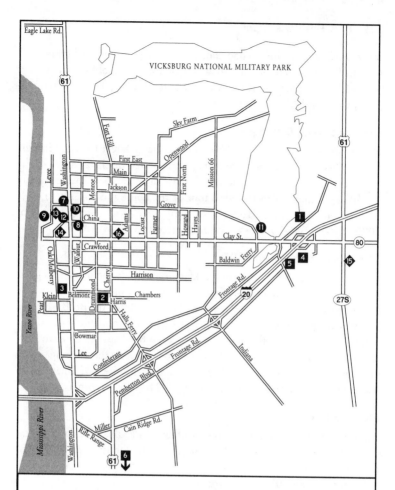

Vicksburg

N

FAMILY LODGING

1. Battlefield Inn
2. Cherry Street Cottages
3. The Corners Mansion
4. The Jameson Inn
5. Holiday Inn
6. Wilson Wood Lodge

ATTRACTIONS

7. Gray & Blue Naval Museum
8. The Great Animal Adventures Children's Museum
9. Mississippi River Adventures Hydro-Jet Boat Cruise
10. Museum of Coca-Cola History and Memorabilia
11. Vicksburg National Military Park
12. Yesterday's Children Antique Doll and Toy Museum

RESTAURANTS

13. Biscuit Company Cafe
14. Burger Village Restaurant
15. Rowdy's Family Restaurant
16. Walnut Hills

make the Battlefield Inn a good choice for overnighting in Vicksburg. And we can't forget to mention the two talking parrots in the lobby. Rates start at $45. 4137 I-20 Frontage Road, Vicksburg; (800) 800-8000 or (601) 638-5077; www.battlefieldinn.com.

Cherry Street Cottages

A comfortable alternative to a hotel room, Cherry Street Cottages has the feel of a bed and breakfast. The cottages are located on the grounds of the Shlenker House, a 1907 Prairie-style home. There are three cottages in all; one has two suites. Stays include a tour of the home and a southern–style breakfast. Rates begin at $100. 2212 Cherry Street, Vicksburg; (601) 636-7086 or (800) 636-7086; www.cherrystreetcottages.com.

The Corners Mansion B&B

Kids are welcome at this bed and breakfast, a stately Victorian with 15 guest rooms, one suite, and a two-bedroom cottage—all of which have private baths. Listed on the National Register of Historic Places, the B&B has some rooms with private porches and views of the Mississippi and Yazoo rivers. Stays include a tour of the mansion, plantation breakfast served in the formal dining room, and a complimentary beverage in the evening. Rates begin at $85 for a double; $160 for a two-bedroom suite. 601 Klein Street, Vicksburg; (601) 636-7421 or (800) 444-7421; www.thecorners.com.

Holiday Inn

Adjacent to the Vicksburg National Military Park, this Holiday Inn features an indoor swimming pool, onsite jogging trail, business services, and room service. Rates begin at $60. 3330 Clay Street, Vicksburg; (601) 636-4551 or (800) 847-0372; www.basshotels.com

The Jameson Inn

This colonial-style inn is nothing fancy, but you can't beat its affordable price and location inside the Vicksburg Factory Outlet Mall. The setup is traditional motel-style with doors opening up to the outside. There is a swimming pool, fitness center and free continental breakfast. Rates average $60 year round. 3975 South Frontage Road, Vicksburg; (800) JAMESON or (601) 619-7799; www.jamesoninns.com.

Wilson Wood Lodge

Once a private residence, this four-bedroom home has been converted into a lodge, complete with nature trails and a private 12-acre lake stocked with bass and bream. An open, grassy area next to the lodge is ideal for bike riding and pick-up soccer games. The lodge is ten miles from Vicksburg. Rates begin at $200 per room per night. 1040 Mallett Road, Vicksburg; (601) 636-0300; www.wilsonwoodlodge.com.

Attractions

Gray & Blue Naval Museum

1102 Washington Street, Vicksburg; (601) 638-6500

Hours: Monday–Saturday, 9 a.m.–5 p.m.

Admission: $2 adults, $1 children

Appeal by Age Group:

Pre-school	Grade School	Teens	Young Adults	Over 30	Seniors
★★★	★★★★	★★★★	★★★★	★★★★	★★★★

Average Touring Time: 30 minutes

Minimum Touring Time: 15 minutes

Rainy Day Touring: Recommended

Author's Rating: ★★★★   Good introduction to the Civil War

Services and Facilities:

Restaurants No	Lockers No
Alcoholic beverages No	Pet kennels No
Disabled access Yes	Rain check N/A
Wheelchair rental No	Private tours Yes
Baby stroller rental No	

Description and Comments   The first thought that went through our minds when we visited this museum was how much glue it took to create all of these models. Many were created by the owner; others were donated to the museum. Regardless, the exhibits include a collection of Civil War gun boats models—the world's largest such collection; a diorama on the Siege of Vicksburg, complete with 2,500 miniature soldiers engaged in battle; a display of "Life on the River" with model steam boats and tow boats; and "The Mississippians" exhibit with miniature naval vessels, all with names connected to Mississippi.

We suggest that you visit the museum before you tour the National Military Park, as the detailed diorama of the Military Park allows you to see how the park is laid out in relation to the river and points of interest. Push buttons let you light up sections at a time.

The Great Animal Adventures Children's Museum

721 China Street, Vicksburg; (601) 629-9920

Hours: Monday–Saturday, 9 a.m.–5 p.m.; Sunday, 1:30–4:30 p.m.

Admission: $2.95 adults, $1.95 children

Appeal by Age Group:

Pre-school	Grade School	Teens	Young Adults	Over 30	Seniors
★★★★	★★★★	★★★★	★★★	★★★	★★★

Average Touring Time: 1 hour

Minimum Touring Time: 30 minutes

Rainy Day Touring: Recommended

Author's Rating: ★★★   The two-headed calf is a hands-down favorite

Services and Facilities:

Restaurants No	Lockers No
Alcoholic beverages No	Pet kennels No
Disabled access Yes	Rain check No
Wheelchair rental No	Private tours Yes
Baby stroller rental No	

Description and Comments   One man's fascination and love for our four-footed friends was the impetus for this museum. The late Dr. Bill Lindley converted an 1888 stable into a tribute to animals, with exhibits housed in former stalls. The exhibits aren't high tech, but high-touch, with hands-on displays that foster an appreciation for animals. There are veterinary tools on display, illustrations locating various body parts, and replicas of animals, including a stuffed horse. Of course, the museum wouldn't be complete without a couple of freaks of nature. This one has a stuffed two-headed calf and a jar with piglets. A special kids area has a clubhouse where sing-alongs are held.

Mississippi River Adventures Hydro-Jet Boat Cruise

P.O. Box 506, Vicksburg; (800) 521-4363 or (601) 638-5443

Hours: Tours daily at 10 a.m., 2 p.m., and 5 p.m.

Admission: $20 adults, $10 children ages 6–12, free for children ages 5 and younger

Appeal by Age Group:

Pre-school	Grade School	Teens	Young Adults	Over 30	Seniors
★★★★	★★★★	★★★★	★★★	★★★	★★★

Average Touring Time: 1 hour

Minimum Touring Time: N/A

Rainy Day Touring: Not recommended

Author's Rating: ★★★

Services and Facilities:

Restaurants No	Lockers No
Alcoholic beverages No	Pet kennels No
Disabled access Yes	Rain check Yes
Wheelchair rental No	Private tours N/A
Baby stroller rental No	

Description and Comments   The only way to experience the mighty Mississippi is to climb aboard a boat and see how she feels up close. This one-hour hydro-jet boat tour lets you do just that. The captain narrates the tour with information about the flora and fauna of the river, along with insight about its historical importance during the Civil War. The tour is five miles down the river and back. If you visit in the summer, keep in mind that there is no air conditioner on board, only a canvas top that is open at the sides and front. Snacks are available at the dock and you can take them with you on the boat. Call ahead if you plan to tour, as it takes at least ten adults for the boat to go out.

Museum of Coca-Cola History and Memorabilia

1107 Washington Street, Vicksburg; (601) 638-6514

Hours: Monday–Saturday, 9 a.m.–5 p.m., Sunday 1:30–4:30 p.m.

Admission: $2.95 adults, $1.95 children ages 12 and younger

Appeal by Age Group:

Pre-school	Grade School	Teens	Young Adults	Over 30	Seniors
★★	★★	★★★	★★★	★★★	★★★

Average Touring Time: 1 hour

Minimum Touring Time: 30 minutes

Rainy Day Touring: Recommended

Author's Rating: ★★★

Services and Facilities:

Restaurants No	Lockers No
Alcoholic beverages No	Pet kennels No
Disabled access Yes	Rain check N/A
Wheelchair rental No	Private tours Yes
Baby stroller rental No	

Description and Comments   In 1894, Vicksburg candy merchant Joseph A. Biedenharn came up with the idea of bottling Coca-Cola and selling it around the rural areas outside the city. This was the first time that Coke was sold in a bottle, a clever idea that changed the way the soft drink was marketed and sold. The museum is housed in Biedenharn's restored candy store and has displays of Coke memorabilia, including the equipment used to bottle the first Coca-Cola. Be sure you visit after meals, because the museum also serves ice cream, homemade candies, and, of course, Coke floats.

Vicksburg National Military Park

3201 Clay Street, Vicksburg; (601) 636-0583 or (601) 636-2199
  www.nps.gov/vick

Hours: Daily, 8 a.m.–5 p.m.; Cairo Museum: November–March, daily, 8:30 a.m.–5 p.m.; April–October, daily, 9:30 a.m.–6 p.m.

Admission: $4 per vehicle for all park activities; $20 for guided car tour

Appeal by Age Group:

Pre-school	Grade School	Teens	Young Adults	Over 30	Seniors
★★	★★★	★★★	★★★★★	★★★★★	★★★★★

Average Touring Time: 1 day

Minimum Touring Time: ½ day

Rainy Day Touring: Not recommended

Author's Rating: ★★★★

Services and Facilities:

Restaurants No	Lockers No
Alcoholic beverages No	Pet kennels No
Disabled access Yes	Rain check No
Wheelchair rental Yes	Private tours Yes
Baby stroller rental No	

Description and Comments   Over 16 miles of woods and pastures make up the Vicksburg National Military Park. It was here that Vicksburg, the "Gibraltar of the Confederacy," eventually fell into Union hands after Northern troops surrounded the town and held its citizens and the Confederate army captive for 47 days, slowly starving them into surrender.

Both sides were heavily vested at Vicksburg—28 states had men fighting here. Today, Confederate and Union lines are identified, with blue markers for the Union and red markers for the Confederacy. In all, there are 1,200 markers, statues, and state memorials.

If your family enjoys American history, spend at least a day in the park, stopping frequently to read the markers along the way. It's almost impossible to see everything at Vicksburg, so we suggest starting at the Visitors Center, where exhibits and an 18-minute film explain the campaign and siege of Vicksburg in detail. Then visit the Gray and Blue Naval Museum, which features a detailed diorama of the park. Both are a good way to decide what sites are the best to visit.

Several sites are of particular interest. The Illinois State Memorial is inscribed with the names of every Illinois soldier present at Vicksburg and is the largest state memorial. The Vicksburg National Cemetery has 17,000 Union soldiers buried here, 13,000 of which are unknown. (Most of the Confederate soldiers were buried in the Vicksburg City Cemetery.) In all, the park has a 16-mile tour road running parallel to the Union and Confederate siege lines.

The Park is also home to the *USS Cairo* complex, which houses a 175-foot long Union gunboat sunk by the Confederacy and raised and restored after 200 years of being underwater. Objects found inside the ship are on display, including cookware, weaponry, sailors' clothing, and photos. A six-minute video tells the story of how the Cairo was sunk by an underwater mine, and how it was salvaged.

Guided and self-guided tours are available for all portions of the park, and in the summer, re-enactments of the skirmishes take place; call ahead for specific times. One note: If your family has already toured several battlefields, you might find that it's hard to keep interest levels high, especially for small children. Either visit this park first and tour it in-depth, or plan only a couple of hours of touring, with plenty of stops in the park.

Yesterday's Children Antique Doll and Toy Museum

1104 Washington Street, Vicksburg; (601) 638-0650

Hours: Monday–Saturday 10:30, a.m.–4 p.m.

Admission: $2 adults, $1 children ages 12 and younger

Appeal by Age Group:

Pre-school	Grade School	Teens	Young Adults	Over 30	Seniors
★★★★	★★★★	★★★★	★★★	★★★	★★★

Average Touring Time: 30 minutes

Minimum Touring Time: 15 minutes

Rainy Day Touring: Recommended

Author's Rating: ★★★

Services and Facilities:

Restaurants No	Lockers No
Alcoholic beverages No	Pet kennels No
Disabled access Yes	Rain check N/A
Wheelchair rental No	Private tours No
Baby stroller rental No	

Description and Comments Either this place will seem scary (there are so many eyes staring back at you) or it will be the favorite stop for doll lovers in your group. There are more than 1,000 dolls, toys, and accessories dating from the 1800s to today on display in this 1836 building. Several French and German bisque dolls are life-size, still dressed in their original costumes. Historical explanations are provided for the famous Alexander doll and composition dolls. A gift shop on site has both antique and new dolls and toys for sale.

Side Trips

Garden for the Blind, Hazelhurst   It's only 30 minutes outside of Jackson, but this garden seems a world away. It started as a labor of love by the McLemore family as a gift to both the sighted and blind employees at Signature Works, the nation's largest employer of the blind and visually impaired. Today, members of the local Garden Club maintain the garden.

Instead of choosing plants for their color, the ones in this garden were chosen for their distinctive fragrances and unusual textures. Sound has also been incorporated into the experience, with wind chimes and a gurgling fountain providing a melodic backdrop.

Give your children the ultimate experience by blindfolding them before you tour; it makes the garden that much more significant. If you call ahead, you can arrange a guided tour of the gardens.

Afterwards, tour the plant and watch as employees make brooms, towels, and other paper products. The guided plant tour takes about two hours. The gardens are across from the plant; garden tours take about 30 minutes. 1 Signature Drive, Hazlehurst; (601) 894-2608; www.signatureworks.com.

Grand Village of the Natchez Indians, Natchez   Don't let the Civil War sites in Mississippi overshadow other historic attractions, in particular the Grand Village of the Natchez Indians. This National Historic Landmark is the location of an important ceremonial mound center for the now-extinct Natchez tribe. In the early 1700s, the French began to explore this area of Mississippi, and though relations between the two groups were friendly at first, they eventually gave way to fighting. The Natchez killed the French garrison at Fort Rosalie, a move that the French retaliated against with such force that it drove the Indians from their homeland.

Today, the site has a museum about the Natchez with artifacts excavated from archaeological digs, a replica of a Natchez Indian hut, and three ceremonial mounds. Open Monday–Saturday 9 a.m.–5 p.m., Sunday 1:30–5 p.m. 400 Jefferson Davis Boulevard, Natchez; (601) 446-6502 or (800) 674-6724; mdah.state.ms.us/hprop/gvni.html.

Family-Friendly Restaurants

BISCUIT COMPANY CAFE

1100 Washington Street, Vicksburg; (601) 631-0099

Meals served:　Lunch and dinner
Cuisine:　American
Entrée range:　$5.95 and up
Kids menu:　No
Reservations:　No
Payment:　All major credit cards accepted

Steaks, pasta, seafood, and po-boys are the house specialties, and a blues band plays at dinner. Located in a historic building overlooking the Mississippi River, the restaurant is close to nearby attractions.

BURGER VILLAGE RESTAURANT

1220 Washington Street, Vicksburg; (601) 638-0202

Meals served:　Breakfast, lunch, and dinner
Cuisine:　American
Entrée range:　$1 and up
Kids menu:　No
Reservations:　No
Payment:　All major credit cards accepted

Being this close to Louisiana has had an influence on Mississippi fare. Here you'll find tasty gumbo, po-boys, red beans and rice, plus other southern favorites like chicken and dumplings, chili, and homemade desserts. Breakfast is served all day.

ROWDY'S FAMILY RESTAURANT

Highways 27 and 80, Vicksburg; (601) 638-2375

Meals served:　Lunch and dinner
Cuisine:　Fish
Entrée range:　$3 and up
Kids menu:　Yes

Reservations: No
Payment: All major credit cards accepted

Grilled and blackened seafood and catfish are the house specialties, along with the homemade pies and cakes. The atmoshpere is just as lively as the name implies.

WALNUT HILLS

1214 Adams Street, Vicksburg; (601) 638-4910

Meals served: Lunch and dinner
Cuisine: Southern
Entrée range: $3.50 and up
Kids menu: No
Reservations: No
Payment: All major credit cards accepted

One of the most popular restaurants in town, Walnut Hills serves southern-style lunches. Everyone sits together around round tables topped with Lazy Susans loaded down with steaming dishes. You can also order from a menu. The fried chicken and homemade bread pudding are fantastic.

Mississippi's Gulf Coast

In recent years, Mississippi's Gulf Coast has made headlines because of its new Las Vegas–style casinos. These upscale gambling resorts can't be ignored, but they are hardly the only reason to visit the coast. The Gulf Coast is home to many natural, historic, and cultural sites. **Beauvoir,** Jefferson Davis' home, is here, along with the **Gulf Coast Gator Ranch** and the **John C. Stennis Space Center.**

The development along the coast has made it hard to distinguish one beach town from the next. **Biloxi** and **Gulfport** have practically merged into one metropolis, and **Bay St. Louis, Pass Christian,** and **Pascagoula** are but short trips down the road.

For families, the 26 miles of beach—the longest manmade beach in the world—is the main attraction, and there are plenty of wet and dry activities to entertain everyone for hours. Parasailing, jet skiing, windsurfing, motor boating, and swimming are some of the activities easily accessed from the beaches.

On the mainland, the beach is relatively undeveloped on the south side of Highway 90, leaving the sand to beach bums. On the north side of Highway 90, which runs parallel to the water, there are restaurants, hotels, and shopping facilities—simply walk across the street for a hiatus from the sun. Another good place to spread out your beach towels is on **West Ship Island,** where the water sparkles a deep aqua and the sand looks like sugar. Take the ferry to the island, tour **Fort Massachusetts,** and play in that beautiful Gulf water.

Note: On the Gulf Coast car-rental rates are among the lowest in the country, rates for hotel rooms rarely rise above $150 during the peak summer season, and the best deals can be had from Thanksgiving through January.

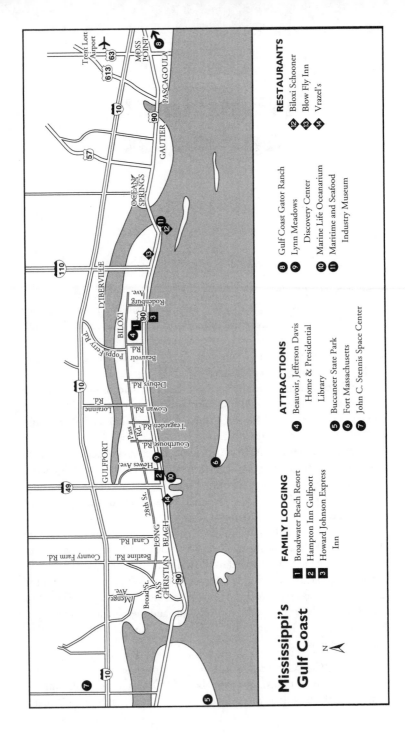

Mississippi's Gulf Coast

N

FAMILY LODGING

1 Broadwater Beach Resort
2 Hampton Inn Gulfport
3 Howard Johnson Express Inn

ATTRACTIONS

4 Beauvoir, Jefferson Davis Home & Presidential Library
5 Buccaneer State Park
6 Fort Massachusetts
7 John C. Stennis Space Center
8 Gulf Coast Gator Ranch
9 Lynn Meadows Discovery Center
10 Marine Life Oceanarium
11 Maritime and Seafood Industry Museum

RESTAURANTS

12 Biloxi Schooner
13 Blow Fly Inn
14 Vrazel's

Family Lodging

Broadwater Beach Resort, Biloxi

Built in 1939, the Broadwater is one of the oldest resorts on the Gulf. Yet that's not to say that it's run-down. Rather, the Broadwater offers spacious, modern rooms and an array of family activities—more than you'll find at newer, swankier competitors. There are ten tennis courts, an 18-hole golf course, three tropical-style swimming pools, and the South's largest covered marina, where Gulf fishing charters leave from the dock. The hotel has a casino, but it located across the street from the hotel. 2110 Beach Boulevard, Biloxi; (228) 388-2211 or (800) 843-7737; www.presidentbroadwater.com.

Hampton Inn Gulfport

Convenient to the Gulf beaches but away from the noise and crowds, Hampton Inn Gulfport offers families an outdoor pool, free continental breakfast, local calls, and in-room movies. Rates begin at $70. 9445 Highway 49; (228) 868-3300 or (800) HAMPTON; www.hamptoninn.com.

Howard Johnson Express Inn

Across the highway from the beach, this Howard Johnson property is brand new. There are suites with Jacuzzis available, and you can request to have a microwave and refrigerator moved to your room if needed. Free amenities include continental breakfast, shuttle to local casinos, access to the fitness room and swimming pool, and a free Crayola Kids Magazine and four-pack of crayons for each child upon check-in. Rates begin at $70. 1712 Beach Boulevard, Biloxi; (228) 432-2000 or (800) 406-1411; www.hojo.com

Attractions

Beauvoir, Jefferson Davis Home & Presidential Library

2244 Beach Boulevard, Biloxi; (800) 570-3818 or (228) 388-9074
www.beauvoir.org

Hours: March 2–September 1, daily 9 a.m.–5 p.m.; September 2–
   March 1, daily 9 a.m.–4 p.m.

Admission: $7.50 adults, $6.50 seniors, $4.50 students, free for children
   ages 5 and younger

Appeal by Age Group:

Pre-school	Grade School	Teens	Young Adults	Over 30	Seniors
★	★★	★★★	★★★	★★★	★★★

Average Touring Time: 1½ hours

Minimum Touring Time: 45 minutes

Rainy Day Touring: Not recommended

Author's Rating: ★★★

Services and Facilities:

Restaurants No	Lockers No
Alcoholic beverages No	Pet kennels No
Disabled access Yes	Rain check Yes
Wheelchair rental Yes	Private tours Yes
Baby stroller rental No	

Description and Comments Beauvoir was the last home of Confederate President Jefferson Davis. It is smaller than you would imagine, but its location under shady oaks and overlooking the Gulf of Mexico no doubt made it a tranquil retreat for Davis and his family. Several family antiques and other memorabilia have survived and are on display in the home.

When Davis died, his widow sold the home to the state on the condition that it be turned into a home for Confederate veterans and their families. Over 2,000 people, including former slaves who fought for the Confederacy, stayed here. In 1947, it became a state museum. The Tomb of the Unknown Confederate Soldier, a cemetery, and an impressive Presidential Library with exhibits about the war and displays on Davis and his family are also located on the grounds. The home is listed on the National Register of Historic Places.

Buccaneer State Park

1150 South Beach Boulevard, Waveland; (228) 467-3822 or (800) GO-PARKS; www.mdwfp.com

Hours: Daily, 8 a.m.–4 p.m.; waterpark is seasonal, 11 a.m.–6:45 p.m.

Admission: $2 per vehicle, $0.50 for each person over 4 years of age

Appeal by Age Group:

Pre-school	Grade School	Teens	Young Adults	Over 30	Seniors
★	★★	★★★	★★★	★★★	★★★

Average Touring Time: 1 day

Minimum Touring Time: ½ day

Rainy Day Touring: Not recommended

Author's Rating: ★★★★ State park activities plus a water park

Services and Facilities:

Restaurants Yes (water park)	Wheelchair rental No
Alcoholic beverages No	Baby stroller rental No
Disabled access Yes	Lockers Yes (water park)

Pet kennels No
Rain check No

Private tours N/A

Description and Comments Its choice location along the Gulf makes this one of Mississippi's most visited state parks. In the 1700s, pirates frequented these shores, and stories circulate even today about buried treasure on the grounds. If your family likes to camp, Buccaneer has both primitive and RV camping sites available, all of which are shady, secluded, and close to laundry, restroom, and picnic facilities. There are picnic facilities with two large pavilions, a nature trail through the coastal forest and wetlands, a new 18-hole disc golf course, two tennis courts, basketball courts, camp store, and game room with video games, pinball machines, and table tennis.

What makes this park different from other state parks is the popular water park. You'll find a wave pool, two plume waterslides, and a toddler's wading pool—all near the campground.

Fort Massachusetts

3500 Park Road, Ocean Springs; (228) 875-0821; www.nps.gov/guis

Hours: Daily, 8 a.m.–sunset; Fort hours: March–October, 9:30 a.m.– 5 p.m.; November–February, 8:30 a.m.–4 p.m.

Admission: Fort: free; Ferry: $16 adults, $14 seniors, $8 children ages 3–10, free for children ages 2 and younger

Appeal by Age Group:

Pre-school	Grade School	Teens	Young Adults	Over 30	Seniors
★★★★	★★★★	★★★★	★★★★	★★★★	★★★★

Average Touring Time: 1 day

Minimum Touring Time: ½ day

Rainy Day Touring: Not recommended

Author's Rating: ★★★★ History and outdoor fun in one trip

Services and Facilities:

Restaurants No
Alcoholic beverages No
Disabled access Yes
Wheelchair rental No
Baby stroller rental No

Lockers No
Pet kennels No
Rain check No
Private tours N/A

Description and Comments Located on one of the barrier islands flanking the Mississippi coast, Fort Massachusetts was built prior to the Civil War and is one of the last masonry forts built by the U.S. Army Corps of Engineers. The fort saw little activity until the war, when it was converted into a Union prison. Now part of the Gulf Islands National Seashore, the fort offers guided and self-guided tours. Take the 70-minute ferry ride from the mainland at the Gulfport Small Craft Harbor.

Gulf Coast Gator Ranch

10300 Highway 90, Pascagoula; (228) 475-6026

Hours: Monday–Saturday, 9 a.m.–5 p.m.; Sunday, 1–5 p.m.

Admission: $10 adults, $5 children; $2 adults and $1 children for gator farm tour only

Appeal by Age Group:

Pre-school	Grade School	Teens	Young Adults	Over 30	Seniors
★★★	★★★★★	★★★★★	★★★★★	★★★★★	★★★★★

Average Touring Time: 2 hours

Minimum Touring Time: 1 hour

Rainy Day Touring: Not recommended

Author's Rating: ★★★★★

Services and Facilities:

Restaurants No	Lockers No
Alcoholic beverages No	Pet kennels No
Disabled access Yes	Rain check No
Wheelchair rental No	Private tours Yes
Baby stroller rental No	

Description and Comments   Alligators—and lots of them. People may flock to the Gulf Coast for sun and sand, but the true coast is a swampland filled with all sorts of mysterious creatures, including beavers, turtles, birds, and, of course, alligators. Boardwalks and pathways let you see these creatures in enclosed natural habitats—if it's hot, they'll most likely be in the water; if it's cold, they'll be lying along the banks.

The ultimate thrill, however, is to board an airboat and head out into the swamps. Here, the gators roam freely, and guides can point out where to best spot them. They'll also point out osprey nests, beaver dams, and alligator nests. While seeing alligators in their natural habitat is certainly a treat, so is the ride on the airboat, a floating contraption powered by a gigantic fan-like motor. Get ready for a noisy, bumpy, and wet ride—exactly the kind your kids will remember long after your vacation is over. One note: The noise and bumpiness of the airboat might unnerve small or shy children.

John C. Stennis Space Center

Building 1200, Stennis Space Center; (228) 688-2370; www.ssc.nasa.gov

Hours: Daily 9 a.m.–5 p.m.

Admission: Free

Appeal by Age Group:

Pre-school	Grade School	Teens	Young Adults	Over 30	Seniors
★★★	★★★★	★★★★	★★★★	★★★★	★★★★

Average Touring Time: 2½ hours

Minimum Touring Time: 1 hour

Rainy Day Touring: N/A

Author's Rating: ★★★★

Services and Facilities:

Restaurants Yes	Lockers No
Alcoholic beverages No	Pet kennels No
Disabled access Yes	Rain check N/A
Wheelchair rental Yes	Private tours No
Baby stroller rental Yes	

Description and Comments   The John C. Stennis Space Center is full of exhibits that demystify the space program and the technology used to send rockets and shuttles into space. As NASA's Center of Excellence for large propulsion systems testing, this is where the main engines used to boost the space shuttle into orbit are tested. Sit in on the deafening firing of a space shuttle main engine test fire, and be prepared to get wet—over one million gallons of water are used to cool down the system, and the steam settles on spectators. Call ahead for testing days and times.

Tours begin in the newly expanded Mississippi Welcome Center, with exhibits about the space program such as a walk-through space station and simulated rides. Guests are then shuttled over to the space center. The Hall of Achievements tells the story of the history of NASA and space flight through films and exhibits like a 154-foot space shuttle fuel tank F-1 rocket engine, a Jupiter-C rocket, and a J-2 rocket. Additionally, other government agencies housed at Stennis have displays, including the Environment Protection Agency, the National Data Buoy Center, and the U.S. Geological Survey.

Lynn Meadows Discovery Center

246 Dolan Avenue, Gulfport; (228) 897-6039; www.lmdc.org

Hours: Tuesday–Saturday, 10 a.m.–5 p.m.

Admission: $5 per person

Appeal by Age Group:

Pre-school	Grade School	Teens	Young Adults	Over 30	Seniors
★★★★★	★★★★★	★★★★★	★★★★	★★★★	★★★★

Average Touring Time: 2 hours

Minimum Touring Time: 1 hour

Rainy Day Touring: Recommended

Author's Rating: ★★★★

Services and Facilities:

Restaurants No	Lockers No
Alcoholic beverages No	Pet kennels No
Disabled access Yes	Rain check No
Wheelchair rental Yes	Private tours No
Baby stroller rental No	

Description and Comments   Voted the 1999 Mississippi Attraction of the Year, the Discovery Center is a hands-on museum where children learn by doing. The museum is especially good for families, as the exhibits facilitate interaction between parents and children as they play with and discuss the various displays.

There are multi-age exhibits designed specifically to be low-technology and high on role playing. For example, at the museum grocery store, you must first work for money, perhaps by stocking the produce section, then after you are paid, you grocery shop for items and try to stay within your budget. Another popular exhibit is the Health Wanted section, featuring R.U. Healthy, a fitness robot, and exhibits that test your reaction time and strength. The History Attic sends kids on a historical scavenger hunt to uncover the secrets of a Mississippi city in the late 1800s. The Super Colossal Climbing Sculpture tests endurance and climbing skills. The Discovery Store is filled with interesting souvenirs, many at prices within range for young allowances.

Marine Life Oceanarium

U.S. 90 and Highway 49 at Joseph T. Jones Memorial Park, Gulfport; (228) 864-2511; www.dolphinsrus.com

Hours: Winter: daily, 9 a.m.–3 p.m.; summer: daily, 9 a.m.–6 p.m.

Admission: $12.75 adults, $9.75 seniors, $7.50 children ages 3–11, free for children ages 2 and younger

Appeal by Age Group:

Pre-school	Grade School	Teens	Young Adults	Over 30	Seniors
★★★★	★★★★	★★★★	★★★★	★★★★	★★★★

Average Touring Time: 2 hours

Minimum Touring Time: 1 hour

Rainy Day Touring: Not recommended

Author's Rating: ★★★★

Services and Facilities:

Restaurants No	Lockers No
Alcoholic beverages No	Pet kennels No
Disabled access No	Rain check Yes
Wheelchair rental No	Private tours No
Baby stroller rental No	

Description and Comments   A local version of SeaWorld, the Oceanarium presents fascinating shows with trained bottlenose dolphins, sea lions, and South American macaws. The dolphin shows are especially captivating, as special stereo equipment allows you to hear the whistles, squeals, and clicks of the dolphins communicating underwater. Before you leave, get your picture taken kissing a sea lion (there is a $5 charge). Other highlights include divers feeding giant loggerhead turtles, sea lions performing in skits, talking birds, and a fun house you can walk through. A new attraction is the interactive dolphin swim, where you can actually get into the water with the dolphins. The show areas are covered with domes but have open sides, so avoid the Oceanarium in stormy weather.

Maritime and Seafood Industry Museum

115 First Street, Biloxi; (228) 435-6320; www.maritimemuseum.org

Hours: Monday–Saturday, 9 a.m.–4:30 p.m.

Admission: $3 adults, $2 seniors and children ages 6–16, free for children ages 5 and younger

Appeal by Age Group:

Pre-school	Grade School	Teens	Young Adults	Over 30	Seniors
★★	★★★★	★★★★	★★★★	★★★★	★★★★

Average Touring Time: 2 hours

Minimum Touring Time: 1 hour

Rainy Day Touring: Recommended

Author's Rating: ★★★★   Different perspective of the Gulf Coast

Services and Facilities:

Restaurants No	Lockers No
Alcoholic beverages No	Pet kennels No
Disabled access Yes	Rain check No
Wheelchair rental No	Private tours Yes
Baby stroller rental No	

Description and Comments   This museum pays tribute to Biloxi's maritime history, starting with the wetland Indians and working all the way to the 1950s. There is particular focus on the Biloxi schooners, those grand working boats that are the backbone of the seafood trade. Exhibits vary from boat building and how the schooners are sailed to seafood factories and the types of jobs people had in them. There are also exhibits on Biloxi's oysters and shrimp. For weather buffs, one room is dedicated to hurricanes and includes a 23-minute film on Hurricane Camille, which wiped out the coast in the '60s.

After indirectly experiencing the schooners and the water from land, steady your sea legs and book a walk-on sail on the museum's very own schooner. This two-and-a-half hour ride begins by motoring out to the channel, then raising the sails for an authentic Biloxi experience. There are no food or drinks sold on board, so take a cooler with your own provisions. Walk-on sails are $20 for adults, $10 for children.

Side Trips

International Checker Hall of Fame, Petal   Founded by checkers guru Charles Walker, the Hall of Fame is a combination reference office and museum for devotees of the game. Exhibits highlight all the countries that play checkers and show how the boards differ from 60 squares up to 120 squares. Trophies and checker memorabilia are on display along with game boards—one was made from an Indian champion who killed an elephant, tanned the hide, and presented the board to Walker as a gift.

Kids are particularly drawn to two things: Guichio, the South American golden spider monkey who greets guests, and the world's largest checker board, where people become game pieces.

Tournaments and championships are held here; call ahead for a schedule of playtimes. Tours are also by appointment. From Highway 42 in Petal, turn right on Chapel Hill Road, left on Leeville Road, and right on Lynn Ray Road; (601) 582-7090.

Walter Anderson Museum of Art, Ocean Springs   Undiscovered until his death in 1965, Walter Anderson captured the flowers and animals of his home state in colorful, surreal paintings so fluid they seem as if they float on the surface. An eccentric man, Anderson would spend weeks at a time in a small cottage on the barrier islands studying his subjects. The cottage has been reassembled in the museum and includes the famed walls he painted in his signature style. A short film profiles Anderson and his work. Open Monday–Saturday, 9:30 a.m.–4:30 p.m. and Sunday, 12:30–4:30 p.m. in winter months; Monday–Saturday, 10 a.m.–5 p.m. and Sunday, 1–5 p.m. during the summer. Cost is $5 adults, $3 seniors and college students, $2 children ages 6–18, free for children ages 5 and younger. 510 Washington Street, Ocean Springs; (228) 872-3164.

Family-Friendly Restaurants

BILOXI SCHOONER

139 Howard Street, Biloxi; (228) 374-8071

Meals served: Breakfast, lunch, and dinner
Cuisine: American/Southern
Entrée range: $5.50 and up
Kids menu: Yes
Reservations: No
Payment: Cash and checks only

Some of the best southern cooking on the Gulf Coast. Po-boys and gumbo are favorites, and a house special is served daily at lunch. The old diner is decorated with photos of 1940s and 1950s fishing schooners.

BLOW FLY INN

1201 Washington Avenue, Biloxi; (228) 896-9812

Meals served: Lunch and dinner
Cuisine: American
Entrée range: $5 and up
Kids menu: Yes
Reservations: Yes
Payment: All major credit cards accepted

The Blow Fly Inn is an automatic favorite for kids—it's one of those places that hands out crayons and menus for pre-dinner entertainment. Buffets are out during lunch; you can also order steak, pasta, poboys, seafood, and ribs. The restaurant is just off the main highway, overlooking Bayou Bernard.

VRAZEL'S

3206 West Beach Boulevard, Gulfport; (228) 863-2229; www.gcww.com/vrazels

Meals served: Lunch and dinner
Cuisine: Seafood
Entrée range: $8.95 and up
Kids menu: Yes
Reservations: Yes
Payment: All major credit cards accepted

Seafood is the house specialty, but you can also get good steaks and chicken entrées for kids. Vrazel's is located directly across form the Grand Casino.

Part Six

North Carolina

Since 1584, when the first English settlers arrived on its shores, people have been visiting North Carolina. And no wonder. Few places in America offer such variety. With mountains, plains, and coastal areas, the state's geography accommodates all types of wanderlust. North Carolina offers skiing in the winter, gorgeous foliage tours in the fall, and boating, swimming, and fishing in the spring and summer.

And that's not to mention the wealth of activities. Almost any sporting event from car racing to golf can be found here; museums devoted to anthropology, art, and natural sciences abound; and both the cities and small towns are meccas for all kinds of shopping.

The majority of North Carolina remains rural, though its cities are of world-class quality. The state's history is also rich. It was an original member of the 13 colonies, a Confederate pacesetter in the Civil War, and a focal point for the Civil Rights struggles of the 1960s. In 1903, Wilbur and Orville Wright took off on the first-ever successful airplane flight from North Carolina soil at **Kill Devil Hills.** Today, sentiment is divided between the progressive urban developments and the more conservative rural areas.

The 300-mile-long Carolina coast, including **Wilmington** and the **Outer Banks,** is perhaps the most popular among tourist destinations. Besides the spectacular views of the Atlantic Ocean, there are three aquariums to visit, historic sites like **Somerset Place** near Creswell, and six operating lighthouses.

In the heartland, North Carolina's cities also keep visitors entertained. Old Salem in **Winston-Salem** is a restored eighteenth-century Moravian town—the first with public water, fire departments, and schools for girls in America. **Discovery Place** in **Charlotte** is the largest museum of science and technology in North Carolina and is adjacent to the **Kelly Space Voyage Planetarium,** the largest planetarium in the country. In **Raleigh,** the **North Carolina Museum of Art** contains one of the most distinguished collections of old masters in the South, and the new Exploris, a museum of the humanities, is billed as the world's first global experience center.

In the summer, the mountains are a welcome respite from the humidity and heat of the Carolina coast. **Sliding Rock** in **Transylvania County** offers a 150-foot natural water slide; **The Great Smoky Mountains National Park,** America's most popular, is a hot spot for hiking and camping; and the **Blue Ridge Parkway,** the nation's most scenic parkway, affords travelers sweeping vistas of the mountains and forests.

There is really no bad time to visit North Carolina. In the winter, some mountain areas get as much as 30 inches of snow a year—great for skiing. But don't expect the temperatures to be bone-chilling; in fact, winter temperatures can be quite mild. In the summer, the heat and humidity along the coast takes some getting used to, but it's no worse than any other place in the South. In the mountains, summers are cool and refreshing with low humidity. The heartland features average winter temperatures of 42 degrees and 77 degrees in the summer.

GETTING THERE

By Plane. The Triangle area, Charlotte, and Winston-Salem have large airports with service from most of the major carriers. Raleigh-Durham International Airport is 11 miles northwest of Raleigh, 10 miles southeast of downtown Durham on I-40, and 20 miles east from Chapel Hill. It has 400 flights daily from ten major carriers (phone (919) 840-2123). The Piedmont Triad International Airport is 20 miles to the east of downtown Winston-Salem, 15 miles northeast of High Point, and 10 miles from downtown Greensboro (phone (336) 665-5600). Charlotte/Douglas International Airport (phone (704) 359-4013) is seven miles from the city and 122 miles from Asheville. It has 500 flights daily on ten major airlines. Asheville Regional Airport is located 15 minutes from downtown with both jet and commuter service provided by major airlines. The Wilmington New Hanover International Airport (phone (828) 681-0051) is a half-mile from downtown at 1740 Airport Boulevard (phone (910) 341-4125).

By Train. North Carolina offers an extensive rail network throughout the state; (800) USA-RAIL; www.amtrak.com.

By Car. North Carolina is well connected via a 78,000-mile highway network, which is the largest state-maintained system in the nation. There are five major interstate highways intersecting the state: I-26 traversing the western part of the state; I-40 from west to east; I-77 from north to south; I-85 from north to south in the central portion of the state; and I-95 from north to south along the eastern border.

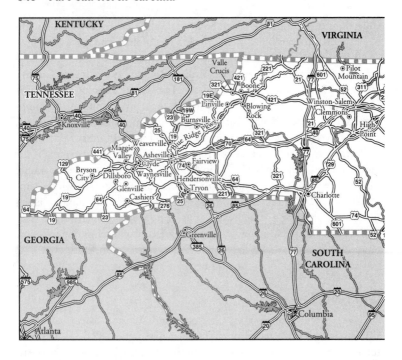

North Carolina law requires all front-seat occupants to buckle up, and children younger than six must be restrained in federally approved safety restraints. Four- and five-year-olds may use safety belts instead of child safety seats mandated for children three and younger. All passengers are required to use safety belts, and the law requires that driving lights should be on whenever your windshield wipers are engaged.

In regard to renting a car, almost every national car rental agency has a counter at the major airports. Rates vary according to agency, mileage, and/or rental period. Traffic information and videos of real-time traffic can be found at www.ncsmartlink.org/triangle.

HOW TO GET INFORMATION BEFORE YOU GO
State

North Carolina Division of Tourism, 301 North Wilmington Street, Raleigh 27601-2825; (800) VISIT-NC, (919) 733.8372; www.visitnc.com

North Carolina Parks & Recreation Division, P.O. Box 27687, Raleigh 27611; (919) 733-4181

NC DOT Ferry Division Information; (800) VISIT-NC; www.ncferry.org

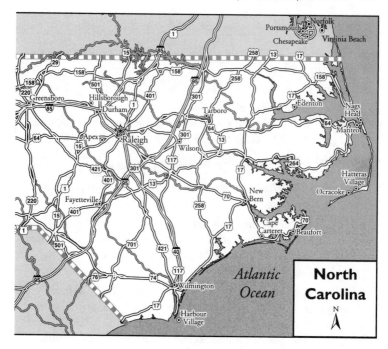

Regional

Blue Ridge Parkway Association, P.O. Box 453, Asheville 28802; (704) 298-0398; www.blueridgeparkway.org

Cherokee Visitor Center, P.O. Box 460, Cherokee 28719; (800) 438-1601; www.cherokee-nc.com

Cape Fear Coast Convention & Visitors Bureau, 24 North Third Street, Wilmington 28401; (800) 222-4757; www.visitwrightsvillebeach.org

Carteret County Tourism Bureau, 3409 Arendell Street, Morehead City 28557; (800) SUNNY-NC or (252) 726-8148

Craven County Convention and Visitors Bureau, 314 Front Street, New Bern 28560; (252) 637-9400; www.nccoast.com

Crystal Coast Visitors Center, 3409 Arendell Street, Morehead City 28557; (800) SUNNY-NC; www.sunnync.com

Great Smoky Mountains National Park Division of Resource Education, 107 Park Headquarters Road, Gatlinburg, TN 37738; (423) 436-1200; www. nps.gov/grsm/homepage.htm or www.nps.gov/grsm

Kids' Beat

- The state bird is the cardinal; the state flower is the dogwood; and the state tree is the pine.

- North Carolina has more salamanders than anywhere else in the world—58 species in all.

- North Carolina is called the "Tar Heel State" because of the state's tar production, or because of the fact that during the Civil War, North Carolina soldiers who couldn't stick their ground and hold off Union troops were said to have forgotten to "tar their heels." Today, the University of North Carolina sports teams are known as the Tar Heels.

- Ocracoke Island is the site where Blackbeard died in a bloody duel with Lt. Richard Maynard of the British Royal Navy. It's rumored that he might have buried gold along the Carolina coast, though none has ever been found.

- Wild ponies can be found on Ocracoke Island. They supposedly arrived on a British ship that came in search of the Lost Colony of Roanoke. Wild horses also roam the northern Outer Banks near Corolla, and Shackleford Banks and Carrot Island near Beaufort.

- Great Smoky Mountains National Park is the largest protected land area east of the Rocky Mountains, covering 276,000 acres in North Carolina.

- Built in 1870, Cape Hatteras Lighthouse is the tallest brick lighthouse in North America.

- Kill Devil Hills is where Wilbur and Orville Wright took the first powered air flight in 1903.

- Jockey's Ridge, north of Nags Head, is the highest sand dune on the East Coast. Tourists come here to hike, hang glide, and fly kites.

- The rare Venus' flytrap, an insect-eating plant, only grows naturally within a 60-mile radius of Wilmington.

- The University of North Carolina was our nation's first state university.

- Mount Mitchell, located about 20 miles northwest of Asheville, is the highest point east of the Mississippi River at 6,684 feet.

North Carolina's Not-to-Be-Missed Attractions

Around the State	Cape Hatteras
	Grandfather Mountain
	Outer Banks
Asheville	Biltmore Estate House and Gardens
	Blue Ridge Parkway
	Great Smoky Mountains
	Grove Park Inn
Charlotte	Discovery Place
	Lowes Motor Speedway
	Reed Gold Mine
Raleigh-Durham-Chapel Hill	Duke Chapel
	Exploris
	Morehead Planetarium
	North Carolina Museum of Natural Science
Wilmington	Battleship *North Carolina*
	Fort Fisher
	North Carolina Aquarium at Fort Fisher
Winston-Salem	Old Salem
	Reynolda House
	Tanglewood Park

Outer Banks Chamber of Commerce, P.O. Box 1757, Kill Devil Hills 27948; (252) 441-8144; www.outerbanks.com

Outer Banks Visitors Bureau, P.O. Box 399, Manteo 27954; (800) 446-6262; outerbanks.org

Pinehurst Area Convention and Visitors Bureau, P.O. Box 2270, Southern Pines 28388; (800) 346-5362; www.pinehurst.com

Swain County Chamber of Commerce, P.O. Box 509-W, Bryson City 28713; (828) 488-3681 or (800) 867-9246; www.greatsmokies.com

Local

Asheville Convention and Visitors Bureau, P.O. Box 1010, Asheville 28802-1010; (828) 258-6101; www.ashevillechamber.org/cvb_top.htm

Charlotte Convention & Visitors Bureau, 122 East Stonewall Street, Charlotte 28202; (800) 231-4636; www.charlottecvb.org

Chapel Hill/Orange County Visitors Bureau, 501 West Franklin Street, Suite 104, Chapel Hill 27516; (888) 968-2060 or (919) 968-2060; www.chocvb.org

Durham Convention & Visitors Bureau, 101 East Morgan Street, Durham 27701; (919) 680-8300 or (800) 446-8604; dcvb.durham.nc.us

Greater Raleigh Convention and Visitors Bureau, Fayetteville Street Mall, Suite 1505, Raleigh 27601; (800) 849-8499 or (919) 834-5900, www.raleighcvb.org

Info Charlotte, Visitor Information Center, 330 South Tyron Street, Charlotte 28202; (704) 331-2700; www.charlottecvb.org

The Winston-Salem Convention and Visitors Bureau, 601 North Cherry Street, Winston-Salem 27101; (800) 331-7018; www.hickory.nc.us/ncnetworks/ws-intr.html

---

More North Carolina Websites

Ag's Cool: North Carolina Agriculture www.agr.state.nc.us/agscool

The Appalachian Trail Home Page www.fred.net/kathy/at.html

Famous North Carolinians ils.unc.edu/nc/famous.html

NC Dot Kids www.dot.state.nc.us/kids

North Carolina Encyclopedia statelibrary.dcr.state.nc.us/nc/cover.htm

North Carolina Lighthouses www.outer-banks.com/lighthouses.cfm

Queen Anne's Revenge, Blackbeard's Flagship www.ah.dcr.state.nc.us/qar

State of North Carolina Kids Page www.secretary.state.nc.us/kids pg/homepage.asp

Listen to the Tweetise Railroad Whistle www.tweetsie-railroad.com/events.html

Virtual Wooly Worm Race www.banner-elk.com/worms

Family Outdoor Adventures

⛺- Camping

♥ - Author's favorite

⛺- *Appalachian National Scenic Trail*   The Appalachian Trail winds 2,160 miles from Georgia to Maine, with 300 miles of trail located in North Carolina—68 miles of which are park. Recognized as part of the national trail system established by Congress in 1968, the Trail is unique in that it was first initiated by volunteers in 1921 and completed by volunteers in 1937. Today, more than 98% of the Trail is public land, and it's considered a wilderness trail intended for foot travel only. Most hikers travel the Trail on weekends or use it for short-term hikes. Those planning to hike it from one end to the other generally start the five- to six-month hike at the southern point in early spring.

For families, there are many entrances that work well for smaller hikes. The Appalachian Trail Conference (www.fred.net/kathy/at.html) provides maps and a variety of trail books with detailed information on various trails, a rating system as to a segment's difficulty, and diaries of trail adventures. Permits are not required to walk the Trail, but overnight camping permits are necessary. Reservations during the summer months are required for some camping areas as well as for the numerous campsites along the Trail. You will also find hostels and other overnight accommodations in nearby towns. Forest Supervisor's Office for North Carolina National Forests, 160-A Zillicoa Street, Asheville 28801; (704) 257-4200; www.nps.gov/aptr.

⛺ - *Blue Ridge Parkway*   This scenic byway connects the Great Smoky Mountains National Park in North Carolina with the Shenandoah National Park in Virginia. The parkway extends 252 miles in North Carolina and offers a wide range of recreational opportunities for families who are interested in mountain culture, scenery, and history. Milepost markers along the Parkway are numbered progressively southward. Using these milepost markers and the Blue Ridge Parkway Association directory (www.blueridgeparkway.org/directory.htm), you can locate a variety of attractions from fishing and golfing to panning for gold, campgrounds, picnic areas, lodging, restaurants, and a variety of other services. Blue Ridge Parkway Association, P.O. Box 2136, Asheville 28802-2136; (828) 271-4779 Ext. 212; www.blueridgeparkway.org.

⛺ - *Cape Hatteras National Seashore*   This popular national park preserves and protects 75 miles along North Carolina's Outer Banks and includes the Cape Hatteras Lighthouse, the tallest brick lighthouse in North America. Storms and the constant washing away of sand along the coast threatened the foundation of the lighthouse, and in 1999 the lighthouse was moved some 2,900 feet inland through the use of hydraulic technology. The lighthouse tower is open to the public on a seasonal basis. Four national park service campgrounds dot the Cape Hatteras National Seashore, providing places to camp along the oceanfront just behind a line of dunes. Campgrounds include grills, bathroom facilities, and parking next to your site. The campgrounds are open from April through October. Outer Banks Visitors Bureau, P.O. Box 399, Manteo 27954; (800) 446-6262; www. nps.gov/caha/capehatteras.htm or www.outerbanks.org.

⋏- *Carolina Beach State Park*   Ten miles north of Wilmington, this park is bordered by the Cape Fear River on one side and the Intracoastal Waterway on the other. It's not a good place to swim, but there are picnic areas, hiking trails, a campground, and a marina. Carolina Beach State Park, P.O. Box 475 Carolina Beach 28428; office: (910) 458-8206, marina: (910) 458-7770; ils.unc.edu/parkproject/cabe.html

⋏ - *The Cherokee Indian Reservation*   Located in western North Carolina, the Cherokee Indian Reservation is home to 12,500 enrolled tribal members. The reservation is adjacent to both the Great Smoky Mountains National Park and Blue Ridge Parkway. Each summer Unto These Hills, recognized as one of the top outdoor dramas, is presented. This drama relates the history of the Cherokee people from about 1540 through their forced removal from this area in the late 1830s. This is a memorable event for even young children in the family. Performances begin in mid-June and last until the end of August. Reserved seating is available for $14; general admission seats are $11 for adults and $5 for children younger than age 12. The Cherokee Historical Association, P.O. Box 398, Cherokee 28719; (828) 497-2111; www.dnet.net/~cheratt.

Chimney Rock Park   Located about 25 miles southeast of Asheville, Chimney Rock Park is situated in beautiful Hickory Nut Gorge. Five-hundred-million-year-old Chimney Rock is a great place to spend time outdoors. Take the 26-story elevator to the top to for a spectacular 75-mile view, or hike the trail to the 404-foot waterfall. Kids will enjoy the park's nature guides to the local geology, birds, and wildflowers. Admission is $10.95 for adults and $5 for children ages 6–12. Travel packages that include accommodations are available. Chimney Rock Park, P.O. Box 39, Chimney Rock 28720; (800) 277-9611; www.chimneyrockpark.com.

♥ - *Grandfather Mountain*   The highest peak in the Blue Ridge is located 75 miles northeast of Asheville. It is the only private park in the world designated by the United Nations as an International Biosphere Reserve. Children of all ages will love the adventurous walk across the Mile High Swinging Bridge. They can also view bears, river otters, panthers, deer, and eagles in spacious natural wildlife habitats and wander through the nature museum. The outdoorsy family will find plenty of hiking adventures along the 13 miles of hiking trails. Open daily 8 a.m.–sunset; weather permitting in winter. Cost is $10 for adults, $5 for children ages 4–12; free ages 4 and younger. (828) 733-2013; www.grandfather-mountain.com.

▲ - *Great Smoky Mountains National Park* Named for the smoky blue haze that covers the mountaintops, the Smoky Mountains are the largest protected land area east of the Rocky Mountains. It is the most visited park in the National Park System. In North Carolina alone, there are 276,000 acres, with 16 peaks rising to 6,000 feet or more.

An abundance of plants and animals live here, many of which are found only in the park's boundaries. Expect to see deer, wild turkeys, grouse, and the occasional bear during your trip, not to mention many of the 4,000 plants that grow wild. Such diversity has contributed to the park's distinction as an International Biosphere Reserve and a World Heritage Site.

The park also boasts a rich cultural history. From the Cherokee Indians to the Scots-Irish settlers, the area is home to a variety of cultures and people. Many historic structures are still standing throughout the area.

Active families can easily spend two weeks hiking, camping, fishing, golfing, and horseback riding in the park, but if you have only one day to explore, a walking/driving tour is your best option. We suggest starting at one of the visitors centers. They provide excellent orientation information that can help you focus your visit toward your family's particular interests. One option for a day trip is to begin with a short walk in the Deep Creek area, slightly north of Bryson City, to Toms Branch and Indian Creek Falls. Drive over to the Blue Ridge Parkway and follow it to Balsam Mountain Road Drive, about nine miles, into the park and past Mile High Overlook. Then head down the well-maintained Heintooga-Roundbottom Road that ends in Cherokee. Newfound Gap and Clingmans Dome Road to Clingmans Dome are also good driving destinations.

Wise travelers will avoid the peak months of June, July, August, and October. Summer, of course, is sometimes the only travel time families have, so that's when the park is the most crowded. October is also a peak month because of the autumn foliage spectacular.

You'll have no trouble finding a place to stay, as hotels are a dime a dozen around the entrances to the park, but you'll need to book in advance, as rooms are quickly reserved during season. Information is available from Swain County Chamber of Commerce, P.O. Box 509-W, Bryson City 28713; (828) 488-3681 or (800) 867-9246; www.greatsmokies.com; and the city of Cherokee, (800) 438-1601; www.cherokee-nc.com.

Inside the park, primitive campsites are nestled in the woods and along rivers. All campgrounds provide cold running water and flush toilets; however, there are no hook-ups available in the park. Most of the campgrounds are open from early spring through the first weekend in November, with fees ranging from $12–20 per night depending on the campground and time of year. Some sites require reservations and may be reserved up to five months in advance through the National Park Service Reservation Service, (800) 365-CAMP; reservations.nps.gov. Pets must be restrained at all times and are not permitted on hiking trails.

If time permits, check in to the park's hands-on educational programs for kindergarteners through eighth graders. Classes about geography, wildlife and their habitats, flora, the history of the park, and other pertinent subjects are presented by specially trained rangers. Some examples include building a log cabin, becoming a nature detective, and tracking red wolves. Information about the programs is available form the park's education office, (423) 436-1292.

There is a limited schedule of programs and events during the spring and fall season and no programs during the months of November through early April. Some attractions are closed or open on a limited basis during the winter months.

The park is accessible from I-40, then west on U.S. Route 19 through Maggie Valley. From Maggie Valley proceed to U.S. 441 North at Cherokee. Follow 441 North into the park. From Atlanta and points south, follow U.S. 441 and 23 North U.S. 441 North leads to the park. The nearest major airport in Tennessee is McGhee-Tyson (TYS) in Alcoa, 45 miles west of Gatlinburg. North Carolina's Asheville Airport is 60 miles east of Cherokee. There is no train or bus service.

For information on camping, hiking, programs, and events, contact the Great Smoky Mountains National Park Division of Resource Education, 107 Park Headquarters Road, Gatlinburg, TN 37738; (423) 436-1200; www.nps.gov/grsm/homepage.htm or www.nps.gov/grsm.

▲ - *Ocracoke Island*   One of the barrier islands of the Outer Banks of North Carolina, Ocracoke Island is accessible only by water or air. Legend has it that in 1718, Blackbeard died on Ocracoke in a bloody duel with Lt. Richard Maynard of the British Royal Navy. Some even speculate that he buried gold along the Carolina coast, though none has ever been found. The famed ponies on Ocracoke are mysteries as well—no one knows for sure how they made it to the island. Ocracoke Island has more than 5,000 preserved acres, including 16 miles of wilderness beach. Whether it's swimming, fishing, surfing, or just enjoying the sunny beach, there is plenty for the whole family to enjoy. Camping facilities are available through two local campgrounds as well as the National Park Service. Several historic commercial buildings and homes in the quaint village of Ocracoke are listed on the National Register of Historic Places, and there are dozens of unique shops to browse. This area is a birdwatcher's paradise, as many migrating water and land birds can be seen on the island and waterways. Outer Banks Chamber of Commerce, P.O. Box 1757, Kill Devil Hills 27948; (252) 441-8144; www.outerbanks.com.

▲ - *The Outer Banks*   The 70 miles of unspoiled beaches from Nags Head all the way to Ocracoke Island make up North Carolina's famed Outer Banks. The coastline is forever shifting due to the weather and the tides, a natural phenomenon that caused many shipwrecks along these parts and earned the area the name the Graveyard of the Atlantic. The Gulf Stream is 12 miles offshore—the closest it comes to land on the East Coast—a factor that makes for world-record deep-sea fishing. A system of shallow sounds also provides marvelous fishing grounds. Activities for the whole family abound from surfing, golfing, and shopping to hiking along nature trails and visiting shipwrecks and historic sites.

If you drive Highway 12 beginning at Corolla in the north and ending at the Ocracoke ferry docks in the south, you'll pass Pea Island National Wildlife Refuge, Cape Hatteras National Seashore, and 16 different resort towns.

Kitty Hawk, "base camp" for the Wright brothers' expeditions to the Outer Banks to test their gliders, has grown into a summer resort area with all of the necessary accommodations and restaurants.

Not to be confused with nearby Kill Devil Hill, where the Wright Brothers Memorial pylon stands, Kill Devil Hills is the largest incorporated municipality in Dare County. Many stories abound regarding the name, but it is generally accepted that it originates from a brand of rum, Kill Devil, that washed ashore during colonial times.

Nags Head, some history books suggest, was named for the high point on Scilly Island, the last sight of old England that early explorers viewed as they left for the New World. However, a more interesting legend about the name is that eighteenth-century "bankers" realized how profitable piracy was and developed their own unique methods. They tied lanterns to their horses' necks and walked them up and down the beach at night, causing ships to change course and run aground. The bankers then pillaged their cargoes. In the 1800s, Nags Head became a resort area and remains so today.

Sir Walter Raleigh, with a charter issued to him by England's Queen Elizabeth I, established a colony on Roanoke Island in 1584. The area today is a focal point of the northern Outer Banks and home to several popular attractions, restaurants, and the fishing village of Wanchese. *The Lost Colony,* the first outdoor drama in the United States, tells the story of the birth of Virginia Dare, the first English child born in the New World. It's a great place for kids to soak up a little history.

Lodging availability on the Outer Banks is limited to mostly rental houses, condominiums, and small motels. Both government and private campgrounds are available. For information on lodging, events, and attractions, contact the Outer Banks Chamber of Commerce, P.O. Box 1757, Kill Devil Hills 27948; (252) 441-8144; www.outerbanks.com.

Skiing   Skiing is primo for both novices and experts in North Carolina, and when you're tired of blowing the slopes, there are plenty of other activities for families in these ski towns, including ice skating, snow tubing, snowboarding, and shopping. Banner Elk, (828) 898-5605; www.banner-elk.com, is a favorite, along with nearby Sugar Mountains, (800) 784-2768; www.skisugar.com. Beech Mountain, www.skibeech.com, has a 5,500-foot summit and is the East's highest ski area, while Sugar Mountain is 5,300 feet and has 18 slopes, including a 1.5-mile run and a 1,200-foot vertical. Appalachian Ski Mountain in Blowing Rock is another place for the family to explore North Carolina skiing, (800) 972-2183; www.blowingrock.org or www.skinorthcarolina.com.

Tweetsie Railroad   Kids young and old will love North Carolina's first theme park that takes you back to the days of the Old West. Hop on board for an unforgettable three-mile journey through scenic mountains and encounters with train robbers. Head over to the Palace Saloon for musical shows complete with can-can girls. And mosey down Main Street for a brush with the local cowpokes and gunslingers. The park offers amusement rides and live entertainment for all ages.

During the summer, the park is open daily 9 a.m.–6 p.m. During the fall (August 25 through October 29), the park is open Friday–Sunday. Admission is $20 for adults, $14 for seniors and children 3 to 12. Highway 321 between Boone and Blowing Rock at the Boone exit; milepost 291 off of the Blue Ridge Parkway; (800) 526-5740; www.tweetsie-railroad.com.

Calendar of Festivals and Events

January

Winter Pastimes, Asheville   The Arts in America's Largest Home offers weekend craft workshops and how-to seminars. Biltmore Estate, U.S. 25, just north of I-40; (800) 624-1575; www.biltmore.com.

N.C. International Jazz Festival   This festival is a series of concerts from the end of January until mid-April, featuring International Jazz musicians. Duke University, Baldwin Auditorium; (919) 687-0288.

February

Annual Native American Pow Wow   A full day of traditional Native American dancing, singing, crafts, food, and socializing. This event takes place at the North Carolina School of Science and Mathematics; 1219 Broad Street, Durham; (919) 660-3663.

March

Annual Star Fiddlers Convention   North Carolina's oldest fiddler's convention has been holding a competition among bluegrass fiddlers from across the South for more than 70 years. The competition takes place the first weekend in March and includes both young and old fiddlers. P.O. Box 101, Star 27356; (910) 428-2972; www.geocities.com/nashville/rodeo/3252.

April

North Carolina Azalea Festival Parade and Master Craft Show   Wilmington has hosted the Azalea Festival for more than 50 years. There's something for everyone—world-class entertainers, a parade, a street fair, garden and home tours, a circus, and a variety of other events. Cape Fear Coast Convention & Visitors Bureau, 24 North Third Street, Wilmington 28401; (800) 222-4757; www.visitwrightsvillebeach.org.

Piedmont Farm Tour, Orange, Chatham and Alamance Counties   Organized by the Carolina Farm Stewardship Association, the farm tour is a great adventure for the whole family. With hands-on, educational programs, the tour includes visits to the goat farm (make goat's-milk soap), produce farms, blueberry fields, a dairy farm, and an old-fashioned garden of flowers. Carolina Farm Stewardship Association, P.O. Box 448, Pittsboro 27312; (919) 542-2402; www.carolinafarmstewards.org.

May

Annual Pleasure Island Spring Festival, Carolina and Kure Beaches   Activities include a dunking booth, an arts and crafts show, a parade, a street dance, and a dog show. Cape Fear Coast Convention & Visitors Bureau, 24 North Third Street, Wilmington 28401; (800) 222-4757 or (910) 458-8434; www.visitwrightsvillebeach.org.

Annual Hang Gliding Spectacular & Air Games, Jockey's Ridge State Park, Nags Head, and Currituck County Airport   Billed as the oldest continuous hang gliding competition in the world, this event includes hang gliding, skydiving, paragliding, and ultralight flying. There are demonstrations and a street show. Beginners can experience flight with a hang gliding lesson on Jockey's Ridge, the East Coast's largest sand dune. Outer Banks Chamber of Commerce, P.O. Box 1757, Kill Devil Hills 27948; (252) 441-8144; www.outerbanks.com.

Artsplosure, Raleigh   This free spring art festival features great live music on three stages, over 100 arts and crafts booths and displays, and Kidsplosure educational activities in the Moore Square area of downtown Raleigh;

(919) 832-8699; www.artsplosure.org. Information is also available from the Greater Raleigh Convention and Visitors Bureau, Fayetteville Street Mall, Suite 1505, Raleigh 27601; (800) 849-8499 or (919) 834-5900; www. raleighcvb.org.

Bimbé Cultural Festival   This is one of the oldest African-American music and arts festivals in the country. It is one of the most comprehensive celebrations of music, art, and dance from African and Caribbean cultures. The event takes place at the Historic Durham Athletic Park. Durham Convention & Visitors Bureau, 101 East Morgan Street, Durham 27701; (919) 680.8300 or (800) 446.8604; dcvb.durham.nc.us.

June

Annual Rogallo Kite Festival, Jockey's Ridge State Park, Nags Head   In honor of Francis M. Rogallo, NASA scientist and inventor of the Flexible Wing, this event is famous for its Kite Auction at Kitty Hawk Kites in Nags Head. Kids will love the competitions, workshops, lessons, and awards, all related to kite flying. Outer Banks Chamber of Commerce, P.O. Box 1757, Kill Devil Hills 27948; (252) 441-8144; www.outerbanks.com.

Annual Wright Kite Festival, Wright Brothers National Memorial, Kill Devil Hills   Enjoy a day filled with fun activities for kids, including making and flying your own kite, yo-yo stunts, workshops, and children's games. Outer Banks Visitors Bureau, P.O. Box 399, Manteo 27954; (800) 446-6262.

Annual Singing on the Mountain, Grandfather Mountain   Experience an old-fashioned, all-day gospel singing, church bazaar, and dinner-on-the-grounds. The event is held in a meadow at the base of Grandfather Mountain; (828) 733-4337 or (828) 733-2013; www.grandfather-mountain.com.

July

Bele Chere, Asheville   North Carolina's largest downtown street festival showcases local, regional, and national talent in music, arts and crafts, drama, and dance. Also featured throughout the weekend are children's performances, (828) 259-5800; www.belechere.com. Information is also available from the Asheville Convention and Visitors Bureau, P.O. Box 1010, Asheville 28802-1010; (828) 258-6101; www.ashevillechamber.org/cvb_top.htm.

Grandfather Mountain Highland Games, Grandfather Mountain   This is a four-day event featuring traditional dancing, piping, athletic achievement, and Gaelic culture. Campsites are available, (828) 733-1333; www.gmhg. org. Information can also be obtained from Grandfather Mountain at (828) 733-2013, www.grandfather-mountain.com.

August

Jimmy V Celebrity Golf Classic, Raleigh   The late Jim Valvano, former North Carolina State University basketball coach, created the Jimmy V Foundation with the support of ESPN in 1993, before dying of cancer at 47 in that same year. This is a great spectator event for both the golfing or basketball family, as it attracts many celebrities and players from the NBA and college basketball leagues. (919) 319-0441; www.golfclassic.org.

EcoCamps for Children, Nags Head Woods Preserve, Nags Head   The Diversity University is designed for children entering kindergarten. The program offers a chance to learn about the animals and plants of Nags Head Woods through stories, songs, and activities. The program is a weeklong activity, with limited enrollment, (252) 441-2525. Information is also available from the Outer Banks Chamber of Commerce, P.O. Box 1757, Kill Devil Hills 27948; (252) 441-8144; www.outerbanks.com.

Herb Festival, Durham   This historical outdoor herb festival features traditional herbal uses and a variety of herb vendors. Duke Homestead State Historic Site and Tobacco Museum, 2828 Duke Homestead Road, Durham; (919) 477-5498; www.ah.dcr.state.nc.us/sections.

Tea Party, Dare County   Sponsored by Dare County Parks and Recreation is designed to gather children in a playful setting to share their dreams and ideas with one another. Boys and girls are asked to come dressed up as pirates. There is no fee for this activity; Dare County Tourist Bureau, P. O. Box 399, Manteo 27954; (800) 446-6262 or (252) 473-1101.

September

Pops in the Park, Raleigh   The North Carolina Symphony performs a family-friendly program of pops music on the lawn of Meredith College; (919) 821-8555.

Bull Durham Blues Festival, Historic Durham Athletic Park   The festival features national, regional, and local blues; (919) 683-1709; www.hayti.org.

Michaelmas, Biltmore Estate   Biltmore's gardens are the setting for a weekend of entertainment and activities celebrating the fall harvest in turn-of-the-century style. The festival includes crafts, dancing, puppetry, and archery demonstrations; (800) 624-1575; www.biltmore.com.

October

International Festival, Raleigh   International foods, cultural exhibits, demonstrations, a world bazaar, ethnic dancing, and music are part of the festivities.

The event is held in the Raleigh Convention Center; (919) 832-4331; www. internationalfestival.org.

North Carolina State Fair, Raleigh   Heralded as the largest event in the state, the fair comes to Raleigh every year for ten days and features craft demonstrations, livestock exhibits, concerts, games, rides, food, and family entertainment; (919) 733-5079.

Forest Festival Day, Great Smoky Mountains, Cradle of Forestry, Pisgah Forest More than 50 craftsmen, exhibitors, and entertainers gather at the Cradle of Forestry to celebrate of our forests and forest heritage. Enjoy mountain music as you stroll the trails at the Cradle, and visit with wood carvers, weavers, quilters, a toy maker, a potter, and a blacksmith. You can also cheer on your favorite lumberjack in the competitions. Cradle of Forestry, 1002 Pisgah Highway, Pisgah Forest; (828) 877-3130; www.cradleof-forestry.com.

November

Christmas at the Biltmore Estate, Biltmore Estate, Asheville   Beginning in November and extending through December, the Biltmore celebrates the season with lavish decorations inspired by the grandeur of the house and its surroundings. (800) 624-1575; www.biltmore.com.

Star of Bethlehem, Morehead Planetarium, Chapel Hill   Beginning in mid-November and extending into the first week of January, the planetarium presents a show of the sky as it was over Bethlehem 2,000 years ago. This event is suitable for children ages 6 and older. Morehead Planetarium, UNC-CH, C.B. #3480, Chapel Hill 27599; (919) 962-1236.

December

Old Salem Christmas and Candle Teas, Winston-Salem   Old and young alike will delight in the old-fashioned Christmas celebration at Old Salem. The celebration includes a tour of Gemeinhaus by candlelight, and, of course, Moravian sugar cakes. Old Salem, Old Salem Road, Winston-Salem; (336) 721-7300; www.oldsalem.org.

Duke Homestead Christmas by Candlelight   The homestead is decorated as the Duke family would have celebrated Christmas. The event features evening tours of the house by costumed interpreters, plus music and refreshments. Duke Homestead State Historic Site and Tobacco Museum; 2828 Duke Homestead Road, Durham; (919) 477-5498, www.ah.dcr.state.nc.us/sections.

Duke Chapel by Candlelight   Duke Chapel is a neo-Gothic centerpiece of Duke University's West Campus. Viewing the chapel can be a memorable event for even young children. The family can enjoy this community event or inquire about other special worship events during the holiday season. Duke Chapel, Chapel Drive (off Duke University Road); (919) 681-1704; www.chapel.duke.edu.

First Night Raleigh   Every New Year's Eve, Raleigh hosts a downtown New Year's Eve festival for the whole family. The activities start early in the day and last until a giant acorn drops at midnight. Plenty of music, arts and crafts, and food for everyone. The Greater Raleigh Convention and Visitors Bureau, Fayetteville Street Mall, Suite 1505, Raleigh 27601; (800) 849-8499 or (919) 834-5900; www.raleighcvb.org.

Asheville

Nestled in the mountains where the Blue Ridge and Great Smoky Mountains meet, Asheville is more than a resort town. In any season you can enjoy the Biltmore Estate, find fabulous mountain views, discover a heritage rich in arts and crafts, or explore endless outdoor adventures. Throughout the year, there are events, festivals, and entertainment to spice up your visit. After a visit in the 1880s with his mother, George W. Vanderbilt described Asheville the most beautiful place in the world. He purchased 125,000 acres and constructed what is now America's largest private residence, the **Biltmore Estate.** From 1890-95, it took hundreds of workers to complete the 250-room French Renaissance–style chateau and surrounding grounds. Vanderbilt's dream to replicate the great estates of Europe brought romance and a distinctive elegance to Asheville. Family and friends traveled from all over the United States and beyond to experience the opulent estate and the splendor of Olmsted's gardens. Management of Vanderbilt's 100,000-acre forest resulted in the establishment of the first forestry school in America.

Asheville, the largest city in western North Carolina, has a reputation as a resort for the wealthy, but it also appeals to middle-class families seeking relief from the summer heat. The **Thomas Wolfe Memorial Home,** a 19-room Queen Anne–style house, is an example of the boarding houses that sprang up to accommodate the visitor of a more modest means. Built in the early 1880s, the house was immortalized in the novel, *Look Homeward, Angel,* written by Asheville's most famous native son, Thomas Wolfe.

Blending of the old and the new, arts and crafts in the Southern Highlands are now a multimillion-dollar handicrafts industry. The traditional coverlets, quilts, furniture, and baskets that put the region on the country's craft map are still being made, but artisans of all types are drawn to the region and are adding a contemporary touch to age-old practices. Since the 1920s, artists have been attracted to the internationally famed **Penland School** and the **John C. Campbell Folk School,** the nation's oldest such school.

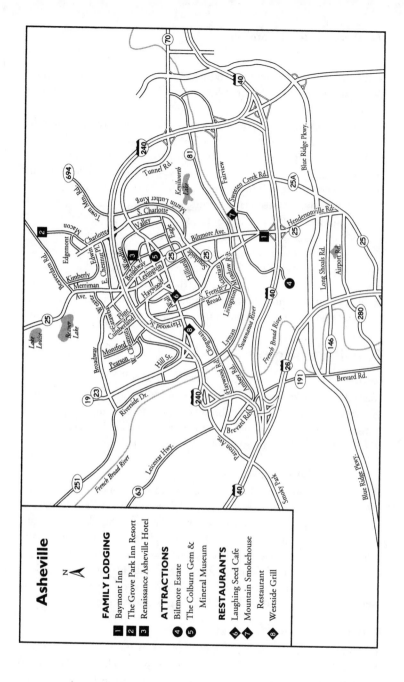

Asheville

N

FAMILY LODGING
1 Baymont Inn
2 The Grove Park Inn Resort
3 Renaissance Asheville Hotel

ATTRACTIONS
4 Biltmore Estate
5 The Colburn Gem & Mineral Museum

RESTAURANTS
6 Laughing Seed Cafe
7 Mountain Smokehouse Restaurant
8 Westside Grill

If you're looking for outdoor adventures, Asheville pleases both the thrill-seeking adventurer and the more faint of heart. Wild rapids and calm waters, backwoods trails and well-worn paths, mountainous rock faces and indoor climbing are all available in Asheville and nearby **Great Smoky Mountains National Park.** And don't forget the area's spectacular fall foliage shows.

Asheville is easily accessible via the nation's most popular scenic highway, the Blue Ridge Parkway. Two major interstates, I-40 and I-26, intersect just outside the city limits. Within 200 miles of Asheville are several major cities: Atlanta and Augusta, Georgia; Charlotte and Winston-Salem, North Carolina; Columbia and Greenville, South Carolina; and Knoxville, Tenessee. Visitors fly into Asheville Regional Airport from all over the world.

Asheville is pleasant in all four seasons. Winter has mild days and enough snow in higher elevations for skiers, and spring and autumn feature warm days and cool nights. Asheville is the perfect place to escape summer's heat—its higher elevations and cool summer air are some of the attributes that made it famous as a health resort at the turn of the century.

Family Lodging

Baymont Inn

Located just blocks from Biltmore Estate and Biltmore Village, accommodations include complimentary breakfast, an indoor swimming pool, and a fitness center. Children stay free in their parents' room. Rates start at $55. 204 Hendersonville Road, Asheville; (929) 274-0101.

The Grove Park Inn Resort

Minutes from downtown Asheville, this 86-year-old grand mountain resort is on the National Register of Historic Places and has a Four Diamond/ Four Star rating. Rooms offer panoramic views of Asheville and the surrounding mountains. There are 510 rooms and an array of activities from golf and tennis to shopping and children's programs. Rates start at $130. Call for information on specials offered year-round. If it's too pricey, at least drop by the lobby to see the massive fireplaces and spectacular veranda view. (800) 438-5800 or (800) 267-8413; www.groveparkinn.com.

Renaissance Asheville Hotel

Two hundred mountain-view rooms—located in the heart of downtown Asheville and within walking distance of an indoor climbing facility, 40 restaurants, and 150 unique shops. Children under 18 stay free. An outdoor swimming pool, golf privileges, and a complimentary breakfast are included. Rates start at $99. 1 Thomas Wolfe Plaza, Asheville; (828) 252-8211 or (800) HOTELS-1; www.renaissancehotels/avlbr.

Attractions

Biltmore Estate

U.S. Highway 25, just north of I-40, Asheville; (800) 624-1575
  www.biltmore.com

Hours: Daily, 9 a.m.–5 p.m.

Admission: $32 adults, $24 children ages 10–15, free for children ages
  9 and younger

Appeal by Age Group:

Pre-school	Grade School	Teens	Young Adults	Over 30	Seniors
★	★★★	★★★★	★★★★	★★★★★	★★★★★

Average Touring Time: 5 hours

Minimum Touring Time: 4 hours

Rainy Day Touring: Recommended

Author's Rating: ★★★★★   Awesome

Services and Facilities:

Restaurants Yes	Lockers No
Alcoholic beverages Yes	Pet kennels No
Disabled access Yes	Rain check No
Wheelchair rental No	Private tours No
Baby stroller rental No	

Description and Comments   America's largest private home is now open
for tours in Asheville. This 250-room mansion, built by George Vanderbilt in 1895, features many acres of gardens and woodlands, a series of
walking trails, restaurants, shops, and an award-winning winery. Wear
comfortable shoes and be ready to walk for miles. The rooms, furniture,
collectibles, gardens, and views are awesome. *Note:* Young children may
tire long before the tour is complete.

The Colburn Gem & Mineral Museum

Pack Place Education, Arts & Science Center, 2 South Pack Square,
  Asheville; (828) 254-7162

Hours: Tuesday–Saturday, 10 a.m.–5 p.m.; Sunday, 1–5 p.m.

Admission: $4 adults, $3 seniors and students, free for children ages 4
  and younger

Appeal by Age Group:

Pre-school	Grade School	Teens	Young Adults	Over 30	Seniors
★	★★★★	★★★	★★	★★★★	★★★

Average Touring Time: 45 minutes

Minimum Touring Time: 30 minutes

Rainy Day Touring: Recommended

Author's Rating: ★★★ The rock hound in the family is sure to find this of interest.

Services and Facilities:

Restaurants No	Lockers No
Alcoholic beverages No	Pet kennels No
Disabled access No	Rain check No
Wheelchair rental No	Private tours Yes
Baby stroller rental No	

Description and Comments   The Colburn Gem & Mineral Museum dazzles visitors with exhibits of mineral crystals and gemstones from North Carolina and around the world. The Collector's Corner is conveniently located in the museum and features items of interest to collectors of all ages. Prices start at $0.25. Proceeds benefit the museum and its ongoing educational activities. Elementary and middle school children especially enjoy these exhibits.

Side Trip

Mount Mitchell   Thirty-three miles northeast on the Blue Ridge Parkway and five miles north on N.C. Highway 128, you can ascend to the highest peak east of the Mississippi, rising to 6,684 feet. There are six hiking trails, including a short trail beginning at the summit parking lot that leads to the stone observation towers. In the museum, kids of all ages will be intrigued by the natural and cultural history of North Carolina's first state park. Enjoy a picnic lunch at one of the two picnic shelters or stop in for a relaxing meal at the restaurant. Tent camping is permitted in each of nine sites offered on a first-come basis; fees are $12 a night. Guided nature walks led by park rangers are available during the summer months. (828) 675-4611.

Family-Friendly Restaurants

LAUGHING SEED CAFE

40 Wall Street, Asheville; (828) 252-3445
www.laughingseed.com

Meals served: Lunch and dinner
Cuisine: International vegetarian
Entrée range: $6.50–13.95
Kids menu: No

Reservations: No
Payment: All major credit cards accepted

Located in the heart of downtown Asheville, Laughing Seed offers international vegetarian cuisine using organic ingredients and newly harvested, locally grown produce. It also serves organic coffees and teas as well as organic wines and a selection of microbrewed and imported beers. If you are unfamiliar with vegetarian dining, you'll find delicious and healthy alternatives here. If you are a seasoned lover of vegetarian food, you've come to the right place. Grilled cheese, pizza, tofu dogs, veggie-burgers, and fruit smoothies are children's favorites. Kids like sitting on the patio and watching the climbers on the wall across the street.

MOUNTAIN SMOKEHOUSE RESTAURANT

802 Fairview Road, Asheville; (800) 850-3718

Meals served: Lunch and dinner
Cuisine: American/Southern
Entrée range: Buffet: $17 adults, $8.50 children ages 6–12, free ages 5 and younger
Kids menu: No
Reservations: No
Payment: All major credit cards accepted

Located near the Biltmore Estate, Mountain Smokehouse Restaurant offers a family–style buffet with barbecue and Southern cooking. You can also enjoy bluegrass music and clogging. Kids age 6–12 eat for half price.

WESTSIDE GRILL

1190 Patton Avenue, Asheville; (828) 252-9605

Meals served: Lunch, dinner, and weekend brunch
Cuisine: American
Entrée range: $5–12
Kids menu: Yes
Reservations: No
Payment: All major credit cards accepted

Near the Biltmore Estate and just four miles from downtown, Westside is a 1950s diner–style restaurant with all-time favorite menu items that kids love, such as meat loaf, fried chicken, pasta, and sandwiches. On the weekends, enjoy Westside's brunches, featuring huge homemade biscuits, pancakes, and more.

Charlotte

Located east of the Catawba River at the crossroads of two Indian trading paths, Charlotte began as a small settlement about 250 years ago. The community grew, and in 1768 it was incorporated and named in honor of the wife of King George III, the reigning British monarch. Local citizens also honored Queen Charlotte when they named their new county Mecklenburg after her German homeland. That's where the city's nickname, "the Queen City," comes from.

The discovery of a 17-pound gold nugget in 1799 brought a rush of prospectors to the area and a reason for establishing a branch of the U.S. Mint. However, the boom was short-lived, and strike-it-richers and other opportunists headed west to California a few years later. The former mint is now the **Mint Museum,** housing an impressive collection of handicraft revival and contemporary pieces.

After the gold rush and bust, the cotton industry brought new prosperity to the region. The Catawba River provided waterpower for development of manufacturing plants and textile mills, and still today, the area is home to 600 textile mills. Charlotte is also a major banking center and a city of skyscrapers, suburban housing developments, and shopping malls.

One of the largest cities in the Piedmont, Charlotte is home base to the NBA Charlotte Hornets, the NFL Carolina Panthers as well as AAA baseball and WNBA basketball. NASCAR fans can take a spin around **Lowe's Motor Speedway** on a tour of the racetrack, or take in a real race during season.

Charlotte is blessed with four distinct seasons and a moderate climate. In spring, Charlotte explodes with the blooms of thousands of dogwoods and pear trees. In autumn, the **Blue Ridge Mountains** come alive with glorious fall color—a must-see if you can plan your trip in October.

The area is easily accessed via Interstates 77 and 85, which intersect Charlotte and link it with the Great Lakes Region, New England, and Florida.

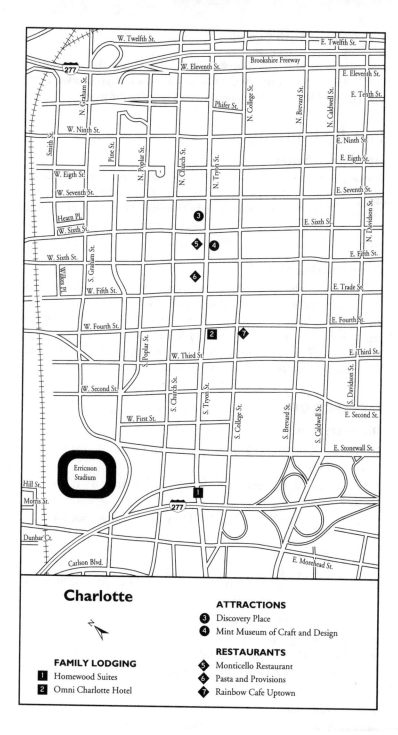

Charlotte

N

FAMILY LODGING

1 Homewood Suites
2 Omni Charlotte Hotel

ATTRACTIONS

3 Discovery Place
4 Mint Museum of Craft and Design

RESTAURANTS

5 Monticello Restaurant
6 Pasta and Provisions
7 Rainbow Cafe Uptown

Interstate 40, running east-to-west across the country, is only an hour north of Charlotte. The Atlantic beaches are three-and-a-half hours away to the east, and the Blue Ridge Mountains are two hours to the west.

Family Lodging

Homewood Suites

Convenient to Lowe's Motor Speedway and other area attractions, Homewood Suites is excellent for families because of its moderate price. Suites have living and sleeping areas plus a full kitchen. There's also an outdoor whirlpool as well as a swimming pool. Rates start at $99. 4920 South Tryon Street, Charlotte; (800) 225-5466.

Omni Charlotte Hotel

The Omni is in the heart of uptown Charlotte, near the Discovery Place, and features 365 guestrooms and suites, a full-service restaurant specializing in American cuisine with a Southern influence, and an on-site fitness center and outdoor pool. The hotel offers theater and sports packages. Rates start at $99, with theater and sports packages available. 101 South Tryon Street, Charlotte; (800) THE-OMNI or (704) 377-0400.

Attractions

Discovery Place

301 North Tryon Street, Charlotte; (800) 935-0553
www.discoveryplace.org

Hours: Open daily except Thanksgiving and Christmas days; hours vary by season

Admission: $6.50 adults, $5 ages 6–12, free for children ages 5 and younger

Appeal by Age Group:

Pre-school	Grade School	Teens	Young Adults	Over 30	Seniors
★★★	★★★★★	★★★★	★★★★	★★★	★★

Average Touring Time: 4 hours

Minimum Touring Time: 2 hours

Rainy Day Touring: Recommended

Author's Rating: ★★★★★ Kids of all ages will find these hands-on exhibits fascinating.

Services and Facilities:

Restaurants Yes	Disabled access Yes
Alcoholic beverages No	Wheelchair rental No

Baby stroller rental No	Rain check No
Lockers No	Private tours No
Pet kennels No	

Description and Comments   Discovery Place is a learn-by-doing science center. It's a fun environment where families can come to experiment, learn, and discover new things about the world, from health science to space exploration. The museum has an ONIMAX theater and the Kelly Space Voyager Planetarium—both quite popular with the younger set. Most visitors spend more time than planned, as there are so many things to see and do. Young children might tire before your visit is complete.

Mint Museum of Craft and Design

220 North Tryon Street, Charlotte; (704) 337-2000
www.mintmuseum.org

Hours: Tuesday–Thursday, Saturday 10 a.m.–7 p.m.; Friday 10 a.m.–9 p.m.; Sunday, noon–5 p.m.

Admission: $6 adults, $4 seniors and students, free for children ages 12 and younger

Appeal by Age Group:

Pre-school	Grade School	Teens	Young Adults	Over 30	Seniors
★★	★★	★★★★	★★★★	★★★★	★★★★

Average Touring Time: 2 hours

Minimum Touring Time: 90 minutes

Rainy Day Touring: Recommended

Author's Rating: ★★★★   Very informative

Services and Facilities:

Restaurants No	Lockers No
Alcoholic beverages No	Pet kennels No
Disabled access Yes	Rain check No
Wheelchair rental No	Private tours Yes
Baby stroller rental No	

Description and Comments   North Carolina is known for its skilled artisans and craftspeople, and this museum highlights their masterpieces along with the history of contemporary studio crafts. Budding artists will be in awe of the exhibits here, but toddlers can lose interest quickly.

Side Trip

Reed Gold Mine State Historic Site, Stanfield   It was here in 1799 that John Reed found a 17-pound gold nugget. As word spread, more nuggets were found and the mine became known for its large, pure nuggets, the largest weighing in at 29 pounds. Families can tour a portion of the underground mine and the ore-crushing mill, take a walk on the Talking Rocks Trail, or pan for gold. The mine is 25 miles from Charlotte. Admission is free, except for a small fee for panning for gold. 9621 Reed Mine Road, Stanfield; (704) 786-8337.

Family-Friendly Restaurants

MONTICELLO RESTAURANT

235 North Tryon Street, Charlotte; (704) 342-1193

Meals served: Breakfast, lunch, and dinner
Cuisine: American/European
Entrée range: $8–45
Kids menu: No
Reservations: Recommended
Payment: All major credit cards accepted

Monticello is conveniently located across from Discovery Place with a street-level view and an eclectic mix of people. If you are on a budget, this may be a bit pricey. As downtown Charlotte is the city's business district, most eateries cater to the business lunch crowd.

PASTA AND PROVISIONS

127 Tryon Street, Charlotte; (704) 342-2200
www.pastaprovisions.com.

Meals served: Lunch
Cuisine: Sandwiches, salads, pasta
Entrée range: $5–15
Kids menu: No
Reservations: No
Payment: All major credit cards accepted

For a quick lunch for the on-the-go family, Pasta and Provisions offers fresh homemade pasta, sandwiches, and salads. This place makes for a quick, convenient downtown pit stop.

RAINBOW CAFE UPTOWN

201 South College Street, Charlotte; (704) 372-2256
www.rainbowcafeuptown.com

Meals served: Breakfast, lunch, and dinner
Cuisine: American
Entrée range: $6–12
Kids menu: No
Reservations: No
Payment: All major credit cards accepted

Conveniently located in downtown, the Rainbow Cafe Uptown uses the finest and freshest ingredients to create daily specials to satisfy everyone's appetite. Selections include a variety of burgers, salads, and pastas.

Raleigh-
Durham-Chapel Hill

The Triangle area refers to three North Carolina cities: Raleigh, Durham, and Chapel Hill. Named for Sir Walter Raleigh, founder of the first English colony, Raleigh is the capital city. Founded in 1792, it has the distinction of being the only state capital established on land specifically purchased for that purpose. The original capitol building burned in 1831, but was rebuilt soon after. Today, this impressive Greek Revival–style building is still standing. Since its early days, Raleigh has grown into a cosmopolitan metropolis with many fine restaurants, shopping, colleges and universities, cultural activities, and sports.

Nearby Durham has a long and colorful history. The area is believed to be the site of an ancient Native American village named Adshusheer. Scots, Irish, and British people began settling the area in the mid-1700s, and between the Revolutionary and Civil wars, large plantations were established. The city was named for Dr. Bartlett Durham, who, in 1849, provided land for a railroad station. After the Civil War, tobacco spawned one of the world's largest corporations and brought riches to the Duke family, who donated $40 million to Trinity College, aptly renamed Duke University. Durham, sometimes referred to as the City of Medicine, is home to Duke University Medical School as well as several world-class pharmaceutical research centers and four major hospitals. Durham is also well known for sports—Duke basketball and the Durham Bulls, a AAA baseball team made famous by the movie *Bull Durham.*

Chapel Hill is a college town, home to the **University of North Carolina,** the country's first state university. Coupled with its close neighbor, Carrboro, the area is home to a fascinating collection of shops and eateries, as well as some of the most progressive music and theater in the state. **Morehead Planetarium** is where early NASA astronauts studied celestial navigation, and **North Carolina Botanical Gardens** is the largest natural garden of it kind in the Southeast.

In both spring and fall the Triangle bursts with color—pinks and whites of the dogwood and azaleas in the spring and the brilliant yellows and orange of fall foliage. Summers can be hot and humid—a good time for indoor activities. Winters are usually mild with only occasional snow.

Getting to the area is easy via the centrally located Raleigh-Durham International Airport, about a 15-mile drive from all three cities. Interstates 85 and 40 connect the communities to the rest of the country.

Atlantic beaches are two-and-a-half hours east of the Triangle, while the mountains are three hours to the west. Pinehurst, with its world-class golf courses, lies 70 miles southwest of Raleigh.

Family Lodging

Holiday Inn Raleigh Durham International Airport

Located near the airport, the Holiday Inn is an ideal base for visiting all three cities in the Triangle. There are 249 guestrooms, a swimming pool, exercise equipment, and van service to Raleigh Durham Airport. Two restaurants are also located on the premises. 4810 Page Road, Exit 282, Raleigh; (919) 941-6000.

Sheraton Capital Center

Located in the heart of downtown, the Sheraton Capital Center is convenient to the capitol building, historic sites, art galleries, museums, shops, and restaurants. The Sheraton has 359 guestrooms, a fitness center, and a restaurant featuring New American Cuisine. 421 South Salisbury Street, Raleigh; (919) 834-9900.

The Velvet Cloak Inn

Adjacent to North Carolina State University, the Velvet Cloak Inn offers a taste of southern charm. Located in the heart of the historic district, the inn is minutes from downtown, shopping, restaurants, and entertainment. The Velvet Cloak Inn has 172 rooms, an on-site restaurant, and a fitness center. Airport shuttle is also available. Kids will like the dramatic doorman, who wears a traditional red velvet topcoat, white gloves, and a tall black stovepipe hat. 1505 Hillsborough Street, Raleigh; (800) 662-8829 or (800) 334-4372.

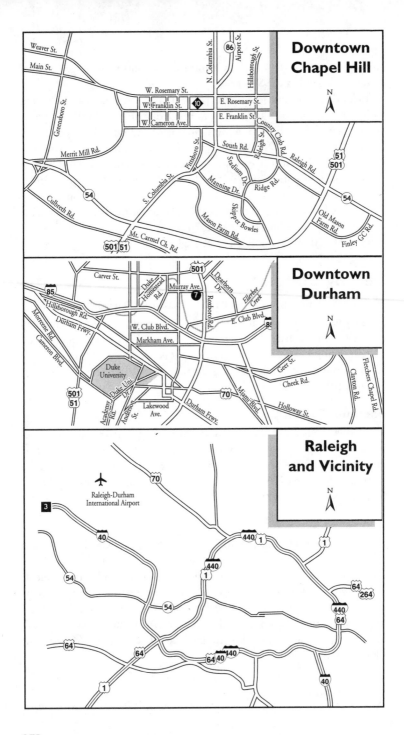

Downtown Chapel Hill

N

Weaver St.

Main St.

Greensboro St.

W. Rosemary St.

N. Columbia St.

86

Airport St.

Hillsborough St.

W. Franklin St. 10

E. Rosemary St.

W. Cameron Ave.

E. Franklin St.

Merrit Mill Rd.

Pittsboro St.

South Rd.

Raleigh St.

Country Club Rd.

Raleigh Rd.

51

501

Culbreth Rd.

54

S. Columbia St.

Stadium Dr.

Manning Dr.

Ridge Rd.

54

Old Mason Farm Rd.

501 51

Mt. Carmel Ch. Rd.

Mason Farm Rd.

Skipper Bowles

Finley GC Rd.

Downtown Durham

N

Carver St.

501

85

Hillsborough Rd.

Durham Frwy.

Morreene Rd.

Cameron Blvd.

Duke Homestead Rd.

Murray Ave. 7

Dearborn Dr.

Roxboro Rd.

Ellerbe Creek

E. Club Blvd.

85

W. Club Blvd.

Markham Ave.

Duke University

Academy Rd.

Duke Univ. Dr.

Anderson St.

Lakewood Ave.

Durham Frwy.

501 51

70

Miami Blvd.

Geer St.

Cheek Rd.

Holloway St.

Clayton Rd.

Fletchers Chapel Rd.

Raleigh and Vicinity

N

✈ Raleigh-Durham International Airport

3

70

40

54

54

54

64

64

64

40

440

1

440

1

440

1

1

64

264

440

64

40

40

1

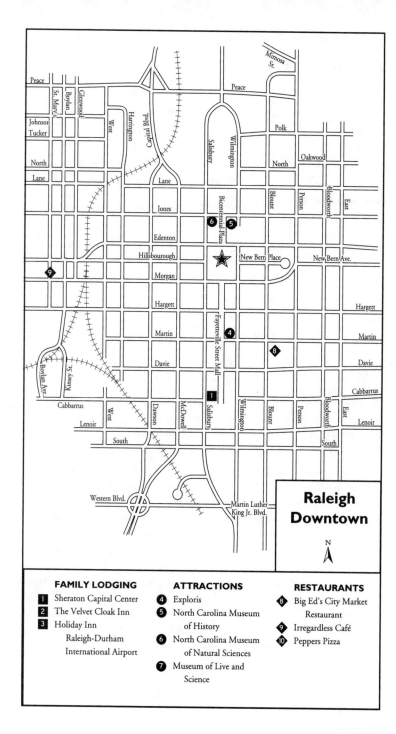

FAMILY LODGING

1. Sheraton Capital Center
2. The Velvet Cloak Inn
3. Holiday Inn
   Raleigh-Durham
   International Airport

ATTRACTIONS

4. Exploris
5. North Carolina Museum
   of History
6. North Carolina Museum
   of Natural Sciences
7. Museum of Live and
   Science

RESTAURANTS

8. Big Ed's City Market
   Restaurant
9. Irregardless Café
10. Peppers Pizza

Attractions

Exploris

201 Hargett Street, Raleigh; (919) 834-4040
  www.exploris.org

Hours: Tuesday–Saturday, 9 a.m.–5 p.m.; Sunday, noon–5 p.m.;
  Monday during the summer, 9 a.m.–5 p.m.

Admission: $6.95 adults, $5.95 seniors, $3.95 children ages 4–11, free
  for children ages 3 and younger

Appeal by Age Group:

Pre-school	Grade School	Teens	Young Adults	Over 30	Seniors
★★	★★★★★	★★★★★	★★★★	★★★★	★★★★

Average Touring Time: 2 hours

Minimum Touring Time: 1 hour

Rainy Day Touring: Recommended

Author's Rating: ★★★★★   Exploris is a fascinating look at the world as
  a community

Services and Facilities:

Restaurants No	Lockers No
Alcoholic beverages No	Pet kennels No
Disabled access Yes	Rain check No
Wheelchair rental No	Private tours No
Baby stroller rental No	

Description and Comments   If you have time to visit only one museum,
Exploris in downtown Raleigh should be the one. Billed as the world's first
global experience center, Exploris is a humanities-based museum that explores our world, ourselves, and others through interactive, interpretive
exhibits. People and Places reveals the interdependent nature of the relationship between people and places, with culture boxes filled with objects
from the daily lives of people around the world. Living in Balance is an
ecology-based exhibit with a water purifying system, global rivers moni-
toring station and a Water Wall. And then there's the Marbles Wall, made
of over one million marbles, that portrays the planet through an image of
the world from space. It's loud, the gift shop has cheap souvenirs for kids,
and the bathrooms are discovery zones in themselves.

Museum of Life and Science

433 Murrary Avenue, Durham; (919) 220-5429
  www.mls.unc.edu.ncmls.ncmls

Hours: Monday–Saturday, 10 a.m.–5 p. m.; Sunday, 1–5 p.m.

Admission: $5.50 adults, $3.50 children ages 3–12

Appeal by Age Group:

Pre-school	Grade School	Teens	Young Adults	Over 30	Seniors
★★★★	★★★★★	★★★★	★★★★	★★★★	★★★★

Average Touring Time: 2 hours

Minimum Touring Time: 1 hour

Rainy Day Touring: Recommended

Author's Rating: ★★★★ The Wings Butterfly House is a delight to old and young alike

Services and Facilities:

Restaurants No	Lockers No
Alcoholic beverages No	Pet kennels No
Disabled access Yes	Rain check No
Wheelchair rental No	Private tours No
Baby stroller rental No	

Description and Comments The Museum of Life and Science is an interactive science-technology center. It includes exhibits on aerospace science and wildlife and their habitats, but the most popular reason for visiting at the moment is the Magic Wings Butterfly House and Insectarium. This facility houses both native and exotic butterflies and plants and is the largest of its kind east of the Mississippi. Visit the Mary Martha Uzzle Emerging Wonders room, where butterflies emerging from their chrysalises are on display, and the Tropical Butterfly Conservatory, a three-story-high home to more than 1,000 rare butterflies from Asia, Africa, and Central and South America. Children of all ages love this place.

North Carolina Museum of History

5 East Edenton Street, Raleigh; (919) 715-0200
  nchistory.dcr.state.nc.us

Hours: Tuesday–Saturday, 9 a.m.–5 p.m.; Sunday, noon–5 p.m.

Admission: Free

Appeal by Age Group:

Pre-school	Grade School	Teens	Young Adults	Over 30	Seniors
★	★★★	★★★	★★★	★★★	★★★★

Average Touring Time: 2 hours

Minimum Touring Time: 1 hour

Rainy Day Touring: Recommended

Author's Rating: ★★★

Services and Facilities:

Restaurants No	Lockers No
Alcoholic beverages No	Pet kennels No
Disabled access Yes	Rain check No
Wheelchair rental Yes	Private tours No
Baby stroller rental No	

Description and Comments While the exhibits at this museum are more traditional in layout and presentation, kids can't seem to get enough of the Sports Hall of Fame. Watch videos of basketball great Michael Jordan or take a virtual racecar ride with Richard Petty on the Lowe's Motor Speedway. Another hit is the Civil War Gallery, where the story of the War Between the States is told through the lives of North Carolinians who fought on both sides. Uniforms, guns, knives, letters, lucky charms, and a wooden leg are among the artifacts on display. The Health and Healing Experiences examine health and healthcare from natural healing to modern technology.

North Carolina Museum of Natural Sciences

Bicentennial Plaza, Raleigh; (919) 733-7450; www.naturalsciences.org

Hours: Monday–Saturday, 9 a.m.–5 a.m.; Sunday, 1–5 p.m.

Admission: Free

Appeal by Age Group:

Pre-school	Grade School	Teens	Young Adults	Over 30	Seniors
★★★	★★★★★	★★★★	★★★	★★★	★★★

Average Touring Time: 2 hours

Minimum Touring Time: 1 hour

Rainy Day Touring: Recommended

Author's Rating: ★★★★★ Don't miss the newest addition, the Terror of the South—a re-created prehistoric battle of dinosaurs complete with sound and special effects

Services and Facilities:

Restaurants No	Lockers No
Alcoholic beverages No	Pet kennels No
Disabled access Yes	Rain check No
Wheelchair rental No	Private tours No
Baby stroller rental No	

Description and Comments The all-new North Carolina Museum of Natural Sciences on Bicentennial Plaza reopened in 1999 as the largest natural history museum in the Southeast. Lifesize dioramas in the nine exhibit halls focus on North Carolina's natural habitats—many of which are home to live critters, including all five pit vipers found in the state. The state's largest dinosaur collection is also on display, with the only acrocanthosaurus in the world. Learning areas like the Discovery Room, Naturalist Center, conservatory, and laboratories engage young minds with hands-on experiments and staffed demonstrations.

Side Trips

Campus Touring   The University of North Carolina, the nation's first state university, is located in Chapel Hill. Families enjoy exploring the campus, visiting numerous buildings, and participating in various events and activities on campus. You can also stroll through the five-acre arboretum created in 1903 on the old campus. For information on a self-guided historic walking tour complete with an audiotape, call (919) 962-1630.

Seeing Stars   Morehead Planetarium in downtown Chapel Hill and adjacent to the UNC campus is a premier facility that has been teaching space science education for nearly 50 years. The planetarium once served as a training center for NASA astronauts. Children of all ages will enjoy the celestial shows. Franklin Street, in the heart of Chapel Hill; (919) 549-6863.

Pinehurst and Southern Pines These courses, 70 miles southwest of Raleigh, shouldn't be missed if there's a golfer in the family. The area has become internationally known for its golf courses and has drawn some of the most distinguished golfers in the world. There are plenty of activities for everyone in the family, from golf and horseback riding to shopping in little boutiques. Package deals are available. Contact the Pinehurst Area Convention and Visitors Bureau at (800) 346-5362.

Family-Friendly Restaurants

BIG ED'S CITY MARKET RESTAURANT

City Market; 220 Wolfe Street, Raleigh; (919) 836-9909

Meals served: Breakfast and lunch
Cuisine: Southern barbecue
Entrée range: $4.95 and up
Kids menu: No
Reservations: No
Payment: All major credit cards accepted

For southern-style cooking at its best, visit Big Ed's in downtown Raleigh's City Market. Big Ed's offers up kids' favorites such as mashed potatoes and gravy, creamed corn, pork chops, and sweet tea. For breakfast, try the grilled biscuits served with blackstrap molasses.

IRREGARDLESS CAFE

901 West Morgan Street, Raleigh; (919) 833-8898

Meals served: Lunch and dinner
Cuisine: American
Entrée range: $8 and up
Kids menu: No
Reservations: No
Payment: All major credit cards accepted

A casual family eatery that uses wholesome, fresh food to create cuisine to satisfy both vegetarians and meat-eaters. The menu changes seasonally. Irregardless Cafe is conveniently located near downtown Raleigh and the NCSU campus.

PEPPERS PIZZA

127 East Franklin Street, Chapel Hill; (919) 967-7766

Meals served: Lunch and dinner
Cuisine: Pizza
Entrée range: $2 and up
Kids menu: No
Reservations: No
Payment: All major credit cards accepted

Peppers is an eclectic local hangout with great pizza and calzone. Kids love to watch their pizza being made through the front window. Ask for the mug of crayons and paper so your little one can create a masterpiece for the back of the menu. Peppers is in the heart of downtown Chapel Hill, near the Morehead Planetarium and UNC campus.

Wilmington/ Cape Fear Coast

Wilmington was once the largest city in the state, partly because of its key location at the mouth of the Cape Fear River. Now it has become the place to summer, with a nice collection of small beaches perfect for families.

Wrightsville Beach is a small island community with fine accommodations and an array of activities—swimming, fishing, sailing, diving, surfing, and water skiing, to name a few. **Carolina Beach State Park** is home to a variety of natural areas along with a killer amusement park. A small family-oriented beach, **Kure Beach,** sits at the southern extreme of U.S. Highway 421.

The **Cape Fear** area can be accessed via Interstates 95 and 40. With the influence of the Atlantic Ocean and the Gulf Steam, the area has four distinct but mild seasons, with summer temperatures usually in the 80s and average winter temperatures around 50.

Family Lodging

Blockade Runner Resort Hotel & Conference Center

The Blockade Runner offers views of the Atlantic Ocean and Wrightsville Sound. The hotel offers sunset and nature cruises and bike and sailboat rentals. Rates begin at $94. Children ages 12 and younger stay free in parents' room. 275 Waynick Boulevard, Wrightsville Beach; (800) 541-1161 or (910) 256-2251; www.blockade-runner.com.

Holiday Inn

With 227 guest rooms, this is one of Wilmington's largest hotels. Conveniences include guest laundry, room service, irons and ironing boards, courtesy van, cable TV, and pay-per-view movies. The Holiday Inn also boasts an Olympic-size outdoor swimming pool. 4903 Market Street, Wilmington; (800) 782-9061 or (910) 799-1440; www.basshotels.com/holiday-inn.

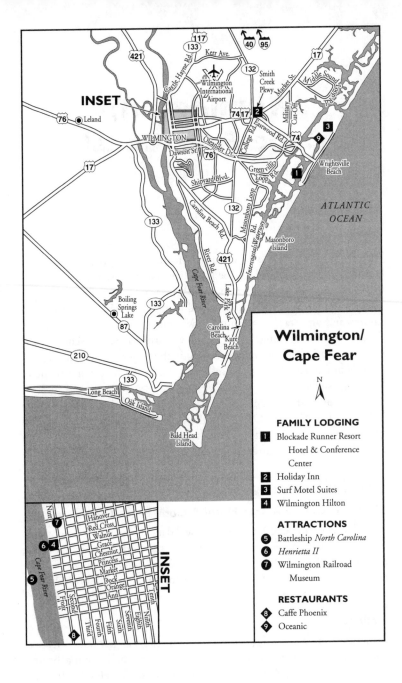

Wilmington/
Cape Fear

N

FAMILY LODGING

1 Blockade Runner Resort
  Hotel & Conference
  Center
2 Holiday Inn
3 Surf Motel Suites
4 Wilmington Hilton

ATTRACTIONS

5 Battleship *North Carolina*
6 *Henrietta II*
7 Wilmington Railroad
  Museum

RESTAURANTS

8 Caffe Phoenix
9 Oceanic

Surf Motel Suites

All rooms are oceanfront suites with fully equipped kitchens, queen beds, and cable TV. An oceanfront pool, sundeck, and shady gazebo are on the hotel grounds. Open year-round. Seasonal, weekly, and monthly rates available. 711 South Lumina Avenue, Wrightsville Beach; (910) 256-2275; www.beachonline.com/surfsuit.htm.

Wilmington Hilton

Situated on the Riverwalk, the Hilton is located in downtown Wilmington. The hotel features 274 guest rooms, half of which overlook the river. There is no charge for children, regardless of age, if they share a room with their parents. Rates start at $120. 301 North Water Street; (800) 445-8667 or (910) 763-5900); www.hilton.com.

Attractions

Battleship North Carolina

On the Cape Fear River, historic downtown Wilmington; (910) 350-1817 www.battleshipnc.com

Hours: May 16–September 15, 8 a.m.–8 p.m.; September 16–May 15, until 5 p.m.

Admission: $6 adults, $4 children ages 6–11; free for children ages 5 and under

Appeal by Age Group:

Pre-school	Grade School	Teens	Young Adults	Over 30	Seniors
★★★	★★★★	★★★★★	★★★★★	★★★★	★★★★★

Average Touring Time: 1½ hours

Minimum Touring Time: 1 hour

Rainy Day Touring: Not recommended

Author's Rating: ★★★★★

Services and Facilities:

Restaurants No	Lockers No
Alcoholic beverages No	Pet kennels No
Disabled access No	Rain check No
Wheelchair rental No	Private tours No
Baby stroller rental No	

Description and Comments   The *North Carolina* is a restored WWII battleship that is permanently moored in the Cape Fear River. Commissioned in 1941, it weighs 44,880 tons, wields nine 16-inch turreted guns, and carries nickel-steel hull armor 16–18 inches thick. This plating helped her survive at least one direct torpedo hit in 1942. The self-guided tour includes nine decks with crew quarters and engine rooms, a museum of WWII exhibits, and a gift shop. Be sure to look out for Old Charlie, the alligator who makes his home near the ship at the river's edge.

Henrietta II

Docked at the Wilmington Hilton; 301 North Water Street,
  Wilmington; (800) 676-0162 or (910) 343-1611

Hours: Most cruises are available from April–October, while others only
  go out during the summer season

Admission: Rates vary according to the type and length of the cruise

Appeal by Age Group:

Pre-school	Grade School	Teens	Young Adults	Over 30	Seniors
★★	★★★★	★★★★	★★★★	★★★★	★★★★★

Average Touring Time: 1½ hours

Minimum Touring Time: 1½ hours

Rainy Day Touring: Recommended

Author's Rating: ★★★★

Services and Facilities:

Restaurants Nearby	Lockers No
Alcoholic beverages Yes	Pet kennels No
Disabled access Yes	Rain check No
Wheelchair rental No	Private tours No
Baby stroller rental No	

Description and Comments   Cruise the Cape Fear River in style on this beautiful riverboat with a variety of options, including a 90-minute narrated sightseeing cruise, narrated lunch cruise, and more. Prepaid reservations are required for cruises that include meals. Call for information on current rates, cruise schedules, and special events.

Wilmington Railroad Museum

501 Nutt Street, Wilmington; (910) 763-2634

Hours: 10 a.m.–5 p.m. Monday–Saturday (except Wednesday when it's
  closed) and 1–4 p.m. Sunday. In the winter months, call for hours.

Admission: $3 for adults, $2 for military personnel and senior citizens
  and $1.50 for children ages 6 to 11. Museum members and children 5
  and younger are admitted free.

Appeal by Age Group:

Pre-school	Grade School	Teens	Young Adults	Over 30	Seniors
★★★	★★★★★	★★★★	★★★★	★★★★	★★★★★

Average Touring Time: 1½ hours

Minimum Touring Time: 1 hour

Rainy Day Touring: Recommended

Author's Rating: ★★★★★

Services and Facilities:

Restaurants Nearby	Lockers No
Alcoholic beverages No	Pet kennels No
Disabled access Yes	Rain check No
Wheelchair rental No	Private tours No
Baby stroller rental No	

Description and Comments   The Railroad Museum will delight anyone fascinated by trains and train culture. For $2 ($1 for children age 6–11 and free for children younger than 6), you can climb into a real steam locomotive and clang its bell. Inside, volunteers are available to guide you through exhibits explaining why the 19th-century Wilmington & Weldon Railroad was called the "Well Done" and that the ghost of beheaded flagman Joe Baldwin is behind the Maco Light. Visitors are encouraged to share their favorite train memories in the museum's "Memories" book. Listed on the National Register of Historic Places, the museum building was the railroad's freight traffic office. In the enormous railroad diorama upstairs, visitors can run the model trains maintained by the Cape Fear Model Railroad Club. Children will also enjoy the railroad theaterette. Contact the museum for information on children's workshops. The museum also invites you to conduct your birthday parties on its caboose; the rental fee includes souvenirs and a tour of the museum. Train-themed refreshments also can be arranged.

Side Trips

Orton Plantation & Gardens   Established as a rice plantation around 1725, this Southern antebellum house and gardens is now a private residence complete with public gardens. The spectacular gardens with 20 acres of live oaks, lawns, ponds, and many varieties of flowers date back to 1920. Wildlife, including alligators, still abound, and the footprints of deer, raccoons, opossum, and other wild animals can be seen. The gardens are open daily March through November and closed Thanksgiving Day and December through February. Admission is $8 for adults, $7 for seniors, and $3 for children. NorthC. Highway 133 between Wilmington and Southport; (910) 371-6851; www.ortongardens.com.

Family-Friendly Restaurants

CAFFE PHOENIX

9 South Front Street, Wilmington; (910) 343-1395

Meals served: Lunch and Dinner
Cuisine: Mediterranean
Entrée range: $6.95 and up
Kids menu: No
Reservations: No
Payment: All major credit cards accepted

Conveniently located in downtown Wilmington, Caffe Phoenix is a quaint storefront restaurant with great pasta and seafood dishes.

OCEANIC

703 South Lumina Avenue, Wrightsville Beach; (910) 256-5551

Meals served: Lunch and dinner
Cuisine: Seafood
Entrée range: $5 and up
Kids menu: No
Reservations: No
Payment: All major credit cards accepted

Not only is the seafood great, but you also get great ocean views—the sunsets are fabulous. After dinner take a stroll out on the pier. Kids will love it during the day, but it's also a great place for a parents' night out!

Winston-Salem

Members of the Moravian Church settled Salem as a central town for their commercial and religious efforts in the South. Their success attracted other settlers to the area, but only Moravians were permitted in the city. The newcomers settled in the surrounding area, which became Forsyth County with Winston as its county seat. After the Civil War, the area experienced tremendous industrial growth, with tobacco, furniture, and textiles becoming the major industries. The two cities merged in 1913 to form the "Twin City" of Winston-Salem.

Old Salem takes you back to days of yesteryear. More than 80 structures have been restored, including a working bakery and a shoemaker's shop. The restored buildings provide a glimpse of how the Moravians lived, worked, and worshipped. An Old Salem Christmas is magical as families come from near and far to celebrate a colonial Yuletide.

Across town is **Reynolda House,** the center of the former estate and model farm created by tobacco magnate Richard Joshua Reynolds and his wife Katharine Smith Reynolds. Constructed in 1917, Reynolda House portrays the lavish lifestyle of the Reynolds' family. Also housed at the center are three centuries of major American paintings, prints, and sculpture. The formal gardens of Reynolda House are magnificent to tour in the spring and summer.

Winston-Salem is located two hours west of Raleigh and a half-hour northwest of Charlotte via U.S. 40. Winston-Salem is also served by several major airlines.

Family Lodging

Brookstown Inn

This Inn, listed on the National Register of Historic Places, was formerly an 1837 cotton mill that supplied material for Confederate uniforms. Children

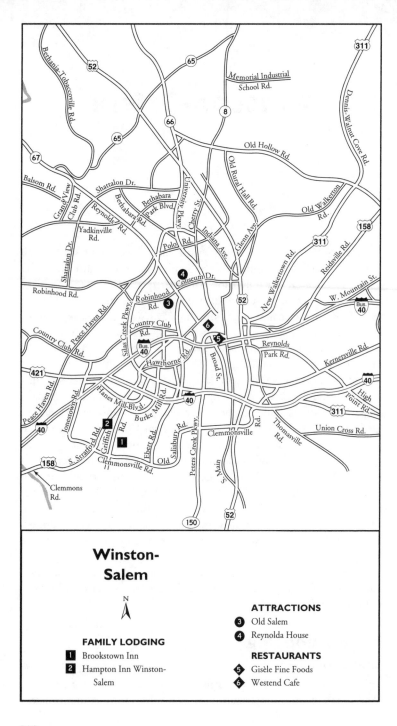

Winston-Salem

N

FAMILY LODGING

1 Brookstown Inn
2 Hampton Inn Winston-Salem

ATTRACTIONS

3 Old Salem
4 Reynolda House

RESTAURANTS

5 Gisèle Fine Foods
6 Westend Cafe

under 12 stay free with parents. The Brookstown Inn is conveniently located near Old Salem and downtown Winston-Salem. Rates start at $90. 200 Brookstown Avenue, Winston-Salem; (919) 725-1120.

Hampton Inn Winston-Salem

Located in the southwest area of town and only a block from Hanes Mall, the Hampton Inn is the only hotel on the new I-40. Hotel amenities include cable TV, in-room refrigerator, and pool. Cribs are also available. Rates start at $77. I-40 at Stratford Road, Winston-Salem; (800) 426-7866.

Attractions

Old Salem

Old Salem Road, Winston-Salem; (336) 721-7300; www.oldsalem.org

Hours: Monday–Saturday 9:30 a.m.–4:30 p.m.; Sunday 1:30–4:30 p.m.

Admission: Old Salem: $10 adults, $5 children ages 6–14; Old Salem and decorative arts museum: $13 adults, $6 children ages 6–14

Appeal by Age Group:

Pre- school	Grade School	Teens	Young Adults	Over 30	Seniors
★★★	★★★★	★★★★	★★★★	★★★★	★★★★

Average Touring Time: 3 hours

Minimum Touring Time: 2 hours

Rainy Day Touring: Not recommended

Author's Rating: ★★★★ A wonderful peek into the daily life of an eighteenth-century town

Services and Facilities:

Restaurants Yes	Lockers No
Alcoholic beverages No	Pet kennels No
Disabled access Limited	Rain check No
Wheelchair rental No	Private tours No
Baby stroller rental No	

Description and Comments You may have toured other restored historic towns, but it's doubtful you'll find one of this magnitude. Children love seeing the costumed hosts and hostesses who show you around and demonstrate crafts practiced by eighteenth-century tradesmen. There are more than 80 restored structures in the original town limits, with buildings like a working bakery, shoemaker's shop, and Single Brother's House.

Note: Those with difficulty walking may find it hard to get around due to rough sidewalks and lots of stairs.

Reynolda House

Reynolda Road, Winston-Salem; (336) 725-5325

Hours: House: Tuesday–Saturday, 8:30 a.m.–4:30 p.m., Sunday
1:30–4:30 p.m.; Gardens: daily 7:30 a.m.–5 p.m.

Admission: House: $6 adults, $5 seniors, $3 students and children; Gardens: free

Appeal by Age Group:

Pre-school	Grade School	Teens	Young Adults	Over 30	Seniors
★★	★★★	★★★★	★★★★	★★★★	★★★★

Average touring time: 3 hours

Minimum touring Time: 2 hours

Rainy Day Touring: Not recommended

Author's Rating: ★★★★   The costume exhibit will be of special interest
to children and teens.

Services and Facilities:

Restaurants Yes	Lockers No
Alcoholic beverages Yes	Pet kennels No
Disabled access Limited	Rain check No
Wheelchair rental No	Private tours No
Baby stroller rental No	

Description and Comments   Reynolda House holds an excellent collection of
furnishings, American art, and vintage clothing. The gardens are both inspiring and relaxing. Children ages seven and younger are not likely to find much
of interest except maybe running around outside on the spacious lawn.

Side Trips

Bethabara   Settled in 1753, Bethabara was North Carolina's first Moravian village. The 175-acre Historic Bethabara Park includes eighteenth-century homes and a church, a reconstructed palisade fort, cabins, and gardens, as well as archaeological ruins. Wetland education trails and a raised
boardwalk are features of the Wildlife Preserve. 2147 Bethabara Road,
Winston-Salem; (336) 924-8191.

Tanglewood Park   Located ten minutes west of Winston-Salem, Tanglewood Park is a public recreational park willed to the citizens of Forsyth
County by William Neal Reynolds, brother of tobacco entrepreneur R. J.
Reynolds. Tanglewood is also home to two championship golf courses.
Other recreational activities include fishing and boat rentals at Mallard Lake,

tennis, and camping. Be sure to stop and smell the roses—all 800 of them. Lodging options include The Manor House, The Lodge, private cottages, and a campground, (336) 778-6300; www.tanglewoodpark.org.

Family-Friendly Restaurants

GISELE FINE FOODS

226 North Marshall Street, Winston-Salem; (336) 761-0674

Meals served: Lunch
Cuisine: American
Entrée range: $4.95 and up
Kids menu: No
Reservations: No
Payment: All major credit cards accepted

On nice days you can enjoy your lunch on the patio. The restaurant is located in the historic Sawtooth Building near Old Salem. Daily specials, soups, salads, and freshly baked breads are house specialties, and kids like the idea of designing their own sandwich.

WESTEND CAFE

926 West Fourth Street; (336) 723-4774

Meals served: Lunch and dinner
Cuisine: American
Entrée range: $6 and up
Kids menu: No
Reservations: No
Payment: All major credit cards accepted.

Located in historic Winston-Salem, Westend Cafe's daily specials and evening menu change often. The lunch menu always serves up their specialty chili, as well as hot dogs, veggie burgers, and create-your-own sandwiches. The extensive dessert menu is sure to please everyone in the family. Everyone enjoys sitting by the fishpond outside the cafe.

Part Seven

South Carolina

Legend has it that when a wealthy Charleston matron was once asked why she so seldom traveled, she quickly replied, "My dear, why should I travel when I'm already here?" After several days in this old city and its surrounding countryside, you, too, might declare that you're staying for good in the Palmetto State.

Few states offer the beauty and culture of South Carolina. Geographically, South Carolina is one of the more northern states of the Deep South, but its ubiquitous palmetto trees and coastal culture make it more akin to Florida or Louisiana. And needless to say, the South Carolina state of mind is on track with the rest of the South when it comes to heritage.

Fort Sumter, located across the harbor from **Charleston,** is the site where the first shots of the Civil War were fired. Like many other parts of the South, Charleston, **Columbia,** and other areas of the state have maintained their heritage through the upkeep of antebellum homes, the preservation of forests and wetlands, and an unfaltering need to continue traditions, such as the waving of the Confederate flag or the recounting of folk stories passed down from African, Native American, and European ancestry.

Like much of Dixie, South Carolina has had to evolve with the times, as a greater number of Americans from the North and the South and immigrants have moved into the state. Charleston has embraced its local "Gullah" culture, while it has simultaneously entertained big-city restaurants and boutiques.

Capital city Columbia has been the breeding ground for some of the most famous members of the good-old-boy government network, like Strom Thurmond, but is also home to the **University of South Carolina,** one of the most respected schools in the world for international business. **Greenville,** located in an otherwise bucolic part of the state, was chosen in 1994 as the first North American location for a BMW plant. Since then, more than 200,000 automobiles have been produced by the German com-

Kids' Beat

- In 1566, the Spanish established Santa Elena, the first European settlement in South Carolina.
- The War Between the States began on April 12, 1861, as the first shots were fired from Fort Sumter in the Charleston Harbor.
- South Carolina's state flower is the yellow jessamine; the state animal is the whitetail deer; the state tree is the palmetto; the state fruit is the peach; and the state beverage is milk.
- Gaffney is home to the "Peachoid," a one-million-gallon water tank painted to resemble a giant peach, visible from I-85.

pany using workers from nearby Greenville and **Spartanburg.** The need for workers created an influx of families from as near as the Carolinas and as far as Europe, bringing their various cultures with them. This immigration has resulted in a wider variety of restaurants, bigger schools, and bustling neighborhoods.

A small state nestled between booming Georgia and North Carolina, South Carolina is often easy to leave off of an itinerary. But, its wealth of culture, from African to antebellum; its attractions, such as the **Charleston Museum** (America's oldest museum) and **BMW Zentrum;** and its natural wonders, such as the **Sumter National Forest** and the **Cape Romain Refuge** and the beaches are all reasons to visit this unique state.

But be prepared: South Carolina has the South's signature heat and humidity during the warmer months. Vacations here are best in mid-spring and fall.

GETTING THERE

By Plane. Flying to South Carolina from other cities within the United States or Canada is easy, as the state has two small international airports in Charleston, (843) 767-7708, and in Greenville/Spartanburg, (864) 877-7426; www.gspairport.com. These airports are served by USAirways, Continental, Midway, and Delta Airlines. In addition to these carriers, Air South and British Airways fly into Charleston International Airport, whereas Comair, Northwest, and TWA serve the Greenville/Spartanburg International Airport. Columbia Metropolitan Airport, (803) 822-5000; www.columbiaairport.com, and Myrtle Beach Airport, (803) 448-1580, are also good choices if you are flying regional airlines such as Atlantic Southeast Airlines, Comair, and USAirways Express.

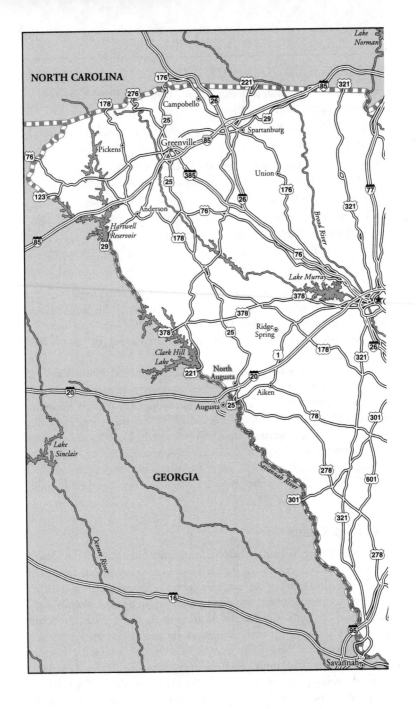

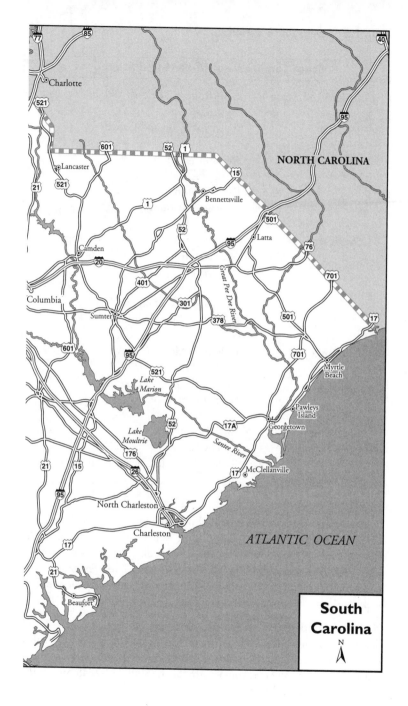

South Carolina's Not-to-Be-Missed Attractions	
Around the State	Cape Romain National Wildlife Refuge
	Riverbanks Zoo and Garden
Myrtle Beach	Alligator Adventure
	Pawleys Island
	Pedro's South of the Border
	Ripley's Aquarium
Charleston	African-American National Heritage Museum
	Charleston Museum
	Fort Sumter
	Magnolia Plantation and Gardens
	South Carolina Aquarium
Columbia	Columbia Museum of Art
	DuPont Planetarium
	Riverbanks Zoo and Garden
	South Carolina State Museum
Greenville	BMW Zentrum
	Greenville Zoo
	Roper Mountain Science Center

Many travelers to South Carolina also choose to fly into Charlotte International Airport or Hartsfield International Airport in Atlanta and drive the short distance to their South Carolina destinations. These out-of-state airports offer more flights, and, in most cases, cheaper fares. For more information on these airports, see the North Carolina and Georgia sections of this book.

By Train. Amtrak makes stops at the major South Carolina cities of Greenville, Columbia, Charleston, and Myrtle Beach, as well as smaller towns such as Camden, Clemson, Florence, and Yemassee. For information on schedules and fares, contact Amtrak at (800) 872-7245 or visit the website at www.amtrak.com.

By Car. South Carolina is traversed by four main interstates: I-26, I-77, I-85, and I-95. I-26 passes through Columbia to Charleston; I-77 runs from

Charlotte, North Carolina, to Columbia; I-85 passes through Greenville and Spartanburg; and, I-95 goes through Dillon and Florence toward Savannah, Georgia, and points south. Take U.S. 17 from North Carolina to Charleston and other destinations on the South Carolina coast.

HOW TO GET INFORMATION BEFORE YOU GO

State

South Carolina Department of Parks, Recreation, and Tourism, 1205 Pendleton Street, Columbia 29201; (803) 734-0193; www.travelsc.com

Regional

Discover Upcountry Carolina Association, 500 East North Street, P.O. Box 3116, Greenville 29602; (864) 233-2690 or (800) 849-4766; www.upcountry-sc.org

Grand Strand Tourism Commission, 1230 Highmarket Street, Georgetown 29440; (843) 546-8502

Lowcountry & Resort Islands Tourism Commission, 1 Lowcountry Lane, P.O. Box 615, Yemassee 29945; (843) 717-3090 or (800) 528-6870; www.lowcountrytravel.org

Old 96 District Tourism Commission, 104½ Public Square, P.O. Box 448, Laurens 29360; (864) 984-2233 or (800) 849-9633; www.old96.org

Olde English Tourism District, P.O. Box 1440, 107 Main Street, Chester 29706; (803) 385-6800 or (803) 728-1842; www.sctravel.net

Pendleton District Historical, Recreational & Tourism Commission, 125 East Queen Street, P.O. Box 565, Pendleton 29670; (864) 646-3782 or (800) 862-1795; www.pendleton-district.org

Local

Charleston Area Convention and Visitors Bureau, 81 Mary Street, P.O. Box 975, Charleston 29402; (843) 853-8000 or (800) 868-8118; www.charlestoncvb.com

Columbia Metropolitan Convention and Visitors Bureau, 1276 Assembly Street, P.O. Box 15, Columbia 29202; (803) 254-0479 or (800) 264-4884

Greenville Convention and Visitors Bureau, Downtown Visitors Center, 206 South Main Street, Greenville 29601; (864) 233-0461 or (800) 717-0023

Myrtle Beach Area Convention Bureau, 1200 North Oak Street, Myrtle Beach 29577; (843) 448-1629 or (800) 488-8998

Spartanburg Convention and Visitors Bureau, 298 Magnolia Street, P.O. Box 1636, Spartanburg 29303; (864) 594-5050 or (800) 374-8326; www.spartanburgsc.org

More South Carolina Websites
South Carolina State House Kids Page www.lpitr.state.sc.us/kids.htm **South Carolina State Symbols and Emblems** www.leginfo.state.sc.us/scinfo/info.html **South Carolina State House Art Collection for Kids** www.lpitr.state.sc.us/chkart.htm **Myrtle Beach Kid's Corner** www.mbchamber.com/kids.htm

Family Outdoor Adventures

⚠ - Camping
♥ - Author's favorite

♥ - *Cape Romain National Wildlife Refuge*   Not to be missed is the Cape Romain National Wildlife Refuge, a veritable paradise for birdwatchers. On over 600,000 acres along the South Carolina coastline, birds as diverse as brown pelicans, yellow warblers, and peregrine falcons make up the majority of residents here. The controlled wetlands area is a nesting ground for loggerhead turtles, and refuge workers work diligently each year to protect turtle eggs from erosion, predators, and curious tourists. Other than wildlife watching, Cape Romain activities include hiking (especially on Bulls Island), biking, and fishing. Camping, fires, and pets are strictly prohibited in the refuge area. 5801 U.S. Highway 17 North, Awendaw; (803) 928-3368.

Cowpens National Battlefield   People often forget about the "other" war that was fought in South Carolina—the Revolutionary War. That's why Cowpens National Battlefield comes as a surprise. This battlefield from the Revolutionary War is the site where Daniel Morgan led colonists to a 1781 victory over the British, in effect turning the tide of war in favor of the Americans. Travelers to this historic field can learn more about the Battle of Cowpens at the on-site Visitors Center, where curators have gathered a collection of portraits, weapons, and other Revolutionary War–era artillery. Reenactments of the battle take place at Cowpens each year on January 17 and July 4. The battlefield trail also has a number of markers, so families can take self-guided tours of the area. Intersection of Highways 11 and 110, Chesnee; (864) 461-2828.

▲ - *Francis Marion National Forest* The Francis Marion National Forest is no longer the old-growth woodland that it used to be. In 1989, many of the forest's large pine and cypress trees were destroyed by the severe winds of Hurricane Hugo. However, many younger trees managed to survive the storm. Today, the Francis Marion is an unusual work-in-progress, a vivid example of nature replenishing itself.

Wildlife viewing is an especially practical activity in the forest, as it is home to otters, bobcats, black bears, beavers, and a colorful array of birds. Visitors to the 250,000-acre forest can also go hiking, horseback riding, or mountain biking on the Swamp Fox Recreation Trail, or go fishing or boating at the Huger or Guilliard Lake Recreation Areas. For camping, try the popular Buck Hall Recreation Area, which has RV hook-ups as well as boat ramps, grills, and on-site toilets and showers. 4931 Broad River Road, Columbia; (843) 887-3257; www.fed.fs.us/r8/fms.

▲ ♥ - *South Carolina Beaches* South Carolina is known for its Atlantic beaches, a fact made evident by the number of oceanside resorts and beachgoers. Myrtle Beach, (843) 238-5325, is ideal for families, as it offers a wide variety of beachside attractions, such as mini-golf, as well as activities like surf fishing, boating, and swimming. Hilton Head Island, (843) 785-3673, an hour and a half from Charleston, is known the world over for its exclusive golf and tennis resorts as well as its unspoiled shores. And then there are coastal locales like Edisto Beach State Park, (843) 869-2756, and Hunting Island State Park, (843) 838-2011, that offer visitors a chance to camp, hike, and fish with little interference from other tourists.

♥ - *South Carolina Golf* It is no wonder that The Palmetto State boasts more than 380 public and private courses, providing more than a year's worth of golfing fun. Golf is a tradition in South Carolina, as the first golf course in the United States, the Carolina Golf Club, was founded in Charleston in 1786. Today, the resorts at nearby Hilton Head are especially known for challenging links. Try the breezy Ocean Course, (800) 925-4653; the Robert Trent Jones Course, (843) 785-1138, ranked fifth in the nation by *Golf* magazine; or, the George Cobb–designed Sea Marsh Course, (800) 925-4653.

Likewise, the Myrtle Beach area is home to some of the state's most famous fairways, and many of the more than 100 courses have hosted PGA tournaments. Play a round at the Championship Course, designed by Rees Jones, (843) 236-8888; the public Man O' War Golf Course, (843) 236-8000; or the Raccoon Run Golf Club, (843) 650-2644.

If you are not planning to stay along the Carolina coast, there are plenty of golfing options inland. The Greenville/Spartanburg area has approximately nine courses, although the Hillandale Golf Course, (864) 250-1700, is the only public course. More than a dozen golf courses are located in the Columbia area. The Northwoods Golf Club, (803) 786-9242, is an ideal public course for young and old.

Make sure to ask your hotel about golf packages, as many include greens fees and accommodations in the price. Most courses also offer discounts of up to 50 percent for younger players.

▲ - *Sumter National Forest* Sumter National Forest offers a host of activities for families, especially along the Chattooga River, which traverses the more than 364,900-acre forest. Families can take to the Chattooga Hiking Trail on foot, bike, or horseback. Walking trails link up with trails from Georgia's Chattahoochee National Forest and North Carolina's Nantahala National Forest. Horse paths connecting to the Chattahoochee Forest allow families to explore as far south as Georgia. Water-based activities on the Chattooga include boating, canoeing, fishing, and whitewater rafting. Camping areas in Sumter range from primitive to deluxe. Good campsites include Parson's Mountain Recreation Area, a 28-acre stretch of land with toilets, showers, grills, and lodging. The heavily wooded Lick Fork Lake area also provides primitive camping opportunities, with access to pit toilets, showers, and picnic tables. The Woods Ferry Recreation Area has approximately 28 sites in which to camp, and seven of these have horse stalls on site. All three camping areas are equipped with at least one boat ramp and are accessible for RVs. 112 Andrew Pickens Circle, Mountain Rest; (864) 638-9568; www.fs.fed.us/r8/fms.

Calendar of Festivals and Events

January

Myrtle Beach Wildlife Expo, Pawleys Island   Animal exhibits, interactive displays, and workshops entertain young and old at this yearly event. All proceeds support wildlife initiatives throughout the state; (843) 237-3899.

Aiken Camellia Show   Over 1,000 camellia blossoms are displayed and judged at this annual event; (843) 649-9586.

Battle Of Cowpens Anniversary Celebration, Chesnee   Cowpens National Battlefield hosts the anniversary of the battle on the weekend closest to January 17. Living-history encampments and tactical demonstrations are part of the activities; (864) 461-2828.

Lowcountry Blues Bash, Charleston   This celebration gets down with more than 50 blues acts appearing in clubs, hotels, theatres, and restaurants; (843) 762-9125.

February

Lowcountry Oyster Festival, Charleston   The oyster is an integral part of Lowcountry cuisine, so each year the city of Charleston celebrates the beloved bivalve with music, eating contests, and other entertainment. Kids can even participate in the Best Dressed Oyster contest. Billed as the world's largest oyster roast, it's your chance to try oysters cooked a number of ways; (843) 577-4030.

Africa Alive, Rock Hill   The diverse cultures of Africa are presented and explored in this weekend family festival. Dancing, storytelling, crafts, and food are among the highlights; (803) 329-2121.

Benedict College African-American Bazaar, Columbia   Harambee!—The Benedict College African-American Bazaar is one of the largest college-sponsored African-American festivals in the nation. Food, children's programs, musical performances, a baking contest, and workshops round out the bazaar; (803) 253-5174.

March

Andrews Gospel Music and Storytelling, Andrews   A celebration of South Carolina's multicultural heritage with gospel music and storytelling; (843) 264-3471.

Renofest, Darlington   This two-day event features the Reno Brothers and other nationally known bluegrass performers; (843) 393-0494.

Edisto Indian Cultural Festival, Ridgeville   Traders, dancers, drummers, and drinks are part of this annual pow-wow; (843) 871-2126.

Georgetown Plantation Tour, Georgetown   This tour showcases the plantations and historic townhouses of this port city; (843) 545-8291.

April

Sap Risin' Children's Festival, Bennettsville   Teaching children about traditional arts, crafts, and skills is the focus of Bennettsville's annual celebration; (843) 479-3869.

Lowcountry Cajun Festival, Charleston   Celebrate South Louisiana culture in Charleston style. Zydeco and Cajun music, crawfish races, authentic Creole and Cajun dishes, and free activities for kids; (843) 762-2172.

World Grits Festival, St. George   A tribute to grits and Southern roots. Crafts, street dancing, clogging, gospel music, live bands, and, of course, grits-grinding and a grits-eating contest are part of the fun; (843) 563-4366.

Riverfest, West Columbia   Spend time along and on the river at this family-oriented festival consisting of a Mayor's 5K River run/walk, celebrity river raft race, food, vendors, live bands, and children's area/activities; (803) 926-0071.

Governor's Frog Jump Festival, Springfield   Unusual activities abound at Springfield's annual festival. A frog-jumping contest, egg-strike contest, horseshoes, carnival, food vendors, crafts, entertainment, bands, and dances will keep you busy for the weekend; (803) 258-3152.

May

Gullah Festival, Beaufort   The Lowcountry Gullah culture and heritage is celebrated each year in the coastal town of Beaufort. Enjoy crafts, art, music, and Gullah cuisine; (843) 525-0628.

Flopeye Fish Festival, Great Falls   This family-friendly party of food and entertainment takes place every Memorial Day weekend; (803) 482-6029.

Hell Hole Swamp Festival, Jamestown   A wonderful family-oriented event with children's games, an adult tobacco-spitting contest, greased pole climbing, a softball tournament, horseshoe pitching, arm wrestling, beauty contests for all ages, a parade, music, a talent contest, exhibits, plus arts and crafts; (843) 257-2233.

Lowcountry Shrimp Festival, McClellanville   A blessing of the fleet ceremony celebrates tradition in this coastal community, and the crowds gather for clam chowder, fish stew, seafood dinners, live entertainment, and other major attractions; (843) 887-3525.

June

Spoleto Festival, Charleston   Spoleto is a celebration of Charleston's artistic roots, with theater, dance, music, opera, and visual arts shows and presentations; (843) 722-2764, www.spoletousa.org.

Harbourfest, Hilton Head Island   Every Tuesday evening during the summer (usually from the beginning of June through the end of August), Hilton Head Island comes alive with food vendors, arts and crafts booths, and live entertainment. A fireworks display caps of the night; (843) 785-1106.

Edisto Riverfest, Walterboro   Guided trips down the black-water Edisto River are the main attractions at this festival. Workshops on canoeing and displays of outdoor gear also are provided; (843) 549-5591.

Juneteenth Celebration, Florence   Juneteenth is the oldest known celebration of the ending of African-American slavery in the United States, dating to

June 19, 1865. The celebration is tribute to African-American freedom, with programs, activities, and entertainment that encourage self-development, self-respect, and respect for all cultures and nationalities; (843) 346-5895.

July

Lexington County Peach Festival, Gilbert   Peach dishes are the main attraction at this annual festival, but you'll also find arts and crafts, live bands, entertainment, and concessions; (803) 892-2473.

Battle Of Huck's Defeat, McConnells   Learn about the Revolutionary War in the Carolina backcountry with this ongoing living history demonstration. British Redcoats and Patriot militia present historical dramas; (803) 684-2327.

Beaufort County Water Festival, Beaufort   South Carolina summers can get hot; this festival is one way to cool down. Water-oriented activities along with entertainment make this one event you'll not want to miss; (843) 524-0600.

September

Come Horse Around Festival, Camden   This is your chance to get up close and personal with Camden's four-legged friends. A parade, demonstrations of equine breeds, entertainment, arts and crafts, and vendors take place on Saturday; on Sunday everyone saddles up for a trail ride through Camden's historic hunt country; (803) 432-2525.

Fall Candlelight Tour of Homes & Gardens, Charleston   Evening walking tours showcase Charleston's homes, gardens, and churches. Guides offer insight on architecture, antiques, and history; (843) 722-4630.

October

Gopher Hill Festival, Ridgeland   Prior to the 1890s, the Town of Ridgeland was known as Gopher Hill because so many gopher tortoises inhabited the area sand hills. This annual festival, named for the now endangered gopher tortoise, offers a parade, arts and crafts, kiddie rides, games, a free outdoor concert with a variety of entertainers, and a turtle race; (843) 726-8126.

Bog-Off Festival, Loris   This Governor's Tourism Award–winning festival began in 1980 and has grown into a fun-filled two-week event. The Bog-Off Festival celebrates Southern hospitality and culture designed around the Lowcountry dish of chicken-bog; (843) 756-6030.

November

Catfish Festival, Society Hill Food, crafts, clowns, a parade, and fun are part of this event. Of course, there are a variety of dishes made with catfish; (843) 332-6401.

Columbia Native American Cultural Festival, Columbia Native American culture is celebrated with dancing, drumming, arts, demonstrations, storytelling, and food; (803) 256-8700.

Children's Garden Christmas & Kid's Walk, Orangeburg This drive-through light display features animated and stationary lights in a variety of shapes and sizes, along with a walking trail with interactive light displays; (803) 533-6020.

Yap Ye Iswa (Day Of The Catawba), Rock Hill Set aside as a way to learn about local Native Americans, this event includes pottery making, beadwork, basket making, hide tanning, blowgun construction, storytelling, herbal workshops, and food; (803) 328-2427.

December

A Holiday Celebration, Myrtle Beach A festival of food and special events, this celebration's highlight is the nautical-themed light display that stretches for miles along the Grand Strand; (843) 626-7444.

Christmas at the Edmondston-Aston House & Middleton Place, Charleston Storytelling, Christmas caroling, a live nativity scene, and craftspeople working in their shops by torchlight are highlights of this holiday event; (843) 556-6020.

Charleston

Literally a diamond in the rough, Charleston is a city of surprising contradictions. Beyond pristine antebellum mansions lie Gullah villages, in-between historic old warehouses are fashionable shops, and mingling on restaurant menus are haute cuisine and Lowcountry fare.

This combination of old and new has made Charleston a favorite destination among travelers of all stripes for over a decade. Among the accolades: Twenty-fourth on *Travel & Leisure's* "Top 25 Cities in the World;" third on *Conde Nast Traveler's* poll of "Top 10 U.S. Cities;" ninth on *Travel & Leisure's* list of "World's Best Values;" and, according to etiquette expert Marabelle Young Stewart, the "Most Mannerly City in America." In fact, Charleston has been mentioned on Stewart's list every year for the 24 years it has been released.

Once you arrive in Charleston, you'll understand what all the hoopla is about. Take a walk along the harbor, where you can enjoy, at once, beautiful views of antebellum mansions and **Fort Sumter.** Spend the morning or the afternoon among the fragrant flowers and singing birds at the **Magnolia Plantation and Gardens.** If rain threatens, make a stop in the **Charleston Museum,** the oldest museum in America. Or, venture over to the **South Carolina Aquarium,** Charleston's newest attraction. Old and new are yours to explore in the Palmetto State's chicest of cities.

Family Lodging

Days Inn Historic District

All 124 rooms of the comfortable Days Inn were renovated in 1999, and now come with fine amenities including two queen-size beds, cable television, a modem jack, and an AM/FM alarm clock/radio. The hotel is located within blocks of shopping and local color on Meeting Street, the historic mansions of the Battery, and the Charleston Visitors Center. An outdoor pool, on-site restaurant, and parking lot (with free parking) round

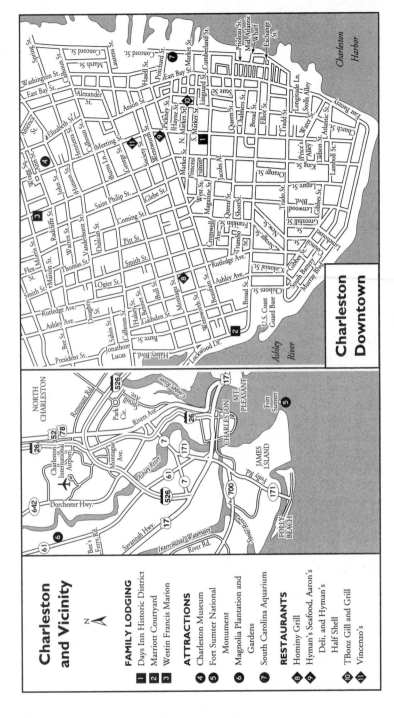

Charleston and Vicinity

N

FAMILY LODGING

1. Days Inn Historic District
2. Marriott Courtyard
3. Westin Francis Marion

ATTRACTIONS

4. Charleston Museum
5. Fort Sumter National Monument
6. Magnolia Plantation and Gardens
7. South Carolina Aquarium

RESTAURANTS

8. Hominy Grill
9. Hyman's Seafood, Aaron's Deli, and Hyman's Half Shell
10. TBonz Gill and Grill
11. Vincenzo's

Charleston Downtown

out the property's facilities. Rates at Days Inn Historic District start at $79. 155 Meeting Street, Charleston; (843) 722-8411 or (800) 544-8313.

Marriott Courtyard Charleston Downtown

This large hotel in the middle of downtown Charleston has 179 rooms and tons of services, including laundry and room service. It is within walking distance of exquisite shops, dining, and historic landmarks and just a few minutes' drive from area beaches and golf courses. Guest rooms have cable/satellite television, in-room movies, a dataport for laptops, an iron and ironing board, and a hairdryer. Cribs are available upon request. Rooms start at $119, and children ages 17 and younger stay free; 35 Lockwood Drive, Charleston; (843) 722-7229.

The Westin Francis Marion

This historic hotel dates back to 1924, when it was the largest hotel in the Carolinas. The hotel is an attraction in itself and is listed in the National Register of Historic Places; it's also near the bustling market area and the Charleston Museum. The Westin Francis Marion was recently restored to its '20s-style elegance, but now features modern amenities like dataports, cable television, irons and ironing boards, and in-room coffee makers with Starbucks coffee. Westin Kids Club provides the young ones with coloring books and bath toys as well as special services for parents, including infant safety kits with plug covers and "running" strollers upon request. Rates start at $150. Kids younger than age 17 stay free; 387 King Street, Charleston; (843) 722-0600.

Attractions

Charleston Museum

360 Meeting Street, Charleston; (843) 722-2996
   www.charlestonmuseum.com

Hours: Monday–Saturday, 9 a.m.–5 p.m.; Sunday, 1–5 p.m.

Admission: $7 adults, $4 children ages 3–12

Appeal by Age Group:

Pre-school	Grade School	Teens	Young Adults	Over 30	Seniors
★★★	★★★	★★★	★★★★	★★★★	★★★★

Average Touring Time: 1½ hours

Minimum Touring Time: 1 hour

Rainy Day Touring: Recommended

Author's Rating: ★★★   Charleston, the South, and America meet here

Services and Facilities:

Restaurants No	Lockers No
Alcoholic beverages No	Pet kennels No
Disabled access Yes	Rain check No
Wheelchair rental No	Private tours Yes
Baby stroller rental No	

Description and Comments   Founded in 1773, the Charleston Museum is the oldest museum in the United States. Exhibits in the museum vary from Native American relics, and colonial-era clothing to and household objects and Civil War memorabilia. The Charleston Museum puts on numerous events for families and kids, examples of which are festivals celebrating the Lowcountry and Gullah heritage of the area, and Amazing Architecture days, when parents and children learn more about the building styles of Charleston through art lessons and demonstrations. Call ahead for information on special activities.

Fort Sumter National Monument

1214 Middle Street, Sullivan's Island (Charleston Harbor); (843) 883-3123
   www.nps.gov/fosu

Hours: Monday–Sunday, times vary

Admission: Boat fees to monument: $10.50 adults, $5.50 ages 6–12

Appeal by Age Group:

Pre-school	Grade School	Teens	Young Adults	Over 30	Seniors
★★	★★★	★★	★★	★★★	★★★

Average Touring Time: 1 hour

Minimum Touring Time: 1 hour

Rainy Day Touring: Not recommended

Author's Rating: ★★★   Best place to view Charleston

Services and Facilities:

Restaurants No	Lockers No
Alcoholic beverages No	Pet kennels No
Disabled access Yes	Rain check No
Wheelchair rental No	Private tours No
Baby stroller rental No	

Description and Comments   Take a boat ride over to the Fort Sumter National Monument to see where the Civil War began. On April 12, 1861, the first shots of the War Between the States were fired from this fort, and from 1863 to 1865, Confederate soldiers kept Fort Sumter out of Union hands for approximately 22 months. Whether you are from the North or the South, you'll want to visit this historic attraction. What's more, the view of Charleston from the fort is unbeatable.

Boat rides from City Marina take only a matter of minutes. Once you pay the fee for the ride, the tour at Fort Sumter is free. A self-guided museum on the fort retells the history of this Charleston landmark.

Magnolia Plantation and Gardens

3550 Ashley River Road, Charleston; (843) 571-1266
www.magnoliaplantation.com

Hours: March–October: 8 a.m.–dusk; November–February opening times vary according to weather

Admission: $10 adults, $9 seniors and college students, $5 children ages 6–12

Appeal by Age Group:

Pre-school	Grade School	Teens	Young Adults	Over 30	Seniors
★★★★	★★★★	★★★★	★★★★	★★★★	★★★★

Average Touring Time: 3 hours

Minimum Touring Time: 2 hours

Rainy Day Touring: Not recommended

Author's Rating: ★★★ The nation's oldest public garden is also one of the prettiest

Services and Facilities:

Restaurants No	Lockers No
Alcoholic beverages No	Pet kennels No
Disabled access Yes	Rain check No
Wheelchair rental No	Private tours Yes
Baby stroller rental No	

Description and Comments Magnolia Plantation and Gardens, the oldest public gardens in America, is continually rated by locals and travelers as one of the treasures of Charleston, and it is not hard to see why. Besides having impeccably manicured lawns, rows and rows of colorful flowers, and interesting architecture, the massive estate is home to a 125-acre bird refuge, an avenue of antebellum-era dwellings, Native American burial mounds, topiary gardens, and a petting zoo. Combine these things with dozens of walking trails and opportunities for biking, canoeing, and picnicking, and you have your day planned.

South Carolina Aquarium

350 Concord Street, Charleston; (843) 720-1990 or (888) 343-9899
www.scaquarium.org

Hours: Daily. March–June and September–October, 9 a.m.—5 p.m.;
July–August, 9 a.m.–7 p.m.; November–February, 10 a.m.–5 p.m.

Admission: $14 adults, $12 seniors and students ages 13–17, $7 ages
4–12, free for children ages 3 and younger

Appeal by Age Group:

Pre-school	Grade School	Teens	Young Adults	Over 30	Seniors
★★★★	★★★★	★★★★	★★★★	★★★★	★★★★

Average Touring Time: 2 hours

Minimum Touring Time: 1½ hours

Rainy Day Touring: Recommended

Author's Rating: ★★★★ Enjoyable for all ages

Services and Facilities:

Restaurants Yes—snack areas	Lockers No
Alcoholic beverages No	Pet kennels No
Disabled access Yes	Rain check No
Wheelchair rental No	Private tours No
Baby stroller rental No	

Description and Comments The newest attraction in Charleston took
more than $22 million to build, so you can believe that the South Carolina
Aquarium has pulled out all the stops. Located at the Charleston Harbor,
the Aquarium houses approximately 10,000 animals, including 11 sea
turtles, 50-pound fish, playful otters, and a myriad collection of reptiles,
amphibians, invertebrates, and water fowl. The Aquarium is separated into
five ecosystems: Mountain Forest, Piedmont, Coastal Plain, Saltmarsh, and
Atlantic Ocean, and each is a spectacle unto its own.

Side Trips

Santa Elena Another famous fort in the vicinity of Charleston is Santa
Elena, (843) 525-2952, also known as Charlesfort. This was the first settlement of South Carolina, and it dates back to the 1500s when it served
as both a French and Spanish outpost. You can tour exhibits that explain
the archaeology of the area or simply take the time to hike Santa Elena's
scenic nature trails. More information, including maps, can be found at
the Parris Island website: www.parrisisland.com.

Beaufort This waterfront community is picturesque with its piers, colorful boats, tall oak trees, and tidy antebellum homes, so much so that it has

served as a movie set for such films as *Forrest Gump* and *The Prince of Tides.* Beaufort is worth a visit for its beauty alone, but its history also provides many attractions. Explore the Beaufort Museum, (843) 525-7077, and view Native-American relics, Lowcountry Gullah treasures, and Revolutionary and Civil War memorabilia. If you would rather soak up the sun instead of history, Beaufort also offers many chances for fishing, swimming, tennis, golf, and more. And while you're at it, stop by for a plate of boiled shrimp, a Beaufort specialty long before the directors of *Forrest Gump* arrived here.

Family-Friendly Restaurants

HOMINY GRILL

207 Rutledge Avenue, Charleston; (843) 937-0930

Meals served: Breakfast, lunch, and dinner
Cuisine: Southern
Entrée range: $4.99–12.49
Kids menu: No
Reservations: No
Payment: All major credit cards

Opened in 1996, this relatively new restaurant has become a local favorite, serving up southern dishes using fresh produce and local seafood. In addition to its tasty breakfast fare, Hominy Grill regularly puts on theme nights, such as Friday Night Fish Fry, and provides all the fixin's for a delicious southern feast. The place is only a few minutes' walk from historic downtown.

HYMAN'S SEAFOOD, AARON'S DELI, AND HYMAN'S HALF SHELL

215 Meeting Street, Charleston; (843) 723-6000
www.hymansseafood.com

Meals served: Breakfast, lunch, and dinner
Cuisine: American, deli, seafood
Entrée range: $5.50–11.95
Kids menu: Yes
Reservations: No
Payment: All major credit cards accepted; personal checks not accepted

This trio of restaurants on Meeting Street will satisfy any appetite or eating preference, be it kosher, vegetarian, carnivore, or seafood. Aaron's serves up delicious New York–style sandwiches piled high with corned beef, pastrami, turkey, or whatever you like. Hyman's Seafood and Hyman's Half Shell serve up local favorites like shrimp-and-grits and she-crab soup, or pasta dishes with fresh seafood. A family could complete a whole day's worth of eating with the selections offered at these three restaurants. All three are open until 11 p.m. each night, and Aaron's opens at 7 a.m. for breakfast.

TBONZ GILL AND GRILL

80 North Market Street, Charleston; (843) 577-2511

Meals served: Lunch and dinner
Cuisine: American
Entrée range: $5.95–14
Kids menu: Yes
Reservations: Accepted
Payment: All major credit cards accepted

This family restaurant has steaks, seafood, and Lowcountry dishes. It's near Market Street shops and the Old Slave Market. Lunch is a particularly good value for families, as you can sample some of Charleston's best crab cakes and steaks for less. Large groups are easily accommodated.

VINCENZO'S

232 Meeting Street, Charleston; (843) 577-7953

Meals served: Lunch and dinner
Cuisine: Italian
Entrée range: $6.95–13.95
Kids menu: No
Reservations: Accepted
Payment: All major credit cards accepted

Classic Italian cuisine including hearty pastas, with red or meat sauce, and pizzas with a variety of toppings. Vincenzo's has been a Charleston fixture for more than 50 years. This restaurant offers a cozy atmosphere and a hearty, sit-down dinner option for families who need to unwind from a day of sightseeing.

Myrtle Beach

When the weather starts to heat up, tourists from all over the East Coast head to South Carolina to enjoy the shore at Myrtle Beach. Part of the "Grand Strand," Myrtle Beach boasts 60 miles of uninterrupted coastline providing numerous opportunities for swimming, fishing, surfing, building sandcastles, or just lazing around in the warm Carolina sun. But there is more to do at Myrtle Beach than soak up the sun and ride the waves.

Families can take advantage of the seaside town's numerous activities, from theaters to zoos to interactive children's museums. Entertainment options are plentiful, especially at **Broadway at the Beach,** a complex of shops, restaurants, theaters, and attractions, such as **Ripley's Aquarium** and the **Discovery IMAX Theater.** The **Children's Museum of South Carolina** and the world's largest reptile zoo, **Alligator Adventure,** provide hours of fun, even on rainy days.

Golfers can enjoy the links at more than 100 area golf courses. Many of Myrtle Beach's hotels and resorts offer golf packages, with opportunities to play a round at a Gary Player or Robert Trent Jones course. If you're not keeping score, then spend some time at one of approximately 47 miniature-golf venues in town.

Myrtle Beach is an entertainment mecca for young and old, but despite the addition of hundreds of shops, grand restaurants, and spectacular sites, the beach is still the reason why approximately 13.5 million tourists and their families flock here annually. It is also why Myrtle Beach was listed in the Surfrider Foundation's Top 10 Urban Beaches for 2000.

Family Lodging

Blue Water Resort

You can't go wrong with this 232-room oceanfront property. Blue Water Resort features four outdoor pools, one indoor pool, a kiddie pool, a lazy river, five whirlpools, and immediate beach access. You'll also find free on-

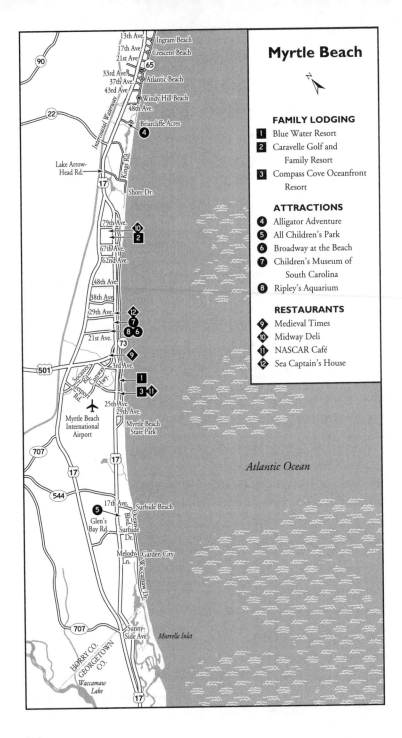

Myrtle Beach

N

FAMILY LODGING

1. Blue Water Resort
2. Caravelle Golf and Family Resort
3. Compass Cove Oceanfront Resort

ATTRACTIONS

4. Alligator Adventure
5. All Children's Park
6. Broadway at the Beach
7. Children's Museum of South Carolina
8. Ripley's Aquarium

RESTAURANTS

9. Medieval Times
10. Midway Deli
11. NASCAR Café
12. Sea Captain's House

site racquetball, a fitness room, and a video arcade. Whether you are staying for two days or two weeks, the resort can accommodate you with a basic oceanview suite or a two-bedroom condo. Amenities at Blue Water vary from room to room, with some having kitchens, dining tables, and lounge areas. All rooms have cable television, private balcony, microwave and refrigerator.Rates range from $35 per night in the off-season to $154 during peak season. Per-week rates start at approximately $450. 2001 South Ocean Boulevard, Myrtle Beach; (800) 845-6994; www.bluewater-resort.com.

Caravelle Golf and Family Resort

This enormous eight-building, 670-room complex caters to families with seven pools, lazy river rides, a video game room, two restaurants, and 720 feet of beachfront. Accommodations range from efficiencies to condominiums, depending on length of stay, and are equipped with microwave, refrigerator, and cable television. All suites and efficiencies have full-size kitchens, and all oceanfront suites feature two remote-control color televisions. Room rates start at $32 in the off-season and $84 during peak vacation time.

The Caravelle Resort offers several packages for golf and entertainment, allowing families to get the most out of a stay at Myrtle Beach. Serious golfers can hit the links at Gary Players' Blackmoor course, the Dunes Golf and Beach Club, or one of more than 80 courses in the area starting at $179 per night per person. Super Saver and Daily Golf specials are also available. Caravelle's entertainment options include the Showtime Package, with tickets to two shows, and the Standing Ovation Package, with tickets to three shows and three dinners. Entertainment packages start at $112.50. 6900 North Ocean Boulevard, Myrtle Beach; (888) 808-7306; www.thecaravelle.com.

Compass Cove Oceanfront Resort

Compass Cove, formerly known as the Swampfox, recently reopened, with renovated rooms and newer amenities. Now, the resort features 92 more accommodation choices, including two-room connecting suites for families. Efficiencies and suites in the Compass Cove tower have room for as many as six people (two adults and four children) and come equipped with color television, double beds, a sleeper sofa, a kitchenette and a microwave. Oceanfront rooms have two televisions.

Compass Cove Oceanfront Resort is loaded with activities for the entire family. Get wet and wild in the resort's seven pools or build sandcastles along 720 feet of pristine beach. Golf and entertainment packages are also available, starting at $149 per night. During the summer, Compass Cove offers a children's program. 2311 South Ocean Boulevard, Myrtle Beach; (800) 326-5224; www.compasscove.com.

Attractions

Alligator Adventure

4898 U.S. Highway 17 South (at Barefoot Landing), Myrtle Beach;
  (843) 361-0789

Hours: Daily, 9 a.m.–10 p.m.

Admission: $11.95 adults, $9.95 seniors, $7.95 children ages 4–12, free
  for children ages 3 and younger

Appeal by Age Group:

Pre-school	Grade School	Teens	Young Adults	Over 30	Seniors
★★	★★★	★★★	★★★	★★★	★★★

Average Touring Time: 2 hours

Minimum Touring Time: 1 hour

Rainy Day Touring: Recommended

Author's Rating: ★★★

Services and Facilities:

Restaurants Yes–in the Barefoot Landing complex	Baby stroller rental Yes
Alcoholic beverages No	Lockers No
Disabled access Yes	Pet kennels No
Wheelchair rental Yes	Rain check No
	Private tours No

Description and Comments   A 1,200-pound crocodile, a 500-pound tortoise, an albino alligator, and tons of slithering snakes, lizards, and reptiles are what you will see at the world's largest reptile zoo. Alligator Adventure also features frogs, komodo dragons, tropical birds, and the capybara, a rodent and the only mammal species in the zoo. Expect to see safari-clad staffers walking around with animals such as the Burmese python or the boa constrictor, offering visitors a rare chance to touch these unusual creatures. Reptile shows are held every two hours, starting at 10 a.m. Squeamish kids (and adults) may want to avoid Alligator Adventure around feeding time, as everything from mice to rabbits to chickens is part of the reptile diet. Feedings take place every two hours, starting at 11 a.m.

All Children's Park

Surfside Beach at South Hollywood and 10th Avenue, Myrtle Beach
  (843) 918-2280

Hours: Dawn to dusk

Admission: Free

Appeal by Age Group:

Pre-school	Grade School	Teens	Young Adults	Over 30	Seniors
★★	★★★	★	★	★★	★★

Average Touring Time: 1 hour

Minimum Touring Time: 20 minutes

Rainy Day Touring: Not recommended

Author's Rating: ★★★

Services and Facilities:

Restaurants No	Lockers No
Alcoholic beverages No	Pet kennels No
Disabled access Yes	Rain check No
Wheelchair rental No	Private tours No
Baby stroller rental No	

Description and Comments   Disabled children will enjoy the barrier-free environment of the All Children's Park. Unlike many playgrounds in the area, All Children's Park does not have a sand floor—rather, it has a rubbery floor surface, making it easier for children (and adults in wheelchairs) to enjoy the park. The design of the park equipment is more ergonomic than most, allowing children of all abilities to play together.

Broadway at the Beach

1325 Celebrity Circle, Myrtle Beach; (843) 444-3200 or (800) FUN-INMB
www.broadwayatthebeach.com

Hours: Daily, 10 a.m.–6 p.m.

Admission: Free; individual attractions have separate admission prices. Call for more details.

Appeal by Age Group:

Pre-school	Grade School	Teens	Young Adults	Over 30	Seniors
★★★★	★★★★	★★★★	★★★★	★★★★	★★★★

Average Touring Time: 3 hours

Minimum Touring Time: 2 hours

Rainy Day Touring: Recommended

Author's Rating: ★★★★   Guaranteed to please all ages

Services and Facilities:

Restaurants Yes– 20	up at Visitors Center
Alcoholic beverages Yes	Baby stroller rental Yes. Rental
Disabled access Yes	available at Children's Carousel
Wheelchair rental Yes, free. Pick	Lockers No

Pet kennels No	Private tours Varies according to
Rain check Varies according to	attraction
attraction	

Description and Comments   This mega-complex on the Grand Strand houses the majority of Myrtle Beach's attractions, shops, and theaters. You can literally spend your entire day and night at Broadway on the Beach. Attractions include Ripley's Aquarium (see below); the IMAX Discovery Theater, (843) 448-4629; and the NASCAR Speedpark, (843) 626-8725. Enjoy breakfast, lunch, or dinner at Broadway at the Beach at one of the theme restaurants, including the NASCAR Cafe, the All-Star Cafe, Planet Hollywood, and Johnny Rocket's. Evening entertainment can be found at the Palace Theater, (843) 448-0588, which features live concerts, plays, and musicals.

Children's Museum of South Carolina

2501 North Kings Highway, Myrtle Beach; (843) 946-9469
   www.bearweb.com/cmsckids

Hours: Tuesday–Saturday, 10 a.m.–4 p.m.

Admission: $4, free for children ages 1 and younger

Appeal by Age Group:

Pre-school	Grade School	Teens	Young Adults	Over 30	Seniors
★★★★	★★★★	★	★	★★★	★★

Average Touring Time: 2½ hours

Minimum Touring Time: 2 hours

Rainy Day Touring: Recommended

Author's Rating: ★★★

Services and Facilities:

Restaurants No	Lockers No
Alcoholic beverages No	Pet kennels No
Disabled access Yes	Rain check No
Wheelchair rental No	Private tours No
Baby stroller rental No	

Description and Comments   On those unfortunate rainy days, pack the kids up and head to the Children's Museum. Featured within approximately 10,000 square feet are the Magic School Bus, making stops through the Solar System; the Children's ER; a Fossil Hunt; and the Giant Bubble, which lets kids blow bubbles while learning the dynamics of how they are formed. The Arts and Crafts Center lets kids tinker around with paint, chalk, and glitter, while the Discovery Lab contains small aquariums, ant farms, and other displays on the animal and plant life of South Carolina.

Ripley's Aquarium

1110 Celebrity Circle, Myrtle Beach; (800) 734-8888
www.ripleysaquarium.com

Hours: Daily, 10 a.m.–6 p.m.

Admission: $13.95 adults, $12.95 seniors, $7.95 ages 5–11, $3.95 children ages 2–4

Appeal by Age Group:

Pre-school	Grade School	Teens	Young Adults	Over 30	Seniors
★★★★	★★★★	★★★★	★★★★	★★★★	★★★★

Average Touring Time: 2 hours

Minimum Touring Time: 1½ hours

Rainy Day Touring: Recommended

Author's Rating: ★★★★

Services and Facilities:

Restaurants No	Lockers No
Alcoholic beverages No	Pet kennels No
Disabled access Yes	Rain check No
Wheelchair rental No	Private tours No
Baby stroller rental No	

Description and Comments   Once you enter into the 330-foot underwater tunnel, you'll understand why Ripley's Aquarium is one of the most popular attractions in the state. Gliding above your head are nine-foot sharks, hundreds of colorful, tropical fish, stingrays, tortoises, and more. Nine live exhibits are dedicated to watery worlds, such as the ocean, Lowcountry wetlands, and the Amazon River. Hourly dive shows provide even more entertainment for the entire family.

Ripley's also offers a Sleep with the Sharks program, a truly unique slumber party. Groups of at least 15 can overnight at the aquarium and take part in a private tour, scavenger hunt, and educational activities. This program is ideal for classes or extended families.

Side Trips

Crook and Chase Theater   Each year from May through October, TNN personalities Crook and Chase broadcast live from Myrtle Beach at the Crook and Chase Theater. The live shows follow the program's usual format and feature celebrities, artists from the world of country music, comedy performances, and more. For information or reservations, call (843) 236-8500.

Beach-Going Wheelchair Program   Everyone can have fun at Myrtle Beach, no matter what their abilities. Throughout the summer (from

Memorial Day through Labor Day), the city offers beach-going wheel-chairs, equipped with a large umbrella and special wheels that travel easily over the sand. There is a one-hour time limit on these chairs, so that all may have the opportunity to enjoy the beach. You can find the beach-going wheelchairs and handicapped parking at the following locations: 5th Avenue North, 8th Avenue North, 8th Avenue South, 24th Avenue North, 54th Avenue North, 72nd Avenue North and 77th Avenue North

Mini Golf   If money or time leave a round of golf off your agenda, why not putt around on a miniature golf course? There are approximately 47 places to play mini golf in Myrtle Beach, offering a fun diversion from laz-ing around on the beach. With names like Captain Hook's Adventure Golf, (843) 626-1430, Mt. Atlanticus Miniature Golf, (843) 444-1008, and Dragon's Lair Fantasy Golf, (843) 444-3215, you and your family are guaranteed to have a ball. Price per person ranges from $4.50 to $6.50.

Pawleys Island   If you're going to laze away your beach vacation on a hammock, why not see first how these relaxing rope loungers are made. The Pawleys Island Rope Hammock has been produced on this small island since 1889, and today you can visit the Original Rope Hammock shop and watch hammock artisans at work, (843) 237-9122 or www.paw-leys.com. Pawleys Island also offers outlet and antique shopping, fabulous fresh seafood restaurants, and miles of unspoiled beach just 15 minutes from the crowds at Myrtle Beach. For more information, contact the Myrtle Beach Area Chamber of Commerce at (843) 626-7444.

Pedro's South of the Border, Dillon   If you have ever traversed the East Coast on I-95, no doubt you have seen the strange signs along the way call-ing you South of the Border. No, you are not close to Mexico, but rather one of the largest Mexican-themed restaurant/park/store–complexes in the country. Pedro's South of the Border is a notorious stop-off for tired travel-ers, but this kitschy attraction has also become a destination unto itself. Just over the North Carolina line, the 350-acre complex vends various wares from Mexico such as baskets, vases, and clothing, plus it has six restaurants and an adjacent hotel with more than 300 rooms. If anything, you will want to stop just to drive through gigantic Pedro's legs, which make up part of the Sombrero Tower. You can also take an elevator ride up to the top of the tower for a stunning view of nothing other than I-95. (800) 845-6011.

Family-Friendly Restaurants

MEDIEVAL TIMES

2904 Fantasy Way, Myrtle Beach; (843) 236-4635
www.medievaltimes.com

Meals served: Dinner
Cuisine: American
Entrée range: $34.75 adults, $18 children ages 12 and younger
Kids menu: No
Reservations: Required
Payment: All major credit cards

Enjoy jousting, dueling, and equestrian performances from the Middle Ages while you feast on a four-course meal fit for a knight. Medieval Times features a prix-fixe menu, which includes the price of two-hour show, dinner, and beverages.

MIDWAY DELI

7827 North Kings Highway, Myrtle Beach; (843) 449-9138

Meals served: Lunch and dinner
Cuisine: Delicatessen
Entrée range: $3.50–5.95
Kids menu: No
Reservations: No
Payment: V, MC

Grab sandwiches for the family and head to the beach for an impromptu picnic. Midway Deli is conveniently located minutes from two area golf courses and the beach, and they provide a quick-bites option for families on the go.

NASCAR CAFE

1808 21st Avenue North, Myrtle Beach; (843) 946-RACE
www.nascarcafe.com

Meals served: Lunch and dinner
Cuisine: American
Entrée range: $8.95–15.95
Kids menu: Yes
Reservations: Recommended

Payment: All major credit cards

NASCAR Cafe redefines the concept of "fast" food. Enjoy mouth-watering favorites like pork chops, fried catfish, and heaping hamburgers. Kids meals cost $5 and come with a drink.

SEA CAPTAIN'S HOUSE

3002 North Ocean Boulevard, Myrtle Beach; (843) 448-8082

Meals served: Breakfast, lunch, and dinner
Cuisine: Seafood
Entrée range: $6.50–24.95
Kids menu: Yes
Reservations: Recommended
Payment: All major credit cards

Enjoy the bounty of the ocean at the popluar Sea Captain's House. Your choice of fresh oyters, clams, crabs, shrimp, etc. can be prepared at least a dozen ways. Kids under 12 can choose from entrées of flounder, shrimp and other seafood combinations, crab cakes, and old-fashioned hamburgers. Breakfast favorites include hotcakes, French toast, and a crabmeat omelet.

Columbia

Families are welcome in Columbia, in part because the city is the state capital and home to a number of free historic and government-related sites. The **South Carolina State House** provides an interesting tour, and the grounds around the capitol building, containing multiple monuments, statues, and an old cannon, provide insight into the history of the state. Likewise, the **South Carolina State Museum** delves into the state's history, stretching as far back as prehistoric times but also covering more recent historical events.

Columbia is also home to kid-friendly attractions like the **Riverbanks Zoo and Gardens** and the **Columbia Museum of Art.** Children can learn about art in the museum's Children's Gallery or take part in demonstrations and activities. The Riverbanks Zoo has all the lions, tigers, and monkeys to excite kids of all ages and many more surprises, such as koala bears and warthogs.

A third factor for families to consider is that Columbia is a college town, home to the **University of South Carolina.** The local university culture helps to bring in exotic restaurants, exclusive art exhibits, multiple musical concerts, and other unexpected goodies—attractions that are affordable and often free.

Family Lodging

Clarion Town House Hotel

This historic hotel located in downtown Columbia puts you within minutes of the Columbia Art Museum, government buildings, the historic district, and the zoo. Rooms are tastefully decorated and are equipped with cable television and a clock radio. Services of the Clarion Town House Hotel include babysitting, laundry, and limited room service. Carolina's Restaurant and Lounge, Clarion's on-site restaurant, serves breakfast, lunch, and dinner daily

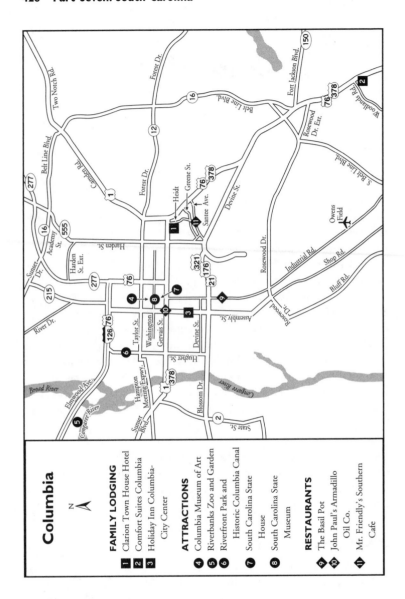

Columbia

N

FAMILY LODGING
1. Clarion Town House Hotel
2. Comfort Suites Columbia
3. Holiday Inn Columbia-City Center

ATTRACTIONS
4. Columbia Museum of Art
5. Riverbanks Zoo and Garden
6. Riverfront Park and Historic Columbia Canal
7. South Carolina State House
8. South Carolina State Museum

RESTAURANTS
9. The Basil Pot
10. John Paul's Armadillo Oil Co.
11. Mr. Friendly's Southern Cafe

until 10 p.m., although numerous eateries are located within walking distance of the hotel. Rates range from $70–200, and children younger than age 17 stay free with parents. 1615 Gervais Street, Columbia; (803) 771-8711; www.clarioninns.com.

Comfort Suites Columbia

Located minutes from downtown, the State Museum, and the Riverbanks Zoo and Gardens, this all-suite hotel has 67 rooms with a bedroom and convenient living area all in one. The suites are equipped with the usual: cable television, clock radio, modem jack, microwave, and mini-refrigerator. Comfort Suites has an indoor pool, a Jacuzzi, and fitness facilities. Rates start at $67, and kids age 18 and younger stay free with parents. 7337 Garner's Ferry Road, Columbia; (803) 695-5555; www.comfortsuites.com.

Holiday Inn Columbia-City Center

Tons of amenities equal a pleasant stay at the Holiday Inn City Center. Newly renovated rooms come with king or two queen beds, cable/satellite television, in-room movies, a two-line phone with a modem jack, voicemail, an iron and ironing board, AM/FM radio alarm clock, and more. The Holiday Inn has an outdoor pool, a fitness center, and a complimentary airport shuttle. Pets stay free, as do children younger than age 17. Rates start at $85; 630 Assembly Street, Columbia; (803) 799-7800 or (888) 979-6800.

Attractions

Columbia Museum of Art

Main and Hampton Streets, Columbia; (803) 799-2810
　www.colmusart.org

Hours:　Tuesday–Saturday, 10 a.m.–5 p.m.; Wednesday until 9 p.m.;
　Sunday, 1–5 p.m.

Admission:　$4 adults, $2 seniors and students

Appeal by Age Group:

Pre- school	Grade School	Teens	Young Adults	Over 30	Seniors
★★	★★★	★★★	★★★	★★★	★★★

Average Touring Time:　1½ hours

Minimum Touring Time:　1 hour

Rainy Day Touring:　Recommended

Author's Rating:　★★★

Services and Facilities:

Restaurants Yes	Lockers No
Alcoholic beverages No	Pet kennels No
Disabled access Yes	Rain check No
Wheelchair rental No	Private tours Yes
Baby stroller rental No	

Description and Comments   The surprising Columbia Museum of Art contains 17 galleries filled with hundreds of paintings from the Italian Renaissance to twentieth-century America. Visitors can also browse furniture, sculpture, and household items that are part of the museum's permanent collection. Budding artists can take part in the Just for Kids or Big Hands/Little Hands interactive art demonstrations.

Riverbanks Zoo and Garden

500 Wildlife Parkway, Columbia; (803) 779-8717
   www.riverbanks.org

Hours: Monday–Sunday, 9 a.m.–4 p.m.; until 5 p.m. during summer

Admission: $6.25 adults, $4.75 seniors, $5 students, $3.75 children
   ages 3–12

Appeal by Age Group:

Pre-school	Grade School	Teens	Young Adults	Over 30	Seniors
★★★★	★★★★	★★★★	★★★★	★★★★	★★★

Average Touring Time: 2½ hours

Minimum Touring Time: 2 hours

Rainy Day Touring: Not recommended

Author's Rating: ★★★★   Rated one of the ten great zoos of America

Services and Facilities:

Restaurants Yes	Lockers No
Alcoholic beverages No	Pet kennels No
Disabled access Yes	Rain check No
Wheelchair rental Yes	Private tours No
Baby stroller rental Yes	

Description and Comments   The cage-free environment of the Riverbanks Zoo and Gardens ensures that both animals and zoo visitors have a good time. Riverbanks Zoo is home to more than 2,000 animals, including not only the usual creatures like lions, tigers, giraffes, and bears, but also more exotic animals like lemurs, koalas, warthogs, Arctic foxes, and the highly endangered black rhino. These unusual residents are the main reason that the Riverbanks Zoo is continually rated among the best in the nation. The 70-acre Botanical Gardens keeps families occupied with its coves of flowers, tropical plants, and exhibits of local archaeological finds.

Riverfront Park and Historic Columbia Canal

Laurel and Huger Streets, Columbia; (803) 733-8331

Hours: Daily, 6 a.m.–9 p.m.

Admission: Free

Appeal by Age Group:

Pre-school	Grade School	Teens	Young Adults	Over 30	Seniors
★★★	★★★	★★★	★★★	★★★	★★

Average Touring Time: 2 hours

Minimum Touring Time: 1 hour

Rainy Day Touring: Not recommended

Author's Rating: ★★★ Relaxing way to spend the day

Services and Facilities:

Restaurants No	Lockers No
Alcoholic beverages No	Pet kennels No
Disabled access Yes	Rain check No
Wheelchair rental No	Private tours No
Baby stroller rental No	

Description and Comments No itinerary is required to visit Riverfront Park and the Columbia Canal. Explore the original Columbia Waterworks and pumphouse or simply stroll, bike, or inline skate through the park.

South Carolina State House

Main and Gervais Streets, Columbia; (803) 734-2430

Hours: Monday–Friday, 9 a.m.–5 p.m.; Saturday, 10 a.m.–5 p.m.; first Sunday of month, 1–5 p.m.

Admission: Free

Appeal by Age Group:

Pre-school	Grade School	Teens	Young Adults	Over 30	Seniors
★	★★	★★	★★	★★	★★

Average Touring Time: 1 hour

Minimum Touring Time: 30 minutes

Rainy Day Touring: Recommended

Author's Rating: ★★

Services and Facilities:

Restaurants No	Lockers No
Alcoholic beverages No	Pet kennels No
Disabled access Yes	Rain check No
Wheelchair rental No	Private tours Yes, on the hour
Baby stroller rental No	and half-hour

Description and Comments The South Carolina State House is an impressive building, with its large Corinthian columns, marble halls, and copper dome. But most people visit the building to view the six marble stars along the exterior walls that mark the spots where Union troops fired cannon during Sherman's destructive Civil War March to the Sea. Older students will likely be interested in the monuments and markers on the grounds of the State House, including a cannon from the battleship *Maine,* the statue of George Washington, and memorials to fallen soldiers.

South Carolina State Museum

301 Gervais Street, Columbia; (803) 898-4921
 www.museum.state.sc.us

Hours: Monday–Saturday, 10 a.m.–5 p.m.; Sunday, 1–5 p.m.

Admission: $4 adults, $3 seniors and college students, $1.50 children
 ages 6–17

Appeal by Age Group:

Pre-school	Grade School	Teens	Young Adults	Over 30	Seniors
★	★★★	★★★	★★★	★★★	★★★

Average Touring Time: 2 hours

Minimum Touring Time: 1 hour

Rainy Day Touring: Recommended

Author's Rating: ★★

Services and Facilities:

Restaurants No	Lockers No
Alcoholic beverages No	Pet kennels No
Disabled access Yes	Rain check No
Wheelchair rental No	Private tours No
Baby stroller rental No	

Description and Comments   South Carolina's long history is presented under one roof at this museum. Examine fossils and bones from prehistoric times and investigate the rich cultural history of the state with exhibits on Native Americans, African-American heritage, and the Revolutionary and Civil wars. In 2003, the museum will open a 150-seat planetarium.

Side Trips

Darlington County Raceway   NASCAR fans will want to make a sidetrip to Darlington, home of the famous Darlington Raceway and Joe Weatherly NMPA Stock Car Hall of Fame. Official NASCAR races are held at the Raceway: the TransSouth Financial 400 each spring and the Pepsi Southern 500 on Labor Day. The adjacent museum has one of the largest collections of stock cars anywhere. It is open daily from 8:30 a.m.–5 p.m.; admission is $3 adults and free for children 12 and younger. 1301 Harry Byrd Highway, Darlington; (843) 395-8821.

DuPont Planetarium, Aiken The University of South Carolina's satellite campus in Aiken is home to the acclaimed DuPont Planetarium. Here, families can explore the heavens in the 45-seat theater, aided by the technology of a variety of telescopes; a Digistar II projector, which explains three-dimensional space travel; and the only known camera obscura, which is able to display space images in real time. Beyond the technical jargon, the staff at the planetarium explains space phenomena with engaging lectures and interactive demonstrations. Especially for kids is the show "Larry Cat in Space," a humorous and elementary look at Earth, the sky, and astronomy through the eyes of a cat. Admission to the Planetarium is $4 for adults, $3 for seniors, and $2 for kids ages 4–17. 471 University Parkway, Aiken; (803) 641-3654.

Family-Friendly Restaurants

THE BASIL POT

928 Main Street, Columbia; (803) 799-0928

Meals served: Breakfast, lunch, and dinner
Cuisine: Vegetarian
Entrée range: $4.50–8.95
Kids menu: No
Reservations: Not necessary
Payment: All major credit cards accepted

This smoke-free vegetarian restaurant is the oldest of its kind in Columbia. The Basil Pot also serves some lean fish and chicken dishes, and bakes its own bread. The spinach lasagna and Mexican pie are especially tasty. A no-frills place just blocks form the capital.

JOHN PAUL'S ARMADILLO OIL CO.

1215 Assembly Street, Columbia; (803) 771-9902

Meals served: Lunch and dinner
Cuisine: American, barbecue
Entrée range: $7.95–24.95
Kids menu: Yes
Reservations: Not necessary
Payment: All major credit cards

Take a trip to the Old West and dine at this finger-lickin' ribs and steak restaurant. John Paul's, located downtown, serves Texas-sized portions of beef, chicken, and pork, and many spicy appetizers, including Armadillo Eggs (cheese-stuffed jalapeño peppers). Items on the kids' menu start at $1.95 and come with thick-cut fries. Over-the-top decor, including vintage signs and chandeliers made of deer antlers, provides for a spirited atmosphere.

MR. FRIENDLY'S SOUTHERN CAFE

2001 Greene Street, Columbia; (803) 254-7828

Meals served: Lunch and dinner
Cuisine: American/southern
Entrée range: $5.95–15.95
Kids menu: No
Reservations: Recommended
Payment: All major credit cards accepted

Enjoy entrées like cornbread catfish and shrimp-and-grits. Lunch is a good value—look for fresh salads, grilled chicken sandwiches, one-third-pound burgers, and daily blue plate specials of steak or chicken starting at $5.45. Near Five Points and the University of South Carolina.

Greenville

The Greenville area has blossomed since German automaker BMW built its United States plant in nearby Greer. The world-famous car manufacturer not only brought thousands of jobs to the area, but also prestige and, therefore, a growing list of new attractions, restaurants, and hotels.

This new influx of money has helped to make Greenville-area sites even better than before. The small **Greenville Zoo** has been able to expand, bringing in traveling exhibits from throughout the United States featuring animals such as lemurs and albino alligators. Meanwhile, the **Roper Mountain Science Center** continues to stimulate and entertain with its interactive science demonstrations and permanent attractions such as the Discovery Room. And, of course, Greenville's newest attraction, **BMW Zentrum,** with its extensive car, motorcycle, and aircraft collection, is drawing in tourists from around the world.

Family Lodging

Crowne Plaza Greenville

This 208-room hotel will put you within reach of Greenville's Roper Mountain Science Center and downtown. Amenities include cable television with Disney, ESPN, and Nickelodeon and in-room movies, coffee makers, hair dryers, irons and ironing boards, separate showers and baths, and modem jacks for laptops. On-site, you'll find an indoor pool, fitness facilities, and a sundeck. Rates range from $69 to $139 per night, and children age 19 and younger stay free with parents. 851 Congaree Road, Greenville; (864) 297-6300.

Hyatt Regency Greenville

If you want to stay in the heart of downtown Greenville, this is the hotel to choose. The high-rise property has 327 rooms, a health club, and an

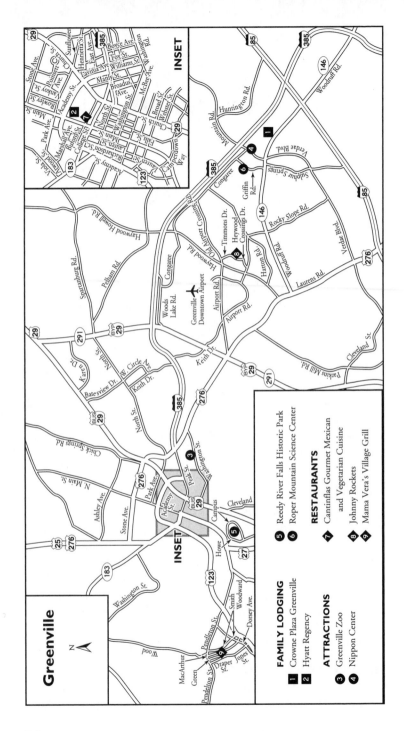

Greenville

INSET

INSET

FAMILY LODGING
1 Crowne Plaza Greenville
2 Hyatt Regency

ATTRACTIONS
3 Greenville Zoo
4 Nippon Center

5 Reedy River Falls Historic Park
6 Roper Mountain Science Center

RESTAURANTS
7 Cantinflas Gourmet Mexican and Vegetarian Cuisine
8 Johnny Rockets
9 Mama Vera's Village Grill

outdoor pool. Services at the Hyatt include laundry, part-time room service, babysitting, and valet parking. Guest rooms come equipped with cable television, in-room movies, voice mail, a dataport for laptops, an AM/FM alarm clock radio, double-sized bath amenities, and more. A restaurant and snack bar are open daily until 10 p.m. Rates start at $69, and children younger than age 17 stay free with parents. 220 North Main Street, Greenville; (864) 235-1234.

Attractions

Greenville Zoo

150 Cleveland Park Drive, Columbia; (864) 467-4300

Hours: Daily, 10 a.m.–4:30 p.m.

Admission: $4 adults, $2 children ages 3–15

Appeal by Age Group:

Pre-school	Grade School	Teens	Young Adults	Over 30	Seniors
★★★	★★★	★★★	★★★	★★★	★★★

Average Touring Time: 2 hours

Minimum Touring Time: 1 hour

Rainy Day Touring: Not recommended

Author's Rating: ★★★   Charming, small zoo

Services and Facilities:

Restaurants No	Lockers No
Alcoholic beverages No	Pet kennels No
Disabled access Yes	Rain check No
Wheelchair rental No	Private tours No
Baby stroller rental No	

Description and Comments   There are more than 100 animals in residence at the Greenville Zoo, including red pandas, elephants, and a white tiger. The year 2000 expansion of the zoo will allow for exhibits of leopards, orangutans, giraffes, and more. You can easily take a day to view areas such as Primate Row, South America, and the Lagoon, but the zoo is also small enough for a short morning or afternoon tour.

Nippon Center and Restaurant Yagoto

500 Congaree Road, Greenville; (864) 288-8471
   www.riceandgrits.com

Hours: Monday–Saturday, 6 a.m.–9:30 p.m.; tours by appointment only

Admission: Free with meal

Appeal by Age Group:

Pre-school	Grade School	Teens	Young Adults	Over 30	Seniors
★	★★	★★	★★★	★★★	★★★

Average Touring Time: 1 hour

Minimum Touring Time: 1 hour

Rainy Day Touring: Not recommended

Author's Rating: ★★★

Services and Facilities:

Restaurants Yes	Lockers No
Alcoholic beverages Yes	Pet kennels No
Disabled access Yes	Rain check No
Wheelchair rental No	Private tours Yes, by appoint-
Baby stroller rental No	ment only

Description and Comments A Japanese mansion and gardens in the heart of the Old South? Indeed, the meticulously landscaped estate of the Nippon Center is a refreshing break from the antebellum plantation homes that dot the Southern states. Walk among fragrant cherry trees, take photographs near a pond of lotus flowers, or meditate in a rock garden. The Nippon Center is an interesting way to introduce older children to other cultures, and you can even plan an afternoon tea ceremony for their entertainment. Tours of the Center are free if dining at the on-site Yagoto Restaurant. This five-star restaurant is expensive, but its cuisine is as authentic as its peaceful surroundings.

Reedy River Falls Historic Park

Howe Street, Greenville

Hours: Daily, dawn–dusk

Admission: Free

Appeal by Age Group:

Pre-school	Grade School	Teens	Young Adults	Over 30	Seniors
★★	★★	★★	★★	★★	★★

Average Touring Time: 1 hour

Minimum Touring Time: 30 minutes

Rainy Day Touring: Not recommended

Author's Rating: ★★

Services and Facilities:

Restaurants No

Alcoholic beverages No

Disabled access Yes

Wheelchair rental No

Baby stroller rental No

Lockers No

Pet kennels No

Rain check No

Private tours No

Description and Comments   This swath of green in the middle of downtown is somewhat apropos for a town called "Greenville." The Reedy River Falls Historical Park contains six landscaped gardens and two waterfalls, all upon the site of the first Greenville settlement of 1776. Reedy River Falls is great for picnics.

Roper Mountain Science Center

402 Roper Mountain Road, Greenville; (864) 281-1188
   www.ropermountain.org

Hours: Monday–Friday, 8 a.m.–5 p.m.; Saturday, 10 a.m.–5 p.m.;
   Sunday, 1–5 p.m.

Admission: $4 adults, $2 seniors, students, and children ages 6–12

Appeal by Age Group:

Pre-school	Grade School	Teens	Young Adults	Over 30	Seniors
★	★★★	★★★	★★★	★★★	★★

Average Touring Time: 2 hours

Minimum Touring Time: 1 hour

Rainy Day Touring: Recommended

Author's Rating: ★★

Services and Facilities:

Restaurants No

Alcoholic beverages No

Disabled access Yes

Wheelchair rental No

Baby stroller rental No

Lockers No

Pet kennels No

Rain check No

Private tours No

Description and Comments   Kids of all ages can explore Star Station One to learn more about the planned International Space Station, or take part in hands-on science experiments and demonstrations. Each Friday, the Science Center invites visitors to its Starry Nights program to gaze at the stars (children must be five or older to attend). Other areas of the center that are worth a look are the Butterfly Garden and the Discovery Room, which houses live reptiles, amphibians, birds, and a honeybee hive.

Side Trips

Paramount's Carowinds, Fort Mill   There are a million things for kids to enjoy at Paramount's Carowinds, such as thrilling roller coasters, soaking water rides, and loads of live dance and music shows. The Zoom Zone and the Animation Station, with Jellystone Garden theme ride and the Scooby-Doo Ghoster Coaster, are perfect for younger children. The park is open daily from mid-March until October, and day prices are $35 for everyone older than age 6 and $23 for children ages 3 to 6. Take I-77; 14523 Carowinds Boulevard, Fort Mill; (800) 888-4386; www.carowinds.com.

BMW Zentrum, Greer   The ultimate museum experience awaits you at BMW Zentrum, the Greenville area's most famous workplace. The plant in Greer houses a museum of BMW memorabilia and an entire range of BMW products, including James Bond's roadster from *Goldeneye,* various Formula One racecars, stealth motorcycles, and jet engines. An adjacent gift shop sells everything from caps to key chains. For families that want to see how the German cars are built from start to finish, BMW Zentrum offers a plant tour.

Note: Children younger than 12 are not permitted to tour the factory. Museum tours are free, but tours of the plant must be arranged in advance. BMW Zentrum is open Tuesday–Friday from 9:30 a.m.–5:30 p.m.; cost is $5 for adults and $3.50 for students. 1400 West Highway 101 South; (800) TOUR-BMW or (864) 989-5537; www.bmwzentrum.com.

Ferne's Miniature Dollhouse Museum and Shop   Doll-lovers will marvel at this collection of more than 400 antique and contemporary dolls at Ferne's Miniature Dollhouse Museum. Also featured at the museum and shop are miniature dollhouses, furnishings, and clothing, from pint-size wicker tables to adorable dresses. The museum and shop are open by appointment only, and are worth the short drive from Greenville. 510 Flat Rock Road; (864) 843-2486.

Family-Friendly Restaurants

CANTINFLAS GOURMET MEXICAN AND VEGETARIAN CUISINE

120 North Main Street, Greenville; (864) 250-1300

Meals served: Lunch and dinner
Cuisine: Mexican/vegetarian

Entrée range: $4.55–9.95
Kids menu: Yes
Reservations: Suggested for groups of five or more
Payment: All major credit cards accepted

Cantinflas specializes in Mexican favorites, such as beef tacos, fajitas, and tamales, and also offers a wide variety of healthy, vegetarian options. Near downtown attractions. The restaurant is named after legendary Mexican clown Cantinflas, whose lively demeanor, the owners say, inspired them to open a warm and welcoming restaurant. This is reflected in the friendly waitstaff. The kids menu has at least seven healthy options starting at $2.95.

JOHNNY ROCKETS

401 Haywood Road, Greenville; (864) 627-0405

Meals served: Lunch and dinner
Cuisine: American
Entrée range: $2.85–4.70
Kids menu: Yes
Reservations: No
Payment: All major credit cards accepted

This 1950s–style chain makes some of the best burgers around. You can also enjoy onion rings, milk shakes, hot dogs, and live entertainment from the staff. Located minutes from downtown Greenville and area golf courses.

MAMA VERA'S VILLAGE GRILL

907 Pendleton Street, Greenville; (864) 239-0218

Meals served: Breakfast and lunch
Cuisine: Italian/American
Entrée range: $1–9.99
Kids menu: Yes
Reservations: No
Payment: All major credit cards accepted

Choose from hearty Italian cuisine or stick-to-your-ribs southern food. Mama Vera's offers a number of $0.99 breakfast specials. All meals are made from scratch daily, and the prices can't be beat. Not far from recreational areas like Reedy River Falls Park.

Part Eight

Tennessee

Fenced in on the west by the mighty Mississippi River and on the east by the Great Smoky Mountains, Tennessee is a natural playground, complete with caves, cliffs, lakes, rapids, wildlife, and plenty of wide-open spaces. "Rocky Top," one of Tennessee's more memorable state songs, describes the state as a laid-back land, free from the pollution and problems of the city: "Ain't no smoggy smoke on Rocky Top, ain't no telephone bills." And, for the most part, this is the case.

Tennessee is also a musical playground. **Memphis'** Beale Street is considered Home of the Blues, and it turned musicians like B.B. King and Bessie Smith into legends. Rock and roll's roots can also be traced back to Memphis, where a young Elvis Presley recorded his first of many classic songs. Thriving **Nashville** is called "Music City USA" and is known for its country tunes. Both **Knoxville** and **Chattanooga** have produced blues and bluegrass artists. Almost every city and town has its own soundtrack.

As a tourist destination, Tennessee beats most other states in the South in sheer number of things to do. In Memphis, you can visit **Graceland,** play at the **Children's Museum,** learn about equality at the **National Civil Rights Museum,** or simply stroll down **Beale Street.** In Nashville, musical museums await, with tours of the **Grand Ole Opry** or the studios of the **Nashville Network.** Chattanooga has the **Choo Choo** and educational venues like the **Creative Discovery Museum** and the impressive **Tennessee Aquarium.** Knoxville is a gateway to the **Great Smoky Mountains** and home to the **World's Fair Park** (brought to the city in 1982), the always-fun **Knoxville Zoo,** and the brand-new **Women's Basketball Hall of Fame Museum.**

Tennessee is an ideal travel destination year round. Fall and spring are the most temperate months to visit. Although summers can be extremely hot, with temperatures well into the 90s, travelers can escape to the cool air of the Smoky Mountains. In winter, these mountains become a winter sports playground, snow permitting.

GETTING THERE

By Plane. Tennessee's largest airports are Memphis International Airport, (901) 922-8000, and Nashville International Airport, (615) 275-1600. Both are served by the major airline carriers—Delta, Continental, USAirways, United, Northwest, and American—and are within minutes of their respective cities. Chattanooga Metropolitan Airport, (423) 855-2200, and McGhee Tyson Airport in Knoxville, (865) 970-2773, are good bets if you are traveling to destinations in the eastern part of the state. However, flights into these regional airports are often preceded by a connection in Memphis or Nashville, and are often on small, puddle-jumper planes, which are noisy and somewhat uncomfortable. Another option if you were going east would be to fly into Nashville International Airport and rent a car. This is a great way to see more of Tennessee, and you will likely save money on your flight.

By Train. Amtrak makes stops in Memphis and Newbern-Dyersburg only. For information on fares and schedules, call (800) USA-RAIL or visit their website at www.amtrak.com.

By Car. Interstate 40 bisects the state horizontally and runs from Memphis through Nashville to Knoxville and beyond. Interstate 24 runs diagonally from Chattanooga to Nashville, whereas I-75 travels northeast from Chattanooga to Knoxville. A majority of Tennessee's attractions can be reached via these highways. Tennessee laws require that all drivers, front-seat passengers, and children ages 4–12 wear seatbelts. Children younger than four must be restrained in a child restraint device. For more information on Tennessee highways and road conditions or to download state and city maps, see the Department of Transportation's website at www.state.tn.us/transport.

HOW TO GET INFORMATION BEFORE YOU GO

State

Tennessee Department of Tourist Development, 320 Sixth Avenue North, Fifth Floor, Rachel Jackson Building, Nashville 37243; (800) 491-TENN; www.tourism.state.tn.us

Tennessee Historical Commission, 2941 Lebanon Road, Nashville 37243-0442; (615) 532-1550

Tennessee Wildlife Resources Agency, P.O. Box 40747, Ellington Agricultural Center, Nashville 37204; (615) 781-6500

Back Roads Heritage Association, 300 South Jackson, Tullahoma 37388; (800) 799-6131

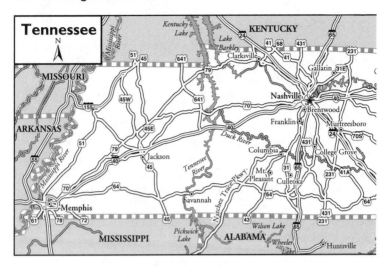

Regional

Upper Cumberland Tourism Association, P.O. Box 2411, Cookeville 38502; (615) 520-1088

East Tennessee Heritage and Community Tourism Development, 531 Henley Street, 703 New State Office Building, Knoxville 37902; (423) 594-5500

Middle East Tennessee Tourism Council, 5616 Kingston Park, Knoxville 37919; or P.O. Box 19806, Knoxville 37939; (423) 584-8553

Northeast Tennessee Tourism Association, Box 415, Jonesborough 37659; (423) 753-4188, Ext. 25 or (800) 468-6882, Ext. 25

Southeast Tennessee Tourism Association, 1001 Market Street, Chattanooga 37402; (423) 756-8687

South Central Tennessee Tourism Organization, 215 Frank Street, Lawrenceburg 38464; (615) 762-6944

Tennessee Natchez Trace Corridor Association, 203 Third Avenue South, Franklin 37064; (615) 794-5555

West Tennessee Heritage and Community Tourism Development, 225 Martin Luther King Drive, Suite 305, Jackson 38301; (901) 426-0888

Memphis Delta Tourism Organization, P.O. Box 53, Collierville 38027; (901) 854-6123

Northwest Tennessee Tourism Organization, P.O. Box 963, Martin 38237; (901) 587-4215

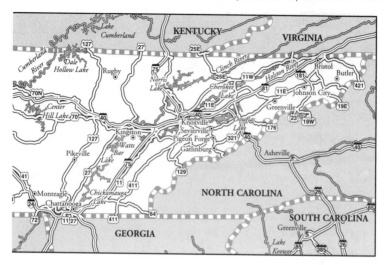

Tourism Association of Southwest Tennessee, 21275 Highway 22 North, Wildersville 38388; (901) 968-6026; www.tast.tn.org

Middle Tennessee Heritage and Community Tourism Development, 320 Sixth Avenue North, Fifth Floor, Rachel Jackson Building, Nashville 37243; (615) 741-9045

Local

Memphis Convention and Visitors Bureau, 47 Union Avenue, Memphis 38103; (901) 543-5300; www.memphistravel.com

Greater Nashville Regional Tourism Council, 501 Union Street, Sixth Floor, Nashville 37219-1705; (615) 862-8828; www.musiccityusa.com

---

Tennessee Websites for Kids

Tennessee symbols www.geobop.com/world/na/us/tn

Knoxville for Kids www.knoxville-tn.com/kids.html

Government Pages for Kids www.state.tn.us/governor/kidslink.htm

Tennessee Titans Kid's Corner www.titansonline.com/kidscorner

State of Tennessee Kid's Pages www.state.tn.us/kids.html

Memphis Kids and Blues co-nect.memphis-schools.k12.tn.us/blues

Nashville Kids nashvillekids.com

Knoxville Kids www.knoxville-tn.com/kids.html

Kids' Beat

- Three U.S. presidents once called Tennessee home: Andrew Jackson (1829–37), James K. Polk (1845–49), and Andrew Johnson (1865–69).

- Tennessee is commonly referred to as the Volunteer State. This nickname originated during the War of 1812, when Tennessee volunteer soldiers, under the command of General Andrew Jackson, fought bravely in the Battle of New Orleans.

- The longest continuously running live radio program in the world is the Grand Ole Opry, which was first broadcast over Nashville's WSM Radio in 1925.

- There are more than 3,800 caves in Tennessee.

- Rhea County, Tennessee, was the site of the controversial Scopes "Monkey Trial" in 1925. The trial's verdict allowed John T. Scopes, and all science teachers thereafter, to teach the theory of evolution in their classrooms.

- Tennessee's state birds are the mockingbird and the bobwhite quail, also known as a partridge; the state flowers are the purple iris and the passionflower; the state tree is the tulip poplar; and the state insects are the firefly and the ladybug.

Chattanooga Convention and Visitors Bureau, 2 Broad Street, Chattanooga 37402; (423) 756-8687 or (800) 322-3344; www.chattanoogacvb.com

Knoxville Convention and Visitors Bureau, 601 West Summit Hill Drive, Suite 200-B, Knoxville 37902-9865; (865) 523-7263 or (800) 727-8045; www.knoxville.org

Family Outdoor Adventures

▲ - Camping
♥ - Author's favorite

▲ - *Cherokee National Forest*   The only National Forest in Tennessee, the Cherokee National Forest was named after the Native American tribe that hid within this vast woodland as U.S. General Winfield Scott was rounding up

Tennessee's Not-to-Be-Missed Attractions	
Around the State	Great Smoky Mountains
Memphis	Beale Street C.H. Nash–Chucalissa Archaeological Museum Graceland Lichterman Nature Center Mud Island River Park National Civil Rights Museum
Nashville	Country Music Hall of Fame and Museum Grand Ole Opry Imaginarium The Parthenon
Chattanooga	Chattanooga Choo Choo Creative Discovery Museum Lookout Mountain Tennessee Aquarium
Knoxville	Knoxville Zoo Women's Basketball Hall of Fame World's Fair Park

Cherokees for exile via the Trail of Tears. In fact, the Eastern Band of the tribe still lives within this area and especially across the border in North Carolina.

The Cherokee National Forest is split by the Great Smoky Mountains and provides over 540 miles of trails for hiking, biking, and horseback riding. However, the area is better known for its whitewater rapids in the Ocoee River Corridor. In 1996, the Centennial Olympics staged its canoe and kayak slalom events along this scenic and challenging waterway. Class III and IV rapids can be found in this area, but there are also family-friendly Class I and II rapids, which serve as an excellent introduction to a wet-and-wild adventure. Contact Ocoee River Whitewater Corridor at (423) 338-5201 and the Ocoee Whitewater Center at (423) 496-5197.

Camping is permitted along the banks of the Ocoee and throughout the Cherokee National Forest. Daily fees range from $5–17, depending on the season. 2800 North Ocoee Street, Cleveland 37311; (423) 476-9700.

♥ - *Cumberland Caverns* Spelunkers list Tennessee as one of their top destinations because of the state's numerous grottos and caverns. Among the most awesome of these is Cumberland Caverns, located between Chattanooga and Nashville. This National Landmark is Tennessee's largest cave and contains one cavern called the Underground Ballroom—a room shaped by nature and used by mankind for thousands of years. Also within Cumberland Caverns, you can examine enormous stalactites and stalagmites (icicle-like formations of dirt and clay), visit an historic saltpeter mine, and listen to the rush of waterfalls. 1437 Cumberland Caverns Road, McMinnville 37110; (931) 668-4396; www.cumberlandcaverns.com.

▲ ♥ – *Great Smoky Mountains National Park* With over nine million visitors per year, the Smokies are the most visited National Park and by far one of the most visited natural attractions in the state. Spanning over 500,000 acres throughout the southeastern tip of Tennessee into western North Carolina, the Smoky Mountains are inspiring and rejuvenating for adults and children alike. A drive along the winding mountain paths is recommended if a camping adventure is not an option. And, with over 800 miles of hiking trails, including stretches of the Appalachian Trail, there are plenty of opportunities to explore the hundreds of plant and animal species indigenous to the area.

If you are planning a camping trip to the Smoky Mountains, there are approximately ten front-country (i.e., developed) and backcountry campground options, each ranging from $10–15 per night depending on the campground type and the time of year. One of the more popular front-country campgrounds in the park is Cades Cove, which includes a visitors center upon its perch of over 1,800 feet. All campgrounds have toilets and cold running water on site, and all but Big Creek Campground accept RVs, though you should call ahead to inquire about RV size limits; (800) 365-CAMP; www.reservations.nps.gov.

Whether you plan to set up camp in the Smokies or just visit them on a day trip, you should take advantage of the opportunity to hike, bike, or fish in the area. Biking is permitted on almost all of the park's unfinished roads and is one of our favorite ways to get some exercise while breathing the fresh mountain air. Anglers must have a Tennessee or North Carolina fishing license, and these must be obtained through local chambers of commerce. The minimum age for a fishing license is 13 in Tennessee (16 in North Carolina). And, while self-led hikes are fun, you may want to arrange an educational, ranger-led hike, which is available in spring, summer, and fall. 107 Park Headquarters Road, Gatlinburg 37738; (423) 436-1200; www.nps.gov/grsm.

Lichterman Nature Center   Escape from the Memphis bustle to this 65-acre wildlife sanctuary and education facility. The center features a three-mile walking trail and picnic areas are set up around the ten-acre lake. Visitors can also participate in environmental education programs, where they will learn about plant and animal life of the mid-South. Lichterman Nature Center is open Tuesday–Saturday 9:30 a.m.–5 p.m. and Sunday 1–5 p.m. 5992 Quince Road, Memphis; (901) 767-7322.

▲ - *Reelfoot Lake State Park*   Often overshadowed by Tennessee's larger natural attractions, Reelfoot Lake State Park in the northwestern corner of the state is a haven for anglers and birdwatchers. In fact, one of the prime winter nesting areas for the American bald eagle is here. Visitors can take guided tours in January and February and per chance view the majestic bird in its natural habitat.

The rest of the year, the Reelfoot Lake area is ideal for fishing. Over 15,000 of its 25,000 acres are comprised of lakes and wetland areas and these contain what is considered the world's largest natural fish hatchery. A number of camping sites are on the grounds, and lodging is in the nearby town of Tiptonville; (901) 253-7756.

♥ - *Tennessee Titans Professional Football*   Tennessee is home to the successful Tennessee Titans franchise from the National Football League. In 1999, the relatively new team made it all the way to the Super Bowl. Football is practically a religion in this state, and watching a game at Adelphia Coliseum in Nashville is one of the great ways to spend a Sunday afternoon or Monday night—if you can get a ticket. One Titans Way, Nashville; (888) 313-8326.

Calendar of Festivals and Events

January

Elvis Presley Birthday Celebration, Memphis   January 8 is the King's birthday, and each year Graceland Mansion throws a party complete with birthday cake. Other events, including live musical concerts, are scheduled over several days to celebrate the life of Elvis and to mark the end of the holiday season; (800) 238-2000; www.elvis-presley.com.

February

Annual Smoky Mountains Storytelling Festival, Pigeon Forge   Folklore is passed down each year at this storytelling festival in Pigeon Forge. Families are encouraged to sit a spell and hear a tale; (865) 429-7350.

March

Mule Day, Columbia   Some have said that what New York City is to stocks, Columbia is to mules. The town celebrates its favorite asset each year with a parade, music, square dancing and clogging performances, and mule shows. Also featured are a flea market and an arts and crafts fair; (931) 381-9557.

April

Dogwood Arts Festival, Knoxville   Here's a festival that celebrates art of all kinds, including music, dance, crafts, photography—and the beginning of spring. Also on view at this time are 60 miles of blossoming dogwood trees; (865) 637-4561; www.korrnet.org/dogwood.

Annual Dolly Parade, Pigeon Forge   Your chance to see Tennessee's favorite daughter, Dolly Parton (and possibly other celebrities), happens each year at the Dolly Parade. Pigeon Forge's way of kicking off spring includes marching bands, floats, and family fun; (865) 429-7350; www.pigeon-forge.tn.us.

Old Time Bluegrass & Fiddler's Championship, Holladay   West Tennessee honors its musical tradition with a bluegrass and fiddling festival. Between the picking, plucking, and grinning, watch parades and enjoy barbecue; (901) 584-3145 or (901) 584-8395; www.bentoncountynet.com.

National Cornbread Festival, South Pittsburg   The South's staple bread is given top billing at the Cornbread Festival. Sample different varieties from the Championship Cook-off, browse tables of arts and crafts exhibits, or take a tour of the town. Children's activities like finger painting and potato-sack races are part of the fun; (423) 837-0022; www.nationalcornbread.com.

May

Memphis in May International Festival, Memphis   Memphis' biggest party of the year lasts the entire month of May. Learn about the year's featured country, catch a show at the Beale Street Music Festival, or chow down on the best barbecue at the World Championship Barbecue Cooking Contest. This promises to have something the whole family will enjoy; (901) 525-4611.

Nashville River Stages, Nashville   A weekend of music at Riverfront Park in downtown Nashville. Over 60 bands appear on six stages; (615) 641-5800; www.nashvilleriverstages.com.

Annual American Indian Celebration & Pow Wow, Knoxville   An opportunity to learn about the many Native American peoples that inhabited this area, the celebration includes pow wow dance ceremonies, craft demonstrations, storytelling, and more; (865) 579-1384.

Running of the Iroquois Memorial Steeplechase, Nashville One of the premier horse-jumping and racing events in Tennessee happens each year at Percy Warner Park. The beautiful May weather is perfect for picnics on the grass; (615) 322-7450; www.iroquoissteeplechase.org.

Gatlinburg Scottish Festival & Games Experience the culture of the Scottish highlands in the Smokies during these festive games. Hear bagpipe musicians and watch border collie competitions, sheep shearing, and a parade of tartans. Or, watch men and women compete in battle-axe throwing, Highland wrestling, and other events. Kids are invited to participate in less challenging games; (865) 457-8242.

June

Ducks Unlimited Outdoor Festival, Memphis Featuring a variety of booths on outdoor activities such as biking, hunting, archery, bird watching, and conservation; (323) 782-2900.

Riverbend Festival, Chattanooga Chattanooga's musical moment in the spotlight comes each year with the Riverbend Festival. Over 100 artists perform in the span of nine days. Also included are fine-arts exhibits, food fairs, and family activities. The end of the festival is marked by a dazzling fireworks display; (423) 265-4112.

International Country Music Fan Fair, Nashville Meet your favorite stars of country music during this weeklong festival and jam session. This is one of Nashville's best events of the year, and, thus, one of the busiest; (615) 889-7503.

Kuumba Festival, Knoxville Usually occurring late June to early July, the lively Kuumba Festival explores African culture through art, dance, and music. Kids will surely love the drum sessions; (865) 525-0961.

July

Gatlinburg Craftsmen's Fair, Gatlinburg Escape to the cool hills of Gatlinburg during the Annual Craftsmen's Fair, where you can watch over 150 artisans from Tennessee and beyond demonstrate their skills. Artworks include unique vases, original paintings, woodcrafts, toys and more; (865) 436-7479; www.craftsmenfair.com.

August

Elvis Week, Memphis If you are in Memphis in mid-August, you will realize how influential the legend of Elvis Presley is on the city and hordes of tourists. The week consists of dozens of events to commemorate the life and career of The King of Rock and Roll, from free musical events to Elvis film screenings. And, on the final day, a candlelight vigil is held to mark Presley's passing; Graceland; (800) 238-2000; www.elvis-presley.com.

Tennessee Walking Horse National Celebration, Shelbyville   Known throughout the world as the most refined of horse breeds, the Tennessee Walking Horse is honored at this celebration. This ten-day event takes place in Shelbyville, just south of Nashville, and ends with the crowning of the World Grand Champion; (931) 684-5915; www.twhnc.com.

September

Tennessee State Fair, Nashville   Ongoing in Nashville since 1906, the Tennessee State Fair is one of the South's biggest fairs. Each fall, the fair features a wide variety of games, livestock and agricultural exhibits, arts and crafts tables, food, and music; (615) 862-8980.

Sequoyah Festival & Pow Wow, Vonore   The tiny town of Vonore, east of Chattanooga, boasts the birthplace of Sequoyah, the Cherokee Nation's best known statesman. The yearly festival celebrates Vonore's indigenous heritage with Native-American dancing, storytelling, craft demonstrations, and games; (423) 884-6246; www.sequoyahmuseum.org.

October

National Storytelling Festival, Jonesborough   A vast number of the nation's most dynamic storytellers are brought together at this decades-old festival. Hear everything from Tennessee folk yarns, to worldly fairy tales, to stories told to the tune of banjos or the beat of African tribal drums; (423) 753-2171 or (800) 952-8392; www.storytellingfestival.net.

November

Annual Pigeon Forge Winterfest Kickoff, Pigeon Forge   The mountain town of Pigeon Forge celebrates the arrival of winter with a two-month festival of games, cook-offs, arts and crafts shows, and musical events; (865) 429-7350; www.pigeon-forge.tn.us.

December

Christmas at Graceland, Memphis   A great time to visit Graceland is around Christmas, when the estate is decorated with Elvis' original Christmas lights. Each room of the mansion also has an ornate Christmas tree; (800) 238-2000; www.elvis-presley.com.

Dickens of a Christmas, Franklin   On the second weekend of December, citizens of the town of Franklin, just south of Nashville, dress up in Victorian costumes and re-create Christmas Past, complete with Dickens' characters, including Scrooge. Carolers stroll through downtown, artisans display their wares, and horse-drawn carriages clip-clop down Main Street. Many restaurants also serve special nineteenth-century menus; (615) 791-9924; www.historicfranklin.com.

Memphis

Memphis contains all the trappings of a chic, cosmopolitan city, with its steel skyscrapers, electrifying music scene, and its role as the number one shipping and distribution center in the country. But if you look closely in the windows on **Beale Street** or past the boutiques clustered around the famed **Peabody Hotel,** you will find that Memphis is a simple southern town whose energy ebbs and flows like the tides of the Mississippi.

Travelers come to Memphis for a variety of reasons. For the music lover, Memphis offers **Elvis Presley's Graceland** estate, one of the most visited attractions in the country. Of course, had it not been for Memphis-based **Sun Recording Studios** and the legacy of Beale Street Blues, the world probably never would have heard of the "King."

Another King attracted followers to Memphis, and, in turn, helped pave the way toward racial equality. Those interested in American history need look no further than Memphis, where in 1968 Martin Luther King, Jr. led hundreds of striking sanitation workers in the fight for living wages, only to be assassinated days later at the infamous Lorraine Motel. The city of Memphis holds keys to the past, as evidenced by the **Chucalissa Indian Village** and several antebellum homes, but it is ever looking toward the future, as the music plays on.

Unless you enjoy large crowds, plan to avoid Memphis during the second week of August, as the annual **"Elvis Week"** takes place then, resulting in heavy traffic and over-the-top hotel prices. What's more, Memphis summers are very hot and humid. September and October are the driest and mildest times of the year as well as the least busy. A trip during the month of May can also be quite enjoyable, as the weather is relatively temperate and the Memphis in May International Festival offers a host of family-friendly activities.

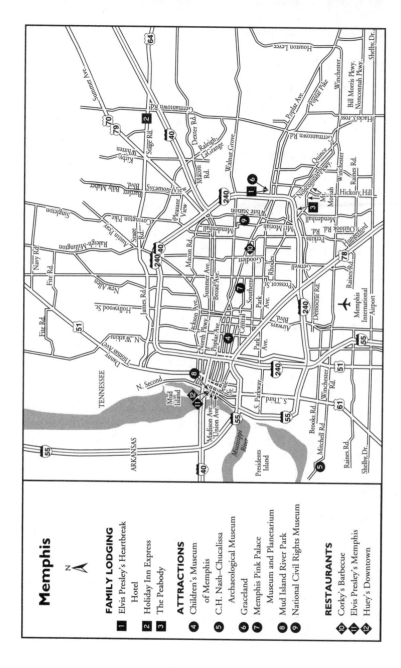

Memphis

N

FAMILY LODGING

1 Elvis Presley's Heartbreak Hotel

2 Holiday Inn Express

3 The Peabody

ATTRACTIONS

4 Children's Museum of Memphis

5 C.H. Nash–Chucalissa Archaeological Museum

6 Graceland

7 Memphis Pink Palace Museum and Planetarium

8 Mud Island River Park

9 National Civil Rights Museum

RESTAURANTS

10 Corky's Barbecue

11 Elvis Presley's Memphis

12 Huey's Downtown

Family Lodging

Elvis Presley's Heartbreak Hotel

You can't help falling in love with this 128-room hotel located directly across the street from Graceland Mansion. For entertainment, the hotel features free in-room Elvis movies and a heart-shaped outdoor swimming pool. Each room comes with a kitchenette (complete with a refrigerator and microwave), cable television, and voice mail–equipped telephone. Regular guest rooms start at $89.95, whereas regular suites are priced at $104.95. If you are feeling a bit more adventurous, the Heartbreak Hotel offers specialty themed suites starting at around $400. Expect these rates to increase in January during the Elvis Birthday Celebration and in August during Elvis Week. On-site parking is available, though the hotel also offers complimentary airport shuttle service. Kids ages 17 and younger stay free with parents. 3677 Elvis Presley Boulevard, Memphis; (877) 777-0606 or (901) 332-1000; www.heartbreakhotel.net.

Holiday Inn Express

Although it is a bit removed from downtown attractions, the Holiday Inn Express is a comfortable option starting at $65. The hotel's 108 rooms and suites are quite spacious and feature a refrigerator, a coffee maker, and an iron and ironing board. Some deluxe suites also have a microwave. All rooms allow disabled access. A free breakfast bar is included in the price of a room. Kids younger than age 19 stay free—and there is plenty to keep them busy at or near the hotel. In-room movies and Nintendo are available for a small fee, and older kids will likely enjoy visiting the Wolfchase Galleria Mall, which is less than a mile away. 8635 Highway 64, Memphis; (901) 372-0000 or (800) HOLIDAY.

The Peabody

If you are willing to shell out the extra bucks, you and your family will relish the luxury of the famed Peabody Hotel. The kids, of course, will love the ducks. The 468-room, 15-suite Peabody is known for its troop of parading ducks, which literally march through the lobby to the elegant fountain every day at 11 a.m. for their daily swim. In terms of amenities, the historic downtown hotel has 24-hour room service, three restaurants, a fitness club, an indoor pool, and shops. Rates for rooms and deluxe suites range from $150 to $270 and require a $30 extra-person fee. 149 Union Avenue, Memphis; (901) 529-4000 or (800) PEABODY; www.peabodymemphis.com.

Attractions

The Children's Museum of Memphis

2525 Central Avenue, Memphis; (901) 458-2678 or (901) 320-3170
  www.cmom.com

Hours: Tuesday–Saturday, 9 a.m.–5 p.m.; Sunday, noon–5 p.m.

Admission: $5 adults and teens; $4 seniors and children ages 12 and
  younger

Appeal by Age Groups:

Pre-school	Grade School	Teens	Young Adults	Over 30	Seniors
★★★★★	★★★★★	★	★	★★	★★

Average Touring Time: 1½ hours

Minimum Touring Time: 1 hour

Rainy Day Touring: Recommended

Author's Rating: ★★★   Child-sized museum = full-sized fun

Services and Facilities:

Restaurants No	Lockers No
Alcoholic beverages No	Pet kennels No
Disabled access Yes	Rain check No
Wheelchair rental No	Private tours Yes
Baby stroller rental No	

Description and Comments   An obvious choice for the young ones, The
Children's Museum of Memphis allows your kids to escape the boring adult
world while simultaneously learning more about it. This restored building,
adjacent to the Liberty Bowl Stadium, houses a kid-sized city with a bank,
post office, grocery store, and more. Children don't realize they are learning,
even when they are "buying" groceries or visiting the neighborhood "dentist."
A full-size fire engine also provides plenty of fun. The museum changes its
exhibits every three to four months; call ahead to learn of upcoming events.

C.H. Nash–Chucalissa Archaeological Museum

1987 Indian Village Drive, Memphis; (901) 785-3160
  www.people.memphis.edu/~chucalissa

Hours: Tuesday–Saturday, 9 a.m.–5 p.m.; Sunday, 1–4:30 p.m.

Admission: $5 adults, $3 seniors and children ages 4–11, free ages 3
  and younger

Appeal by Age Group:

Pre-school	Grade School	Teens	Young Adults	Over 30	Seniors
★	★★★	★★★★★	★★★★★	★★★★★	★★★★★

Average Touring Time: 1½ hours

Minimum Touring Time: 1 hour

Rainy Day Touring: Not recommended

Author's Rating: ★★★★ Fascinating look at Native American life

Services and Facilities:

Restaurants No	Lockers No
Alcoholic beverages No	Pet kennels No
Disabled access Yes	Rain check No
Wheelchair rental No	Private tours Yes
Baby stroller rental No	

Description and Comments　Just outside downtown Memphis lies the Chucalissa Archaeological Museum, which documents the life of Native American tribes once living in the area. Inside the museum, glimpse artifacts of early Choctaw tribes or look on as Native American staff members demonstrate traditional weaving, pottery making, and other crafts. Outside is a reconstructed, fifteenth-century Choctaw village, which offers insight into the daily lives of Mississippian-era tribes.

The museum offers a number of special events, including Archaeology Days, and it recently set up an archaeological explorer post that gives children a hands-on learning experience. We found the history lesson was enjoyable for adults, too.

Graceland, Home of Elvis Presley

3734 Elvis Presley Boulevard, Memphis; (901) 332-3322, (800) 238-2000, or TDD (901) 344-3146; www.elvis-presley.com

Hours:　Open Monday–Saturday, 9 a.m.–5 p.m.; Sunday, 10 a.m.–4 p.m.; mansion closed Tuesdays November–February

Admission:　Mansion tour: $10 adults, $9 seniors, $5 ages 7–12, free ages 6 and younger; Platinum tour (admission to all attractions): $19.50 adults, $17.55 seniors, $11 ages 7—12, free for children ages 6 and younger

Appeal by Age Group:

Pre-school	Grade School	Teens	Young Adults	Over 30	Seniors
★★★	★★★	★★★★★	★★★★★	★★★★★	★★★★★

Average Touring Time: 2 hours

Minimum Touring Time: 1 hour

Rainy Day Touring: Recommended

Author's Rating: ★★★★★ See how America's King once lived

Services and Facilities:

Restaurants Yes	Wheelchair rental Yes
Alcoholic beverages Yes	Baby stroller rental Yes
Disabled access Yes, except for	Lockers Yes
two rooms in the mansion and	Pet kennels No
the airplane tour. Ask for spe-	Rain check Yes
cial discounts.	Private tours Yes

Description and Comments Make no mistake, this should be your first stop in Memphis, as it is one of the longest and most enjoyable tours in the city. Even if you aren't an Elvis fan, you should see what all the hype is about.

The Graceland Mansion tour is exhaustive, but if you are strapped for time, this tour alone will give you a comprehensive glimpse into the lavish life of Elvis Presley. In the mansion, see the music room, dining room, TV room, pool room, and the well-known "jungle" den. You can also visit Elvis' trophy building, which contains his overwhelming collection of awards, stage costumes, gold records, and more. Complimentary headsets are given with the price of admission, and we especially enjoyed hearing the voices of Elvis and Priscilla guiding us through the audio tour.

Also on the 14-acre estate is the Automobile Museum and Elvis' custom jet, the "Lisa Marie." Although kids will like some aspects of the mansion tour (the music room and trophy building), they will delight in touring Elvis' private plane and seeing his impressive car collection, featuring his 1955 pink Cadillac,. At least five candy-colored, shined-to-perfection vintage vehicles are on display in the Automobile Museum, as are Elvis' Harley Davidson, leather motorcycle jacket, and driver's license. The "Lisa Marie" jet is also impressive, with its full-sized living room and bedroom. Both tours are self-guided with video screens.

Finally, there is the Sincerely Elvis Museum, which features Presley's personal effects, from his off-stage wardrobe to photographs and home movies. The collection is interesting, but can be skipped if you're not a die-hard Elvis fan.

Memphis Pink Palace Museum & Planetarium

3050 Central Avenue, Memphis; (901) 320-6320 or (901) 763-IMAX
www.memphismuseums.org

Hours: Monday through Thursday, 9 a.m.– 4 p.m.; Friday through Saturday, 9 a.m.–9 p.m.; Sunday, Noon–6 p.m.

Admission: Museum: $6 adults, $5.50 seniors, $4.50 children ages 3–12; museum and planetarium: $7.50 adults, $7 seniors, $6 children; museum, planetarium and IMAX: $11 adults, $10 seniors, $8 children

Appeal by Age Group:

Pre-school	Grade School	Teens	Young Adults	Over 30	Seniors
★★	★★★	★★★	★★★	★★★	★★★

Average Touring Time: 4 hours

Minimum Touring Time: 2 hours

Rainy Day Touring: Recommended

Author's Rating: ★★★   Planetarium and IMAX provide hours of entertainment

Services and Facilities:

Restaurants No	Lockers No
Alcoholic beverages No	Pet kennels No
Disabled access Yes	Rain check No
Wheelchair rental No	Private tours No
Baby stroller rental No	

Description and Comments   Within this complex, visitors find natural and cultural history exhibits, including an exact replica of Piggly Wiggly, the first full-service grocery store founded by entrepreneur Clarence Saunders. Incidentally, Saunders built the Pink Palace Mansion in 1923 with his grocery fortune. The museum also features dinosaur fossils, historical dioramas, Civil War artifacts, and more. The adjacent Planetarium and IMAX theater are two of the best rainy-day attractions for adults and kids. Explore the earth and stars while being thoroughly entertained.

Mud Island River Park

125 North Front Street, Memphis; (901) 576-7241, (800) 507-6507, or TDD (800) 848-0298; www.mudisland.com

Hours: Open second week of April–October: Tuesday–Sunday, 10 a.m.–5 p.m.; Memorial Day–Labor Day until 8 p.m.

Admission: $8 adults, $4 seniors and children ages 4–11, free for children ages 3 and younger

Appeal by Age Group:

Pre-school	Grade School	Teens	Young Adults	Over 30	Seniors
★★	★★★	★★★	★★★	★★★	★★★

Average Touring Time: 1½ hours

Minimum Touring Time: 1 hour

Rainy Day Touring: Not recommended

Author's Rating: ★★   An interesting look at how the mighty river shaped the area

Services and Facilities:

Restaurants Yes

Alcoholic beverages No

Disabled access Yes

Wheelchair rental No

Baby stroller rental No

Lockers No

Pet kennels No

Rain check No

Private tours Yes

Description and Comments The only museum dedicated to a river, the Mud Island River Park features indoor and outdoor exhibits showcasing the Mississippi River. In the 18-gallery Mississippi River Museum, visitors learn about the cultures that sprang up along the banks of the river from Illinois to Louisiana. Also on display are a full-sized replica of an 1870s-era steamboat, Native American artifacts, and a presentation on the birth of blues and rock and roll and the Mississippi's role in inspiring them. The World War II–era fighter plane, the "Memphis Belle," is also worth a glimpse, as the bomber was one of the more successful planes deployed over Europe.

Most impressive, however, is the park's River Walk. With over 800,000 gallons of water pumping each minute, the River Walk re-creates the flow of the lower Mississippi at a 30-inch-to-one-mile scale. Pass over bridges or follow the path of the river until it spills out into the park's 1.3-million-gallon Gulf of Mexico.

The museum is located across the harbor from downtown Memphis, and in order to get there you must board the monorail. (The price of the monorail is included in admission.) Park at the intersections of Front Street and Poplar Avenue, then enjoy a smooth ride with a bird's-eye view of the Memphis skyline.

The National Civil Rights Museum

450 Mulberry Street, Memphis; (901) 521-9699
www.civilrightsmuseum.org

Hours: September–May: Monday–Saturday, 10 a.m.–5 p.m.; Thursday, 9 a.m.–8 p.m.; Sunday, 1–5 p.m.; June–August: Monday–Saturday, 10 a.m.–6 p.m.; Thursday, 9 a.m.–8 p.m.; Sunday, 1–6 p.m.; closed every Tuesday

Admission: $6 adults, $5 seniors and students, $4 children ages 6–12, free for children ages 5 and younger

Appeal by Age Group:

Pre-school	Grade School	Teens	Young Adults	Over 30	Seniors
★	★★★	★★★★★	★★★★★	★★★★★	★★★★★

Average Touring Time: 2 hours

Minimum Touring Time: 1 hour

Rainy Day Touring: Recommended

Author's Rating: ★★★★★ An interactive museum with a message

Services and Facilities:

Restaurants No

Alcoholic beverages No

Disabled access Yes

Wheelchair rental No

Baby stroller rental No

Lockers No

Pet kennels No

Rain check No

Private tours No

Description and Comments Now more than ever the words and ideas of Martin Luther King, Jr. and his followers are worth listening to, and the National Civil Rights Museum is the place to hear them. The first museum of the American Civil Rights Movement is housed in the historic Lorraine Motel, site of the assassination of Martin Luther King, Jr. on April 4, 1968. There are a number of exhibits and interactive displays that allow visitors to experience the hardships of African-Americans during segregation. Learn about the March on Washington, the Montgomery Bus Boycott and Rosa Parks, Brown vs. the Board of Education, and other landmark rulings. You can also listen to the many rousing speeches of Dr. Martin Luther King, Jr. Visitors are granted access to hotel rooms 306 and 307, the rooms outside of which Dr. King was assassinated.

Undoubtedly, you will be as moved by this museum as we were. For older kids, this educational laboratory will hopefully give them an understanding of the world that we live in today, and how far we have yet to go. Although off the beaten "fun-museum" path, the National Civil Rights Museum embodies the culture of African-American Memphis as much as anything on Beale Street.

Side Trips

The Pyramid What is that gleaming triangular-shaped building in the distance? It's the Memphis Pyramid Arena, a tribute to the city's namesake of Memphis, Egypt. Construction on the 32-story Pyramid began in 1989 and was completed in 1991, in time for the Judds' Farewell Concert. The Pyramid is home to the University of Memphis basketball team and it is the venue of choice for many large conventions and concerts. Arena tours take place Monday through Friday (when an event is not scheduled) at noon, 1 p.m., and 2 p.m. Cost is $4 for adults, $3 for children and seniors. Parking is free during the tour. One Auction Avenue, Memphis; (901) 521-9675, Ext. 340.

Slavehaven/Burkle Estate Museum If you have time—and if your kids were inspired by the National Civil Rights Museum—we suggest that you round out your tour with a visit to the Slavehaven/Burkle Estate Museum. The original struggle for equality among Africans in America has roots in this way station on the Underground Railroad route. The antebellum mansion, built in 1849 by abolitionist Jacob Burkle, features a series of trap doors and secret cellars, some of which lead to passages that twist and turn as far as the banks of the Mississippi. There are also other artifacts that date to the days when Memphis was one of the largest slave-trading markets in the country. 826 North Second Street, Memphis; (901) 527-3427.

Beale Street Historic District   Beale Street is the heart, and especially the soul, of Memphis. But with so many museums, restaurants, shops, and historical sites to visit on this busy stretch, deciding where to go can be a dizzying experience. For younger children, this grown-up area can be a bit boring; still, this is where Memphis was born, and you should make a point of walking in the footsteps of W.C. Handy, Elvis Presley, and B.B. King, to name a few.

The Memphis Music Hall of Fame contains memorabilia from the world of Memphis music, including original recordings from W.C. Handy, Elvis, and artists from the STAX and Sun labels. Museum displays feature photographs, biographies, and musical instruments from Memphis artists. Admission is $7.50 for adults, $2.50 for children ages 7–14. 97 South Second Street, Memphis; (901) 525-4007.

To find out more about the history of Memphis, visit the Center for Southern Folklore. This well-known Beale Street museum focuses on Memphis' role as a major commercial and cultural center of the South. Museum guests can enjoy art displays, films, and daily live music played by artists from all genres. The center also offers walking tours of Beale Street. 130 Beale Street, Memphis; (901) 525-3655; www.southernfolklore.com.

If you come across a small, wood-frame house while walking down Beale, you are more than likely staring at the humble home of the "Father of the Blues." The W.C. Handy House Museum displays a sizable collection of Handy's personal items. Admission is $2 for adults, $1 for children. The museum is open daily until 5 p.m. 352 Beale Street, Memphis; (901) 522-1556.

The newest attraction on Beale Street fits in quite nicely with the other musically themed sites. Gibson Guitar Memphis is both a museum and factory devoted to the highly revered Gibson guitar. Would-be musicians can test-drive pricey guitars or purchase one of a number of stringed beauties at the Gibson store. Also featured at the museum is the Smithsonian's Rock 'n' Soul Museum—a must-see. 145 Lt. George West Lee Avenue, Memphis; (800) 4-GIBSON.

Take a tour of Sun Studio to see where artists like Jerry Lee Lewis, B.B. King, and Elvis recorded many of their hits. The studio has rare photographs, memorabilia, and vintage recording equipment. It is open daily. Admission is $8; free for children ages 12 and younger. 706 Union Avenue, Memphis; (901) 521-0664 or (800) 441-6249; www.sunstudio.com.

A fixture on Beale Street since 1876, A. Schwab is the place to stock up on postcards, souvenirs, snacks, fireworks, and other inexpensive novelty items. The store's motto is, "If you can't find it at Schwab's, you're better off without it." The dry goods store is open every day but "the Lord's Day," (901) 523-9782.

Shiloh National Military Park   A couple hours drive east of Memphis will bring you to Shiloh, the scene of one of the bloodiest battles in the War Between the States. Within the 4,000-acre park you can visit the Shiloh National Cemetery and well-preserved, prehistoric Indian mounds. Families can use battlefield maps to guide them around the park or get a tour from a ranger (available Memorial Day through Labor Day). Plan on spending much of the day at the park (approximately four to five hours), though you can take the tour in as little as two hours. Shiloh National Military Park costs $4 per family and is open daily 8 a.m.–5 p.m. 1055 Pittsburg Landing, Shiloh 38376; (901) 689-5696.

Family-Friendly Restaurants

CORKY'S BAR-B-Q

5259 Poplar Avenue, Memphis; (901) 685-9744 or (800) 9-CORKYS
www.corkysbbq.com

Meals served: Lunch and dinner
Cuisine: American/barbecue
Entrée range: $3.99–17.99
Kids menu: Yes
Reservations: No
Payment: All major credit cards accepted

Barbecue lovers are urged to stop at Memphis' famous Corky's Restaurant. This full-service dining establishment has barbecue pork shoulder, ribs, pulled chicken sandwiches, and a range of other items that go well with tangy barbecue sauce. Corky's Kids' Menu includes spaghetti, grilled cheese, and "drummies," deep-fried chicken drumsticks.

ELVIS PRESLEY'S MEMPHIS

126 Beale Street, Memphis; (901) 527-6900
www.epmemphis.com

Meals served: Lunch and dinner
Cuisine: American
Entrée range: $10–19
Kids menu: Yes
Reservations: Recommended for dinner
Payment: All major credit cards accepted

Complete your Elvis experience with a meal at Elvis Presley's Memphis, one of the most entertaining dining spots in town. The '50s-style restaurant features avariety of contemporary southern cuisine, such as pork chops, pecan-crusted catfish, and meat loaf. Meanwhile, kids can feast on "Love Me (chicken) Tenders," grilled cheese, spaghetti, or Elvis' signature peanut butter and banana sandwich. In addition to great food, there is musical entertainment Wednesday through Saturday night and a Gospel Brunch on Sunday.

HUEY'S DOWNTOWN

77 South Second Street, Memphis; (901) 527-2700

Meals served: Lunch and dinner
Cuisine: American
Entrée range: $8–15
Kids menu: Yes
Reservations: Not accepted
Payment: All major credit cards accepted

As winner of the Best Burger in Memphis for over a decade, Huey's is the place to get juicy burgers, golden french fries, and typical American eats. Kids' meal options are limited, but the mini-corndogs are always a hit.

Nashville

From the **Country Music Hall of Fame** and the **Grand Ole Opry** to **The Nashville Network,** the city of Nashville is country through and through. But there is more to Music City USA than honky tonks and country line dancing.

Nashville is the Tennessee state capital, and the city contains a number of museums and historical sites for visitors who want to learn more about this Southern state's past. Tour the **Tennessee State Capitol** or take a walk through the 19-acre **Bicentennial Mall State Park.** A short drive outside of Nashville takes you to the **Hermitage,** the mansion home of Andrew Jackson, the seventh president of the United States. You can even get a glimpse of ancient Greece, as Nashville is home to the world's only full-scale replica of Athens' **Parthenon.**

If you have come to this city for the music, you won't be disappointed. The Country Music Hall of Fame and Museum offers hours of country entertainment with its collection of memorabilia from stars like Patsy Cline and Johnny Cash. And if you want to see a living legend of country music, you can still visit the Grand Ole Opry.

The **Nashville Toy Museum** and the Imaginarium are attractions that will certainly excite kids of all ages. The Toy Museum features dolls, models of ships, trains and planes, toy soldiers, and vintage teddy bears. Equally as entertaining is the hands-on **Imaginarium,** where kids can escape to theme worlds, such as a dinosaur room, outer space, or a pirate ship. For the long, hot days of summer, families can head over to **Nashville Shores,** the areas own beach-like recreation area featuring pools, slides, water games, and picnic tables.

Family Lodging

AmeriSuites Nashville/Opryland

Intended for business travelers, the AmeriSuites, south of Nashville in Brentwood, is also ideal for families. The 126-suite hotel has six wheelchair-

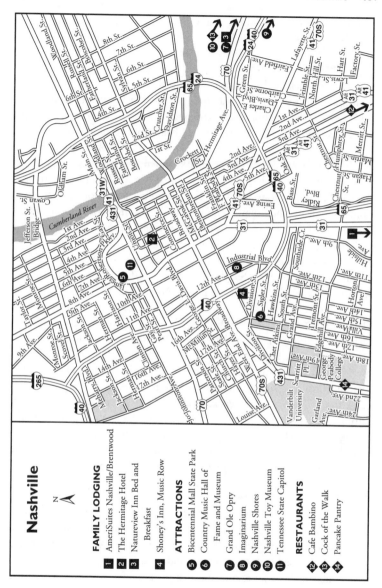

Nashville

N

FAMILY LODGING
1. AmeriSuites Nashville/Brentwood
2. The Hermitage Hotel
3. Natureview Inn Bed and Breakfast
4. Shoney's Inn, Music Row

ATTRACTIONS
5. Bicentennial Mall State Park
6. Country Music Hall of Fame and Museum
7. Grand Ole Opry
8. Imaginarium
9. Nashville Shores
10. Nashville Toy Museum
11. Tennessee State Capitol

RESTAURANTS
12. Cafe Bambino
13. Cock of the Walk
14. Pancake Pantry

accessible rooms starting at $89 per night during the off-season (rates increase during Fan Fair). All rooms have a refrigerator, microwave, and 25-inch television/VCR. On-site movie rentals will keep kids occupied. A complimentary continental breakfast buffet is served daily. AmeriSuites also creates a community atmosphere for its guests with its daily popcorn meet-

and-greet session in the lobby. Near Opry Mills shopping. 220 Rudy's Circle, Nashville; (615) 872-0422.

The Hermitage Hotel

One of the oldest and most storied of Nashville hotels, the Hermitage is within steps of the Tennessee capitol. Named after President Andrew Jackson's estate, which, confusingly enough, is just outside of the city, the hotel was built in 1910 and is the only beaux arts structure in Tennessee. The impressive all-suite inn recently underwent a $4 million renovation and has been restored it to its original grandeur.

Suite rates at the Hermitage Hotel range from $109–179 throughout the year, but this is considered quite a bargain given the hotel's prime location. One- or two-bedroom accommodations feature a living room, refrigerator and 25-inch television, equipped for cable and pay-per-view movies. Children younger than 18 stay free with parents.

The award-winning Capitol Grille is on the premises and is a great place to sample some nouveau Southern cuisine. Go during lunch when prices are reasonable; 231 Sixth Avenue North, Nashville; (615) 244-3121.

Natureview Inn Bed and Breakfast

If a visit to Andrew Jackson's Hermitage is on the agenda and you want to get away from the big-city hotels, you should consider this quaint bed and breakfast situated on five lush acres east of Nashville. This country inn has two fully furnished suites, one that sleeps four and one that sleeps six. Rates range from $75–95 (extra-person charge is $15), and increase dramatically during Fan Fair. A pool is on the premises, and the grounds provide ample hiking and horseback riding opportunities. A gourmet breakfast is served daily, but guests must make reservations for dinner if they plan to eat at the inn. 3354 Old Lebanon Dirt Road, Mt. Juliet; (615) 758-4439.

Shoney's Inn, Music Row

This is the closest hotel to all the action on Nashville's Music Row. Shoney's Inn has 147 rooms, including six suites, three of which allow disabled access. Standard rooms come with the typical amenities, whereas more comfortable suites are equipped with a microwave and refrigerator. Rates run from $72 for a double to $129 for a suite, but that price can be twice as much during June's Fan Fair. Family restaurant Shoney's is the nearest restaurant.

The hotel is located off the interstate, but is within walking distance of Music Row, the Country Music Hall of Fame, and various gift shops. Downtown Nashville is five minutes from Shoney's Inn, and the hotel provides a trolley so guests can easily access downtown restaurants and entertainment. An outdoor pool is welcoming during the humid summer months. Kids younger than 18 stay free with parents, and AARP discounts are available; 1501 Demonbreun, Nashville; (615) 255-9977.

Attractions

Bicentennial Mall State Park

598 James Robertson Parkway, Nashville; (615) 741-5280

Hours: Daily, dawn to midnight

Admission: Free when special events are not scheduled

Appeal by Age Group:

Pre-school	Grade School	Teens	Young Adults	Over 30	Seniors
★★★	★★★	★★★	★★★	★★★	★★★

Average Touring Time: 2 hours

Minimum Touring Time: 1½ hours

Rainy Day Touring: Not recommended

Author's Rating: ★★★ A "fresh" tour of Tennessee history

Services and Facilities:

Restaurants Adjacent to park		Lockers No	
Alcoholic beverages No		Pet kennels No	
Disabled access Yes		Rain check No	
Wheelchair rental No		Private tours No	
Baby stroller rental No			

Description and Comments If you want to come away from your trip to Tennessee knowing a bit more about the great state, stroll over to the Bicentennial Mall State Park. This 19-acre outdoor history museum, situated north of the State Capitol, features the Walk of Counties and the Wall of History, a 200-foot granite map of Tennessee. No fewer than 31 fountains, symbolizing the state's major waterways, decorate the downtown park, making for a serene and relaxing atmosphere after a long day of touring.

Make your way to the visitors center first to get ideas on how to best view the park. Or, if you visit on a Saturday, grab some fresh produce at the Nashville Farmer's Market, located adjacent to the park, and spend the afternoon munching on peaches as you meander.

During the summer months, a number of outdoor events are held at the 2,000-seat Bicentennial Mall Amphitheater. Country concerts and lively plays are the usual fare, offering ideal evening entertainment options for families. However, admission to the park is not free during these times.

Country Music Hall of Fame and Museum

4 Music Square East, Nashville; (615) 256-1639
www.countrymusichalloffame.org

Hours: Daily, 9 a.m.–5 p.m.

Admission: $10.75 adults; $4.75 children ages 6–11; free for children
ages 5 and younger

Appeal by Age Group:

Pre-school	Grade School	Teens	Young Adults	Over 30	Seniors
★	★★	★★★	★★★	★★★	★★★

Average Touring Time: 3 hours

Minimum Touring Time: 2 hours

Rainy Day Touring: Recommended

Author's Rating: ★★★   Fun look at the music and musicians that made
Nashville

Services and Facilities:

Restaurants No	Lockers No
Alcoholic beverages No	Pet kennels No
Disabled access Yes	Rain check No
Wheelchair rental No	Private tours No
Baby stroller rental No	

Description and Comments   The world of country music past and present
is brought to you through displays of original sheet music, sound recordings, an exhibit of over 3,000 stage costumes, and more. See rare memorabilia from Hank Williams (one of the Hall's first inductees), Elvis Presley's "solid gold" Cadillac, and George Strait's cowboy hat. You can also
watch old country music broadcasts and walk through an exhibit devoted
to country music in the movies. One notable piece of memorabilia from
the latter is the mechanical bull that John Travolta rode in *Urban Cowboy.*

Work is currently underway for a new, bigger museum, scheduled to
open spring 2001. And, as the popularity of country music grows, thanks
to stars like Lee Ann Rimes, Shania Twain, Garth Brooks, and Alan Jackson, the museum is going to need all the extra space it can get.

Grand Ole Opry

2802 Opryland Drive, Nashville; (615) 889-6611

Hours: Showtimes: Friday, 7:30 p.m.; Saturday, 6:30 and 9:30 p.m.

Admission: $16–20, depending on location within hall (subject to
change); tickets can be purchased by phone one week in advance.

Appeal by Age Group:

Pre-school	Grade School	Teens	Young Adults	Over 30	Seniors
★★	★★★	★★★★	★★★★	★★★★	★★★★

Average Touring Time: 2 hours

Minimum Touring Time: 2 hours

Rainy Day Touring: N/A

Author's Rating: ★★★ Discover Music City's roots

Services and Facilities:

Restaurants No	Lockers No
Alcoholic beverages No	Pet kennels No
Disabled access Yes	Rain check No
Wheelchair rental No	Private tours No
Baby stroller rental No	

Description and Comments The world's longest radio show goes on, and you can be part of the action. Every Friday and Saturday night, celebrity performers from the world of country music entertain a live audience of approximately 4,400 and a broadcast audience of millions. The world-famous Grand Ole Opry has brought country music to the ears of Americans for over 73 years. Come see superstars, Hall of Famers, legends, and hot new stars perform on the stage of the Grand Ole Opry House, a 4,400-seat broadcast studio. Here is your chance to see these performers take the stage in a relatively intimate setting. If you are unable to make it to the Opry House, you can watch The Nashville Network's broadcast of the show every Saturday night. Most every hotel room in the city carries the network.

Imaginarium

1111 Laurel Street, Nashville; (615) 254-3334

Hours: Daily, 10 a.m.–5 p.m.

Admission: $4.50 ages 2 and older

Appeal by Age Group:

Pre-school	Grade School	Teens	Young Adults	Over 30	Seniors
★★★★	★★★★	★	★	★★	★★

Average Touring Time: 3 hours

Minimum Touring Time: 2 hours

Rainy Day Touring: Recommended

Author's Rating: ★★★ Stimulating museum for kids

Services and Facilities:

Restaurants No

Alcoholic beverages No

Disabled access Yes

Wheelchair rental No

Baby stroller rental No

Lockers No

Pet kennels No

Rain check No

Private tours No

Description and Comments Let the kids romp around in this 9,000-square-foot interactive learning museum. There are no less than ten themed areas, including a rainforest, an aquarium, a fire station, an art studio, and a pirate ship. The Imaginarium even has a special section for toddlers. Although the museum is all about kids, parents will enjoy watching children discover and play.

Nashville Shores

4001 Bell Road, Hermitage; (615) 889-7050

www.nashvilleshores.com

Hours: May–October daily, 10 a.m.–6 p.m.; Saturday until 8 p.m.

Admission: $11.95 adults; $8.95 children ages 3–12, free for children ages 2 and younger

Appeal by Age Group:

Pre-school	Grade School	Teens	Young Adults	Over 30	Seniors
★★★★★	★★★★★	★★★★	★★★★	★★★	★★

Average Touring Time: 4½ hours

Minimum Touring Time: 3 hours

Rainy Day Touring: Not recommended

Author's Rating: ★★★★ An enjoyable day in the sun

Services and Facilities:

Restaurants Yes

Alcoholic beverages No

Disabled access Yes

Wheelchair rental No

Baby stroller rental No

Lockers Yes

Pet kennels No

Rain check No

Private tours No

Description and Comments If the kids have been unusually well behaved, treat them to a day at Nashville Shores, the area's water theme park, located in nearby Hermitage. The little tykes will have fun getting wet on such wild attractions as the Tennessee Twisters, a rough-and-tumble water slide pair stretching 700-feet, or on Big Ol' Splash, an enormous pond filled with child-size lily pads. Also on site are miniature golf, three pools, sandy beaches, and Jet Skis available for rental for older children and adults. Picnic areas scattered about the park allow families to enjoy a day at the ocean smack-dab in the middle of Tennessee. (Note, however, that it is prohibited to bring in your own food or beverages.)

Nashville Toy Museum

2613 McGavock Pike, Nashville; (615) 883-8870

Hours: Daily, 9 a.m.–5 p.m.

Admission: $3.50 adults, $3 seniors, $1.50 children ages 6–12, free for children ages 5 and younger

Appeal by Age Group:

Pre-school	Grade School	Teens	Young Adults	Over 30	Seniors
★★★	★★★	★★	★★	★★	★★

Average Touring Time: 1½ hours

Minimum Touring Time: 30 minutes

Rainy Day Touring: Recommended

Author's Rating: ★★★   Great site for train lovers

Services and Facilities:

Restaurants No	Lockers No
Alcoholic beverages No	Pet kennels No
Disabled access Yes	Rain check No
Wheelchair rental No	Private tours No
Baby stroller rental No	

Description and Comments   Both kids and adults will be dazzled as they watch miniature trains chug through complex track layouts around the museum. This small museum also has a collection of toy soldiers, toy bears from around the world, model planes and ships, and antique dolls. This interesting assortment of old and new playthings span a time period of at least 150 years.

Next door to the Toy Museum you will find the Train Store, where hundreds of model trains and railroad components are for sale. Both of these attractions are located two blocks from Briley Parkway across from the Opryland Hotel.

Tennessee State Capitol

Charlotte Avenue, between Sixth and Seventh Avenues, Nashville; (615) 741-2692

Hours: Monday–Friday, 9 a.m.–4 p.m.

Admission: Free

Appeal by Age Group:

Pre-school	Grade School	Teens	Young Adults	Over 30	Seniors
★	★★	★★	★★	★★	★★

Average Touring Time: 30 minutes

Minimum Touring Time: 30 minutes

Rainy Day Touring: Recommended

Author's Rating: ★★ Historic statehouse is worth a visit

Services and Facilities:

Restaurants No	Lockers No
Alcoholic beverages No	Pet kennels No
Disabled access Yes	Rain check No
Wheelchair rental No	Private tours No
Baby stroller rental No	

Description and Comments Built in 1859, the Tennessee State Capitol has been a part of the Nashville skyline since before the Civil War. Most of the Greek Revival–style building looks the way it did when it was built, though the library and Supreme Court chamber have been restored.

Side Trips

The Parthenon Just as Memphis has its Pyramid, Nashville has its Parthenon. Long known as the "Athens of the South" because of the many colleges and universities within town, Nashville's nickname is also due in part to this full-scale re-creation of the famous Greek temple. The building now houses the city's fine-art museum as well as a monumental sculpture of goddess Athena Parthenos. At 42 feet high, the Athena is thought to be one of the largest indoor sculptures in the world. Admission is $2.50 for adults, $1.25 for seniors and children ages 4–17, and free for ages 3 and younger. Open Tuesday–Saturday 9 a.m.–4:30 p.m. and limited Sunday hours April–September. West End and 25th Avenue (Centennial Park), Nashville; (615) 862-8431.

Opryland USA When this well-known amusement park shut its doors in 1997, many people were disappointed. But several years and millions of dollars later, the site where Opryland once stood has been transformed into **Opry Mills,** a shopping and entertainment complex. Of interest at the new mall are dozens of outlet stores, including Banana Republic, Gap, and Liz Claiborne retailers, and a number of unique shops and restaurants. Young children will adore the Build-A-Bear Workshop, where they can design and create their own stuffed animals, and the Rainforest Cafe, a theme restaurant that features animated creatures and simulated waterfalls. Other fun stops include the NASCAR Silicon Motor Speedway, a virtual racecar ride, and the IMAX 3-D Theater. 2802 Opryland Drive, Nashville; (615) 514-1100; www.oprymills.com.

The Hermitage Tennessee native son Andrew Jackson was one of the nation's most decorated soldiers, and his accomplishments on the battlefield led him to become the seventh president of the United States. During the time that Jackson lived in Tennessee, both before and after his presidency, he resided at the Hermitage. Jackson purchased this grand estate outside of Nashville in 1804, and on the grounds he built an enviable mansion named Tulip Grove. Over the years, the land gained a couple of log cabins, landscaped gardens, a church, and, ultimately, a cemetery. Today, a visit to the Hermitage entails a tour of the mansion, circa-1804 log cabins, formal gardens, and Confederate Cemetery. A restaurant and gift shop are also on site. Admission to the Hermitage is $9.50 for adults, $8.50 for seniors, and $4.50 for children ages 6–12. Reduced admission is available on January 8 (to commemorate the Battle of New Orleans) and March 15 (Jackson's birthday). 4580 Rachel's Lane, Hermitage; (615) 889-2941; www.thehermitage.com.

Tennessee Antebellum Trail Begin your tour of this 90-mile loop in Nashville and travel through historic Maury and Williamson counties. See how pre-Civil War Tennesseeans lived at more than 50 plantation homes, battlefields, and noteworthy attractions. Nine homes are open to the public, including the Belle Meade Plantation, the Belmont Mansion, Traveller's Rest, and The Athenaeum. Information and a road map are available from the Tennessee Antebellum Trail Society, (800) 381-1865.

Family-Friendly Restaurants

CAFE BAMBINO

734 Thompson Lane, Nashville; (615) 383-4383

Meals served: Breakfast, lunch, and dinner
Cuisine: Continental bistro/Italian
Entrée range: $2–8
Kids menu: Yes
Reservations: Not required
Payment: All major credit cards accepted

Even if you visit all of the wonderful, kid-friendly attractions in Nashville, there will come a time when your little one needs to take a break from it all. Enter Cafe Bambino, a coffeehouse with a child's area that includes a chalkboard, Legos, and more. Parents and grandparents can sip on a cappuccino while the kids enjoy supervised fun. The cafe offers an assortment of healthy pastas, sandwiches, and baked goods.

COCK OF THE WALK

2624 Music Valley Drive, Nashville; (615) 889-1930

Meals served: Lunch and dinner
Cuisine: Seafood
Entrée range: $9–12
Kids menu: Yes
Reservations: Recommended
Payment: All major credit cards accepted

This popular restaurant serves some of the best catfish in town. You can also enjoy grilled chicken, fried shrimp, and a good old-fashioned burger. The restaurant offers a small kids menu with a choice of either fried chicken or fried catfish for only $4.95. Near Opry Mills shopping complex.

PANCAKE PANTRY

1796 21st Avenue South, Nashville; (615) 383-9333

Meals served: Breakfast and lunch
Cuisine: American
Entrée range: $4–8
Kids menu: No
Reservations: No
Payment: All major credit cards accepted

If breakfast does not come complimentary with your hotel accommodations, you will rejoice when you come across Nashville's famous Pancake Pantry. This breakfast joint serves pancakes hundreds of ways, from the plain buttermilk variety to a stack smothered in whipped cream and fruit. You can also get eggs, home fries, and other breakfast and lunch items, but nothing beats the hotcakes. Be prepared to stand in long lines on weekends, as the Pantry is a favorite breakfast spot for locals and tourists alike. You will realize that the wait was worth it when you're slowly drizzling blueberry syrup over a hot, buttery stack of homemade pancakes.

Chattanooga

Chattanooga's claim to fame has long been its **Choo Choo,** and this Tennessee landmark is still a great reason to visit the city. However, Chattanooga has been on the rise for quite some time, with its restructuring of downtown and its focus on the natural beauty of the region. In 1998, *U.S. News and World Report* designated Chattanooga as one of six "smart cities" in North America, due to its efforts to beautify its downtown and waterfront. The area by the Tennessee River now boasts the popular **Children's Discovery Museum** and the **Tennessee Aquarium.**

Family Lodging

Chattanooga Choo Choo Holiday Inn

If you are in town to see the famous train, the Chattanooga Choo Choo Holiday Inn puts you within steps of the landmark. The downtown all-suite hotel is located within the original walls of Chattanooga's Terminal Station, dedicated in 1909. Within the hotel complex are several restaurants, one indoor and two outdoor pools, a Jacuzzi, shops, and parking. Complimentary downtown shuttle service is available just outside the hotel lobby. All rooms are rather spacious and are wheelchair accessible. Parents—the Holiday Inn has a babysitting service for when you want a night just for the two of you. Rates start at $109, and children younger than age 17 stay free with parents.

The historic hotel also offers rooms aboard one of 48 restored Victorian railcars. The luxurious accommodations come equipped with the same amenities as the regular suites—cable television, modern furnishings—but cost up to $40 extra per night. For true train lovers, the experience is worth it. 1400 Market Street, Chattanooga; (800) 872-2529 or (423) 266-5000; www.choochoo.com.

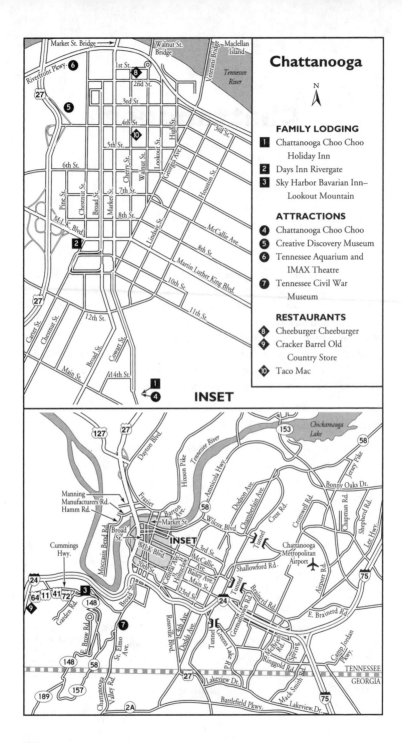

Chattanooga

N

FAMILY LODGING

1. Chattanooga Choo Choo
   Holiday Inn
2. Days Inn Rivergate
3. Sky Harbor Bavarian Inn–
   Lookout Mountain

ATTRACTIONS

4. Chattanooga Choo Choo
5. Creative Discovery Museum
6. Tennessee Aquarium and
   IMAX Theatre
7. Tennessee Civil War
   Museum

RESTAURANTS

8. Cheeburger Cheeburger
9. Cracker Barrel Old
   Country Store
10. Taco Mac

Days Inn Rivergate

This is a no-nonsense hotel located within walking distance of Chattanooga's downtown attractions, including the Tennessee Aquarium and the Chattanooga Choo Choo. The 137-room hotel has five wheelchair accessible rooms, an outdoor pool, and cable-equipped color televisions in all rooms. Free parking is available to all hotel guests, as the Rivergate specializes in accommodations for families and tour groups. All-American diner Denny's, open 24-hours, is next to the hotel. Room rates range from $45–99, and kids 18 and younger stay free with parents. 901 Carter Street, Chattanooga; (423) 266-7331.

Sky Harbor Bavarian Inn–Lookout Mountain

Overlooking the lush hills of the Smoky Mountains, the Sky Harbor Bavarian Inn puts you near the natural wonders of the Chattanooga area. Located on Lookout Mountain near Ruby Falls and Rock City Gardens, the pet-friendly, country hotel features rooms with kitchenettes, including microwaves, coffee makers and refrigerators, cable television, and well-appointed furnishings. Sky Harbor also has a restaurant, an outdoor pool, a Jacuzzi, and free parking. Unfortunately, most rooms at the Bavarian Inn are not wheelchair accessible. Standard room rates range from $68–115. 2159 Old Wauhatchie Pike, Lookout Mountain; (423) 821-8619.

Attractions

Chattanooga Choo Choo

1400 Market Street, Chattanooga; (423) 266-5000
www.choochoo.com

Hours: Daily, 8 a.m.–6 p.m.

Admission: Free

Appeal by Age Group:

Pre-school	Grade School	Teens	Young Adults	Over 30	Seniors
★★★	★★★	★★★	★★★	★★★★	★★★★

Average Touring Time: 1 hour

Minimum Touring Time: 30 minutes

Rainy Day Touring: Not recommended

Author's Rating: ★★★ See the train that made the city famous

Services and Facilities:

Restaurants Yes	Disabled access Yes
Alcoholic beverages Yes	Wheelchair rental No

Baby stroller rental No   Rain check No
Lockers No   Private tours No
Pet kennels No

Description and Comments   What remains of the Chattanooga Choo Choo continues to draw thousands of visitors each year. The 24-acre complex, located on the grounds of the old Terminal Station (now restored as the Holiday Inn), is made up of intricate gardens, including rose, herb, and butterfly gardens; a 1924 New Orleans trolley car; several restaurants; and a number of boutiques. The rail cars on the property are indeed vintage cars from the Choo Choo era, but they now exist as two-room hotel suites in the Holiday Inn.

Creative Discovery Museum

321 Chestnut Street, Chattanooga; (423) 756-2738
www.cdmfun.org

Hours: September–May: Tuesday–Saturday, 10 a.m.–5 p.m.; Sunday, noon–5 p.m.; May–September: daily, 10 a.m.–6 p.m.

Admission: $7.75 adults, $4.75 children ages 2–12

Appeal by Age Group:

Pre-school	Grade School	Teens	Young Adults	Over 30	Seniors
★★★★	★★★★	★	★	★★	★★

Average Touring Time: 2 hours

Minimum Touring Time: 1½ hours

Rainy Day Touring: Recommended

Author's Rating: ★★★★   Creative, interactive programs keep kids entertained

Services and Facilities:

Restaurants No   Lockers No
Alcoholic beverages No   Pet kennels No
Disabled access Yes   Rain check No
Wheelchair rental No   Private tours No
Baby stroller rental No

Description and Comments   Let kids pretend to be musicians, inventors, scientists, or artists at the Creative Discovery Museum, the fully hands-on children's attraction in downtown Chattanooga. Museum guides provide paint, clay, musical instruments, kid-sized science lab tools, and more so toddlers can discover their hidden talents. Also at the Creative Discovery Museum is the Little Yellow House, an indoor tree house with a musical porch, small-scale make-believe kitchen, and other fun stuff to let toddlers' imaginations run wild. The museum features special monthly events, such as walk-up art and music lessons and theater performances for families, so call ahead to find out what's new.

Tennessee Aquarium and IMAX Theatre

One Broad Street, Chattanooga; (423) 265-0608 or (800) 262-0695
www.tnaqua.org

Hours: Daily, 10 a.m.–6 p.m.

Admission: $16.25 adults, $9.95 children ages 3–12 (includes IMAX film and aquarium admission); aquarium only: $11.95 adults, $6.50 children; IMAX only: $6.95 adults, $4.95 children

Appeal by Age Group:

Pre-school	Grade School	Teens	Young Adults	Over 30	Seniors
★★★★	★★★★	★★★★	★★★★	★★★★	★★★★

Average Touring Time: 2½ hours

Minimum Touring Time: 2 hours

Rainy Day Touring: Recommended

Author's Rating: ★★★★ Combined exhibits appeal to entire family

Services and Facilities:

Restaurants No	Wheelchair rental No
Alcoholic beverages No	Baby stroller rental No
Disabled access Yes (theater provides audio and video accessibility for sight or hearing impaired)	Lockers No
	Pet kennels No
	Rain check No
	Private tours No

Description and Comments The world's largest freshwater aquarium is appropriately located in Chattanooga, given the city's unique position near the Tennessee River and the Appalachian Mountain chain. The aquarium features exhibits with more than 575 species of fish, reptiles, amphibians, and other sea creatures. There are also several exhibits that contain fowl indigenous to the region, such as wood ducks and yellow-billed cuckoos, and a special ecosystem designed for the museum's only mammalian residents, the river otters.

The adjacent IMAX Theatre projects 3D films about the universe or Earth and its creatures. Crystal-clear sound and larger-than-life images make you feel like you're walking with dinosaurs, swimming with dolphins, or exploring outer space. The whole family will enjoy the experience.

Tennessee Civil War Museum

3914 St. Elmo Avenue, Chattanooga; (423) 821-4954

Hours: Monday–Saturday, 8 a.m.–6 p.m.; Sunday, noon–5 p.m.

Admission: $6.50 adults, $6 seniors, $5.50 ages 8–12, free for children ages 7 and younger

Appeal by Age Group:

Pre-school	Grade School	Teens	Young Adults	Over 30	Seniors
★	★★★	★★★	★★★	★★★	★★★★

Average Touring Time: 2½ hours

Minimum Touring Time: 1½ hours

Rainy Day Touring: Recommended

Author's Rating: ★★ A comprehensive, fascinating collection of Civil War artifacts

Services and Facilities:

Restaurants No	Lockers No
Alcoholic beverages No	Pet kennels No
Disabled access Yes	Rain check No
Wheelchair rental No	Private tours No
Baby stroller rental No	

Description and Comments This museum just outside of Chattanooga houses of one of the largest collections of Civil War memorabilia anywhere. Interactive touch-screens and an on-site historian help to re-create the events of the War Between the States, as do displays of uniforms, cannon, medals, canteens, and other personal effects. Not surprisingly, the Tennessee Civil War Museum focuses mainly on the history of the Confederate Army, but exhibits also explain the contributions of men, women, and African-Americans who fought on both sides.

Side Trip

Lookout Mountain A few minutes drive down Interstate 24 takes you to the attractions of Lookout Mountain (www.lookoutmtnattractions.com). Here, you can see the natural wonders that have brought so many people to the Chattanooga area over the years, including Rock City Gardens and Ruby Falls. From atop Rock City, you can see the vast valley in which Chattanooga lies, and on a clear day, no fewer than seven states. Rock City Gardens is also where you can see a 1,000-ton balanced rock, which has remained in this precarious position for thousands of years. Ruby Falls, inside Lookout

Mountain, features a 145-foot sparkling waterfall and enormous natural caverns. Both Lookout Mountain attractions open daily at 8:30 a.m. Rock City information is available at (706) 820-2531; www.seerockcity.com. Ruby Falls information is available at (423) 821-2544; www.rubyfalls.com.

Family-Friendly Restaurants

CHEEBURGER CHEEBURGER

138 Market Street, Chattanooga; (423) 265-4108

Meals served: Lunch and dinner
Cuisine: American
Entrée range: $3–8
Kids menu: Yes
Reservations: Not required
Payment: All major credit cards accepted

Cheeburger Cheeburger serves—what else?—cheeseburgers and hamburgers, but it also offers chicken sandwiches and heaping salads. Child-sized portions of hamburgers or cheeseburgers are available, as are chicken fingers and grilled cheese. All items on the kid's menu cost $3.95 and come with french fries and a drink. Located across the street form the Tennessee Aquarium.

MANDARIN GARDEN

5450 Highway 153, Chattanooga; (423) 877-8899

Meals served: Lunch and dinner
Cuisine: Chinese
Entrée range: $6.95–23
Kids menu: No
Reservations: Not required
Payment: All major credit cards

Mandarin Garden has an extensive menu of beef, seafood, poultry, and vegetarian entrées, prepared according to classic Hunan, Szechuan, and Peking recipes. Families can save money by ordering the family dinner, which comes with servings of fried rice, egg rolls, wonton or hot and sour soup, and a heaping bowl of their favorite dinner item. The restaurant is minutes from the Tennessee Aquarium and the Chattanooga Choo Choo.

TACO MAC

423 Market Street, Chattanooga; (423) 267-8226

Meals served: Lunch and dinner
Cuisine: Tex-Mex
Entrée range: $6–12
Kids menu: Yes
Reservations: Not required
Payment: All major credit cards accepted

This lively restaurant comes to Chattanooga by way of Atlanta, and, indeed, it is best known for its large selection of beer and late-night dining. But Taco Mac is also an ideal family establishment, as it serves up a variety of dishes that everyone can agree upon. Adults can snack on heaping plates of nachos, indulge in tacos or enchiladas, or sample some of the restaurants famous buffalo wings. Kids have a choice of quesadillas, mini corndogs, chicken fingers, spaghetti, and more. All kids' plates cost $2.99 and come with a drink, fruit, and a cookie. The place is not far from the Riverfront and the Tennessee Aquarium.

Knoxville

The city of Knoxville has had its day in the sun at least twice during its existence. From 1796 to 1815, this east Tennessee town served as the state capital and was the center of western colonial life. Fast forward more than 150 years later and Knoxville became the center of the universe for at least one summer, as it hosted the 1982 World's Fair. Soon after the international exposition ended, Knoxville shrank back into relative anonymity for a while until it emerged as a vibrant city with a revamped downtown, based largely on the remnants of the buildings left from the World's Fair. Today, Knoxville is known as a convention town, a college town, a center for African-American life, and a gateway to the Great Smoky Mountains.

Family Lodging

Hampton Inn East

The location of Hampton Inn East allows guests to enjoy the attractions of Knoxville or the Smoky Mountains. The Hampton Inn is within minutes of World's Fair Park and the Knoxville Zoo. It's also convenient for visiting destinations farther afield, such as Dollywood or the parks of the Great Smoky Mountains. And, although this hotel sits just outside of Knoxville proper, amenities are comparable to or better than those of downtown hotels.

Rooms come equipped with coffee makers, refrigerators, dataports, cable television, and comfortable furnishings. On the hotel grounds you will find an indoor pool, an outdoor pool, an exercise room, a playground for children, and services like guest laundry. Room rates for the Hampton Inn East start at $68 per night, and children younger than 17 stay free with parents. 814 Brakebill Road, Knoxville; (865) 525-3511 or (800) 526-2462.

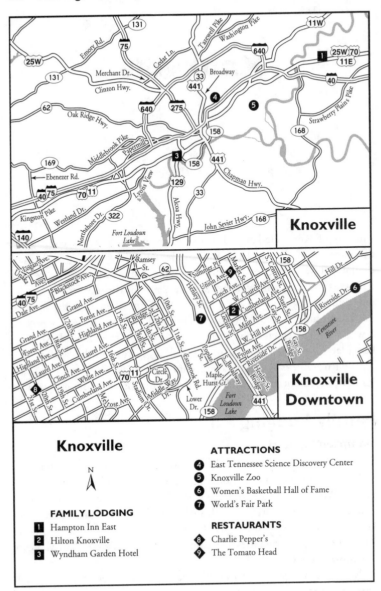

Knoxville

N

FAMILY LODGING

1 Hampton Inn East
2 Hilton Knoxville
3 Wyndham Garden Hotel

ATTRACTIONS

4 East Tennessee Science Discovery Center
5 Knoxville Zoo
6 Women's Basketball Hall of Fame
7 World's Fair Park

RESTAURANTS

8 Charlie Pepper's
9 The Tomato Head

Hilton Knoxville

If you want to stay in the heart of Knoxville, within walking distance of such attractions as the Sunsphere and the Tennessee River, accommodations at the Hilton are ideal. The comfortable guest rooms feature adjustable thermostats, cable television, and voice-mail, and some have small kitchenettes. A number of the hotel's rooms connect, allowing parents and kids to have their own private space. The Hilton also boasts an exercise facility, an outdoor pool, and Jack's Steakhouse Restaurant. Other recreation within minutes of the hotel includes a driving range, bowling alley, and playground. Rates for the Hilton start at $89 per night double occupancy. 501 West Church Avenue, Knoxville; (865) 523-2300.

Wyndham Garden Hotel

In a quiet neighborhood near the University of Tennessee campus, the Wyndham Garden Hotel offers accommodations for business travelers and families. The 137-room hotel has a heated outdoor pool, fitness center, spa, and complimentary parking. All rooms are wheelchair accessible and are equipped with alarm clock/radios, coffee makers, cable television, voice mail, and modem ports. Room rates range from $75–120 per night, and children younger than 17 stay free with parents; 208 Market Place Lane, Knoxville; (800) WYNDHAM.

Attractions

East Tennessee Science Discovery Center

516 North Beaman Street, Knoxville; (865) 594-1494
    www.korrnet.org/etdc/etdc.html

Hours: Monday–Friday, 9 a.m.–5 p.m.

Admission: $3 adults, $2 students, free for children ages 5 and younger

Appeal by Age Group:

Pre-school	Grade School	Teens	Young Adults	Over 30	Seniors
★★	★★★	★★	★★	★★	★★

Average Touring Time: 1½ hours

Minimum Touring Time: 1 hour

Rainy Day Touring: Recommended

Author's Rating: ★★★   Small center makes science fun

Services and Facilities:

Restaurants No	Lockers No
Alcoholic beverages No	Pet kennels No
Disabled access Yes	Rain check No
Wheelchair rental No	Private tours No
Baby stroller rental No	

Description and Comments   Learn the technology behind holograms, electricity, lasers, and microscopes, or just enjoy playing with these scientific instruments. The Science Discovery Center features a first-rate planetarium, giant whisper dishes, a collection of fossils, and a live insect zoo, which includes tarantulas and giant hissing cockroaches. Children and adults will be fascinated by this one-of-a-kind, hands-on museum.

The Knoxville Zoo

I-40, Exit 392, Knoxville; (865) 637-5331
  www.knoxville-zoo.org

Hours: Monday–Friday, 9:30 a.m.–4:30 p.m.; Saturday–Sunday,
  9:30 a.m.–5:00 p.m.

Admission: $7.95 adults, $4.95 ages 3–12, free for children ages 2 and
  younger

Appeal by Age Group:

Pre-school	Grade School	Teens	Young Adults	Over 30	Seniors
★★★★	★★★★	★★★★	★★★★	★★★★	★★★★

Average Touring Time: 3 hours

Minimum Touring Time: 2 hours

Rainy Day Touring: Not recommended

Author's Rating: ★★★★

Services and Facilities:

Restaurants Yes	Lockers No
Alcoholic beverages No	Pet kennels No
Disabled access Yes	Rain check No
Wheelchair rental No	Private tours No
Baby stroller rental No	

Description and Comments   The whole family will enjoy a day at the zoo, especially the Knoxville Zoo. Exotic animals such as red pandas, black bears, snow leopards, and white rhinos are featured among nearly 1,000 animals from around the world. The zoo also has lions, tigers, elephants, gorillas, reptiles, and other animals on several dozen rolling green acres just outside of Knoxville.

Women's Basketball Hall of Fame

700 Hall of Fame Drive, Knoxville; (865) 633-9000
  www.wbhof.com

Hours: Memorial Day–Labor Day: Monday–Saturday, 9 a.m.–8 p.m.;
  Sunday, noon–8 p.m.; Labor Day–Memorial Day: Monday–Thursday,

10 a.m.–6 p.m.; Friday and Saturday, 10 a.m.–8 p.m.; Sunday, noon–6 p.m.

Admission: $7.95 adults, $5.95 seniors and ages 6–15, free for children ages 5 and younger

Appeal by Age Group:

Pre-school	Grade School	Teens	Young Adults	Over 30	Seniors
★	★★	★★★	★★★	★★★	★★

Average Touring Time: 2 hours

Minimum Touring Time: 1½ hours

Rainy Day Touring: Recommended

Author's Rating: ★★★ Refreshing focus on women in sports

Services and Facilities:

Restaurants No	Lockers No
Alcoholic beverages No	Pet kennels No
Disabled access Yes	Rain check Yes
Wheelchair rental No	Private tours No
Baby stroller rental No	

Description and Comments Young women will definitely be inspired by the Women's Basketball Hall of Fame, which is aptly placed in Knoxville, home of the very successful University of Tennessee Lady Volunteers college basketball team. Featured within the museum are biographies on past players from college, the Olympics, and professional teams. There are also three indoor basketball courts and an interactive model of a locker room. The Hall of Fame looks at the interesting history of women's basketball, such as the long-skirted uniforms players once wore.

World's Fair Park

810 Clinch Avenue, Knoxville; (423) 524-1796

Hours: Varies according to attraction

Admission: Varies according to attraction

Appeal by Age Group:

Pre-school	Grade School	Teens	Young Adults	Over 30	Seniors
★★	★★★	★★★	★★★	★★★	★★★

Average Touring Time: 2 hours

Minimum Touring Time: 1½ hours

Rainy Day Touring: Not recommended

Author's Rating: ★★

Services and Facilities:

Restaurants Yes	Lockers No
Alcoholic beverages No	Pet kennels No
Disabled access Yes	Rain check No
Wheelchair rental No	Private tours No
Baby stroller rental No	

Description and Comments   On the site of the 1982 World's Fair, Knoxville has built a number of noteworthy attractions, incorporating many of the buildings that were used for this international exposition. The Knoxville Museum of Art houses an extensive collection of American art and regularly presents exhibitions from famous artists from around the globe. The museum also stages family days, where children and parents can take part in art lessons and workshops. Admission is $7 for adults, $5 for children ages 12–17, and free for kids age 11 and younger. The museum opens Tuesday through Saturday at 10 a.m.. and on Sunday at noon.

The Sunsphere is one of the most recognizable sites on the Knoxville skyline, and you can visit the observation deck of this structure leftover from the 1982 World's Fair. A suggested donation for the visit to the top of the Sunsphere is $4 for adults and $2 for children. If you want to know even more about the Sunsphere and the history of the World's Fair, visit the Sunsphere Museum. Entry to the museum is free, and exhibits include information on the building of the Sunsphere and the history of the World Expos from 1815 to the present.

Side Trips

Gatlinburg   When winter hits, many skiers throughout Tennessee and across the South come to Gatlinburg. This idyllic mountain village has first-class skiing and hiking, and its views of the snow-capped Smokies are rarely equaled. The town has a number of family-friendly activities in which to participate year round, including horseback riding, mountain biking, fishing, and golfing. For more information about Gatlinburg, contact the Chamber of Commerce at (800) 900-4148.

Dollywood, Pigeon Forge   A day of wholesome family fun is only a short drive from Knoxville in Pigeon Forge. Here, you will find Dollywood, the east Tennessee amusement park owned by country star Dolly Parton. At Dollywood, you can ride roller coasters, swoosh through the water on log rides, watch a live musical performance, or take part in arts and crafts showcases. Also featured at the park is Imagination Forest, which includes an interactive tree house and plenty of room for kids to jump, climb, and mingle with one another. Dollywood is open each year from April through October (dates and times vary). For more information, call (800) DOLLY-WOOD or visit the park's website at www.dollywood.com.

Family-Friendly Restaurants

CHARLIE PEPPERS

716 20th Street, Knoxville; (865) 524-8669

Meals served: Lunch and dinner
Cuisine: Tex-Mex
Entrée range: $7–10
Kids menu: Yes
Reservations: Not required
Payment: All major credit cards accepted

This local favorite features spicy southwestern cuisine, including tacos, burritos, chimichangas, and fajitas. Just blocks from the University of Tennessee campus, Charlie Peppers is an ideal restaurant if your itinerary includes the university, Morningside Park, or the Knoxville Zoo. Kids' meals start at $2.99, and choices include half of a "wagon wheel" (a quesadilla), miniature corn dogs, spaghetti, hamburgers, or cheeseburgers. All kids' meals come with a fruit cup, drink, and cookie.

THE TOMATO HEAD

12 Market Square, Knoxville; (865) 637-4067

Meals served: Lunch and dinner
Cuisine: American/vegetarian
Entrée range: $5–7
Kids menu: Yes
Reservations: Not required
Payment: MC, V

As an alternative to unhealthy fast food, The Tomato Head offers fresh salads, sandwiches, and vegetarian entrées for families on the go. Diners can choose from a vegetarian menu, including stir-fry tofu and Asian-inspired dishes, or go for a three-cheese sub, loaded with fresh vegetables. Tomato Head's kids' menu contains selections from the adult menu at smaller portions, with prices ranging from $2–3.50. Kids can choose a pasta plate, cheese toast, or a sampler plate with pasta, fresh veggies, fruit, and juice.

Index